PN4193.O4 W673 2012
The words of our time :
33663005184490
CYP

DATE DUE

THE WORDS
OF OUR TIME

Prime Minister David Cameron addressing the House of Commons, 2011.

THE WORDS OF OUR TIME

SPEECHES THAT MADE A DIFFERENCE 2001–2011

—

JOHN SHOSKY

Biteback Publishing

First published in Great Britain in 2012 by
Biteback Publishing Ltd
Westminster Tower
3 Albert Embankment
London
SE1 7SP

ISBN 978-1-84954-177-0

10 9 8 7 6 5 4 3 2 1

A CIP catalogue record for this book is available from the British Library.

Front cover photo credits: Barack Obama © US Army; Nelson Mandela © Library of
the London School of Economics and Political Science; Aung San Suu Kyi © Htoo Tay Zar,
Open Myanmar Photo Project; Tony Blair © Remy Steinegger, World Economic Forum;
Vladimir Putin © Sebastian Dcrungs, World Economic Forum; and Bill Clinton © Ralph
Alswang, ralphphoto.com. Back cover photo: Crowd © Jeffrey Beall; Frontispiece photo:
Reproduced by kind permission of the Parliamentary Recording Unit.

Set in Adobe Garamond Pro and Gotham by Namkwan Cho
Cover design by Namkwan Cho

Printed and bound in Great Britain by
CPI Group (UK) Ltd, Croydon CR0 4YY

To Al Blume, Peter Loehr and Tom DeYarman

TABLE OF CONTENTS

THE WAR ON TERRORISM

GLOBALISATION

ACKNOWLEDGEMENTS

I first gave thought to the construction of speeches as a fourteen-year-old freshman at Roncalli High School in Pueblo, Colorado, a private Catholic school. The memories of that time linger, still fresh and alive.

It just shows how good teachers influence their students. My first speech teacher and mentor was Brother Al Blume, a great guy, who passionately loved rhetoric and public speaking. He had tremendous insight into the process of drafting and presenting speeches, talking with me for hours about words and techniques that made a speech stand out, becoming memorable. We met in a practice room and I would give a speech on a topic he assigned. Then we would analyse it together. We did this every week, sometimes every day. I made notes on yellow three-by-five cards, some of which I still have in my files or tucked away in books. Brother Al had suffered a stroke, so the words came with difficulty. But he carried on, even though each word he spoke was a painful act of will. There was great insight in those words, a true recognition of the power of persuasion.

His instruction was enhanced, magnified and quickly pushed into action by Brother Peter Loehr, a towering figure in my life, who understood the vast impact of great speeches. Brother Peter was in charge of our debate team and its amazing coaching staff, which included the legendary Homer Bisel, who had won a national championship, and his wife, Ruth, who taught us the humanity of public speaking. Richard Amman was a wonderful coach, too. He seemed able easily and competently to handle any aspect of instruction. Some of the students were good role models, like my heroes Bill Davis and Steve Henson.

Brother Peter took us to tournaments where we were fortunate to compete against talented speakers from other schools, teams from all over Colorado, and sometimes from other states. It was a process of trial by fire, learning by doing, slowly overcoming fear and ignorance. He was the first person who made me realise the profound power of a great speech, how the right words could instantly change the world. His guidance on preparation and reading spilled over into wide-ranging recommendations. I remember one day, the last day of the school year, he encouraged me, in my mother's presence, to read more demanding novels. He made it a personal challenge, telling me I could accomplish more and learn more quickly. I had already read some classics by

Bram Stoker and Herman Melville, which I thought was pretty good going at my age. But I gravitated to political or economic texts. He wanted me to develop a love of literature. So Brother Peter recommended Boris Pasternak, Leo Tolstoy, Jack London and others, a turning point in my life. In particular, I will be forever grateful for his mentioning Pasternak, as *Dr Zhivago* became my favourite novel. He had those books right there, ready for my inspection, a sizeable stack of imposing names and formidable reading. My mother wrote out a cheque and bought that stack of books, that very day, providing me with a summer's (and a lifetime's) foundation for exploring great literature. What an amazing gift, an act of love. After that, in our home, we had a framed picture of Brother Peter, whom we recognised as a brilliant teacher and caring friend. I still have that picture up in my office today.

Roncalli High School closed after my freshman year, so I moved to another school, this time East High School, a public institution. Tom DeYarman, my new speech, debate and economics instructor, spent three years explaining the process of persuasion, and taught me the fundamentals of audience analysis. Mr DeYarman was a talented and inspirational teacher, a source of endless information, providing subtle patience and encouragement. He understood precisely how to motivate me to read and research, and to think about arguments and speeches. I still talk to him. He helps me see issues with greater clarity and deeper insight. Recently, he was elected to our school's 'Hall of Fame'. This is a rare honour for a teacher, a public recognition of his extraordinary influence on thousands of students.

I dedicate the book to all three of them: Brother Al Blume, Brother Peter Loehr and Tom DeYarman. I do so with admiration, respect, friendship and thanks. And much appreciation! I'm not sure how they ever put up with me.

Once I started this book, several people were very helpful. Thanks to Lisa Anderson for extraordinary efforts in reviewing and editing the language. Many thanks to James Stephens and Sam Carter of Biteback Publishing for their editorial guidance and infinite patience. Reuben Cohen gave this manuscript a careful examination. Thanks. Of course, any remaining problems are my responsibility.

Also, thanks to Iain Dale and Shane Greer for approving this book for publication.

Over the last year I benefited from on-topic conversations with Dana Pohedra, Rachel Phillips, Cherie Clawsen, Shane Greer, Matthew Richardson, Renée Lorraine, Suzanne Ruscio, Lee Toliver, Jim Stanfield, Vanessa Moore, Robert Barnard, Anne Sutherland, Rom Harré, Michael Anderson, Carla Proctor, Mark Carmel, Matt Peterson, David Quayle and Cliff Henke. I also want to thank the former Lord Mayor of London, Alderman Sir Michael Bear and Rose Corona, a friend and in-demand orator, for a number of vivid and stimulating conversations about public speaking and manuscript preparation. As always, there was some extremely valuable discussion with Rick Teske. He helped give the project structure and form. I owe him. Rick brings an architect's eye to public speaking, helping to see a speech's foundation and scaffolding, as well as a deep understanding of how the persuasive process turns speech into action. This combination of strengths makes him a profoundly insightful critic. Many thanks. I also thank my friends and colleagues at Roncalli Communications: Bertram Collier, Winston Shosky, Kylie Shepherd, Frederick Katz and Juno O'Neel.

I worked on part of this manuscript at Linacre College, University of Oxford. Thanks to the principal, fellows and students of the college for their hospitality and encouragement. Linacre is my second home, a vibrant and electric community of scholars. I owe much to the Principal Emeritus, Paul Slack, Principal Nick Brown, Susan Jones and Anne Keene, as well as my friends in the Development Office. I must also mention the encouragement and support offered by my good friend and mentor, Rom Harré. I wouldn't have undertaken this project without his excellent advice and stern directives. Rom also is a good model for clear writing.

Thanks to all those who gave permission for the publication of these speeches. I especially want to recognise Baroness Thatcher for allowing publication of a speech under her copyright.

INTRODUCTION

SPEECHES THAT MAKE A DIFFERENCE

In a way, writing a great speech should be easy. Put the words on paper and tell an audience how you feel about an issue. Share your ideas. After all, talking heads and political pundits talk and talk and talk. The Internet and television give us endless access to conversation. It seems like the world is one enormous, infinite, inescapable dialogue, fractured, splintered and fragmented into billions of smaller ones.

We talk all the time, sometimes even when we are asleep. And we do communicate ideas and feelings, sometimes most of all when doing so unconsciously. We are constantly expressing ourselves on topics as varied as food and climate change, football and music, movies and relationships, power and poverty, life and death.

Yes, we talk a lot in seemingly endless conversations. But, then, try to write or give a speech. Shock. Worry. Fear. Risk. Potential disaster. It's not easy. A great speech is a rarity, a powerful, profound connection between speaker, audience and message that changes our world, becomes history.

Speechwriting is one of the most demanding literary disciplines, a necessary part of culture, business, religion and politics that requires skill in audience analysis, word choice, sentence construction, argument development, storytelling and salesmanship. The speaker must often present a dangerous problem, offer a compelling reason for change, suggest a set of solutions that will alleviate those problems, and motivate an audience to join together in a unified effort to tackle the problem immediately, regardless of the personal inconvenience or risk of harm. Even something as seemingly natural as a toast at a wedding or remarks at a golf tournament can be challenging. The challenge remains, perhaps magnifies, when CNN or the BBC is covering the speech or thousands of journalists are filing stories based on the remarks. And, in addition to a specific message, there must be a broader vision of a better world, something that justifies the action, a worldview bigger than the needs or wants of one person, a call to unified action that will benefit most, if not all, people. Ronald Reagan – sometimes called 'the great communicator' – said that every speech must offer hope to its audience.

Then there is the delivery of the speech; the delivery must touch the emotional and satisfy the rational in a very human bonding of faith, trust and belief. A great speech reaches into the soul itself. There must be an appropriate tone, pleasing depth and warmth to the voice, meaningful changes in rate and volume, profound use of emphasis, non-verbal gestures that complement and reinforce the message and the intelligence behind the delivery to maximise the effect of every word. There must be a profound authenticity to the speaker; he or she must emit the impression of someone who has experience and knowledge, one who has lived their own message and understands its importance, a person who is honest, bold, confident and dedicated to solutions that will make the world a better place. The dynamic underlying all of this must be a powerful engagement with the audience, moving as many people as possible to a point of collective agreement to act. The speaker becomes a leader for the group, but in doing so becomes a voice of collective assent, which means the speaker is giving voice to the hopes, aspirations and dreams of the audience, speaking the words they would eventually like to speak, demanding that the audience's needs be given a priority, and that action will be taken to satisfy the audience.

So a speaker is a leader, organiser, seer, advocate, coalition builder, faith-healer and magician-illusionist. And because Aristotle said that people come to a speech primarily to assess the character of the speaker, those who give great speeches are also role models, inspirational figures and teachers. Some speakers even reach the status of celebrity, turning a speech into an event, in some cases reaching rock-star proportions.

Just to show that everything I've written so far is more rule inviting exception, some speeches aren't difficult at all – they just seem to write themselves, a remarkable rarity, flowing out of the fingers into the computer, forcing themselves on a speaker, demanding that the audience listen, and, once given, refuse to go away. The speaker becomes a mouthpiece, an oracle, the vehicle for something larger than person or place. The speech is a conjurer's creation that defies control or limitation, and throws itself out into the world. Sometimes the speaker is confounded by the energy and reach of a speech, wondering 'Where did that come from?' And they may honestly not know!

In our time, a great speech must remain in the language of the common man, using the strength of simplicity with the purpose of shared meaning, becoming a conversation that highlights, educates, discusses, eliminates and urges solutions to problems. In a great speech, the speaker talks to an audience, leads them, becomes one with them, their representative and champion.

When it all works, the highest compliment is to say that the speech has 'impact'. Great speeches have impact. The speech is effective because it all comes together, persuasively uniting an audience around a set of actions, motivating the audience to act immediately to change the world. And they do more than commit to action; they perform it.

A great speech raises large issues, addresses the concerns of the moment and looks into the future, involves context and setting, requires the right speaker, a message that reaches out to the audience with impact, a receptive audience that is willing to think and feel in concert with the intentions of the speaker, and a bit of luck, too, with few mistakes through a demonstration of speaker competence and preparation. No wonder few people can write and give a great speech. It is amazing that anyone can. Discounting luck and natural talent, both in short supply, it takes a lot of thought, work, empathy, sensitivity, insight, developed skill, self-awareness and courage to produce a great speech.

I think few speeches meet this set of needs. Every day thousands of speeches are given in London alone; thousands more in Paris, Strasbourg, Hong Kong, Tokyo, Washington and New York, thousands worldwide. Multiplied over the year, there are tens of millions of speeches. The vast, vast majority do nothing at all and change nothing. When the speech is over it evaporates into the ether, instantly forgotten. I recently heard a speech where the speaker started the conclusion by saying 'And, now, finally, at last, in the end...' with the triple emphasis of stopping, doing nothing to give weight to the words of the speech, which dissolved within seconds of saying 'Thank you'. The audience could not have told you what the speech said. It did nothing to convince the mind, win the heart or touch the soul. Such convoluted emptiness is, sadly, all too typical.

A small minority of speeches have potential but come up short. These speeches create a strong impression at the moment of delivery and briefly stay in the brain, but fade into insignificance within hours or days. The speech itself seems important. There is some motivation after it is over. However, conflicting ideas and experiences push the speech to the back of the brain, where it dies a silent death.

The best speeches refuse to be forgotten. They simply will not go away, demanding to be heard. A mere handful of speeches stand apart. For one thing, they continue to persuade and engage long after delivery. These are speeches that make history, that turn words into action. They become part of the zeitgeist, inserting themselves into our national and global conversations. They define the cutting edge on an issue. They channel thinking, moving it into new territory. They tell us how to see and feel. They persuade us to act. They become part of us. They become the words of our time. In this volume you will find 50 examples.

How do they do that?

GREAT SPEECHES CHANGE THE WORLD

The greatest of speeches literally create new realities. Their language turns into action. After the words have been spoken, the world becomes a different place. The power of that dynamic is the dazzling and seductive allure of words. Speechwriters look to a speech like John F. Kennedy's 1961 Inaugural Address with envy, searching the words for the philosopher's stone that turned simple, mostly monosyllabic words into verbal gold. Winston Churchill mobilised a nation with his 'fight them on the beaches' speech after Dunkirk. Resignation speeches such as Richard Nixon's or Geoffrey Howe's are a form of action. As they are delivered, the words of such addresses become truths. Every leader is aware of this and uses a speech to transform the world. That is a cardinal characteristic of a great speech.

GREAT SPEECHES ARE SIMPLE

Most great speeches have a simple message, a view that can often be condensed into a phrase of a few words. When Ronald Reagan said 'Mr Gorbachev, tear down this wall,' the message was very clear. Neil Kinnock said, 'You can't play politics with people's jobs.' That is crystal clear, simple in message and meaning. Entire speeches can be simple, like Lincoln's Gettysburg Address or Elie Wiesel's speech at Auschwitz, where he said, 'Listen to the silent screams.' Earl Spencer's eulogy for his sister is powerfully direct and heartfelt.

GREAT SPEECHES BRING OUT THE BEST IN THE AUDIENCE

Aristotle thought that speeches should be used to craft good character in the audience, ennobling and enriching the community. Great speeches appeal to our better instincts. They attempt to establish common ground. They touch our sympathy and our humanity. Great speeches ask us to embrace freedom, show respect, protect human rights, listen to others, reason well, prize mutual regard and empower the community. Some words appear often in great speeches: virtue, goodness, duty, equality, egalitarianism, human rights, dignity, tolerance and charity. These are words to live by. They are words that can help make the community and its citizens better.

GREAT SPEECHES ARE BOLD

Words of qualification can take the life out of a sentence. These qualifying 'weasel words', make the assertion less powerful. These words are the lovechildren of bureaucrats, lawyers and others who fear overstatement or provocation. When Nelson Mandela was released from prison, he said that 'Our struggle has reached a decisive moment. We call on our people to seize this moment, so that the process towards democracy is rapid and uninterrupted. We have waited long enough for freedom!' Those sentences are profound and powerful. Imagine if they had been 'weaselled': 'Our struggle may have reached a moment when something may happen. We might call on our people to potentially act, so the process towards democracy may be rapid and possibly uninterrupted. We have waited a long time for freedom. It might be better if we didn't have to wait for much longer!' Most modern speech language is so qualified and 'weaseled' that it doesn't say much. In fact, that last sentence is too weaselled itself. The vast majority of speeches say nothing. They are qualified to the point of meaninglessness.

GREAT SPEECHES ARE PERSUASIVE

I believe that every act of communication is persuasive, that there is no such thing as an informative speech. Every speech is an act of persuasion, simply because the audience is asked to believe the speaker, if nothing else. Great speeches are persuasive messages, designed to convince the audience to do something *now*. They convey a sense of urgency. The audience is asked to use their reasoning and experience to understand a problem, agree with the diagnosis of the problem, accept and support a set of solutions for positive change. When Margaret Thatcher asks the audience to help rollback the 'frontiers of the State', she is not offering information or explaining a problem. She wants agreement, acceptance of actions, and performance of those actions. If she doesn't attempt to persuade, then she is allowing an important, unique opportunity to pass by, which is a criminal offence in public speaking, the very definition of wasting the audience's time. She knows this, which is why she uses every fact, story, experience and word to persuade the audience to advocate for less government, lower taxes, more individual freedom and more personal responsibility. Every great speech has an agenda.

GREAT SPEECHES ARE WELL WRITTEN

Winston Churchill received the Nobel Prize for Literature. His speeches certainly helped him win that award. A possibly apocryphal story tells of Churchill and President Franklin Delano Roosevelt giving consecutive radio addresses from the White House during the War. Upon seeing Churchill's text, the President complained to his aides about the inferiority of his speech to the Prime Ministers.' The chastened writers are said to have replied, 'Sorry, Mr President, the problem is the old man rolls his own.' I believe he is the only Nobel Literature Prize Laureate whose speeches are mentioned as part of the winning body of work by the Nobel Committee. Churchill's speeches were masterpieces of the craft. Prose or poetry writers should be good speechwriters. William Shakespeare wrote literate speeches demonstrating the highest linguistic craftsmanship. Alexander Solzhenitsyn gave a great speech at Harvard years after winning his Nobel Prize. Unfortunately, most speeches are not considered for their literary style or merit. You don't find books of collected speeches classified as 'literature', although they are as creative, imaginative and provocative as any novel. Sometimes a critic will talk about a line in a speech and consider it as poetry. But good speeches have subtle poetry and cadence underneath, and great speeches are almost always, on the surface, well-written prose. So speeches should be evaluated for their literary style and quality. Perhaps the reason some people see speeches differently is because of the overt use of persuasion by politicians, clergy and businesspeople. In other words, the speeches are found wanting in serious literary achievement because of the speakers themselves, who by using words for persuasion may taint those words as self-serving or propaganda. The subject matter is also disqualifying in the minds of some: political speeches cannot be literature, although political novels have been among the best examples of the literary craft.

In fairness, many great novels are guilty of similar associations and have persuasive content. Perhaps speeches are rejected as literature because they are written primarily for the 'mind's ear', not the 'mind's eye'. (Although some poetry is also guilty of being so intended, such as the *Iliad*, Shakespeare's sonnets or contemporary performance poetry.) Also, plays are primarily for the ear, not the eye. If Harold Pinter and Tom Stoppard are literary figures, then surely Martin Luther King, Jr and Tony Blair should shine in the same literary light. I would like to see a prize given by an august, public, respected *literary* body for the best-written speech each year, a Booker Prize level award for speech *writing*. I am certain that the literary quality of speeches would rise dramatically if public attention were given to their style and quality. Place speeches under a literary spotlight. This does not mean that speeches would be praised for their 'sugary' content or 'pretty words'. Rather, as with novels and poetry, quality would be determined by craftsmanship and effectiveness of language use. The craft of speechwriting needs a champion with influence and clout, someone who is willing to elevate the attention and seriousness given to the wording of speeches. I realise that the last few lines will be received with derision by some readers. But think of the original promise of public speaking in Athenian democracy. Aristotle held that eloquence was a civic duty, that the polity benefited from good speaking and clear discourse. Such efforts could bring out the best in citizens, ennobling them, enriching the community, making the city-state better, more virtuous and more human.

GREAT SPEECHES TELL US SOMETHING AUTHENTIC ABOUT THE SPEAKER

In a great speech we get insight into the speaker. We learn something about their view of the world, their decision-making, their values, their hopes, their commitments and their passions. A great speech unifies and uses inclusive language, but it also offers a glimpse into the mind, heart and soul of the speaker. That is one reason a great speech is effective: it establishes a sympathetic and empathic link between speaker and audience. In my own work, I always tell a speaker to give the audience a 'piece of themselves', to share a very personal moment with the audience.

GREAT SPEECHES ARE PART OF OUR COLLECTIVE CONSCIENCE

Great speeches become part of our national and international dialogue, whether in business, politics, culture or general conversation. To know these speeches is to know ourselves. They made us who we have become. The speeches on the war in Iraq are part of us. The aspirations for democracy in Burma and Cuba are our hopes, too. We need to understand the voices for change in Bolivia and Brazil. The rise of India is one of the central facts of the twenty-first century. China is becoming an economic and military superpower. Political leaders in France and Germany tackle problems similar to those in the United Kingdom and the United States. We are all living the words which describe and explain the international monetary crisis. These words are the ones we use to frame problems and act upon them. Interestingly, these words are more than familiar to us; they define us. They offer a way of thinking about the years to come. For example, consider the direction and velocity of Tony Blair's 2001 Party Conference speech or his resignation speech. Years later, these words are still trying to take the audience into the future.

GREAT SPEECHES KEEP DOING THEIR JOB

Great speeches carry us into the future. They move the frontiers, taking us into previously unknown territory. There is a gravitational pull, constant and steady in most cases, of much higher velocity in others. These words won't leave us alone. They keep working, keep persuading, long after the speech is over. Consider the powerful pull of Dr King's speech on the Washington Mall. The 'I Have a Dream' speech has been part of revolutions in South America and Africa and was explicitly mentioned in South Africa's transition from apartheid and in the election of an African-American President in the United States. That speech is still at work, still on the job. It may well be that the 'I Have a Dream' speech will become immortal, relevant and vital as long as people strive for equality and freedom.

In this volume we start with remarks by Aung San Suu Kyi. After years of house arrest, she has much to say to joyous followers who have a singular moment of jubilation at her release. That speech reminds us of the power of words, and also the struggle to find the right words at an unexpected moment. After that there are speeches on race, morality, governance, war, terrorism, international economics, tension between neighbours, developmental concerns, rising tiger economies, multiculturalism, biomedical research and remembrance. One of the last speeches, Margaret Thatcher's video remarks at the funeral of Reagan, recalls an earlier era, demonstrating from a distance the way words and actions can make a difference. Reagan and Thatcher's speeches became the words of their time. In a generation to come, someone will give a eulogy for this era. When they do that, they will be mindful of our language, the way we used words for action. They will talk about the words of our time. Great speeches are part of our living modern history. They are the words of the present and remain the words of our story, setting a course for the time to come. By looking at great speeches, we can better see where we have come from, who we are and where we will go.

———

Please note: The speeches that follow have been lightly edited. Spelling has been standardised to UK English. The major change has been to create or change paragraph separation. For example, in the British party conference speeches, and in the other speeches by Tony Blair, David Cameron, Nick Clegg, Michael Bear and George Osborne the rally-type one-line presentation, still found on web sites that provide these speeches, has been re-structured into paragraphs to allow for the continuity of the message to be understood in a reading format. This involved judgement calls. Often I myself am uncomfortable with the results, with paragraphs that are not exactly well-developed or inter-connected. Single sentences are joined together into paragraphs wherever necessary to better capture the coherent flow of the speech. I left Ed Miliband's speech alone so the reader could see the one-liner style in action. Words have not been changed nor have sentences been removed, except where indicated. But I admit that the paragraphs could have been structured differently, and my efforts are simply a best attempt.

Each speech begins with short biographical information and comments about the setting. Sometimes there may be a few lines about interesting aspects of the content or the technique used in speechwriting. Little needs to be said because the speeches themselves, as part of their historical moment, usually recreate the content and controversy. The speaker seems to recognise the singular moment as part of the point and purpose of the words. These speeches speak for themselves.

Obviously, there will be disagreement over the speeches selected for this volume. Did I leave out other great speeches? Were some of those speeches better or more important than those included in this volume? Who made you the arbiter of a speech's greatness? Fair questions. I know any list is subject to second-guessing, even questions of sanity. For example, Barack Obama's remarks in 2004 at the Democratic Party National Convention are a clear omission. However, given the widespread availability of those remarks, reproduction here would be redundant. Certainly each of the speeches in this collection stands out ... demands attention. These are speeches that won't go away, refuse to be forgotten.

I am pleased to provide them for you. I hope you find the collection useful. Thanks for reading this book and making these speeches a part of your life.

AUNG SAN SUU KYI

'THE HARD LIFE MUST BE WORTHWHILE'

—

REMARKS AFTER RELEASE FROM HOUSE ARREST

RANGOON, BURMA, 14 NOVEMBER 2010

*A*ung San Suu Kyi, daughter of the assassinated 'father of modern Burma', Aung San, is General Secretary of the Burmese National League for Democracy. The ruling military authorities placed her under house arrest in 1989, and although her party scored a landslide victory in the 1990 general election, winning 80 per cent of the seats, the junta rejected the election result. Suu Kyi remained under house detention for fifteen of the next twenty-one years. This resulted in near-permanent separation from her late husband, Dr Michael Aris, who was diagnosed with prostate cancer in 1997. When it transpired that Dr Aris's condition was termi-nal, the Burmese government refused to issue him an entry visa to make a farewell visit, encouraging Suu Kyi to instead travel to the UK. Suu Kyi declined, fearing that she would not be subsequently permitted to re-enter her home country, and did not see her husband prior to his death. Her charismatic manner, devotion to democracy in Burma, and physical courage in the face of a military dictatorship have made Suu Kyi a symbol of pro-democracy movements and struggles around Asia and the world. She was awarded the Nobel Peace Prize in 1991.

Under increasing domestic and international pressure, the Burmese authorities finally released Suu Kyi on 13 November 2010. In a special election on 1 April 2012, she won her seat in Pyithu Hluttaw, the lower house of the Burmese Parliament, representing the constituency of Kawhmu Township. The following remarks were given to a massive throng of supporters on her first full day of freedom. Evidently, the conditions of her release forbade direct criticism of the military government. So she discusses the way democracy can be implemented on a grassroots level, from the ground up. As she explains her view, members of the audience, overcome by *excitement and joy, shout to her. In turn, she responds to some of these comments. So the speech weaves in and out of any prepared remarks, interspersed with impromptu comments, leading to broken threads of thought. The speech is hopeful, sincere and authentic. It is electric and historic. This speech shows the power of words … why they matter. After more than twenty years of suppression, honest speech breathes life into a democratic movement. This speech also shows the character of the speaker. In a situation like this, Suu Kyi is not hiding behind a careful media image. The audience can see right into her heart, mind and soul.*

—

I have to begin by thanking you for your support. We haven't seen each other for a long time but I am happy to see that our mutual faith remains strong, it fortifies me. In order to do our work, we must know what the people want – you do know what you want, don't you? Well it's fine to know what you want but you must also know how you are going to achieve what you want. I believe that politics must be learned. I have often said, in my talks with the youth, I don't believe there is such a thing as good people or bad people, or smart or stupid people, I only believe that there are people who can learn and people who can't. I believe that we, the people, can learn very well. It's not enough to know what you want but also to know how to achieve it with integrity. I say this not to patronise, I say from experience that no matter what the goal, if the path is without integrity, it will lose its way and be destroyed. This is why we must achieve what we want with integrity.

I know you have lots of questions to ask me and I want to hear the voices of the people but I can't hear through the cacophony. I believe that I will now have the chance to listen to the voices of the people. While under restriction, I listened to foreign radio broadcasts to hear what the people are saying. It's very tiresome to listen to the radio for five to six hours a day but I do this out of regard for the people. So I believe that I am, to a degree, aware of the wishes of the people. I don't believe I know everything. This is not possible. So the people must make their voices heard by us. This will help us help the people. I believe that the people now realise that nothing can be accomplished without the participation of the people. Because nothing can be accomplished without the people's participation, we would like to create a democracy network across the world, of the people and by the people. It is only when we strive with this mentality, can we serenely achieve our democratic goals. In short, it means we have a lot of work to do. You will not get anything without working for it.

We Burmese blame it all on luck. But do you know what luck means? Luck means you reap what you sow. So if there is anything you want, you have to work to achieve it. We cannot simply bribe the people and promise them the impossible. We will try hard and pave the road that the people want. We will pave it together and we will take that road together. It's not right that one person paves the road while the other stands idly by. Speaking of paving roads, maybe I picked an inappropriate analogy. It was a slip of the tongue. What I mean is that we will walk the road that leads to the democratic goals. We will walk on it together, we will pave it together. It is only [by] this way, [that] we can reach our goals. Don't wait for others to do it for you. We will not 'force' you to do it [alluding to forced labour]. If you do not put your mind and soul into achieving it, otherwise, who knows whether it will end up with the tar being stolen [alluding to the shoddy quality of the roads being built because of corruption].

I know that your show of support is not without expectation. The burden of these expectations is great and the responsibilities are immense. But I am not one to shy away from responsibility. But I am afraid of not being able to live up to my responsibilities. I will do my utmost to live up to these responsibilities and call on the people to help us, to advise us, to point out our shortcomings. Pointing out shortcomings, if done in sincere goodwill, is very helpful. It will help us help the people achieve their aspirations.

I would like to ask the people to please communicate with us openly and courageously. Please don't have any qualms about talking to us. We won't do anything to you. If we are not in agreement, we will let you know. This is the basis of democracy – that of freedom of speech. But freedom to speak is not the same as freedom to be abusive. Well, there may be a bit of admonition. It is very important to be able to achieve mutual understanding. To be able to exchange views. We have to practise this and improve on this.

Upon my release, the main change that I have seen is that there is a proliferation of camera-phones. I see camera-phones all over the place. This shows the development of communication. This development must be used for the good of the majority. Communication brings understanding. Please use communication to foster mutual understanding and unity. Show me your phones; let's see how many there are. My, there are so many. I used a phone like this for the first time yesterday. Six years ago these did not exist here. I did not even know where to talk into – the phone was so ... I will have to put up a sign for those who cannot hear me [reportedly the speaker held up a sign, in blue felt-tip, reading: 'I love the Burmese people' with a tick beside it and her name beneath].

But it is not enough just to say you love me, you have to work. So I thought what love means. Love means the desire for mutual happiness and the implementation of that desire. It is not enough to keep repeating 'I love you'. If you want to give me that bouquet, pass it on. Why are you holding on to it? [the speaker received a bouquet].

I want to ask the people, to tell us what's on your mind. You can deliver the letter here, if you don't trust the postal service. I want to know what's on your mind. What has been in your mind over the past six years, what has changed? I can't know all of this at once. I have to study it. It's not feasible to speak to all of you individually. If possible, I'd like to hand over the mike to you and listen to what each of you has to say. It's not going to end. But I like that. It's so boring to be the only one to speak. If there is an exchange of dialogue, it creates harmony and is more beneficial. I feel that it is not democratic if one person does all the talking. Let's try it out. I will simply point to one of you in the crowd and ask you to say a few words.

[Persons from the crowd said, 'We want to have a free democracy.' Others screamed, 'I love Amay Suu' or 'We love Amay Suu.']

It looks like we will need a 'Speakers' corner'. To be able to hear the voices of the people.

[Addressing a commotion in the crowd]: What is the problem over there? Can I help? Is it because people at the back are pushing? Please have discipline. Don't be so impatient. There will be other opportunities for us to talk. This will not be the only occasion. There will be many others. That is why. Let's be patient.

I thank you for your patience. As I said just now, there is so much to do so you must save your strength. Well, it's been twenty years of having a hard life, so you must be used to it. I don't want you to continue to have a hard life. Having a hard life isn't the point. The point is that the hard life must be worthwhile, and then one can have endurance. So you must save your strength to make it all worthwhile.

I want to tell you not to be dejected. Sometimes there may be some things in our country that will make you feel dejected. Surely you must feel that we have not gotten anywhere or that there has been no development. But there is no reason to feel dejected. We must strive hard.

Perseverance is important. We must continue to persevere from the start to the finish. The work is never done. Even if something is finished, there will be something else. Building a nation is like this, one thing after the other has to be done. There will never be full satisfaction of the people but we must strive to achieve a measure of satisfaction. I cannot promise this, but with the trust, dependence and support of the people, I will be fortified because I cannot do it alone. I don't want to do it alone. Doing it alone is not democracy. I have no intention to do it alone. I will do it with the majority, with the people of this country, and with the global community that have shown us goodwill and support. We will do it with everybody. We have to keep this firmly in mind. Courage is not what some people think, to be up in arms and being a hero. Courage means the resolve to achieve one's goals. We must have this kind of courage. Go to the movies if you want a hero. Courage is a daily task. Don't we people have to muster the courage to face each day? We have to use this courage beneficially and effectively for our country.

It's not enough to think only of oneself or one's own family. I want to reiterate this. Please don't have the attitude that politics do not concern you. My father has said that before, that you may not be concerned with politics but politics will be concerned with you, you can't avoid this. Everything is politics. Politics is not just coming here and supporting us. The housewife, who is cooking at home, also has something to do with politics because she is struggling to feed her family with the money she has. Struggling to send children to school is politics. Everything is politics. No one is free of politics. So saying that politics does not concern you and that you do not wish to be involved in politics is a lack of awareness of politics. So I ask the people to try and understand politics and to teach us. We must teach one another. Unless the people teach us what democracy is, we will make mistakes.

What is important in a democracy is that the people at the back must be able to keep those who are working in the front under control. This is democracy. The people, who are the majority, must have the right to keep the rulers, who are the minority, under control. This is democracy. So I will accept it if the people keep me under control. But of course, I do not like it if those, who are not of the people, keep me in control. But then, I only say this in passing. During the time of my detention I had a lot of interaction with the people who were in charge of my security. They have been good to me. I have to say what the truth is. Since one must show appreciation to those who are deserving, I say with sincerity that I am grateful to those who were in charge of my security. I want the people to be able to have mutual understanding and gratitude. A revered monk once said when I was young, that those who were worthy of gratitude and those who showed gratitude were hard to find. I found the latter hard to accept. I thought that human beings were capable of showing gratitude. But that is not true. There are some who show ingratitude. What does showing gratitude mean? It means just to have mutual recognition.

[To commotion in the crowd]: Well, you have to have a little forbearance. There is no question why you have to be angry just because someone stood up. As I said in front of my compound [yesterday], those in front must have forbearance and understanding of those at the back and likewise, those at the back must have forbearance and understanding of those in the front.

So now I want to know how the people are going to embark on a journey of politics. So if we have to depend on the people, we must have an exchange of views. I will continue to work for national reconciliation among the people, among all of us. There is no one that I cannot work or talk with. If there is a will to work together, it can be done. If there is a will to talk to one another, it can be done. I will take this path. On taking this path, I declare that we need the might of the people. I ask you to support us with the might of the people. Whatever we decide, we will let the people know. I haven't finished consulting with the National League for Democracy [NLD], but I will not only work with the NLD. I will work with all democratic entities and I would like the people to encompass us. We will tell the people, explain to them what our decisions are. There may be things that we decide which the people may not like. But this is natural. Not everyone can be of the same opinion. Accepting that there can be a difference of opinion is a democratic principle.

Why do we do this? We must gain the trust of the people, not the votes of the people. We will gain the understanding and support of the people. I apologise that I cannot clarify this further at this stage but it would be reckless of me if I were to start announcing one activity after the other, just after my release.

In the meantime, we would like to hear the voices of the people. We will decide how to proceed after listening to the voices of the people. But as I have said, we will use the might of the people and work with all the democratic forces and we will work for national reconciliation. In doing so, we will do it in a way that would bring the least damage to the people. I can't guarantee that there will be no damage at all. If I were to do so, it's another form of bribery to say that by following us, there will be no sacrifice. But we will and the least damaging way. There may be some sacrifice, we have suffered, our colleagues have suffered, so I ask you for a little forbearance if you have to sacrifice anything. You can't simply want something without sacrifice.

[Responding to someone in the crowd]: If you say you had forbearance for too long, what was it that you had to forbear? It is important to differentiate between right and wrong and to have the courage to stand by what is right, but what is right can be relative to the occasion. My father used to say that he was not afraid to stand before the court of his conscience. Since I have stood before the court, I am not afraid to stand before the court of my conscience every day. I ask the people to stand before the court of their conscience to find the answer as to whether one is undertaking what should be done. If you can do this, your might will increase immensely. Remember if might is not used rightly, it is a menace. Might that is used rightly cannot be overcome by anyone.

Let us now have a little test of your empathy, understanding and forbearance of one another. The people over there are complaining that they cannot hear. I am about to finish speaking. So can I suggest that the people in front make way for the people on the other side?

So now you can hear can't you? So if one group of people were to always remain in one place – that's not good.

Now that's fair isn't it?

So now I would like to thank all of you who took the trouble to come here and to show your support. We have repeatedly said that we depend on the might of the people and we cannot succeed without the might of the people. This might of the people must be used systematically. When the people in front stand up for too long the people in the back get annoyed. The people in the front shouldn't be standing up for too long. The people in the back should also have a little forbearance if they are standing up for just a while. Well, so what, but it's different if they are standing up too long of course.

I would like to repeat what I said that we have to work together to achieve success. You will not succeed just by wishing and hoping. You must be able to know how to achieve your aspirations and have the courage and ability to do so. We will find the best way. That is to find a way that avoids bringing suffering to the people as much as possible to achieve these goals. I am a fervent believer in national reconciliation. I believe that this is the path we should take. Let me openly tell the people here that I have no grudge against the people who kept me under restriction. I believe in human rights and the rule of law. I will always strive for this. I don't harbour hatred of anyone. I have no time for this. I have too much to do to harbour any hatred. The people in charge of keeping me under restriction were good to me. This is the truth and I value this and I am grateful.

Likewise in every aspect I would like everyone to have good interactions with one another. How wonderful would it be if the people were also treated as nicely as I was? But of course I don't mean that the people should be put under house arrest.

So I would like to plead, 'Please don't put the people under house arrest like I was, but please be nice to the people just as you were nice to me.'

We must value the good things and be grateful of things that are worthy of gratitude. Just because one doesn't like it, it does not mean that everything is bad. There are good things and there are bad things. So don't be angry if people say you are doing bad things. If you don't want the people to say this, then just don't do anything bad. Just as I value what is good and am grateful, I am not hesitant to say so. It's so rewarding to be able to give recognition to someone worthy of gratitude. I want to do this. I want to be so grateful so just do things that are worthy of gratitude and I will sing your praises all day. So I want to thank each and every one of the people. Of course, I would end up with a sore throat.

So let me say thank you. Keep up your strong resolve. People say that the courage of the Burmese is like straw fire. I don't like this. This shouldn't be so. A human being must have all its manifestations and live in human dignity. Do you want human rights? The Universal Declaration of Human Rights begins by saying that everyone is born with inherent dignity. This dignity must be upheld. The dignity commensurate with these rights must be upheld. I don't wish to make a one-sided statement by repeating what should be done for the people.

There are also things that the people must do. Everyone must know his or her responsibility and be able to fulfil them. Only then will our country develop. So it goes without saying that whether or not our country has developed, is something that the people will know more than I do. But rather than blaming who is at fault for this lack of development, I would only like to ask for the opportunities for us to work together hand in hand. I don't like the people having to hold out their hands to beg. I shall not hold out my hands to beg and I believe that my people do not wish to hold out their hands to beg. I believe that people want the right to development so we must work to give the people the right to development. There must be opportunities for people to be able to feed themselves to the full.

We shall proceed in consultation with democratic entities and the NLD shall not go it alone but hand in hand with [the] majority. Furthermore, the majority must be encompassed by the people. We cannot do it without the people and we ask for their assistance. I ask for your faith and support. So keep up your strength. I feel bad to ask you to eat up [to keep up your strength] since I hear that you do not have enough to eat. I ask you to keep up your physical and mental strength. It is with this strength we shall work together to reach our goal. I would have to say that there are some of us who have lost sight of that goal. But to have to walk the path to reach this proper goal is priceless.

Man is mortal. One day it will all be over, but before it is over, how one has led one's life is the most important. So I take this opportunity to honour those of our colleagues and comrades who have given their lives to the cause for democracy; to honour our colleagues and comrades who are still in prison. Let us pray that they will be released as soon as possible.

BARACK OBAMA

'TO FORM A MORE PERFECT UNION … WE CAN MOVE BEYOND SOME OF OUR OLD RACIAL WOUNDS'

—

REMARKS ON RACE, POLITICS AND RELIGION

PHILADELPHIA, PENNSYLVANIA, 18 MARCH 2008

Born in Hawaii in 1961 to a Kenyan father of Muslim ancestry and an American mother, Barack Obama studied at Columbia University and Harvard Law School, becoming editor of the prestigious Harvard Law Review. After a career in the private sector that included teaching at the University of Chicago's Faculty of Law and years as a community organiser, Obama entered politics, winning a seat in the Illinois State Senate. After a failed primary campaign for the Democratic Party's nomination for a seat in the United States House of Representatives (US House, 1st District, Illinois), he launched a successful 2004 bid for one of the state's two seats in the United States Senate. A shambolic campaign on the Republican side resulted in a landslide victory for Obama, whose much-praised keynote address at the 2004 Democratic National Convention was perhaps the most dramatic introduction of an up-and-coming politician to a national audience since then-Senator John F. Kennedy narrowly lost the Vice-Presidential nomination to Senator Estes Kefauver in 1956. Like Kennedy, Obama is credited with rhetorical gifts that lent his campaigns an inspirational quality and attracted legions of devoted volunteers, including many students and young people.

Despite having denied any intention to contest the Presidency in 2008, a burgeoning draft-Obama movement convinced him to enter the race, resulting in a gripping, hard-fought primary battle with then-Senator Hillary Clinton, who had long been the presumptive frontrunner. He emerged as the surprise Democratic nominee, facing US Senator John McCain, Republican of Arizona, in the Presidential election. Obama was elected President in November 2008 and sworn into office in January 2009.

In the course of the primary campaign, Obama's association with Reverend

Jeremiah Wright attracted widespread criticism. Reverend Wright, Pastor Emeritus of Trinity United Church of Christ, is known for his inflammatory rhetoric from the pulpit, including a 2003 sermon featuring the repeated words 'God Damn America' and speaking of the 9/11 attacks as 'America's chickens coming home to roost'. In this speech, then-Senator and Presidential candidate Obama explains his view of the role of race, politics and religion in America. In some published accounts, this speech has been given the title 'A More Perfect Union'. In 2010, President Obama won the Nobel Peace Prize. He is running for a second Presidential term in the 2012 election.

This speech has become an important document about the separation of church and state, as well as a personal statement about faith, influence and loyalty. It is also a deep discussion about racism in America. The first line is appropriate for the range of topics and the setting, Philadelphia.

———

'We the people, in order to form a more perfect union.'

Two hundred and twenty-one years ago, in a hall that still stands across the street, a group of men gathered and, with these simple words, launched America's improbable experiment in democracy. Farmers and scholars; statesmen and patriots who had travelled across an ocean to escape tyranny and persecution finally made real their declaration of independence at a Philadelphia convention that lasted through the spring of 1787.

The document they produced was eventually signed but ultimately unfinished. It was stained by this nation's original sin of slavery, a question that divided the colonies and brought the convention to a stalemate until the founders chose to allow the slave trade to continue for at least twenty more years, and to leave any final resolution to future generations.

Of course, the answer to the slavery question was already embedded within our Constitution – a Constitution that had at its very core the ideal of equal citizenship under the law; a Constitution that promised its people liberty, and justice, and a union that could be and should be perfected over time.

And yet words on a parchment would not be enough to deliver slaves from bondage, or provide men and women of every colour and creed their full rights and obligations as citizens of the United States. What would be needed were Americans in successive generations who were willing to do their part – through protests and struggle, on the streets and in the courts, through a civil war and civil disobedience and always at great risk – to narrow that gap between the promise of our ideals and the reality of their time.

This was one of the tasks we set forth at the beginning of this campaign – to continue the long march of those who came before us, a march for a more just, more equal, more free, more caring and more prosperous America. I chose to run for the presidency at this moment in history because I believe deeply that we cannot solve the challenges of our time unless we solve them together – unless we perfect our union by understanding that we may have different stories, but we hold common hopes; that we may not look the same and we may not have come from the same place, but we all want to move in the same direction – towards a better future for our children and our grandchildren.

This belief comes from my unyielding faith in the decency and generosity of the American people. But it also comes from my own American story.

I am the son of a black man from Kenya and a white woman from Kansas. I was raised with the help of a white grandfather who survived a Depression to serve in Patton's Army during World War II and a white grandmother who worked on a bomber assembly line at Fort Leavenworth while he was overseas. I've gone to some of the best schools in America and lived in one of the world's poorest nations. I am married to a black American who carries within her the blood of slaves and slaveowners – an inheritance we pass on to our two precious daughters. I have brothers, sisters, nieces, nephews, uncles and cousins, of every race and every hue, scattered across three continents, and for as long as I live, I will never forget that in no other country on Earth is my story even possible.

It's a story that hasn't made me the most conventional candidate. But it is a story that has seared into my genetic make-up the idea that this nation is more than the sum of its parts – that out of many, we are truly one.

Throughout the first year of this campaign, against all predictions to the contrary, we saw how hungry the American people were for this message of unity. Despite the temptation to view my candidacy through a purely racial lens, we won commanding victories in states with some of the whitest populations in the country. In South Carolina, where the Confederate Flag still flies, we built a powerful coalition of African-Americans and white Americans.

This is not to say that race has not been an issue in the campaign. At various stages in the campaign, some commentators have deemed me either 'too black' or 'not black enough'. We saw racial tensions bubble to the surface during the week before the South Carolina primary. The press has scoured every exit poll for the latest evidence of racial polarisation, not just in terms of white and black, but black and brown as well.

And yet, it has only been in the last couple of weeks that the discussion of race in this campaign has taken a particularly divisive turn.

On one end of the spectrum, we've heard the implication that my candidacy is somehow an exercise in affirmative action; that it's based solely on the desire of wide-eyed liberals to purchase racial reconciliation on the cheap. On the other end, we've heard my former pastor, Reverend Jeremiah Wright, use incendiary language to express views that have the potential not only to widen the racial divide, but views that denigrate both the greatness and the goodness of our nation; that rightly offend white and black alike.

I have already condemned, in unequivocal terms, the statements of Reverend Wright that have caused such controversy. For some, nagging questions remain. Did I know him to be an occasionally fierce critic of American domestic and foreign policy? Of course. Did I ever hear him make remarks that could be considered controversial while I sat in church? Yes. Did I strongly disagree with many of his political views? Absolutely – just as I'm sure many of you have heard remarks from your pastors, priests, or rabbis with which you strongly disagreed.

But the remarks that have caused this recent firestorm weren't simply controversial. They weren't simply a religious leader's effort to speak out against perceived injustice. Instead, they expressed a profoundly distorted view of this country – a view that sees white racism as endemic, and that elevates what is wrong with America above all that we know is right with America; a view that sees the conflicts in the Middle East as rooted primarily in the actions of stalwart allies like Israel, instead of emanating from the perverse and hateful ideologies of radical Islam.

As such, Reverend Wright's comments were not only wrong but divisive, divisive at a time when we need unity; racially charged at a time when we need to come together to solve a set of monumental problems – two wars, a terrorist threat, a falling economy, a chronic health care crisis and potentially devastating climate change; problems that are neither black or white or Latino or Asian, but rather problems that confront us all.

Given my background, my politics, and my professed values and ideals, there will no doubt be those for whom my statements of condemnation are not enough. Why associate myself with Reverend Wright in the first place, they may ask? Why not join another church? And I confess that if all that I knew of Reverend Wright were the snippets of those sermons that have run in an endless loop on the television and YouTube, or if Trinity United Church of Christ conformed to the caricatures being peddled by some commentators, there is no doubt that I would react in much the same way

But the truth is, that isn't all that I know of the man. The man I met more than twenty years ago is a man who helped introduce me to my Christian faith, a man who spoke to me about our obligations to love one another; to care for the sick and lift up the poor. He is a man who served his country as a US Marine; who has studied and lectured at some of the finest universities and seminaries in the country, and who for over thirty years led a church that serves the community by doing God's work here on Earth – by housing the homeless, ministering to the needy, providing day care services and scholarships and prison ministries, and reaching out to those suffering from HIV/AIDS.

In my first book, *Dreams From My Father*, I described the experience of my first service at Trinity:

'People began to shout, to rise from their seats and clap and cry out, a forceful wind carrying the reverend's voice up into the rafters... And in that single note – hope! – I heard something else; at the foot of that cross, inside the thousands of churches across the city, I imagined the stories of ordinary black people merging with the stories of David and Goliath, Moses and Pharaoh, the Christians in the lion's den, Ezekiel's field of dry bones. Those stories – of survival, and freedom, and hope – became our story, my story; the blood that had spilled was our blood, the tears our tears; until this black church, on this bright day, seemed once more a vessel carrying the story of a people into future generations and into a larger world. Our trials and triumphs became at once unique and universal, black and more than black; in chronicling our journey, the stories and songs gave us a means to reclaim memories that we didn't need to feel shame about ... memories that all people might study and cherish – and with which we could start to rebuild.'

That has been my experience at Trinity. Like other predominantly black churches across the country, Trinity embodies the black community in its entirety – the doctor and the welfare mom, the model student and the former gang-banger. Like other black churches, Trinity's services are full of raucous laughter and sometimes bawdy humour. They are full of dancing, clapping, screaming and shouting that may seem jarring to the untrained ear. The church contains in full the kindness and cruelty, the fierce intelligence and the shocking ignorance, the struggles and successes, the love and yes, the bitterness and bias that make up the black experience in America.

And this helps explain, perhaps, my relationship with Reverend Wright. As imperfect as he may be, he has been like family to me. He strengthened my faith, officiated my wedding, and baptised my children. Not once in my conversations with him have I heard him talk about any ethnic group in derogatory terms, or treat whites with whom he interacted with anything but courtesy and respect. He contains within him the contradictions – the good and the bad – of the community that he has served diligently for so many years.

I can no more disown him than I can disown the black community. I can no more disown him than I can my white grandmother – a woman who helped raise me, a woman who sacrificed again and again for me, a woman who loves me as much as she loves anything in this world, but a woman who once confessed her fear of black men who passed by her on the street, and who on more than one occasion has uttered racial or ethnic stereotypes that made me cringe.

These people are a part of me. And they are a part of America, this country that I love.

Some will see this as an attempt to justify or excuse comments that are simply inexcusable. I can assure you it is not. I suppose the politically safe thing would be to move on from this episode and just hope that it fades into the wood-work. We can dismiss Reverend Wright as a crank or a demagogue, just as some have dismissed Geraldine Ferraro, in the aftermath of her recent statements, as harbouring some deep-seated racial bias.

But race is an issue that I believe this nation cannot afford to ignore right now. We would be making the same mistake that Reverend Wright made in his offending sermons about America – to simplify and stereotype and amplify the negative to the point that it distorts reality.

The fact is that the comments that have been made and the issues that have surfaced over the last few weeks reflect the complexities of race in this country that we've never really worked through – a part of our union that we have yet to perfect. And if we walk away now, if we simply retreat into our respective corners, we will never be able to come together and solve challenges like health care, or education, or the need to find good jobs for every American.

Understanding this reality requires a reminder of how we arrived at this point. As William Faulkner once wrote, 'The past isn't dead and buried. In fact, it isn't even past.' We do not need to recite here the history of racial injustice in this country. But we do need to remind ourselves that so many of the disparities that exist in the African-American community today can be directly traced to inequalities passed on from an earlier generation that suffered under the brutal legacy of slavery and Jim Crow.

Segregated schools were, and are, inferior schools; we still haven't fixed them, fifty years after *Brown v. Board of Education*, and the inferior education they provided, then and now, helps explain the pervasive achievement gap between today's black and white students.

Legalised discrimination – where blacks were prevented, often through violence, from owning property, or loans were not granted to African-American business owners, or black homeowners could not access Federal Housing Administration mortgages, or blacks were excluded from unions, or the police force, or fire departments – meant that black families could not amass any mean-ingful wealth to bequeath to future generations. That history helps explain the wealth and income gap between black and white, and the concentrated pockets of poverty that persist in so many of today's urban and rural communities.

A lack of economic opportunity among black men, and the shame and frus-tration that came from not being able to provide for one's family, contributed to the erosion of black families – a problem that welfare policies for many years may have worsened. And the lack of basic services in so many urban black neighbourhoods – parks for kids to play in, police walking the beat, regular garbage pick-up and building code enforcement – all helped create a cycle of violence, blight and neglect that continue to haunt us.

This is the reality in which Reverend Wright and other African-Americans of his generation grew up. They came of age in the late fifties and early sixties, a time when segregation was still the law of the land and opportunity was systematically constricted. What's remarkable is not how many failed in the face of discrimination, but rather how many men and women overcame the odds; how many were able to make a way out of no way for those like me who would come after them.

But for all those who scratched and clawed their way to get a piece of the American Dream, there were many who didn't make it – those who were ultimately defeated, in one way or another, by discrimination. That legacy of defeat was passed on to future generations – those young men and increasingly young women who we see standing on street corners or languishing in our prisons, without hope or prospects for the future. Even for those blacks who did make it, questions of race, and racism, continue to define their worldview in fundamental ways. For the men and women of Reverend Wright's generation, the memories of humiliation and doubt and fear have not gone away; nor has the anger and the bitterness of those years. That anger may not get expressed in public, in front of white co-workers or white friends. But it does find voice in the barbershop or around the kitchen table. At times, that anger is exploited by politicians, to gin up votes along racial lines, or to make up for a politician's own failings.

And occasionally it finds voice in the church on Sunday morning, in the pulpit and in the pews. The fact that so many people are surprised to hear that anger in some of Reverend Wright's sermons simply reminds us of the old truism that the most segregated hour in American life occurs on Sunday morning. That anger is not always productive; indeed, all too often it distracts attention from solving real problems; it keeps us from squarely facing our own complicity in our condition, and prevents the African-American community from forging the alliances it needs to bring about real change. But the anger is real; it is powerful; and to simply wish it away, to condemn it without understanding its roots, only serves to widen the chasm of misunderstanding that exists between the races.

In fact, a similar anger exists within segments of the white community. Most working- and middle-class white Americans don't feel that they have been particularly privileged by their race. Their experience is the immigrant experience – as far as they're concerned, no one's handed them anything, they've built it from scratch. They've worked hard all their lives, many times only to see their jobs shipped overseas or their pension dumped after a lifetime of labour. They are anxious about their futures, and feel their dreams slipping away; in an era of stagnant wages and global competition, opportunity comes to be seen as a zero sum game, in which your dreams come at my expense. So when they are told to bus their children to a school across town; when they hear that an African-American is getting an advantage in landing a good job or a spot in a good college because of an injustice that they themselves never committed; when they're told that their fears about crime in urban neighbourhoods are somehow prejudiced, resentment builds over time.

Like the anger within the black community, these resentments aren't always expressed in polite company. But they have helped shape the political landscape for at least a generation. Anger over welfare and affirmative action helped forge the Reagan Coalition. Politicians routinely exploited fears of crime for their own electoral ends. Talk show hosts and conservative commentators built entire careers unmasking bogus claims of racism while dismissing legitimate discussions of racial injustice and inequality as mere political correctness or reverse racism.

Just as black anger often proved counterproductive, so have these white resentments distracted attention from the real culprits of the middle-class squeeze – a corporate culture rife with inside dealing, questionable account-ing practices, and short-term greed; a Washington dominated by lobbyists and special interests; economic policies that favour the few over the many. And yet, to wish away the resentments of white Americans, to label them as misguided or even racist, without recognising they are grounded in legitimate concerns – this too widens the racial divide, and blocks the path to understanding.

This is where we are right now. It's a racial stalemate we've been stuck in for years. Contrary to the claims of some of my critics, black and white, I have never been so naive as to believe that we can get beyond our racial divisions in a single election cycle, or with a single candidacy – particularly a candidacy as imperfect as my own.

But I have asserted a firm conviction – a conviction rooted in my faith in God and my faith in the American people – that working together we can move beyond some of our old racial wounds, and that in fact we have no choice if we are to continue on the path of a more perfect union.

For the African-American community, that path means embracing the burdens of our past without becoming victims of our past. It means continuing to insist on a full measure of justice in every aspect of American life. But it also means binding our particular grievances – for better health care, and better schools, and better jobs – to the larger aspirations of all Americans – the white woman struggling to break the glass ceiling, the white man who's been laid off, the immigrant trying to feed his family. And it means taking full responsibility for own lives – by demanding more from our fathers, and spending more time with our children, and reading to them, and teaching them that while they may face challenges and discrimination in their own lives, they must never succumb to despair or cynicism; they must always believe that they can write their own destiny.

Ironically, this quintessentially American – and yes, conservative – notion of self-help found frequent expression in Reverend Wright's sermons. But what my former pastor too often failed to understand is that embarking on a programme of self-help also requires a belief that society can change.

The profound mistake of Reverend Wright's sermons is not that he spoke about racism in our society. It's that he spoke as if our society was static; as if no progress has been made; as if this country – a country that has made it possible for one of his own members to run for the highest office in the land and build a coalition of white and black, Latino and Asian, rich and poor, young and old – is still irrevocably bound to a tragic past. But what we know – what we have seen – is that America can change. That is the true genius of this nation. What we have already achieved gives us hope – the audacity to hope – for what we can and must achieve tomorrow.

In the white community, the path to a more perfect union means acknowledging that what ails the African-American community does not just exist in the minds of black people; that the legacy of discrimination – and current incidents of discrimination, while less overt than in the past – are real and must be addressed. Not just with words, but with deeds – by investing in our schools and our communities; by enforcing our civil rights laws and ensuring fairness in our criminal justice system; by providing this generation with ladders of opportunity that were unavailable for previous generations. It requires all Americans to realise that your dreams do not have to come at the expense of my dreams; that investing in the health, welfare, and education of black and brown and white children will ultimately help all of America prosper.

In the end, then, what is called for is nothing more, and nothing less, than what all the world's great religions demand – that we do unto others as we would have them do unto us. Let us be our brother's keeper, Scripture tells us. Let us be our sister's keeper. Let us find that common stake we all have in one another, and let our politics reflect that spirit as well.

For we have a choice in this country. We can accept a politics that breeds division, and conflict, and cynicism. We can tackle race only as spectacle – as we did in the O.J. Simpson trial – or in the wake of tragedy, as we did in the aftermath of Katrina – or as fodder for the nightly news. We can play Reverend Wright's sermons on every channel, every day and talk about them from now until the election, and make the only question in this campaign whether or not the American people think that I somehow believe or sympathise with his most offensive words. We can pounce on some gaffe by a Hillary Clinton supporter as evidence that she's playing the race card, or we can speculate on whether white men will all flock to John McCain in the general election regardless of his policies.

We can do that.

But if we do, I can tell you that in the next election, we'll be talking about some other distraction. And then another one. And then another one. And nothing will change.

That is one option. Or, at this moment, in this election, we can come together and say, 'Not this time.' This time we want to talk about the crumbling schools that are stealing the future of black children and white children and Asian children and Hispanic children and Native American children. This time we want to reject the cynicism that tells us that these kids can't learn; that those kids who don't look like us are somebody else's problem. The children of America are not those kids, they are our kids, and we will not let them fall behind in a twenty-first century economy. Not this time.

This time we want to talk about how the lines in the Emergency Room are filled with whites and blacks and Hispanics who do not have health care; who don't have the power on their own to overcome the special interests in Washington, but who can take them on if we do it together.

This time we want to talk about the shuttered mills that once provided a decent life for men and women of every race, and the homes for sale that once belonged to Americans from every religion, every region, every walk of life. This time we want to talk about the fact that the real problem is not that someone who doesn't look like you might take your job; it's that the corporation you work for will ship it overseas for nothing more than a profit.

This time we want to talk about the men and women of every colour and creed who serve together, and fight together, and bleed together under the same proud flag. We want to talk about how to bring them home from a war that never should've been authorised and never should've been waged, and we want to talk about how we'll show our patriotism by caring for them, and their families, and giving them the benefits they have earned.

I would not be running for President if I didn't believe with all my heart that this is what the vast majority of Americans want for this country. This union may never be perfect, but generation after generation has shown that it can always be perfected. And today, whenever I find myself feeling doubtful or cynical about this possibility, what gives me the most hope is the next generation – the young people whose attitudes and beliefs and openness to change have already made history in this election.

There is one story in particularly that I'd like to leave you with today – a story I told when I had the great honour of speaking on Dr King's birthday at his home church, Ebenezer Baptist, in Atlanta.

There is a young, twenty-three-year-old white woman named Ashley Baia who organised for our campaign in Florence, South Carolina. She had been working to organise a mostly African-American community since the beginning of this campaign, and one day she was at a roundtable discussion where everyone went around telling their story and why they were there.

And Ashley said that when she was nine years old, her mother got cancer. And because she had to miss days off work, she was let go and lost her health care. They had to file for bankruptcy, and that's when Ashley decided that she had to do something to help her mom.

She knew that food was one of their most expensive costs, and so Ashley convinced her mother that what she really liked and really wanted to eat more than anything else was mustard and relish sandwiches. Because that was the cheapest way to eat.

She did this for a year until her mom got better, and she told everyone at the roundtable that the reason she joined our campaign was so that she could help the millions of other children in the country who want and need to help their parents too.

Now Ashley might have made a different choice. Perhaps somebody told her along the way that the source of her mother's problems were blacks who were on welfare and too lazy to work, or Hispanics who were coming into the country illegally. But she didn't. She sought out allies in her fight against injustice.

Anyway, Ashley finishes her story and then goes around the room and asks everyone else why they're supporting the campaign. They all have different stories and reasons. Many bring up a specific issue. And finally they come to this elderly black man who's been sitting there quietly the entire time. And Ashley asks him why he's there. And he does not bring up a specific issue. He does not say health care or the economy. He does not say education or the war. He does not say that he was there because of Barack Obama. He simply says to everyone in the room, 'I am here because of Ashley.'

'I'm here because of Ashley.' By itself, that single moment of recognition between that young white girl and that old black man is not enough. It is not enough to give health care to the sick, or jobs to the jobless, or education to our children.

But it is where we start. It is where our union grows stronger. And as so many generations have come to realise over the course of the two-hundred and twenty-one years since a band of patriots signed that document in Philadelphia, that is where the perfection begins.

VÁCLAV HAVEL

'A SENSE OF SOLIDARITY'

—

REMARKS TO THE CUBAN PEOPLE

FLORIDA INTERNATIONAL UNIVERSITY, MIAMI, FLORIDA,
23 SEPTEMBER 2002

Václav Havel (5 October 1936 – 18 December 2011), playwright, essayist and politician, was an active dissident during the years of communism in Czechoslovakia. The author of over twenty widely translated works of drama and non-fiction, Havel was a signatory of the pro-democracy Charter 77 Manifesto and a founding signatory of the Prague Convention on European Conscience and Communism. Following the collapse of communism in 1989 he was elected President of Czechoslovakia, a post he held until the secession of Slovakia under the leadership of nationalist Prime Minister Vladimír Mečiar in 1992. Havel was elected President of the Czech Republic the following year, serving for a decade. Throughout his presidency he remained a vocal critic of countries that continued to deny basic freedoms to their citizens. Seen as an international symbol of the ongoing struggle for democracy and human rights, Havel was voted 4th in Prospect *magazine's 2005 global poll of the world's top 100 intellectuals. His death was much-lamented around the world.*

Havel often argued for a moral politics, a 'living in truth'. Respect for human rights, freedom and dignity is needed in Cuba, just as in Central and Eastern Europe in 1989. For him, the communist government of Cuba is repellent precisely because of its oppression, lies and cult of personality. Unlike many, Havel is willing to speak out for liberty and justice in Cuba.

—

Mr President, distinguished guests, ladies and gentlemen, and to all those citizens of Cuba who are listening to us, I am here in Florida for the first time in my life, and Florida is also the last state in the United States – and the last place on the whole American continent – that I will be visiting as President of my country. It was my own choice to come to Florida, and I have chosen it, among other things, because it is from here that I want to extend my greetings to all Cubans – both to those who live here, and to those who live at home, in Cuba.

Every modern, freedom-loving person feels, or at least ought to feel, a sense of solidarity both with those who are prevented from living in their home country or from freely visiting it, and with those who are forced to live in their country in a state of constant fear, and who cannot leave it and return to it of their own free will.

But there are people who should naturally feel this kind of solidarity far more intensively than others. I am referring to those of us who experienced first-hand, on our own skins, as it were, the oppressive weight of life under a totalitarian system of the communist type, or who may even have tried to resist that system and, in doing so, experienced just how important the solidarity and help offered by people from freer countries was.

I think that one of the most diabolical instruments for subjugating some people and fooling others is the special communist language. It is a language full of subterfuge, ideological jargon, meaningless phrases and stereotypical figures of speech. To people who have not seen through its mendacity or who have never had to live in a world manipulated by it, this language can appear very attractive. At the same time, in others, this very same language can evoke fear and horror and force them into permanent state of dissimulation.

In my country, too, entire generations of people once let themselves be led astray by this kind of language with its fine words about justice, peace and the necessity of fighting against those who, allegedly in the interests of evil foreign powers, resisted the power that spoke this language. The great advantage of this language lies in the fact that all its parts are firmly bound together in a closed system of dogmas that excludes anything that does not fit. Any idea with a hint of originality or independence – as well as any word that is not part of the official vocabulary – is labelled an ideological diversion – almost, it would seem, before anyone can express it. The web of dogmas deployed to justify any arbitrary action by the ruling power, therefore, usually takes a utopian form – that is, an artificial construct that contains a whole set of reasons why everything that does not fit the structure or that reaches beyond it must be suppressed, forbidden or destroyed for the sake of some happy future.

The easy thing to do is to accept this language, to believe in it or, at least, to adapt to it. It is very difficult to maintain one's own point of view, though common sense may tell you a hundred times over that you are right, as long as that means either revolting against the language of the powers that be, or simply refusing to use it. A system of persecutions, of bans, of informers, of compulsory elections, of spying on one's neighbours, of censorship and, ultimately, of concentration camps is hidden behind a veil of beautiful words that have utterly no shame in calling enslavement a 'higher form of freedom', of calling independent thinking a way of 'supporting imperialism', or labelling the entrepreneurial spirit a way of 'impoverishing one's fellow humans' and calling human rights a 'bourgeois fiction'.

My country's experience was simple: when the internal crisis of the totalitarian system grows so deep that it becomes clear to everyone, and when more and more people learn to speak their own language and reject the hollow, mendacious language of the powers that be, it means that freedom is remarkably close, if not directly within reach. All of a sudden, it seems that the king is naked and the mysterious radiant energy that comes from free speech and free actions turns out to be more powerful than the strongest army, police force, or party organisation, stronger than the greatest power of a centrally directed and centrally devastated economy, or of the centrally controlled and centrally enslaved media, those chief propagators of the mendacious language of the official utopia.

Our world, as a whole, is not in the best of shape and the direction it is headed in may well be quite ambivalent. But this does not mean that we are permitted to give up on free and cultivated thinking and to replace it with a set of utopian clichés. That would not make the world a better place, it would only make it worse. On the contrary, it means that we must do more for our own freedom, and that of others.

May all Cubans live in freedom and enjoy independence and prosperity!

To all those who have not lost the will to resist arbitrary force and lies, may your dreams be fulfilled!

And may Oswald Payá Sardinas, the great champion of human rights in Cuba, be awarded the Nobel Peace Prize, and may this award strengthen the courage of all the Cuban people to take up non-violent resistance against an oppressive regime!

Thank you for being here and for listening to me.

TONY BLAIR

'WE ARE AT OUR BEST WHEN AT OUR BOLDEST'

—

REMARKS AT THE LABOUR PARTY CONFERENCE

BLACKPOOL, UNITED KINGDOM, 1 OCTOBER 2002

Tony Blair was elected to the UK House of Commons in 1983, representing the constituency of Sedgefield. He became leader of the Labour Party in 1994, following the sudden death of his predecessor in that office, John Smith. Restyling the party as 'New Labour', he embarked on a series of symbolic and substantive party reforms, most famously amending Clause IV of the Labour Party's constitution, which had, since 1918, committed the party 'To secure for the workers by hand or by brain the full fruits of their industry and the most equitable distribution thereof that may be possible upon the basis of the common ownership of the means of production, distribution and exchange, and the best obtainable system of popular administration and control of each industry or service.' This sweeping mandate for nationalisation, Blair argued, was an embarrassing anachronism an electoral albatross. He persuaded the party membership to drastically revise the clause, incorporating an acceptance of free markets while maintaining a commitment to the redistribution of wealth. This was a defining moment in Labour's recovery from a series of disastrous electoral defeats in 1979, 1983, 1987 and 1992. His rhetoric placed a new emphasis on supporting middle-class aspirations and the financial sector.

In 1997, Blair led his party to an historic electoral victory, winning 418 of 659 seats in the House of Commons, Labour's best ever election result, and was appointed Prime Minister. Under his leadership Labour won the next two general elections, though with declining majorities. In 2007 he resigned from the party leadership and office of Prime Minister.

In these remarks he sets the agenda for his party as it moves into the new *millennium. The language here has been extensively borrowed by politicians in all of Britain's major political parties, as well as in the United States and elsewhere. Many words and phrases have been pillaged by hundreds of politicians. Style has been influential, too. Note Blair's use of word economy. He understands the power of the right word. I have often said that he has 'intelligence behind the words', which means that he knows the reason for each word in the speech and he knows what he wants to do with it. Thus, he can get more out of a speech than most speakers, who use more words but say less. In a short period of time he can take the listener on a journey of ideas and experience to end at a point of collective agreement. He also knows how to persuade with patriotism, binding citizens together through language and symbols. And he has a vision for Great Britain, the destination of this journey together. The paragraph construction is my own. The original speech was published with each sentence standing alone.*

———

The paradox of the modern world is this: we've never been more interdependent in our needs; and we've never been more individualist in our outlook.

Globalisation and technology open up vast new opportunities but also cause massive insecurity.

The values of progressive politics – solidarity, justice for all – have never been more relevant; and their application never more in need of modernisation. Internationally, we need a new global partnership, that moves beyond a narrow view of national interest. At home, it means taking the great progressive 1945 settlement and reforming it around the needs of the individual as consumer and citizen for the twenty-first century. What we did for the Labour Party in the new clause IV, freeing us from outdated doctrine and practice, we must now do, through reform, for Britain's public services and welfare state.

We are at a crossroads: party, government, country. Do we take modest though important steps of improvement? Or do we make the great push forward for transformation?

I believe we're at our best when at our boldest. So far, we've made a good start but we've not been bold enough. Interdependence is obliterating the distinction between foreign and domestic policy. It was the British economy that felt the aftermath of 11 September. Our cities who take in refugees from the 13 million now streaming across the world from famine, disease or conflict.

Our young people who die from heroin imported from Afghanistan. It is our climate that is changing.

Today, a nation's chances are measured not just by its own efforts but by its place in the world.

Influence is power is prosperity. We are an island nation, small in space, 60 million in people but immense in history and potential. We can take refuge in the mists of Empire but it is a delusion that national identity is best preserved in isolation, that we should venture out in the world only at a time of emergency.

There is a bold side to the British character. And there is a cautious side. Both have their time and season. Caution is often born of common sense, a great British trait. But there are times when caution is retreat and retreat is dangerous. Now, at the start of the twenty-first century, is a time for reaching out. The cold war is over. The US is the only superpower. The Americans stand strong and proud, but at times resented. Europe is economically powerful but not yet politically coherent. Russia is breaking free from its past but still carrying the burden. For China and India, power is only a matter of time. For the moment, Japan is changing, South America struggling, Asia emerging; Africa impoverished; the Middle East unstable.

The world can go in two ways. Countries can become rivals in power, or partners. Partnership is the antidote to unilateralism. For all the resentment of America, remember one thing.

The basic values of America are our values too, British and European, and they are good values. Democracy, freedom, tolerance, justice. It's easy to be anti-American. There's a lot of it about but remember when and where this alliance was forged: here in Europe, in World War II when Britain and America and every decent citizen in Europe joined forces to liberate Europe from the Nazi evil.

My vision of Britain is not as the fifty-first state of anywhere, but I believe in this alliance and I will fight long and hard to maintain it. I'm not saying we always apply our values correctly.

But I've lost count of the number of supposedly intelligent people who've said to me. You don't understand the Serbs. They're very attached to Slobodon Milošević. No they weren't. The Afghans are different. They like religious extremism. No they didn't. The Iraqis don't have the same tradition of political freedom. No they don't but I bet they'd like to.

Our values aren't Western values. They're human values, and anywhere, anytime people are given the chance, they embrace them. Around these values, we build our global partnership. Europe and America together. Russia treated as a friend and equal. China and India seeking not rivalry but cooperation and for all nations the basis of our partnership not power alone but a common will based on common values. Applied in an even-handed way. Some say the issue is Iraq. Some say it is the Middle East Peace Process. It's both. Some say it's poverty. Some say it's terrorism. It's both. I know the worry over Iraq. People accept Saddam is bad.

But they fear it's being done for the wrong motives. They fear us acting alone. So the United Nations route. Let us lay down the ultimatum. Let Saddam comply with the will of the UN.

So far most of you are with me. But here is the hard part. If he doesn't comply, then consider.

If at this moment having found the collective will to recognise the danger, we lose our collective will to deal with it, then we will destroy not the authority of America or Britain but of the United Nations itself. Sometimes, and in particular dealing with a dictator, the only chance of peace is a readiness for war.

But we need coalitions not just to deal with evil by force if necessary, but coalitions for peace, coalitions to tackle poverty, ignorance and disease. A coalition to fight terrorism and a coalition to give Africa hope. A coalition to re-build the nation of Afghanistan as strong as the coalition to defeat the Taliban. A coalition to fight the scourge of AIDS, to protect the planet from climate change every bit as powerful as the coalition for free trade, free markets and free enterprise.

And yes, what is happening in the Middle East now is ugly and wrong. The Palestinians living in increasingly abject conditions, humiliated and hopeless; Israeli civilians brutally murdered.

I agree UN resolutions should apply here as much as to Iraq. But they don't just apply to Israel. They apply to all parties. And there is only one answer. By this year's end, we must have revived final status negotiations and they must have explicitly as their aims: an Israeli state free from terror, recognised by the Arab world and a viable Palestinian state based on the boundaries of 1967.

For Britain to help shape this new world, Britain needs to be part of it. Our friendship with America is a strength. So is our membership of Europe. We should make the most of both.

And in Europe, never more so than now. The single currency is a fact, but will Europe find the courage for economic reform? Europe is to become 25 nations, one Europe for the first time since Charlemagne, but will it be as a union of nation states or as a centralised super-state?

It has taken the first steps to a common defence policy, but will it be a friend or a rival to NATO?

The answers to these questions are crucial to Britain. They matter to the British economy, our country, our way of life. And the way to get the right answers, is by being in there, vigorous, confident, leading in Europe not limping along several paces behind. That's why the Euro is not just about our economy but our destiny. We should only join the Euro if the economic tests are met. That is clear. But if the tests are passed, we go for it.

Interdependence is the core reality of the modern world. It is revolutionising our idea of national interest. It is forcing us to locate that interest in the wider international community. It is making solidarity – a great social democratic ideal – our route to practical survival. Partnership is statesmanship for the twenty-first century. We need now the same clarity of vision for our country.

I have learned this in five years of government. The radical decision is usually the right one. The right decision is usually the hardest one. And the hardest decisions are often the least popular at the time.

The starting point is not policy. It's hope. I sometimes think the whole of politics can be reduced to a battle between pessimism and hope. Because from hope comes change. At times, in Britain we lack self-belief. Britain is a great country. On the way up. Fourth largest economy in the world. The best mortgage, inflation and unemployment figures for a generation. Long-term youth unemployment now down to 5,400 for the whole of Britain. Compare that with three million unemployed under the Tories and then understand the difference a Labour government can make. As a result, the welfare bills of failure are falling; so we can spend £6 billion a year more today on pensioners than in 1997 and that's also the difference a Labour government makes. In arts and culture, we lead the world in awards, prizes and talent. Our armed forces are the best anywhere. Our school system has now been judged, by the most authoritative international analysis, among the top eight in the world, above France and Germany.

More students than ever before go to university. Our universities are widely regarded as the best in Europe.

I understand the anxiety of students affected by the marking down of their A levels.

We are totally committed to helping them. But perhaps mistakes like this can be avoided if in future, when our students do well, we praise the students, thank the teachers instead of thinking we must have failed, when actually we've done better.

For all the attacks on the NHS, listen to this story of a woman who has breast cancer. Screened because she was one of the 140,000 extra now checked a year. Who saw a consultant within two weeks. Saw him because now every urgent patient suspected of cancer has to be seen within two weeks. Treated within four weeks because that is now the maximum time for breast cancer treatment. Five years ago, even two years ago, none of that would have been guaranteed.

That's what we meant when in 1997 we said Britain was going to get better. That's what the Tories hate. They sneer at the investment. Pessimism about Britain is now the official strategy of the Tories. The purpose is not just to undermine the government, but to undermine government, to destroy the belief that we can collectively achieve anything, to drench progress in cynicism, to sully the hope from which energy, action and change all spring. Now they've gone 'compassionate'. Know what it means? We are going to run down your schools but we feel really bad about it. We're going to charge you to see a GP but we really wish we weren't.

We're going to put more children in poverty but this time we'll honestly feel very guilty about it.

In Opposition, Labour was trying to escape policies we didn't believe in. It was a journey of conviction. Today's Tories are trying to escape policies they do believe in. Theirs is a journey of convenience and it fools no one least of all themselves. There's no cause for pessimism, we should believe in ourselves and use that self-belief to choose now and irrevocably the path of reform.

The twentieth century was a century of savage slaughter, insane ideology, and unparalleled progress. Progress won in the end. Governments used collective power through the state, to provide opportunity for the masses. But in time the institutions of that power became huge interests in their own right. And the people became more prosperous, more assertive, more individualist. Eventually, the 1980s saw a reaction by the individual against collective power in all its forms.

Now with globalisation, a new era has begun. People are no less individualist, but they are insecure. Modern prosperity may be greater but modern life is pressure and stress. Twentieth-century collective power was exercised through the Big State. Their welfare was paternalistic, handing down from on high. That won't do today. Just as mass production has departed from industry, so the monolithic provision of services has to depart from the public sector.

People want an individual service for them. They want government under them not over them.

They want government to empower them, not control them. And they want equality of both opportunity and responsibility. They want to know the same rules that apply to them, apply to all. Out goes the Big State. In comes the Enabling State. Out goes a culture of benefits and entitlements. In comes a partnership of rights and responsibilities.

That's why we need reform. Reform is just a word. It has no meaning in itself. It's the purpose of it that matters. I will tell you why I am passionate about reform. Because poor public services and welfare are usually for the poorest. The better-off can buy a better education or move to a better area or know a better doctor; or find a better job. Those great governments of 1906 and 1945 did great things. They inherited a situation where the majority were have-nots and made them haves. But prosperity never reached all the way down. We went from being a 30-70 country to being a 70-30 one. Today it's not enough. Not morally. Not economically where we need every last drop of potential to be fulfilled, if Britain is to succeed.

Let me spell it out. In education, we need to move to the post-comprehensive era, where schools keep the comprehensive principle of equality of opportunity but where we open up the system to new and different ways of education, built round the needs of the individual child. We need an NHS true to the principle of care on the basis of need, not ability to pay, but personalised, built around the individual patient. Both require an end to the 'one size fits all' mass production public service. The purpose of the twentieth-century welfare state was to treat citizens as equals.

The purpose of our twenty-first century reforms must be to treat them as individuals as well.

And we can't make that change by more bureaucracy from the centre, by just flogging the system harder.

We need to change the system. It means putting power in the hands of the patient or parent, which is what Alan [Johnson] and Estelle [Morris] are doing. Why shouldn't an NHS patient be able to book an appointment for an operation at their convenience, just like they could if they paid for it? 'At the time I want, with the doctor I want' was Margaret Thatcher's reason for going private. Why shouldn't it be the right for every citizen and why shouldn't it be done within the NHS? Why shouldn't our best hospitals be free to develop their services within the NHS as foundation hospitals? Why shouldn't there be a range of schools for parents to choose from: from specialist schools to the new City Academies, to faith schools, to sixth forms and sixth form colleges offering excellent routes into university and skilled employment? Why shouldn't good schools expand or take over failing schools or form federations? It means power in the hands of the professionals. Why shouldn't nurses prescribe medicines or order x-rays? Why shouldn't classroom assistants and IT specialists be every bit as important as teachers in the future? Why should a consultant who does thirty NHS operations a week not be paid more than one who does ten? Why should a teacher who wants to stay in the classroom and is superb at it not be paid the same as a Head of Department?

Every time the reform is tough, just keep one thing in mind: the child in a school where barely any pupils take A levels, where only 20 per cent get good GCSEs and where the majority know they will just end up as one of the 7 million British adults who can't even read or write properly.

The only difference between that child and mine is one had a chance in life and the other had none. If the status quo was good enough, that child would be a figment of our imagination.

The fact that such children do exist – thousands of them every year in Britain – is why reform is the road to social justice, not its denial.

Do you know what really holds back change? The pessimism that says: go on, you can't really have top-quality services for all. It's like the Tories who argue you dumb down if 50 per cent of young people go to university though of course three quarters of middle-class children already do.

As if God distributed ability by class background. I visited the Beswick estate in East Manchester on Saturday with John Prescott. Three years ago going down.

Now on the way up. Massive investment. The primary school results dramatically improved.

Were the boys and girls in 2002 brighter than their brothers and sisters in 1999? Rubbish.

All that's changed is that for the first time in their lives, people are giving them a bit of hope, a bit of belief, a bit of confidence that they're every much as entitled to a start in life as the middle-class child five miles up the road.

We reject old Tory pessimism. But we on the left have our own pessimism. It's that if we change a cherished institution, we betray it. If we deliver a service in a different way, we trash its founding principles. I agree competition should not be on the basis of cutting wages or employment protection. Demoralised staff don't perform at their best. We should value our public servants. I don't just mean the doctors, nurses, teachers and police. I mean the porters, cleaners, secretaries, administrators, the dinner ladies, the care assistants who day in and day out give time and effort and commitment way beyond their contractual duty.

I say to the trade unions: work with us on the best way of delivering the service and we will work with you on ending the two-tier workforce.

But let me make one thing plain. We are the only government anywhere in the Western world that this year, next year, the year after, is increasing both health and education public spending as a percentage of national income. The only one. That is our commitment to public services.

We said schools and hospitals first. We're building them. Lots of them. And I am not going to go to parents and children and patients in my constituency or any other and say I'm sorry because there is an argument going on about PFI we're going to put these projects on hold. They don't care who builds them. So long as they're built. I don't care who builds them. So long as they're on cost, on budget, and helping to deliver a better NHS and better State schools for the people of Sedgefield and every other constituency in the land. Between 1979 and 1997, ten new hospitals were built. Through PFI since 1997, fifteen new hospitals built and a hundred on the way. Five hundred and fifty schools are being re-built or modernised. In Glasgow, the whole of the secondary school system is being re-built with twelve brand new schools. All under PFI. And every single part of the service remains universal and free at the point of use.

Come on: this isn't the betrayal of public services. It's their renewal.

All that is happening is that here, as round the rest of the world, we are dividing means and ends. The ends, universal provision, remain the same. The means of delivery, partnership between public, private and voluntary sectors and between state and citizen, change. Pensions is probably the biggest current worry for the workforce. And transport probably the worst area of public services. Over the coming months, we will present long-term proposals for both.

But there is no way government through the general taxpayer can do it all.

People still have 1945 expectations of government. They want it to do things for them. In fact today, government can only do things with them. It's the same for the economic role for government. We can empower but we can't run people's lives or their business. In fact the greatest hope for social democracy is the coming together of the social and the economic case for developing human potential. Investment in people, helping them to learn new skills and technology, to start a business or help their business to grow.

But it has to be a partnership. And that applies to all walks of life. I know the plight of the farming community. It is serious. I have spent five years working on it. We are putting more money into it than the rest of British industry combined. We'll carry on doing it. But it's time this money is used to reform farming so that it has a future, rather than to prop up the failed practices of the past.

And I want to stress our commitment to British science. We face a choice. We can use our huge strengths in this area to become world leaders. Or we can be deterred by the Luddite tirades.

I have made that choice for Britain. Two billion pounds extra over three years. And I was proud to have made that choice when I sat waiting to be interviewed by David Frost on Sunday, watching an interview with the American actor Christopher Reeve who said he wanted to thank Britain and the British people for taking a lead on research which could help him and others like him all over the world.

But the other side of government helping the citizen is the citizen's responsibility to others. Partnership is also citizenship for the twenty-first century.

I don't have the toughest job in government. David Blunkett does. On asylum, where big reform is needed urgently. And on crime. I still hear from time to time this nonsense that crime is not a real Labour issue, and all we have to do is deliver on poverty and opportunity. Of course we have to do that. But try telling a 92-year-old pensioner, a Labour supporter for the last seventy years, that she'll have to wait for the Tories to get tough on the young thugs who battered her. That's not a conversation I'm prepared to have. We're the first government since the war under which crime has fallen not risen. Does that reassure everyone? No. There is less of a chance today of being a victim of crime than at any time for twenty years. Does everyone believe it? No. We have increased the numbers of police to record numbers, toughened the law on everything from rape to benefit fraud. Does that mean everyone feels safer? No. Why? Because the problem is not just crime. It is disrespect. It is anti-social behaviour. It is the drug dealer at the end of the street and no one seems to be able to do anything about it. This is not only about crime. It is about hard-working families who play the rules seeing those who don't, getting away with it. The street crime initiative has been one of the most successful exercises in partnership between government and police in living memory. Not my words, but those of the Chief Constables. But what was fascinating was not the initiative itself, but what it uncovered.

Outdated identity parades taking weeks if not months to organise. Defendants who didn't answer to their bail and never got punished for it. Police officers told it was a breach of civil liberties to check whether defendants were obeying bail conditions. It's not civil liberties. It's lunacy. Drug addicts with previous offences routinely bailed though everyone knew what they would be doing between bail and trial. Magistrates unable to remand persistent young offenders in custody because no places existed in prison or secure accommodation. The whole system full of excellent people, worn down and worn out. Step by step David and his team, working with the police, are putting it right. Later this year we will introduce the Criminal Justice and Sentencing Reform Bill. It will re-balance the system emphatically and in favour of the victims of crime. Old rules will be swept away; court procedures simplified; sentencing built round the offender as well as the offence, with those on drugs getting treatment or custody. More police on the beat. More Community Support Officers. Instant fines for anti-social behaviour. Parents of truants who refuse to cooperate with the school will be fined or lose benefit. Anti-social tenants and their anti-social landlords who make money out of abusing Housing Benefit, while making life hell for the community, should lose their right to it. Those who assault teachers or nurses should go to jail.

And from early next year, wealthy drug dealers or organised criminals with money in their bank account or a home or an asset of any sort but no lawful means of support will have it taken from them unless they show it was come by lawfully not through crime. For a hundred years, our Criminal Justice System like our welfare system was based on a messy compromise between liberals and authoritarians. The liberals tended to view crime as primarily about social causes and the welfare system primarily about giving to the poor. The authoritarians wanted harsh penalties and as ungenerous a benefit system as possible. The compromise was a Criminal Justice System weighted in favour of the defendant but with harsh penalties for the convicted; and a passive welfare system with mean benefits.

In short, the worst of all worlds.

In its place, a new contract between citizen and community. We give opportunity to all.

We demand responsibility from all. We are investing heavily in the biggest anti-poverty strategy of any government for half a century. On top of record investment in education, we've introduced the New Deal, the Working Families Tax Credit, record increases in Child Benefit and Income Support, Sure Start.

To the majority who are reasonably well off, these are just words. To people who need them, they can be transforming. I saw it last week in Hackney, where a woman said till Sure Start came along she felt trapped in her council flat, looking after her child. Now the child had a creche to go to; the mother had a network of friends and contacts; she got a job. She was happy. I've seen it at Ferryhill in my own Sedgefield constituency. It is a great feeling. You're the local MP.

But you're also the Prime Minister. And the government you lead has created centres like those all over the country. And you can see the impact for the better on the lives of people who elected you. And what was brilliant about Sure Start at Ferryhill wasn't just the fantastic new facilities, the crèche and nursery, the help and advice for families. It was the buzz of mums and dads, staff and helpers taking control, not just of their own lives but of the community, making those lives and that community better.

That is what we mean by the redistribution of power, wealth and opportunity to the many not the few. The modern welfare state must be active, not passive, put partnership in place of paternalism. That's what a modern civic society, with reformed public services and welfare, can do.

But it also means changes to politics itself. The same issues that confront our public services – collapse of deference, rise of individualism, a desire for involvement – apply in equal measure to the conduct of politics.

I don't have all the answers. I don't have all the levers. The other parties. Local politicians.

The media. Pressure groups. Anyone with a vested interest in a healthy democracy has a role to play here. For us, I accept a big majority means a big responsibility to make Parliament more relevant and do more in Parliament. And our very political strength means that when voters get disengaged the challenge is for us to find out why and do something about it. Next time, we want to win but we want to do it on a turnout of more than 59 per cent. Our relations too, Party leadership and members, has to change. You've lost your love of discipline for its own sake.

I've lost my love of popularity for its own sake. Soon, we will present proposals to you for the renewal of our membership base, policy discussion and our links with other parties around the world. The alternative is a return to self-destruction, the perennial disease of centre-left governments. Never let us fall for the far left's eternal delusion: that if there is dissatisfaction with a moderate centre-left government this can be manipulated into support for a far-left government. It results only in one thing. Always has. Always will: the return of a right-wing Tory government. Displeasing people; pockets of disillusion; impatience and frustration. These are not the hallmarks of this Labour government. They are the hallmarks of government.

The test is to listen, adapt and move forward. Up to 1997, do you know how many years of the twentieth century Labour was in power with a substantial majority? Nine. By the end of this Parliament, we will have doubled it. We learned the hard way.

But now we have to show that we have the capacity not only to learn but to transform, to show what a liberated modern social democracy can do. We can do it. I'm an optimist.

Why? Because there is change happening. Ten years ago people asked would Labour ever win again. Now, they ask it of the Tories. Ten years ago, they asked if we were fit to manage the economy. Now thanks to the vision and brilliance of Gordon Brown, we have succeeded beyond any previous Labour or Tory government. Not by chance. Every part of it – from the first years of discipline, through to Bank of England independence through to reform of tax and benefits to make work pay – was a bold choice. The right-wing never deserved their reputation for economic competence. And we've made sure they'll never have exclusive rights to it again. Ten years ago, claims that the minimum wage would cost a million jobs were the centrepiece of John Major's election campaign: now it's the law, business and trade unions agree it, and the Tories have to pretend they were in favour of it all along. At our best when at our boldest. For four elections, anyone who said investment before tax cuts was brave but doomed. In 2001, we did it and it is those who oppose the investment who are on the run. The New Deal was savaged by the Tories, challenged politically, challenged legally, challenged by business. Now it's in its sixth year, over a million people have been helped by it and not one Tory candidate dares to stand up and say we should abolish it.

At our best when at our boldest. Remember how devolution would break up Britain? And now there is a Scottish Parliament and a Welsh Assembly, the nationalists are running from their separatism and not a single party in Britain proposes going back. And in Northern Ireland, for all the difficulties, Republicans and Unionists sit in government together and the principle of consent is accepted North and South on the island of Ireland for the first time in eighty years.

At our best when at our boldest. And remember how for a hundred years we tried to reform the House of Lords and now the reform is happening, the hereditary peers are leaving and the attack is that it doesn't go far enough? The equal age of consent passed massively in the House of Commons. The first black Cabinet Minister. Record numbers of women Cabinet Ministers. Record numbers of women MPs.

From progress here to life and death, abroad, it is happening. A month ago I visited Beira District Hospital in Mozambique. There are as many doctors in the whole of Mozambique as there are in Oldham. I saw four children to a bed, sick with malaria. Nurses dying of AIDS faster than others can be recruited. Tens of thousands of children dying in that country needlessly every year. I asked a doctor: what hope is there? Britain is our hope, he said. Thanks to you we have debt relief. Thanks to you we have new programmes to fight AIDS and malaria. Thanks to you the docks at Maputo are being rebuilt and we can sell our goods abroad.

When you tire of knocking on the door, putting the leaflet in the envelope, wonder what it's all about and what it's all for, reflect on that doctor, feel proud of what you do, and understand that's what we elect a Labour Government for. We haven't just nailed the myths about Labour of old; we've created some legend of achievement about New Labour too.

We've been at our best when we've been at our boldest. And now we need to be again.

And all it takes, is for us to do what we believe in. We believe in a school system of equal opportunity for all. But we don't yet have it. We believe in an NHS with equal access for all; but not all get it. We believe in punishing the guilty and acquitting the innocent but it's not what happens. We believe in ridding Britain of child poverty but children are still poor. We believe in Europe but we're not yet at the centre of it. There's nothing wrong with the old principles but if the old ways worked, they'd have worked by now. If you believe in social justice, in solidarity, in equality of opportunity and responsibility, then believe in the reforms to get us there.

Now is the time. To quicken the march of progress not mark time. What started with the renewal of the Labour Party only ends with the renewal of Britain. Pessimism or hope. Despair or confidence. Decline or renewal.

At our best when at our boldest. This is not the time to abandon our journey of modernisation but to see it through.

TONY BLAIR

'BRITAIN IS NOT A FOLLOWER. IT IS A LEADER'

—

RESIGNATION SPEECH

SEDGEFIELD, UNITED KINGDOM, 10 MAY 2007

*I*n 2007, after ten years as Prime Minister and three general election victories, Tony Blair resigned from government and the party leadership. As generally expected, he was succeeded by former Chancellor of the Exchequer Gordon Brown. Brown had reluctantly refrained from opposing Blair in the 1994 Labour leadership election, and his resulting resentment became a regular subject of press speculation, leaks and counter-leaks throughout the course of Blair's years in office. At first close friends and allies in opposition, the two became bitter rivals and leaders of opposing factions within the Labour Party in government, with Brown considered the more 'authentic' Labour man and socialist, as opposed to Blair's centrism. Brown's supporters alleged that Blair had broken repeated promises to stand down as leader at an earlier date and speculation continues as to whether the two agreed a formal deal over the leadership and timescale for a handover from Blair to Brown in 1994, at a famous, now-defunct, North London restaurant named Granita.

The speech is the end of an era. Literally, the speaking of the words marked a turning point in British politics. The content is a retrospective of the glory years of New Labour, as well as a concession of the corrosive effect of the war in Iraq and the voter fatigue of a decade in power. The paragraph construction below is my own.

—

I have come back here, to Sedgefield, to my constituency, where my political journey began and where it is fitting it should end. Today I announce my decision to stand down from the leadership of the Labour Party. The Party will now select a new leader. On 27 June I will tender my resignation from the office of Prime Minister to the Queen. I have been Prime Minister of this country for just over ten years. In this job, in the world today, that is long enough, for me, but more especially for the country. Sometimes the only way you conquer the pull of power is to set it down.

It is difficult to know how to make this speech today. There is a judgement to be made on my premiership. And in the end that is for you, the people, to make. I can only describe what I think has been done over these last ten years and, perhaps more important, why. I have never quite put it like this before. I was born almost a decade after the Second World War. I was a young man in the social revolution of the 60s and 70s. I reached political maturity as the Cold War was ending, and the world was going through a political, economic and technological revolution. I looked at my own country, a great country – wonderful history, magnificent traditions, proud of its past, but strangely uncertain of its future, uncertain about the future, almost old-fashioned. All of that was curiously symbolised in its politics. You stood for individual aspiration and getting on in life or social compassion and helping others. You were liberal in your values or conservative. You believed in the power of the state or the efforts of the individual. Spending more money on the public realm was the answer or it was the problem. None of it made sense to me. It was twentieth-century ideology in a world approaching a new millennium.

Of course people want the best for themselves and their families, but in an age where human capital is a nation's greatest asset, they also know it is just and sensible to extend opportunities, to develop the potential to succeed, for all – not an elite at the top. People are, today, open-minded about race and sexuality, averse to prejudice and yet deeply and rightly conservative with a small 'c' when it comes to good manners, respect for others, treating people courteously.

They acknowledge the need for the state and the responsibility of the individual.

They know spending money on our public services matters and that it is not enough. How they are run and organised matters too.

So 1997 was a moment for a new beginning, for sweeping away all the detritus of the past. Expectations were so high, too high – too high, in a way, for either of us. Now in 2007, you can easily point to the challenges, the things that are wrong, the grievances that fester. But go back to 1997. Think back. No, really, think back. Think about your own living standards then in May 1997 and now. Visit your local school, any of them round here, or anywhere in modern Britain.

Ask when you last had to wait a year or more on a hospital waiting list, or heard of pensioners freezing to death in the winter, unable to heat their homes. There is only one government since 1945 that can say all of the following: 'More jobs, fewer unemployed, better health and education results, lower crime and economic growth in every quarter' – this one. But I don't need a statistic. There is something bigger than what can be measured in waiting lists or GCSE results or the latest crime or jobs figures. Look at our economy – at ease with globalisation, London the world's financial centre. Visit our great cities and compare them with ten years ago. No country attracts overseas investment like we do. Think about the culture of Britain in 2007. I don't just mean our arts that are thriving. I mean our values, the minimum wage, paid holidays as a right, among the best maternity pay and leave in Europe, equality for gay people. Or look at the debates that reverberate round the world today – the global movement to support Africa in its struggle against poverty, climate change, the fight against terrorism.

Britain is not a follower. It is a leader. It gets the essential characteristic of today's world – its interdependence. This is a country today that for all its faults, for all the myriad of unresolved problems and fresh challenges, is comfortable in the twenty-first century, at home in its own skin, able not just to be proud of its past but confident of its future. I don't think Northern Ireland would have been changed unless Britain had changed, or the Olympics won if we were still the Britain of 1997.

As for my own leadership, throughout these ten years, where the predictable has competed with the utterly unpredicted, right at the outset one thing was clear to me. Without the Labour Party allowing me to lead it, nothing could ever have been done. But I knew my duty was to put the country first. That much was obvious to me when just under thirteen years ago I became Labour's Leader. What I had to learn, however, as Prime Minister was what putting the country first really meant.

Decision-making is hard. Everyone always says: 'Listen to the people.' The trouble is they don't always agree. When you are in opposition, you meet this group and they say: 'Why can't you do this?' And you say: 'It's really a good question. Thank you.' And they go away and say: 'It's great, he really listened.' You meet that other group and they say: 'Why can't you do that?' And you say: 'It's a really good question. Thank you.' And they go away happy you listened.

In government, you have to give the answer – not an answer, the answer. And, in time, you realise putting the country first doesn't mean doing the right thing according to conventional wisdom or the prevailing consensus or the latest snapshot of opinion. It means doing what you genuinely believe to be right. Your duty is to act according to your conviction.

All of that can get contorted so that people think you act according to some messianic zeal.

Doubt, hesitation, reflection, consideration and re-consideration, these are all the good companions of proper decision-making. But the ultimate obligation is to decide. Sometimes the decisions are accepted quite quickly. Bank of England independence was one, which gave us our economic stability. Sometimes, like tuition fees or trying to break up old monolithic public services, they are deeply controversial, hellish hard to do, but you can see you are moving with the grain of change round the word. Sometimes, like with Europe, where I believe Britain should keep its position strong, you know you are fighting opinion, but you are content with doing so.

Sometimes, as with the completely unexpected, you are alone with your own instinct.

In Sierra Leone and to stop ethnic cleansing in Kosovo, I took the decision to make our country one that intervened, that did not pass by, or keep out of the thick of it. Then came the utterly unanticipated and dramatic – September 11th 2001 and the death of 3,000 or more on the streets of New York. I decided we should stand shoulder to shoulder with our oldest ally. I did so out of belief. So Afghanistan and then Iraq – the latter, bitterly controversial. Removing Saddam and his sons from power, as with removing the Taliban, was over with relative ease. But the blowback since, from global terrorism and those elements that support it, has been fierce and unrelenting and costly.

For many, it simply isn't and can't be worth it. For me, I think we must see it through. They, the terrorists, who threaten us here and round the world, will never give up if we give up. It is a test of will and of belief. And we can't fail it.

So, some things I knew I would be dealing with. Some I thought I might be. Some never occurred to me on that morning of 2 May 1997 when I came into Downing Street for the first time. Great expectations not fulfilled in every part, for sure. Occasionally people say, as I said earlier: 'They were too high, you should have lowered them.' But, to be frank, I would not have wanted it any other way. I was, and remain, as a person and as a Prime Minister, an optimist. Politics may be the art of the possible – but at least in life, give the impossible a go. So of course the vision is painted in the colours of the rainbow, and the reality is sketched in the duller tones of black, white and grey.

But I ask you to accept one thing. Hand on heart, I did what I thought was right. I may have been wrong. That is your call. But believe one thing if nothing else. I did what I thought was right for our country. I came into office with high hopes for Britain's future. I leave it with even higher hopes for Britain's future. This is a country that can, today, be excited by the opportunities not constantly fretful of the dangers. People often say to me: 'It's a tough job' – not really. A tough life is the life the young severely disabled children have and their parents, who visited me in Parliament the other week. Tough is the life my dad had, his whole career cut short at the age of forty by a stroke. I have been very lucky and very blessed. This country is a blessed nation.

The British are special. The world knows it. In our innermost thoughts, we know it. This is the greatest nation on earth.

It has been an honour to serve it. I give my thanks to you, the British people, for the times I have succeeded, and my apologies to you for the times I have fallen short. Good luck.

DAN HANNAN

'A DEVALUED PRIME MINISTER, OF A DEVALUED GOVERNMENT'

—

REMARKS BEFORE THE EUROPEAN PARLIAMENT

STRASBOURG, FRANCE, 26 MARCH 2009

A uthor and journalist Dan Hannan was elected to the European Parliament in 1999 representing South East England for the Conservative Party. He is a vocal advocate of euroscepticism, a primarily right-wing ideology that opposes moves towards greater European Union integration, in some cases proposing Britain's actual withdrawal from the EU. Following his election, Hannan took an active part in the victorious campaign for a 'no' vote in the 2000 Danish referendum on the introduction of the Euro. After his re-election to the European Parliament in 2009, Hannan agitated for the withdrawal of the UK Conservative Party from the transnational European People's Party-European Democrats, the Parliament's centre-right bloc, on the grounds that the wider European membership represented by parties such as Germany's Christian Democratic Union (CDU) supported the creation of a European super-state.

This withdrawal led to the establishment of a new, anti-federalist bloc in the European Parliament, the European Conservatives and Reformists (now known as the Alliance of European Conservatives and Reformists or AECR), including a number of nationalist and right-wing parties from around the EU. The group faced widespread condemnation for granting membership to Latvian MEP Robert Zile of the National Alliance, as he had participated in events commemorating the Latvian Legion, which fought alongside the Waffen-SS in World War II. Hannan argued that Zile was simply showing his respect for all of Latvia's war dead, but the controversy intensified scrutiny of the new bloc. Further criticism followed the inclusion of Polish Nationalist Michał Kamiński in the AECR. Accused of anti-Semitism in the British press, Kamiński was *defended by the Chief Rabbi of his native Poland. However, then-Conservative MEP Edward McMillan-Scott maintained that Kamiński had 'anti-semitic, homophobic, and racist links', and stood against him in elections for one of the Vice-Presidencies of the European Parliament. McMillan-Scott defeated Kamiński and was eventually expelled from the Conservative Party, joining the UK Liberal Democrats.*

Dan Hannan is incumbent Secretary-General of the AECR. These remarks were given in the presence of then British Prime Minister Gordon Brown, who was sitting in the chamber and is the subject of reference. The intensity and directness of these remarks were considered shocking at the time of delivery. In some circles it became known simply as 'The Speech'. Hundreds of thousands of people watched the speech on YouTube. Hannan confronts the Prime Minister with a record of the government's failure. The speech became a point of reference in the 2010 British elections.

———

Prime Minister, I see you've already mastered the essential craft of this Parliament – that being to say one thing in this chamber, and a very different thing to your home electorate. You've spoken here about free trade, and amen to that; who would have guessed, listening to you just now, that you were the author of the phrase 'British Jobs for British Workers', and that you have subsidised – where you have not nationalised outright – swathes of our economy, including the car industry and many of the banks.

Perhaps you would have more moral authority in this house if your actions matched your words.

Perhaps you would have more legitimacy in the councils of the world if the United Kingdom were not going into this recession in the worst condition of any G20 country.

The truth, Prime Minister, is that you have run out of our money. The country as a whole is now in negative equity. Every British child is born owing around £20,000. Servicing the interest on that debt is going to cost more than educating the child.

Now once again today you tried to spread the blame around, you spoke about an international recession; an international crisis. Well, it is true that we are all sailing together into the squall – but not every vessel in the convoy is in the same dilapidated condition. Other ships used the good years to caulk their hulls and clear up their rigging – in other words, to pay off debt – but you used the good years to raise borrowing yet further. As a consequence, under your captaincy, our hull is pressed deep into the water line, under the accumulated weight of your debt. We are now running a deficit that touches almost 10 per cent of GDP – an unbelievable figure. More than Pakistan, more than Hungary – countries where the IMF has already been called in.

Now, it's not that you're not apologising – like everyone else, I've long accepted that you're pathologically incapable of accepting responsibility for these things. It's that you're carrying on, wilfully worsening the situation, wantonly spending what little we have left. Last year, in the last twelve months, 125,000 private sector jobs have been lost – and yet you've created 30,000 public sector jobs. Prime Minister you cannot go on forever squeezing the productive bit of the economy in order to fund an unprecedented engorging of the unproductive bit.

You cannot spend your way out of recession or borrow your way out of debt. And when you repeat, in that wooden and perfunctory way, that our situation is better than others, that we're well placed to weather the storm, I have to tell you, you sound like a Brezhnev-era Apparatchik giving the party line. You know, and we know, and you know that we know that it's nonsense. Everyone knows that Britain is the worst placed to go into these hard times. The IMF has said so. The European Commission has said so. The markets have said so, which is why our currency has devalued by 30 per cent – and soon the voters, too, will get their chance to say so.

They can see what the markets have already seen: that you are a devalued Prime Minister, of a devalued government.

DAVID CAMERON

'THIS COUNTRY NEEDS CHANGE'

—

REMARKS AT THE CONSERVATIVE
PARTY CONFERENCE

BIRMINGHAM, UNITED KINGDOM, 6 OCTOBER 2010

David Cameron was elected to Parliament as a Conservative representing the constituency of Witney in 2001. In the 2005 Conservative Party leadership election, he won an upset victory over the presumed favourite, David Davis. His victory in the leadership race was generally attributed to his extemporaneous 2005 Conservative Party Conference address, and an unwise, risqué photo opportunity on Davis's part, featuring buxom women wearing T-shirts with the slogan 'It's DD for me'.

In 2010, Cameron went on to defeat Prime Minister Gordon Brown in a general election that produced a 'hung parliament' – no single party held an overall majority. After four days of negotiations, Cameron emerged as Prime Minister at the head of a Conservative/Liberal Democrat coalition government, Britain's first formal coalition since World War II. In these remarks he explains his agenda as Prime Minister. This speech has become the benchmark for understanding and evaluating his time in office. The paragraph structure is my own, linking together sentences that were presented as stand-alone one-liners.

—

It is an honour and a privilege to stand here, before the party I lead, before the country I love, as the Conservative Prime Minister of the United Kingdom.

I want to tell you today, in the clearest terms I can, what we must do together. And what we can achieve together.

But first let's remember where we've come from. Three defeats. Thirteen party conferences.

Four thousand seven hundred and fifty-seven days in the wilderness. Remember what they said about us? They called us a dead parrot.

They said we had ceased to be. That we were an ex-party. Turns out we really were only resting.

And here we are. Back serving our country. Together in the national interest. Giving Britain the good, strong government it deserves.

There are so many we need to thank for that. The British people. You have given us a chance and we will work flat out to prove worthy of that chance. I want to say a big thank you to those who led this party before me. William Hague got us back on our feet. Iain Duncan Smith helped us get back our heart. Michael Howard gave us back our confidence. I know that I am standing here as Prime Minister because they stood up for this party in good times and bad and I will always remember that. And it is impossible to pay tribute to previous leaders of this party, without mentioning the greatest peacetime Prime Minister of the twentieth century. Next week, Margaret Thatcher celebrates her 85th birthday. She'll be doing it in Downing Street and I know everyone in this hall will want to wish her well. But there are some very special people I'd like to thank: you, the people of this party. I can't thank all of you individually – but I am going to single one of you out. His name is Harry Beckough. Harry joined our party in 1929 to fight Stafford Cripps. Since then, across 81 years and 21 elections, Harry has been with us. When Churchill warned of an iron curtain, Harry was with us. When this country had never had it so good, Harry was with us. When a lady refused to turn, Harry was with us. This year, when we fought the general election, Harry – aged ninety-six – was there, manning the loud hailer on the battle bus in Marlborough. And I'm delighted to say, Harry is with us here today. I tell you something – this is a party for all generations. Harry, without people like you we wouldn't be here – and our party wouldn't be in government. So thank you for everything you've done – and all you represent.

I'll never forget the night of May 6th. Watching the results coming in. The Tories back in the North. Winning in Wales. Sweeping across West Yorkshire. Taking seats we hadn't won in decades: Carlisle. Cannock. Thurrock. The end of a Labour government that had done so much damage. But, also, as I drove to London, there was that growing sense that we just weren't going to make it across the winning line. I went to bed at about 7am in a hotel, wishing like anything I was at home with Sam and the little ones, not knowing where it was all heading. I woke up two hours later and felt sure of the answer. The country wants leadership, not partisanship. Try the big thing. Do the right thing. Succeed and you can really achieve something. Fail and, well, at least you tried. I know there are a few who say that we should have sat tight, waited for our opponents to fall out and brought in a minority government. But a minority government would have limped through Parliament, unable to do anything useful for our country. The voters left us with a hung parliament and they wanted us to respond responsibly, to do the right thing, not play political games.

So I set out to form a strong, stable, coalition government. And I want to thank Nick Clegg for what he did. There were loads of phone calls and meetings in those five hectic days in May.

My daughter Nancy asked at breakfast one morning: 'Daddy, why are you spending so much time with this man Nick Leg?' Nick and I didn't agree about everything. He wanted clearer pledges on PR. I wanted them on the family. When I told him what I really thought of the European Parliament he said 'my God it's worse than I thought'. But we recognised we could work together. Not just lots of shared values, like wanting a country that is more free, more fair, more green, more decentralised. But a shared way of trying to do business. Reasonable debate, not tribal dividing lines. Give and take. Respect when you disagree. Trust. A sense that politics shouldn't be so different from the rest of life, where rational people do somehow find a way of overcoming their disagreements. Nick Clegg is not just sitting in government trying to win a few concessions here and there. The Liberal Democrats are proper partners, getting stuck in, making big decisions, shaping what we do and taking responsibility. That's why we can form a proper government and you can be proud of what we've done together. Now I know there will be compromise and I know we'll have to do things we might not like. Next May, there'll be a referendum on electoral reform. I don't want to change our voting system any more than you do.

But let's not waste time trying to wreck the bill – let's just get out there and win the vote.

Because you know what? At its best this party always puts country first. We'll leave the vested interests to others.

And no, we're not about self-interest either. This is the party of the national interest and with this coalition that's what we're showing today. People wondered what a coalition could achieve.

But just look at what we are achieving already – together, in the national interest. Conservative policies, policies you campaigned on, policies we are delivering. Two hundred new academies. Ten thousand university places. Fifty thousand apprenticeships. Corporation tax – cut. The jobs tax – axed. Police targets – smashed. Immigration – capped. The third runway – stopped. Home Information Packs – dropped. Fat cat salaries – revealed. ID Cards – abolished. The NHS – protected. Our aid promise – kept. Quangos – closing down. Ministers' pay – coming down. A bank levy – coming up. A cancer drugs fund – up and running. Six billion pounds of spending saved this year. An emergency budget to balance the books in five years. An EU referendum lock to protect our sovereign powers every year. For our pensioners – the earnings link restored. For our new entrepreneurs – employees' tax reduced. And for our brave armed forces – the operational allowance doubled.

Look what we've done in five months. Just imagine what we can do in five years. In five years' time, our combat troops will have left Afghanistan. This Party has steadfastly supported our mission there, and so will this government. But that does not mean simply accepting what went before. In our first few weeks in office, we set a clear new direction. Focused. Hard-headed.

Time-limited. We are not in Afghanistan to build a perfect democracy. No dreamy ideas. Just hard-headed national security – pure and simple. Almost every terrorist who took part in 9/11 was trained by al Qaeda in Afghanistan. If we left tomorrow those training camps could easily come back, because Afghans are not yet capable of securing their own country. But we will not stay a day longer than we need to. British combat forces will not remain in Afghanistan after 2015. By then they will have been there for fourteen years and in Helmand province for nine – three years longer than World War Two. For those who have served; for those who bear the scars; and for those who will never come home, this country has gratitude beyond words.

This government has set a new direction right across our foreign policy. Our principles are simple. Don't neglect important relationships. Already we are restoring ties with India; with allies in the Gulf; with our friends in the Commonwealth. Don't make commitments without the right resources. Today we're geared up to fight old wars. We have armoured brigades ready to repel Soviet tanks across the German plain. But we struggled to provide enough helicopters for our soldiers in Afghanistan, for the real war we are really fighting.

Since becoming Prime Minister nothing has shocked me more than the complete mess of the Defence budget we inherited. So our Defence Review will match our commitments with the resources we've got. This will mean some big changes. But I promise you this: I will take no risks with Britain's security. That's why, when more and more countries have or want nuclear weapons, we will always keep our ultimate insurance policy, we will renew our nuclear deterrent based on the Trident missile system.

But Britain's reputation is not just about might. It's about doing what is right. When this country has got it wrong, we'll admit it, as I did when I apologised for Bloody Sunday. When there's a cloud hanging over our reputation, we'll address it, as we have done by setting up an inquiry into whether this country was complicit in the mistreatment of detainees.

We will always pursue British interests. But there are some red lines we must never cross. Like the sight of the man responsible for the Lockerbie bombing, the biggest mass murderer in British history, set free to get a hero's welcome in

Tripoli. No. It was wrong, it undermined our standing in the world, and nothing like that must ever happen again.

When I walked into Downing Street as Prime Minister, I was deeply conscious that I was taking over the heaviest of responsibilities, not least for the future of our United Kingdom. Tony Blair, Gordon Brown – and John Major before them – worked hard to bring lasting peace to Northern Ireland and I will continue their work. And as the threat of dissident Republican terrorism increases, I want to make it clear that we will protect the people of our country with every means at our disposal.

And I want to make something else clear. When I say I am Prime Minister of the United Kingdom, I really mean it. England, Scotland, Wales, Northern Ireland – we're weaker apart, stronger together, so together is the way we must always stay.

But there is another side to life as Prime Minister. Like being made to watch the England football team lose, 4–1 to Germany, in the company of the German Chancellor. It's a form of punishment I wouldn't wish on anyone. I have to say, she is one of the politest people I have ever met, every time their players scored another goal, she would turn to me and say, 'I really am terribly sorry.' It's brought a whole new element to Anglo-German diplomatic relations: whatever you do, don't mention the score.

But however different life has got as Prime Minister, there's one thing that for me has stayed the same.

My belief about how this country needs to change.

Let's start by being honest with ourselves. The mess this country is in – it's not all because of Labour. Of course, they must take some of the blame.

All right – they need to take a lot of the blame.

Let me just get this off my chest. They left us with massive debts, the highest deficit, overstretched armed forces, demoralised public services, endless ridiculous rules and regulations and quangos and bureaucracy and nonsense. They left us a legacy of spinning, smearing, briefing, backbiting, half-truths and cover-ups, patronising, old-fashioned, top-down, wasteful, centralising, inefficient, ineffective, unaccountable politics, 10p tax and ninety days detention, an election bottled and a referendum denied, gold sold at half price and council tax doubled, bad news buried and Mandelson resurrected, pension funds destroyed and foreign prisoners not deported, Gurkhas kept out and extremist preachers allowed in.

Yes, they deserve some blame and we'll never let them forget it.

But the point I want to make is this. The state of our nation is not just determined by the government and those who run it. It is determined by millions of individual actions – by what each of us do and what we choose not to do. Yes, Labour failed to regulate the City properly.

But they didn't force those banks to take massive risks with other people's money. Yes, Labour tried to boss people around and undermined responsibility. But they weren't the ones smashing up our town centres on a Friday night or sitting on their sofas waiting for their benefits. Yes, Labour centralised too much and told people they could fix every problem. But it was the rest of us who swallowed it, hoping that if the government took care of things, perhaps we wouldn't have to. Too many people thought 'I've paid my taxes, the state will look after everything'. But citizenship isn't a transaction – in which you put your taxes in and get your services out. It's a relationship – you're part of something bigger than you, and it matters what you think and feel and do.

So to get out of the mess we're in, changing the government is not enough. We need to change the way we think about ourselves, and our role in society. Your country needs you. And today I want to tell you about the part we've all got to play, and the spirit that will take us through. It's the spirit I saw in a group of NHS maternity nurses in my constituency who told me they wanted to form a co-op to use their own ideas and their nous to help new parents. It's the spirit you see just down the road in Balsall Heath, where local residents' street patrols have turned a no-go area into a place where people can once again feel safe. It's the spirit that just today, has seen some of our leading social organisations come together to set up a new Citizen University, to help give people the skills they need to play a bigger part in society. It's the spirit of activism, dynamism, people taking the initiative, working together to get things done.

Sometimes that spirit gets taken a little too far. I got a letter from a six-year-old girl called Niamh with a pound coin stuck to it. And there was a note from her mum which said ... 'Dear Mr Cameron ... after hearing about the budget, Niamh wanted to send you her tooth fairy money to help.'

There we are, George – nearly there.

Niamh: thank you.

What I'm talking about, the spirit we need, is the big society spirit – and here's why I think its time has come. All over the world, governments are wrestling with the same challenges.

Not just building prosperous, competitive economies, providing good public services and paying for pensions but creating strong societies, improving quality of life, ensuring that everyone feels they belong. The countries that succeed will be those that find new ways of doing things, new ways of harnessing the common good, better alternatives to the old-fashioned state, and we're on the right side of that argument. Here at home, at this year's election, the result may not have been clear-cut when it came to the political parties. But it was clear enough when it came to political ideas. The old way of doing things – the high-spending, all-controlling, heavy-handed state – those ideas were defeated. Statism lost ... society won.

That's what happened at the last election and that's the change we're leading.

From state power to people power.

From unchecked individualism to national unity and purpose.

From big government to the big society.

The big society is not about creating cover for cuts. I was going on about it years before the cuts. It's not government abdicating its role, it is government changing its role. It's about government helping to build a nation of doers and go-getters, where people step forward not sit back, where people come together to make life better. Of course the cynics and the defeatists will say it can't be done, that we're stuck in some inevitable decline. But that's what they said in the seventies.

They were wrong then – and we'll prove them wrong again.

We can build a country defined not by the selfishness of the Labour years but by the values of mutual responsibility that this party holds dear. A country defined not by what we consume but by what we contribute. A country, a society where we say: I am not alone. I will play my part. I will work with others to give Britain a brand new start.

Over the coming months we will need that spirit as we face up to our financial responsibilities. Everyone knows that this government is undertaking a programme of spending cuts. I know how anxious people are. 'Yes', they say: 'of course we need to cut spending. But do we have to cut now, and by this much? Isn't there another way?'

I wish there was another way.

I wish there was an easier way.

But I tell you: there is no other responsible way.

Back in May we inherited public finances that can only be described as catastrophic. This year, we will borrow more money than we spend on the NHS. Just think about that. Every doctor's salary. Every operation. Every heating bill in every hospital. Every appointment. Every MRI scan. Every drug. Every new stethoscope, scalpel, hospital gown. Everything in our hospitals and surgeries – paid for with borrowed money, much of it from abroad. And then think about the interest. This year, we're going to spend £43 billion on debt interest payments alone. Forty-three billion pounds – not to pay off the debt – just to stand still. Do you know what we could do with that sort of money? We could take eleven million people out of paying income tax. We could take every business in the country out of corporation tax. That's why we have acted decisively – to stop pouring so much of your hard-earned money down the drain.

And it's stopped us slipping into the nightmare they've seen in Greece, confidence falling, interest rates rising, jobs lost and in the end, not less but more drastic spending cuts than if you'd acted decisively in the first place.

Our emergency budget showed the world that Britain is back on the path of fiscal responsibility. It took us out of the danger zone – and the man we have to thank for that is George Osborne. The world has backed us. Our credit rating – the mark of trust in our economy – has been preserved. The International Monetary Fund, the G20, yes even the EU. They support what we're doing.

There's just one group of people who don't: You guessed it, the people who mortgaged Britain to the hilt in the first place – Labour. Labour's plan is just to halve the deficit over four years.

Let me tell you what that means. It means that even after years of cuts, not only would the national debt still be growing, it would be growing as a share of our national income. The problem would still be getting worse. And as a result, the cuts would be bigger, not smaller, because the interest payments on that debt would be higher. That's why it's right to deal with this problem now, and right to deal with it properly. And I promise you that if we pull together to deal with these debts today, then just a few years down the line the rewards will be felt by everyone in our country. More money in your pocket. More investment in our businesses. Growing industries, better jobs, stronger prospects for our young people.

And the thing you can't measure but you just know it when you see it, the sense that our country is moving forwards once again. The big society spirit means facing up to this generation's debts, not shirking responsibility.

And here I want to say something to the people who got us into this mess. The ones who racked up more debt in thirteen years than previous governments did in three centuries. Yes you, Labour. You want us to spend more money on ourselves, today, to keep racking up the bills, today, and leave it to our children – the ones who had nothing to do with all this – to pay our debts tomorrow? That is selfish and irresponsible. I tell you what: these Labour politicians, who nearly bankrupted our country, who left a legacy of debts and cuts, who are still in denial about the disaster they created, they must not be allowed anywhere near our economy, ever, ever again.

Reducing spending will be difficult. There are programmes that will be cut. There are jobs that will be lost. There are things government does today that it will have to stop doing. Many government departments will have their budgets cut by on average 25 per cent over four years.

That's a cut each year of around 7 per cent.

Of course, that's big. But let's remember, a lot of businesses have had to make the same or bigger savings in recent years. And when we're done with these cuts, spending on public services will actually still be at the same level as it was in 2006. The spending cuts we do have to make, we'll make in a way that is fair. Fairness includes protecting the service we most rely on – the health service. We said five years ago we were the party of the NHS and now in government, by protecting NHS spending from cuts, we are showing it. And as we work to balance the budget, fairness includes asking those on higher incomes to shoulder more of the burden than those on lower incomes. I'm not saying this is going to be easy, as we've seen with child benefit this week. But it's fair that those with broader shoulders should bear a greater load.

And I think it's time for a new conversation about what fairness really means. Here's what I think. Yes, fairness means giving money to help the poorest in society.

People who are sick, who are vulnerable, the elderly – I want you to know we will always look after you. That's the sign of a civilised society and it's what I believe. But you can't measure fairness just by how much money we spend on welfare, as though the poor are products with a price tag, the more we spend on them the more we value them. Fairness means supporting people out of poverty, not trapping them in dependency.

So we will make a bold choice. For too long, we have measured success in tackling poverty by the size of the cheque we give people. We say: let's measure our success by the chance we give. Let's support real routes out of poverty: a strong family; a good education; a job. So we'll invest in the early years, help put troubled families back on track, use a pupil premium to make sure kids from the poorest homes go to the best schools not the worst, recognise marriage in the tax system and most of all, make sure that work really pays for every single person in our country.

Remember last year? When you stood up to show how angry you were about the injustice of some low-paid single mothers going out to work and losing 96p for every extra pound they earned? Well after months of hard work, I can tell you Iain Duncan Smith has found a way to end that system. So to that single mother struggling and working her heart out for her children, we can now say: We're on your side; we'll help you work; we will bring that injustice to an end.

Here's something else about fairness. Fairness isn't just about who gets help from the state. The other part of the equation is who gives that help, through their taxes. Taking more money from the man who goes out to work long hours each day so the family next door can go on living a life on benefits without working – is that fair? Fairness means giving people what they deserve – and what people deserve depends on how they behave. If you really cannot work, we'll look after you. But if you can work, but refuse to work, we will not let you live off the hard work of others.

Tackling the deficit is what we have to do. But transforming our country is what we passionately want to do. Here again we need the big society spirit – of activism and dynamism. We need it to get growth.

Let me tell you what I believe. It will be the doers and grafters, the inventors and the entrepreneurs who get this economy going. Yes, it will be the wealth-creators – and no, those aren't dirty words. When you think of a wealth-creator, don't think of the tycoon in a glass tower. Think of the man who gets up and leaves the house before dawn to go out and clean windows. Think of the woman who sits up late into the night trying to make the figures add up to make sure she can pay her staff. I can't tell you how much I admire people who leave the comfort of a regular wage to strike out on their own. I'll always remember what the owner of a small business told me once. He said, 'When I was starting out the government didn't lift a finger to help me. Then as soon as I start making money they're all over me trying to take it away.'

That is completely the wrong way round. We need to get behind our wealth-creators. That's what we're doing. Dealing with the deficit so interest rates stay low. Slashing red tape.

Cutting the small-business profits rate, corporation tax and national insurance contributions for new businesses.

But I don't think our job ends there. I don't believe in laissez-faire. Government has a role not just to fire up ambition, but to help give it flight. So we are acting to build a more entrepreneurial economy. Tens of thousands of university and apprenticeship places and a new generation of technical schools. A new Green Investment Bank, so the technologies of the future are developed, jobs created and our environment protected. Big infrastructure projects like high-speed rail, super-fast broadband, Carbon Capture and Storage. A £1 billion regional growth fund to stimulate enterprise in those areas where the private sector is weak. And as we've announced this week, a New Enterprise Allowance that gives money and support to unemployed people who want to start their own business.

And there's another way we're getting behind business – by sorting out the banks. Taxpayers bailed you out, now it's time for you to repay the favour and start lending to Britain's small businesses again.

Just as we need the big society spirit to get our economy going, we need it in our society too. Social change is where this coalition has its beating, radical heart. This is what drives us.

To change forever the way this country is run. We're going to start by taking power away from central government and giving it to people. On May 11th a great shadow was cast over the empire of the quangocrats, the bureaucrats and the power-hoarders. He is the enemy of the bureaucratic state. Public chum number one. The big man on the side of the people. Eric Pickles.

Eric has come in to government and hit the ground sprinting, leading the most radical shift in power this country has seen for decades. More freedom for local councils, to keep more of the money when they attract business to their area, to finance big new infrastructure projects and to run new services. More power for neighbourhoods, to keep local pubs open, stop post offices from closing, to run local parks, to plan the look, shape and feel of their area. New powers to you, to choose the hospital you get treated in, the school your child goes to. And because information is power, we're bringing transparency to government.

All those things the last government kept from you, who spends your money, what they spend it on, what the results are, where the waste is, we're putting it in your hands. After all, it's your money – so you should see where it's going. This is not about a bit more power for you and a bit less power for central government – it's a revolution. Let's leave Labour defending the status quo, the vested interests, the unions, the quangocrats, the elites, the establishment. We are the radicals now, breaking apart the old system with a massive transfer of power, from the state to citizens, politicians to people, government to society. That is the power shift this country needs today.

And let me tell you why we desperately need this change.

It's because the old way, of just pouring money into public services from on high, didn't make the difference it promised to. Health inequalities got worse. Almost four in ten children left primary school unable to read, write and do maths properly. There were nearly a million violent crimes a year. So if anyone tells you that all we need to improve our hospitals and schools or keep our streets safe is more money, tell them, been there, done that and it didn't work.

So this is what radicalism means. No more top-down, bureaucrat-driven public services. We're putting those services in your hands. The old targets and performance indicators that drove doctors, nurses and police officers mad – they're gone. All that bureaucracy that meant nothing ever happened – we're stripping it away. The big, giant state monopolies – we're breaking them open to get new ideas in. Saying to the people who work in our public services – set up as a co-operative, be your own boss, do things your way. Saying to business, faith groups, charities, social enterprises – come in and provide a great service. Already, businesses are getting people trained and ready for work. GPs are coming together to deliver local NHS services. And next year, the first generation of free schools will open in the state sector.

But as with any radical changes, there's going to be opposition. I want to give you an idea of the mentality we're fighting. Ed Balls, the man who used to be in charge of education in our country, said one of the dangers of our schools policy was that it would create 'winners'. Winners? We can't have that. The danger that your child might go to school and turn out to be a winner. Anti-aspiration. Anti-success. Anti-parents who just want the best for their children.

What an unbelievable attitude from this Labour generation. Now I've heard people say there are some places where reform can't go – like law and order. I disagree. Of course the state has a clear role, to score a line between right and wrong; to punish those who step over it, and to do it in a way that gives people confidence. That's why I have no time for those who sneer at public attitudes to punishing criminals. Offenders who should go to prison will go to prison.

Justice must be done. But we also have to recognise where the state is failing on crime. We spend £41,000 a year on each prisoner – and within a year of leaving half of them reoffend. There are 150,000 people in Britain today who get their heroin substitutes on the state, their addictions maintained by the taxpayer. We have police officers who spend more time on paperwork than they do on patrol.

It's here that reform is needed most. So let's get our best charities to help rehabilitate offenders, our best social enterprises to get people off drugs. Let's get more local people – who know their streets – to be special constables. And let's get our police officers out from behind their desks and on the streets fighting crime. I've seen what the police do for us – how they put themselves in the line of danger to keep us safe. So I want to give them more freedom. But in return for that freedom, police are going to have someone new to answer to. Not Ministers – people.

You.

On the way are new elected police commissioners that you can vote in – and kick out. Neighbourhood beat meetings where you hold the police to account. I say to every policeman and woman in the country – don't be afraid of these changes. The more you've been controlled by the central state, the less people have respected you. I want to change that. More freedom for you to be out on the streets, policing the way you know best – and in a way local people support, that will mean more respect for the vital work that you do.

This is the reform our public services need. From top-down to bottom-up. From state power to people power. The big society spirit blasting through.

But the big society needs you to give it life. People already do so much to help others. Three weeks ago volunteers were asked to come forward to help with the 2012 Olympic Games. You know how many applications have come in? One hundred thousand. Together we're going to make these Olympics great for Britain and great for the world. And on the way we're going to throw everything we can into winning that bid for the 2018 World Cup.

There is such an appetite out there for people to play their part. Our job is to help them, encourage them, break down the barriers that stop them. So let's scrap the health and safety rules that put people off. Let's get community organisers to stimulate social action in our poorest areas. Let's get going with National Citizen Service so more teenagers get some purpose in their lives. And today I can announce International Citizen Service, to give thousands of our young people, those who couldn't otherwise afford it, the chance to see the world and serve others. Last century, America's Peace Corps inspired a generation of young people to act, and this century, I want International Citizen Service to do the same.

That's the big society spirit, around the world and back here at home. So that great project in your community – go and lead it. The waste in government – go and find it. The new school in your neighbourhood – go and demand it. The beat meeting on your street – sign up. The neighbourhood group – join up. That business you always dreamed of – start up. When we say 'we are all in this together' that is not a cry for help, but a call to arms.

Society is not a spectator sport. This is your country. It's time to believe it. It's time to step up and own it.

So mine is not just a vision of a more powerful country. It is a vision of a more powerful people.

The knowledge in the heart of everyone – everyone – that they are not captive to the circumstances of their birth, they are not flotsam and jetsam in the great currents of wealth and power, they are not small people but big citizens. People that believe in themselves. A Britain that believes in itself. Not a promise of a perfect country. Just an achievable future of a life more fulfilled and fulfilling for everyone.

At this time of great national challenge, two parties have come together to help make it happen. Yes, this is a new kind of government, but no, not just because it's a coalition. It is a new kind of government because it is realistic about what it can achieve on its own, but ambitious about what we can all achieve together. A government that believes in people, that trusts people, that knows its ultimate role is not to take from people but to give, to give power, to give control, to give everyone the chance to make the most of their own life and make better the lives of others.

Yes, we will play our part – but the part you play will mean even more. Your country needs you.

It takes two. It takes two to build that strong economy. We'll balance the budget, we'll boost enterprise, but you start those businesses that lead us to growth. It takes two to build that big society. We'll reform public services, we'll devolve power, but you step forward to seize the opportunity. Don't let the cynics say this is some unachievable, impossible dream that won't work in the selfish twenty-first-century – tell them people are hungry for it. I know the British people and they are not passengers – they are drivers. I've seen the courage of our soldiers ... the spirit of our entrepreneurs ... the patience of our teachers ... the dedication of our doctors ... the compassion of our care workers ... the wisdom of our elderly ... the love of our parents ... the hopes of our children.

So come on: let's pull together. Let's come together. Let's work, together, in the national interest.'

NICK CLEGG

'WE WILL NOT LOSE OUR SOUL'

—

REMARKS AT THE LIBERAL PARTY CONFERENCE

LIVERPOOL, UNITED KINGDOM, 20 SEPTEMBER 2010

Nick Clegg won election to the European Parliament in 1999, sitting for the Liberal Democrats. He returned to the UK to seek election to the House of Commons, winning the Parliamentary seat of Sheffield Hallam in 2005. After a shambolic few years that saw one Liberal Democrat leader, Charles Kennedy, resign under pressure from his colleagues owing to an admitted drinking problem, and his successor, Menzies ('Ming') Campbell fail to find traction with the British electorate, a further leadership election was held in 2007. Seen as the frontrunner when campaigning began, Nick Clegg won a narrow victory over Chris Huhne, who was later forced to resign from the coalition Cabinet in February 2012 after being charged with perverting the course of justice over a 2003 traffic offence. Some claim that if late-arriving ballots had been included in the leadership election count, Huhne would have been the victor.

The 2010 election produced a paradoxical result for the Liberal Democrats. The campaign featured Britain's first televised debates between the three main party leaders. Clegg was judged the winner of the first debate in much press commentary and most opinion polls, leading to a phenomenon dubbed 'Cleggmania'. The Liberal Democrats briefly jumped from third place to first in some opinion polls, and Clegg's sudden popularity was compared to Barack Obama's in the 2008 US Presidential race. However, it transpired that Clegg had peaked too early, and although the Liberal Democrats increased their share of the national popular vote, winning 23 per cent overall, owing to the vagaries of Britain's simple plurality or 'first past the post' electoral system, the party actually lost seats in Parliament.

With no party having won an overall majority, Nick Clegg led the Liberal

Democrats into a coalition government with David Cameron's Conservatives, and took the Cabinet post of Deputy Prime Minister.

This speech sets out his view of the coalition, explaining his vision of what the Liberal Democrats can achieve in government. This was surely the most important speech of his Party Conference and perhaps the most important Liberal Party/Liberal Democrat speech of the post-war era. The paragraph structure is mine, again trying to link one-line sentences.

—

Two and a half years ago, I stood in this very hall to make my first speech as leader of our party. I said that the chance for change was within our reach, and we had to seize it. That chance came.

Perhaps not quite in the way many of us could have expected. But the chance came and you – we – responded with real courage and conviction. Cynics expected us to back away. Instead, we confounded those who said that coalition government was impossible. We created a government which will govern and govern well for the next five years.

Of course there are those who will condemn us. We are challenging years of political convention and tradition and our opponents will yell and scream about it. But I am so, so proud of the quiet courage and determination which you have shown through this momentous period in British political history.

Hold our nerve and we will have changed British politics for good. Hold our nerve and we will have changed Britain for good.

Just think what we've done already. We've ended the injustice of the richest paying less tax on investments than the poorest do on their wages. We've guaranteed older people a decent increase in their pension. In November, we will publish a Freedom Bill to roll back a generation of illiberal and intrusive legislation. By Christmas, Identity Card laws will be consigned to the history books. From New Year's Day, the banks will pay a new levy that will help fill the black hole they helped create. On 1 April 900,000 low earners will stop paying income tax altogether. In May, the people of Britain will get to choose their own voting system. And this time next year, there will be a pupil premium so the children who need the most help, get the most help.

We've always been the face of change. We are now the agents of change. And every single person in this room is part of that change. Actually there's one contribution you all made to the success of the coalition negotiations that you probably aren't aware of. Our formidable negotiating team got all the training they needed battling out policy right here on the conference floor.

Some things are different in government. Some are the same. I still think the war in Iraq was illegal. The difference is lawyers now get anxious when I mention it. I still believe in our commitments to the developing world. The difference is I get to make those commitments at a UN summit and make them happen. I still campaign for political reform. The difference is I'm now legislating for it as well. The only real problem is I'm still trying to explain to my children that going from leader to Deputy PM isn't a demotion.

We will take risks in government. But we will never lose our soul. We haven't changed our liberal values. Our status is different but our ambition is the same.

Remember the four big promises we made in the election campaign? For the first time in my lifetime, Liberal Democrats are able to deliver on those promises.

We promised no tax on the first £10,000 you earn. We've already raised the personal allowance by £1000. And in the coming years we will go further to put money back in the pockets of millions of low earners.

We promised more investment in the children who need the most help at school. It will happen at the start of the next school year.

We promised a rebalanced, green economy, a new kind of growth. Already we're taking action on the banks. We've set up a regional growth fund. There will be a Green Investment Bank to channel money into renewable energy. These are the first steps to rewire our economy. New jobs, new investment, new hope.

And we promised clean politics. We're giving people the chance to change our voting system, cleaning up party funding and finally, a century after it should have happened, we are going to establish an elected House of Lords.

Those pledges we made, together, in the election of 2010, will be promises kept in the election of 2015. The Coalition Programme, which commits the government to making all these changes, is not the Liberal Democrat manifesto. But it is not the Conservative manifesto either. It is our shared agenda. And I stand by it. I believe in it. I believe it will change Britain for good.

Now, some say we shouldn't have gone into government at a time when spending had to be cut. We should have let the Conservatives take the blame. Waited on the sidelines, ready to reap the political rewards. Maybe that's what people expected from a party that has been in opposition for 65 years. People have got used to us being outsiders, against every government that's come along. Maybe we got used to it ourselves. But the door to the change we want was opened, for the first time in generations.

Imagine if we had turned away. How could we ever again have asked the voters to take us seriously? Labour left the country's coffers empty. So the years ahead will not be easy. But you do not get to choose the moment when the opportunity to shape your country comes your way. All you get to choose is what you do when it does. We chose a partnership government.

The truth is I never expected the Conservatives to embrace negotiation and compromise. But they did and it does them credit. David Cameron showed he could think beyond his party and help build a new kind of politics. The election result didn't give a single party the mandate to govern. It gave all parties the mandate to govern differently. We answered that call. And one of the most remarkable surprises of this coalition government is that our parties are not, despite so many cynical predictions, simply settling for the lowest common denominator between us.

Instead, we have become more than the sum of our parts. For those of us who believe in plural politics, that's not a surprise. In life, two heads are usually better than one. And in politics, too, when the country faces grave challenges – the deficit, the threat of climate change, a war in Afghanistan, millions of children trapped in disadvantage – two parties acting together can be braver, fairer and bolder than one party acting alone.

The new politics – plural politics, partnership politics, coalition politics – is the politics our nation needs today. The Liberal Democrats and the Conservatives are and always will be separate parties, with distinct histories and different futures. But for this Parliament we work together: to fix the problems we face and put the country on a better path. This is the right government for right now.

Our first job, however, is a difficult one. Balancing the budget. I did not come into politics to make spending cuts. But it is the only choice if we want to steer Britain out of the economic mess Labour made. The only choice if we want to bring back hope and optimism to our nation. We are gripped by a crisis, and it's the worst kind: it's invisible.

You can't see the debts mounting up.

Walk the high street, go to work, talk to your friends, you won't see the signs of our debts or our deficit. The numbers sound alarming, but in the end they're just numbers. It doesn't feel like we can't afford things.

So how did this debt crisis happen? Put simply, over the course of the recession, 6 per cent of our economy disappeared. The shock was so profound that even now the economy is growing, we are poorer today than we thought we would be. All the old predictions about our future economy – predictions on which spending plans had been based – have turned out to be wrong. We can't keep spending money as if nothing had changed.

The problems are there. They are real. And we have to solve them. It's the same as a family with earnings of £26,000 a year who are spending £32,000 a year. Even though they're already £40,000 in debt. Imagine if that was you. You'd be crippled by the interest payments. You'd set yourself a budget. And you'd try to spend less. That is what this government is doing.

This isn't new for Liberal Democrats. Speak to councillors who've led councils across the country; they know what it's like to pick up the pieces after Labour spent a community dry. Newcastle, Sheffield, Lambeth, Southwark, and right here in Liverpool. Our council leaders know the poorest are the ones that suffer when the finances get out of control and money has to be spent on debts. They know there is nothing fair about denying you have a problem and leaving it for the next generation to clear it up. Would you ask your children to pay your credit card bill?

I've heard some people say that the cuts we are making are somehow taking Britain back to the 1980s, or the 1930s. Dismantling the state. It isn't true. Even when all the cuts have happened, we will still be spending 41 per cent of our national income – the same amount we were spending in 2006.

The Spending Review is about balance and responsibility not slash and burn. Of course, I wish there was a pain-free alternative. Who wouldn't? But whatever Labour say now, there isn't one. Not even in Alistair Darling's old plans – they too would have meant massive cuts. Delay won't solve the problems – in fact, it would make them worse.

We could have decided to go more slowly but it would have worsened not eased the pain. Because every day you ignore a deficit, it gets harder to fix. The debts mount up and you have to pay interest on them. Already we are spending £44bn a year on interest alone. Under Labour's plans, that would have risen to nearly £70bn. A criminal waste of money that shouldn't be lining the pockets of bond traders. It should be paying for police, care workers, hospitals and schools.

That's why this government's aim is that by the time of the next election, our debt problems will be solved; our debts falling as a proportion of national income. We will have wiped the slate clean for a new generation.

In making these changes we will learn from the mistakes of previous recessions.

We will not repeat the mistakes of the 1980s in which whole communities were hollowed out. I know from my constituents in Sheffield how worried people are that cuts will hurt the North in the way the industrial changes of the 1980s did. So let me say to everybody in those communities, in Scotland and in Wales, many of whose lives were torn apart. Yes, it will be difficult, but it will not be like the 80s. We will not let that happen. We will make these cuts as fairly as possible.

Finding money for the pupil premium to help children get the best start in life. Reforming welfare to help people get back to work.

We will not let capital spending – investment in new buildings, infrastructure and repairs – be swept away as it has in the past. We have a billion-pound Regional Growth Fund targeted specifically at creating growth in those areas of the country that have been dependent on public sector jobs. We've offered a National Insurance tax break to employers who set up new companies outside London and the wider South East. And we are determined to wean the economy off Labour's lopsided obsession with financial services in the City of London. Rebalancing our economy – so opportunity is never again concentrated only in the south-east corner of our island. So no matter what your background or where you live, you have the opportunities you crave.

The destination is the right one but getting there is going to be hard. To those thousands of people who work in the public sector, who do such an outstanding job in our schools, hospitals, police forces and local councils, I say this:

I know these are very unsettling times for you. I will not disguise the fact that we need to take difficult decisions today to ensure there are good, affordable public services tomorrow. We have protected the funding for the NHS, the biggest public service of all.

We will provide more, not less, money for the children in our schools who need the most help. But I know you will be thinking: why should you have to make any sacrifices to deal with a recession you didn't cause?

Why are the bankers who helped create the mess not taking more of the blame? Why should you have to accept a pay freeze, or changes to your pension, when the richest still get away with paying little or no tax at all? I agree.

That's why we imposed a levy on the banks in our first budget. It's why we're working hard with our friends in Europe and beyond on the idea of a financial activities tax on profits, pay and bonuses. It's why we're going to be forcing the banks to own up about the ludicrous pay and bonuses they give out. It's why our Banking Commission is looking at whether to split the banks up completely to keep our economy safe. And it's why we're working flat out to get the banks lending again to small businesses, the lifeblood of our economy.

We have done more in five months than Labour ever did to sort out the greed and the recklessness of the banks. Our approach is simple: they helped bring down our economy. It must never happen again.

People who avoid and evade paying their taxes will no longer get away with it either. We all read the headlines about benefit fraud. We all agree it's wrong when people help themselves to benefits they shouldn't get. But when the richest people in the country dodge their tax bills that is just as bad. Both come down to stealing money from your neighbours.

We will be tough on welfare cheats. But unlike Labour, we'll be tough on tax cheats too. We will crack down on the super-rich who hide away money overseas. We will take on organised crime gangs set up to avoid tax. And we will prosecute five times as many tax cases as Labour ever did.

So the message is loud and clear: Just as the public sector must be made affordable, the banks must be held to account. And tax avoiders and evaders must have nowhere to hide.

I want to make something crystal clear about the coming Spending Review. It is not an ideological attack on the size of the state. There is one reason and one reason only for these cuts: As Liam Byrne said in that infamous letter: there isn't any money left.

It's not smaller government I believe in. It's a different kind of government: a liberating government. This government will transform the state. Reversing generations of centralisation. Putting power into people's hands. Because the job of government is not to run people's lives. It is to help people to run their own.

I want Britain to have the best schools and hospitals in the world. But that doesn't mean we should be controlling them all from Whitehall. Governments that have the arrogance to imagine that 100 ministers and 1,000 civil servants can fix the country all by themselves. Governments like that fail.

So we will restore power to people, families, communities, neighbourhoods and councils. Turning the tide of centralisation and for the first time giving power away. Councils, like all parts of government, are going to have to make do with less money in the years ahead. But they will have more freedom than ever before.

Labour rattled on about decentralisation, but they held the purse strings tight. We are different; we are liberal. Because we will put local government back in charge of the money it raises and spends. That's why in our first budget we unlocked more than a billion pounds of ring-fenced grants. That's why we will end central capping of Council Tax. That's why we will allow councils to keep some of the extra business rates and council tax they raise when they enable new developments to go ahead.

And I can announce today that we will be giving local authorities the freedom to borrow against those extra business rates to help pay for additional new developments. This may not make the pulses race, even at a Liberal Democrat conference. But I assure you it is the first step to breathing life back into our greatest cities.

Our leaders in Sheffield say it could allow the redevelopment of derelict mines in the Don Valley; our leaders in Newcastle believe this could help them create a new science park; in Leeds they argue the Aire Valley could be transformed. But whether in Newcastle, in Sheffield, in Leeds or indeed in every city in the UK, what matters most is that finally, they will be in the driving seat, instead of waiting for a handout from Whitehall. Local people, local power, local change.

The same approach – financial freedom – is governing our relationship with Scotland and Wales, too. That's why we are taking forward the Calman Commission to give Scotland real freedom and responsibility over its own money. And why, if the referendum for more devolution in Wales is successful, we will take forward a similar process for the Senedd. Giving the nations of the UK the freedom they deserve.

Putting power in local hands is one of the many things Labour never really understood. The Labour leadership candidates are trying to rewrite history. But we remember. Civil liberties destroyed on an industrial scale. A widening gap between rich and poor. Failure to act on the environment. Locking up more children than anywhere else in Western Europe. Kowtowing to the banks. A foreign policy forged in George Bush's White House. The invasion of Iraq.

And then, on top of all that, they brought the country to the brink of bankruptcy. Writing cheques, even in the final days of their government, that they knew would bounce. This country could not have borne five more years of Labour.

Has anyone else lost track of the books Labour people keep publishing? Never in the field of political memoirs, has so much been written by so few about so little. They went from nationalisation to serialisation. From 'The Third Way' to a third off at the bookshop.

And the next generation is still fighting the same backstabbing battles instead of talking about the future for Britain. We held a public consultation about the Spending Review. We had 100,000 ideas from members of the public about how to cut waste and do things more effectively. And not a single idea from the Labour Party.

I want to say something to whoever is elected as the next Labour leader. You cannot duck difficult choices forever. All you have done in the last four months. is carp and complain. But a decent opposition has to provide a decent alternative. Your party let people down in government. Until you face up to your responsibility for the state we're in you'll let people down in opposition too.

Labour did some good things, of course they did. But just think what they could have done, with enormous majorities, thirteen years and money to spare. The best opportunity for real fairness there has been in my lifetime. But, imprisoned by timidity, they squandered a golden age.

We must now take up the challenge that Labour ducked. We must do more, even though they left us with less. When faced with the daunting task of reducing our deficit, the temptation might have been to go slow elsewhere. One difficult task at a time – that would have been the cautious response. But it wasn't our response.

Because I believe at times of great difficulty, great things can still be done. At times of great difficulty, great things must be done. Some say we've bitten off more than we can chew. I say there's no time to wait. We could wait to solve the welfare crisis, but every day people struggle to get back into work. We could wait to give our children a better start at school, but they only get the chance to grow up once. We could wait to reform our prisons, but every day offenders leave prison and go straight back to crime. We could wait to cut the deficit, but every day, we spend £120m servicing our debts, and that's £120m we can't spend on our children.

We have four years and seven months before the next election. One thousand six hundred and ninety days. We're not going to waste a single second. There is no time for the old go-slow, timid governments of the past. We're keeping our eyes on the horizon, not on the headlines. Building, brick by brick, day by day, the changes Britain needs.

Of course the ambition of these reforms will provoke controversy. I know some people, for instance, are worried about our plans for expanding Academies, as we heard this morning.

It wouldn't be a Liberal Democrat conference if we didn't have a motion that provoked strong passions on both sides. The great thing is that all Liberal Democrats share a passion for education. When it comes to lasting fairness, education is everything.

So I want to be really clear about what the government is proposing. It's not Labour's academies programme: a few schools singled out for preferential treatment – a cuckoo in the nest that eats up attention and resources. We're opening up the option of Academy freedom to all schools. Because if one head teacher is free to run their classes in the way they know is best, why shouldn't all head teachers be free?

My vision is that every school, in time, will be equal, every school equally free. But there's one freedom new schools shouldn't have. Freedom to select. The whole concept of our reforms falls apart if you use it to expand selection – because instead of children and parents choosing schools, you get schools choosing children. So we have made it absolutely clear: we will allow people to set up new schools but we will not allow them to pick and choose the brightest. No to more selection.

Welfare reform will be controversial too. Benefit reform is difficult in times of plenty, but essential when money is tight. Labour's welfare system simply isn't fair. It pays people to live without hope of a better life instead of paying to help them build a better life. A liberal welfare system is different. It's built around work. I believe in work. Work is essential to a person's sense of self-worth, their identity.

We will only build the fair, mobile society we want if we make it easy for everyone to get out to work and get on in life. And that's what this government will do.

So the immediate future will not be easy, but the long-term prize is great. I want you to imagine what you will say to people when you knock on their door at the next general election.

Imagine how it will feel to say that in government, Liberal Democrats have restored civil liberties, scrapped ID cards, and got innocent people's DNA off the police database. Imagine how it will feel to say that our government has taken action to cut reoffending, and cut crime, while stopping Labour's mass incarceration of children.

We will have withdrawn our combat troops from Afghanistan, our brave servicemen and women having completed the difficult job we asked them to do.

You will be able to explain that finally, we have a fair tax system where the rich pay their share, and the lowest earners pay no income tax at all.

Our banking levy will have raised £10bn, reckless bonuses for short-term gain will have ended, and banks will be lending responsibly again.

Imagine how it will feel to visit home after home that our Green Deal has made warm and affordable to heat.

You'll be able to tell people they have a new right to sack MPs who do wrong, and that the party funding scandals of the past are history.

You'll be campaigning alongside Liberal Democrat candidates for the House of Lords.

And if the British people say yes to the Alternative Vote in the referendum next May – forcing MPs to work harder for your vote – then you will also be able to say that the clapped-out politics of first past the post* is gone for good.

To those who are angry now about the difficult decisions needed to balance the budget you'll be able to show that those decisions have set us on a better course with new growth and jobs that last.

And, finally, you'll be able to say that all this has been delivered by a totally new way of doing politics. Never again will anyone be able to frighten the voters by claiming that coalition government doesn't work. Liberal, plural politics will feel natural; the sane response to a complex and fast-changing world. Just imagine how different our country will be.

Britain in 2010 is anxious, unsure about the future, but Britain in 2015 will be a different country. Strong, fair, free and full of hope again. A country we can be proud to hand on to our children. That is the goal we must keep firmly fixed in our minds. That is the prize.

The years ahead will not be easy but they will make the difference our country needs. Stick with us while we rebuild the economy. Stick with us while we restore our civil liberties, protect our environment, nurture our children and repair our broken politics. Stick with us and together we will change Britain for good.

---

*'First past the post' is a commonly used term for the simple plurality electoral system used in the United Kingdom and United States, as opposed to contests involving run-offs or proportional representation. In a multi-party election, simple plurality voting can lead to seats being won on small minority votes, and has led to the chronic under-representation of the third party in the UK House of Commons (the Liberal Democrats and their predecessors for the past sixty-five years). In the 1983 general election, the Liberal-Social Democrat Alliance won 25.4 per cent of the national vote, and only 3.5 per cent of seats in the Commons, as first past the post works to the benefit of parties with a strong regional base, such as Labour in the North and the Conservative Party in the Southeast of England, while Liberal Democrat support tends to be more evenly distributed across the UK, excepting a minor fiefdom in the Southwest of England and some large but sparsely populated areas of Scotland and Wales.

ED MILIBAND

'THE NEW GENERATION OF LABOUR IS DIFFERENT'

—

REMARKS AT THE LABOUR PARTY CONFERENCE

MANCHESTER, UNITED KINGDOM, 28 SEPTEMBER 2010

Ed Miliband was elected as a Labour member of the House of Commons in 2005 representing Doncaster North. He served in various governmental and Cabinet positions from 2007–2010, rising to the office of Secretary of State for the newly created Department of Energy and Climate Change in 2008. Following Labour's 2010 general election defeat and the resignation of Gordon Brown, Miliband announced his candidacy for the Labour leadership. This made for an unusual and intriguing intra-party election, as his main rival was his older brother, David (referred to in the speech below), a fellow Labour MP who had served as Foreign Secretary in Gordon Brown's Cabinet. The elder Miliband was considered the frontrunner by most of the press and political establishment when the campaign began.

Miliband's surprise defeat of his older brother was made possible by the electoral college with which Labour Party leaders are elected, allocating a third of the vote each to lay party members, Labour members of the Commons and European Parliament, and to trade unions and socialist societies affiliated to the party. David Miliband led among the general and Parliamentary membership, but his younger brother's union support proved decisive in a close race (50.65 per cent to 49.35 per cent in the final run-off on a preferential ballot). Miliband's reliance on union support led many in the party and beyond to question his democratic credentials as leader. His brother has left frontline politics for the time being.

This was Ed Miliband's first conference speech as leader of the party and the opposition in the House of Commons. It provides a counterpoint by which to evaluate and contrast the previous speeches by Cameron and Clegg. I have not tried to group *sentences together in this case. The reader can see the use of one-line stand-alone sentences in this speech. Note the similarities to the Party Conference speech given by Blair in 2002. The stand-alone sentences are another acknowledgement of this influence. The single-sentence structure allows for applause lines, functioning to turn the speech into a rally. The trick is to make the rally speech thoughtful, visionary and compelling. Blair was able to do this consistently, with amazing skill. Miliband is mindful of the need for these lines to inspire, persuade and energise his core Labour Party audience. The lines must also reach out to those who are potential converts to his party, or at least willing to reject the coalition government and vote for Labour in a future election.*

—

Conference, I stand here today ready to lead: a new generation now leading Labour.

Be in no doubt. The new generation of Labour is different. Different attitudes, different ideas, different ways of doing politics.

Today I want to tell you who I am, what I believe and how we are going to do the most important thing we have to do – win back the trust of the country.

We all of us share a deep conviction which brought us into this party and into this hall.

But each of us has our own individual story. And I want to tell you about mine.

In 1940, my grandfather, with my Dad, climbed onto one of the last boats out of Belgium.

They had to make a heartbreaking decision – to leave behind my grandmother and my father's sister. They spent the war in hiding, in a village sheltered by a brave local farmer. Month after month, year upon year, they lived in fear of the knock at the door.

At the same time, on the other side of Europe, my mother, aged five, had seen Hitler's army march into Poland.

She spent the war on the run sheltering in a convent and then with a Catholic family that took her in. Her sister, her mother and her.

My love for this country comes from this story. Two young people fled the darkness that had engulfed the Jews across Europe and in Britain they found the light of liberty.

They arrived with nothing. This country gave them everything.

It gave them life and the things that make life worth living: hope, friendship, opportunity and family.

And they took hope and opportunity. They worked hard; they got on.

My Dad learned English, paid his way moving furniture during the day, and studying at night at technical college. He joined the Navy to fight for our country and afterwards he wanted to go to university. He did.

My Mum built a life here after the war, for all of us. I know nobody more generous, nobody more kind, nobody more loving and nobody more relieved that this contest is over, than my Mum.

The gift my parents gave to me and David are the things I want for every child in this country. A secure and loving home. Encouragement and the aspiration to succeed.

In those ways my family was just like every other. But in some ways it was different.

I suppose not everyone has a dad who wrote a book saying he didn't believe in the Parliamentary road to socialism.

But you know, it wasn't a cold house. It was warm, full of the spirit of argument and conviction, the conviction that leads me to stand before you today, the conviction that people of courage and principle can make a huge difference to their world.

What my parents learned in fear, they passed on to us in an environment of comfort and security.

And there was one more lesson that I learned. We do not have to accept the world as we find it. And we have a responsibility to leave our world a better place and never walk by on the other side of injustice.

Freedom and opportunity are precious gifts and the purpose of our politics is to expand them, for all our people.

That faith is not something I chose. It's not something I learned from books, even from my Dad's books.

It was something I was born into.

And that is why David and I have devoted our lives to politics.

And it is why I will commit to you here and now. My beliefs will run through everything I do. My beliefs, my values are my anchor and when people try to drag me, as I know they will, it is to that sense of right and wrong, that sense of who I am and what I believe, to which I will always hold.

Conference, I am so honoured that you chose me to lead your party and I know you share those values.

And I am proud that every day, day in and day out, in every village, and every town and city in the land, you work to put those values into practice.

Conference, can I thank you for the heroic work you did at the election.

The reason we denied the Conservative Party a majority was because of the incredible work of Labour and trade union members the length and breadth of our country.

From Birmingham Edgbaston to Westminster North and from Edinburgh

South to the Vale of Clwyd, it was your dedication, your energy and your determination to fight for the communities you love that beat the Ashcroft millions.

And let me thank everyone, not just Labour Party members, but thousands of ordinary members of the public who drove the BNP out of Barking and Dagenham.

But let's face facts. We had a bad result. We had a very bad result. And we are out of government.

And let me tell you, there is nothing good about opposition.

Every day out of power is another day when this coalition can wreak damage on our communities, another day when we cannot change our country for the better.

And let us resolve today that this will be a one-term government. That is the purpose of my leadership of this party.

But to achieve that we must go on our own journey.

And that is why the most important word in politics for us is 'humility'.

We need to learn some painful truths about where we went wrong and how we lost touch.

We must not blame the electorate for ending up with a government we don't like, we should blame ourselves.

We have to understand why people felt they couldn't support us.

We have to show we understand the problems people face today.

This will require strong leadership. It won't always be easy. You might not always like what I have to say.

But you've elected me leader and lead I will.

This country faces some tough choices. And so do we. And we need to change.

You remember. We began as restless and radical. Remember the spirit of 1997, but by the end of our time in office we had lost our way.

The most important lesson of New Labour is this: Every time we made progress we did it by challenging the conventional wisdom.

Think of how we took on the idea that there was a public ownership solution to every problem our society faced.

We changed Clause IV. We were right to do so.

Think of how we emphasised being tough on crime was as important as being tough on the causes of crime. We were right to do so.

Think of how we challenged the impression that we taxed for its own sake and that we were hostile to business. We were right to change.

And think of how we challenged the idea of a male-dominated Parliament with all-women shortlists and made the cause of gender equality central to our government. We were right to do so.

And the reason Tony and Gordon took on conventional wisdom in our party was so they could change the country.

We forget too easily what a radical challenge their ideas were to established ways of thinking about Britain and how they reshaped the centre ground of politics.

They were reforming, restless and radical.

The old way of thinking said that economic efficiency would always come at the price of social justice.

With the minimum wage, tax credits, the New Deal, they showed that was wrong.

I am proud that our government lifted hundreds of thousands of children out of poverty, hundreds of thousands of pensioners out of poverty, proud that we created the highest levels of employment in Britain's history.

The old way of thinking said that public services would always be second-class. But we defied the conventional wisdom.

I come from a generation that suffered school lessons in portacabins and crumbling hospitals. I tell you one thing, for the eighteen years they were in power the Tories did nothing to fix the roof when the sun was shining.

Our legacy is a generation for whom newly built schools and modernised hospitals are an everyday fact of life.

I am proud of the fact that because of what we did, yes we did save the National Health Service in this country.

The old way of thinking said that you couldn't change attitudes towards gay men and lesbians.

Let me tell you that last month I was privileged to be in this great city, at Pride, to see not just thousands of people marching but thousands of people lining the street in support.

We should be proud that our commitment to equality means we have couples forming civil partnerships across the country and celebrating with their family and friends.

The old thinking told us that for 300 years, the choice was either the break-up of the United Kingdom or Scotland and Wales run from London.

We should be proud that Labour established the Scottish Parliament and the Welsh Assembly.

And we should make sure that after next May's elections we re-elect Carwyn Jones as the First Minister in Wales and we elect Iain Gray as the new First Minister in Scotland.

And I am so, so proud that, against all the odds, we helped deliver peace in Northern Ireland. And it will be one of Tony Blair's great legacies to this country.

The old thinking told us that the challenges of the world were too big and our country too small to make a difference.

But thanks to our leadership around the world, development spending is now heading towards our goal, forty million more children are going to school each day, and two hundred million are protected from malaria. And that would never have happened without the leadership of Gordon Brown as Chancellor and then Prime Minister.

Tony and Gordon had the courage to take on established attitudes and institutions – and change Britain.

It is that courage that made us such a successful political force.

But our journey must also understand where it went wrong. I tell you, I believe that Britain is fairer and stronger than it was thirteen years ago.

But we have to ask, how did a party with such achievements to its name end up losing five million votes between 1997 and 2010?

It didn't happen by accident.

The hard truth for all of us in this hall is that a party that started out taking on old thinking became the prisoner of its own certainties.

The world was changing all around us – from global finance to immigration to terrorism – New Labour, a political force founded on its ability to adapt and change – lost its ability to do so.

The reason was that we too often bought old, established ways of thinking and over time we just looked more and more like a new establishment.

Let me say to the country:

You saw the worst financial crisis in a generation, and I understand your anger that Labour hadn't changed the old ways in the City which said deregulation was the answer.

You wanted your concerns about the impact of immigration on communities to be heard, and I understand your frustration that we didn't seem to be on your side.

And when you wanted to make it possible for your kids to get on in life, I understand why you felt that we were stuck in old thinking about higher and higher levels of personal debt, including from tuition fees.

You saw jobs disappear and economic security undermined, I understand your anger at a Labour government that claimed it could end boom and bust.

And I understand also that the promise of new politics of 1997 came to look hollow after the scandal of MPs' expenses. And we came to look like a new establishment in the company we kept, the style of our politics and our remoteness from people.

I stand before you, clear in my task: to once again make Labour a force that takes on established thinking, doesn't succumb to it, speaks for the majority and shapes the centre ground of politics.

And I tell you this: if we are not this party, nobody will be.

This new generation that leads our party is humble about our past and idealistic about our future.

It is a generation that will always stand up for the mainstream majority.

It is a generation that will fight for the centre ground, not allow it to be dominated or defined by our opponents.

And it is a generation which thirsts for change.

This week we embark on the journey back to power.

It will be a long journey involving hard thinking for our party.

We do not start that journey by claiming we know all the answers now.

We do so by setting a direction of change.

Let me tell you what kind of country I want to see:

This generation wants to change our economy so that it works better for working people and doesn't just serve the needs of the few at the top.

This generation wants to change our society so that it values community and family, not just work, because we understand there is more to life than the bottom line.

This generation wants to change the way government works because it understands the power of the state to change lives but also how frustrating it can be if not reformed.

This generation wants to change our foreign policy so that it's always based on values, not just alliances.

And this generation knows very profoundly that to change Britain we need a new politics.

Above all, I lead a new generation not bound by the fear or the ghosts of the past.

As we emerge from the global economic crisis, we face a choice: we can return to business as usual or we can challenge old thinking to build the new economy we need.

Let me say, I believe strongly that we need to reduce the deficit.

There will be cuts and there would have been if we had been in government.

Some of them will be painful and would have been if we were in government.

I won't oppose every cut the coalition proposes.

There will be some things the coalition does that we won't like as a party but we will have to support.

And come the next election there will be some things they have done that I will not be able to reverse.

I say this because the fiscal credibility we earned before 1997 was hard-won and we must win it back by the time of the next general election.

I am serious about reducing our deficit.

But I am also serious about doing it in a way that learns the basic lessons of economics, fairness and history.

Economics teaches us that at times of recession governments run up deficits.

We were too exposed to financial services as an economy so the impact of the crash on the public finances was deeper on us than on others.

We should take responsibility for not building a more resilient economy.

But what we should not do as a country is make a bad situation worse by embarking on deficit reduction at a pace and in a way that endangers our recovery.

The starting point for a responsible plan is to halve the deficit over four years, but growth is our priority and we must remain vigilant against a downturn.

You see when you cancel thousands of new school buildings at a stroke, it isn't just bad for our kids, it's bad for construction companies at a time when their order books are empty.

It's not responsible, it's irresponsible.

When you deprive Sheffield Forgemasters of a loan, a loan from government which would be paid back, you deprive Britain of the ability to lead the world in new technology.

It's not responsible, it's irresponsible.

And when you reduce your economic policy simply to deficit reduction alone you leave Britain without a plan for growth.

It's not responsible, it's irresponsible and we should say so.

No plan for growth means no credible plan for deficit reduction.

And nor should we reduce the deficit without learning the basic lessons of fairness.

We must protect those on middle and low incomes. They did nothing to cause the crisis but are suffering the consequences.

I say the people who caused the crisis and can afford to do more should do more: with a higher bank levy allowing us to do more to protect the services and entitlements on which families depend.

And we should learn the basic lessons of history.

After 1945, we had the biggest debt we have ever had.

That generation cut the deficit but they had a bigger vision: for a new economy and a good society.

True patriotism is about reducing the debt burden we pass on to our kids. But Mr Cameron, true patriotism is also about building an economy and a society fit for our kids to work and live in.

You were the optimist once, but now all you offer is a miserable, pessimistic view of what we can achieve. And you hide behind the deficit to justify it.

But I have a different ambition, to emerge from the global economic crisis tackling the deficit, but also learning the much deeper lessons that this generation must learn.

It is a huge challenge to change our economy for the future and the same old thinking will lead to the same old results: an economy too dependent on financial services, too many people stuck in low pay and dead-end jobs and growing inequality.

We need a plan for change. A plan to reform the banks, invest in the industries of the future and support the small businesses and entrepreneurs who can be the lifeblood of our economy.

The new generation in my party understands the fundamental New Labour lesson that we must build prosperity as well as redistributing it.

And it also knows that there are huge vested interests and huge barriers to the wealth-creators in this country, particularly small businesses and the self-employed.

These must be tackled. I tell you this, I will make Labour the party of enterprise and also the party of small business.

And I want British businesses, large and small, to be able to make the most of the advantages of globalisation.

New Labour was right to be enthusiastic about the opportunities that come in a more connected world: the movement of goods and services, the chance to travel, the new markets for our companies.

But this new generation recognises that we did not do enough to address concerns about some of the consequences of globalisation, including migration.

All of us heard it. Like the man I met in my constituency who told me he had seen his mates' wages driven down by the consequences of migration.

If we don't understand why he would feel angry – and it wasn't about prejudice – then we are failing to serve those who we are in politics to represent.

I am the son of immigrants. I believe that Britain has benefited economically, culturally, socially from those who come to this country.

I don't believe either that we can turn back the clock on free movement of labour in Europe. But we should never have pretended it would not have consequences.

Consequences we should have dealt with.

We have to challenge the old thinking that flexible labour markets are always the answer.

Employers should not be allowed to exploit migrant labour in order to undercut wages.

And if we have free movement of labour across Europe we need proper labour standards in our economy, including real protection for agency workers.

And, as every democratic country recognises, it is vital that workers have a voice that speaks for them.

I remember during this campaign I met some school dinner ladies. They had to buy their own uniforms, their shift patterns were being changed at a moment's notice; frankly, conference, they were being exploited.

So they looked to their union to help them. They weren't interested in going on strike, they loved the kids they served and wanted to serve their schools. But they wanted someone to help them get basic standards of decency and fairness.

Responsible trade unions are part of a civilised society, every democratic country recognises that.

But all of us in this movement bear a heavy responsibility. We want to win an argument about the danger this coalition poses to our economy and our society.

To do so we must understand the lessons of history.

We need to win the public to our cause and what we must avoid at all costs is alienating them and adding to the book of historic union failures.

That is why I have no truck, and you should have no truck, with overblown rhetoric about waves of irresponsible strikes.

The public won't support them. I won't support them. And you shouldn't support them either.

But it is not just from trade unions that I want to see responsibility.

This new generation demands responsibility from business too.

During this campaign, I have met some extraordinary people doing amazing service for our country.

I remember a care worker I met in Durham.

She worked hard and with dedication, looking after our Mums, Dads and grandparents when they couldn't look after themselves anymore.

She is doing one of the most important jobs in our society, and if it was my Mum or Dad, I would want anyone who cared for them to be paid a decent wage.

But she was barely paid the minimum wage – and barely a few pence extra for higher skills.

She told me that she thought a fair wage would be seven pounds an hour because, after all, she would get that for stacking shelves at the local supermarket.

I believe in responsibility in every part of our society.

That's why I believe in not just a minimum wage but that the foundation of our economy in the future must be a living wage.

And we need a tax system for business that rewards responsibility:

To pay a living wage.

To provide high-quality apprenticeships and family-friendly employment.

And we need responsibility at the top of society too. The gap between rich and poor does matter.

It doesn't just harm the poor, it harms us all.

What does it say about the values of our society, what have we become, that a banker can earn in a day what the care worker can earn in a year?

I say: responsibility in this country shouldn't just be about what you can get away with.

And that applies to every chief executive of every major company in this country.

And, just as businesses have responsibility to ensure fair pay, so those who can work have a responsibility to do so.

This is one of the hardest issues for our party because all of us know in our communities people who are in genuine need and who worry about the impact of new medical tests, or changes to rules on them.

At the same time, let's be honest, we also know there are those for whom the benefits system has become a trap.

That is not in their interests or the interests of us as a society and we are right when we say it must be challenged.

Reforming our benefits system is not about stereotyping everybody out of work, it's about transforming their lives.

Real help matched with real responsibility.

That is why on welfare, I will look closely at whatever the government comes forward with: not arbitrary cuts to benefits but a genuine plan to make sure that those in need are protected and that those who can work have the help they need to ensure they do so.

Work is a central part of life. But it is not all that matters.

We all care about making a living but we don't just care about that.

Here is our generation's paradox: the biggest ever consumers of goods and services, but a generation that yearns so much for the things that business cannot provide.

Strong families. Time with your children. Green spaces. Community life. Love and compassion.

New Labour embraced markets in our economy and was right to do so.

But let's be honest. We became naive about them.

We must never again give the impression that we know the price of everything and the value of nothing.

We must be on the side of communities who want to save their local post office, not be the people trying to close it.

We must be on the side of people trying to protect their high street from looking like every other high street, not the people who say that's just the forces of progress.

And we must be on the side of those who are dismayed by the undermining of the local pub with cut-price alcohol from supermarkets.

We must shed old thinking and stand up for those who believe there is more to life than the bottom line.

We stand for these things not because we are social conservatives but because we believe in community, belonging and solidarity.

And I tell you this: the good life is about the things we do in our community and the time we spend with family.

I feel this so deeply since the birth of my son sixteen months ago.

As we rebuild our economy, we must think how we protect families up and down this country.

Families can't do the best job if they are stressed out, working sixty or seventy hours a week, can't be there when the kids get home from school, doing two or three jobs.

We've got to change our culture on working time not just for the good of families, but because it is through family that we learn right from wrong, develop ambitions for ourselves and show kindness and respect for others that is the foundation of our society.

When I look at some of the challenges we face as a country – from gangs to teenage pregnancy – it is only a government that stands up for families that are trying their best to bring up their kids that can offer answers.

So as we rebuild our economy we must think about how we protect and nourish the things that matter to families and to family life.

This new generation also wants to challenge the way we think about the state and what it can achieve.

I believe profoundly that government must play its part in creating the good society.

But our new generation also knows that government can itself become just such a vested interest. That unless reformed, unless accountable, unless responsive, government can impede the good society.

Our new generation, hungry for change, is unwilling to see that happen.

Like millions of people around the country, I went to my local comprehensive. I know the value of a good school, a good teacher.

And I know there are many parents frustrated, with a school that doesn't suit your child or live up to your hopes.

There are amazing secondary schools in my constituency and amazing teachers and head teachers. But one of them was consistently failing its pupils.

And it pained me as an MP to see those kids being consistently let down. Now that school has been taken over, the kids' life chances transformed.

That is what good public service reform is all about.

My generation recognises too that government can itself become a vested interest when it comes to civil liberties.

I believe too in a society where individual freedom and liberty matter and should never be given away lightly.

The first job of government is the protection of its citizens. As Prime Minister I would never forget that.

And that means working with all the legitimate means at our disposal to disrupt and destroy terrorist networks.

But we must always remember that British liberties were hard-fought and hard-won over hundreds of years.

We should always take the greatest care in protecting them.

And too often we seemed casual about them.

Like the idea of locking someone away for ninety days – nearly three months in prison – without charging them with a crime.

Or the broad use of anti-terrorism measures for purposes for which they were not intended.

They just undermined the important things we did like CCTV and DNA testing.

Protecting the public involves protecting all their freedoms.

I won't let the Tories or the Liberals take ownership of the British tradition of liberty.

I want our party to reclaim that tradition.

So too in our foreign policy the new generation must challenge old thinking.

We are the generation that came of age at the end of the Cold War.

The generation that was taught that the end of history had arrived and then saw 9/11 shatter that illusion.

And we are the generation that recognises that we belong to a global community: we can't insulate ourselves from the world's problems.

For that reason, right now this country has troops engaged in Afghanistan.

They represent the very best of our country.

They and their families are making enormous sacrifices on our behalf and we should today acknowledge their service and their sacrifice.

Our troops are there to stabilise the country and enable a political settlement to be reached so that Afghanistan can be stable and we can be safe.

I will work in a bipartisan way with the government to both support our mission and ensure Afghanistan is not a war without end.

But just as I support the mission in Afghanistan as a necessary response to terrorism, I've got to be honest with you about the lessons of Iraq.

Iraq was an issue that divided our party and our country. Many sincerely believed that the world faced a real threat. I criticise nobody faced with making the toughest of decisions and I honour our troops who fought and died there.

But I do believe that we were wrong. Wrong to take Britain to war and we need to be honest about that.

Wrong because that war was not a last resort, because we did not build sufficient alliances and because we undermined the United Nations.

America has drawn a line under Iraq and so must we.

Our alliance with America is incredibly important to us but we must always remember that our values must shape the alliances that we form and any military action that we take.

So many of the world's problems need functioning international institutions. The days in which any country could achieve their goals on their own are over.

There can be no solution to the conflicts of the Middle East without international action, providing support where it is needed, and pressure where it is right to do so.

And let me say this, as Israel ends the moratorium on settlement building, I will always defend the right of Israel to exist in peace and security. But Israel must accept and recognise in its actions the Palestinian right to statehood.

That is why the attack on the Gaza flotilla was so wrong.

And that is why the Gaza blockade must be lifted and we must strain every sinew to work to make that happen.

The government must step up and work with our partners in Europe and around the world to help bring a just and lasting peace to the Middle East.

But to achieve all these things – a different economy, a different society and reform of the state – we must change our politics too.

Let's be honest, politics isn't working.

People have lost faith in politicians and politics.

And trust is gone.

Politics is broken.

Its practice, its reputation and its institutions.

I'm in it and even I sometimes find it depressing.

This generation has a chance – and a huge responsibility – to change our politics. We must seize it and meet the challenge.

So we need to reform our House of Commons and I support changing our voting system and will vote Yes in the referendum on AV.

Yes we need to finally elect the House of Lords after talking about it for so long – about a hundred years.

Yes we need more decisions to be made locally, with local democracy free of the constraints we have placed on it in the past and free of an attitude which has looked down its nose at local government.

And I want to congratulate all our local councillors and tell you: I will be shoulder to shoulder with you at next May's local elections.

And the following year, we will be proud not only of the Olympics in London, but proud too to see them presided over by the next Mayor of London. Ken Livingstone. And let me also congratulate Oona on the campaign that she fought.

Let's be honest, changing our institutions won't be enough to restore trust on its own.

Look, in the end, it's politicians who have to change.

This generation must reject the old ways of doing politics. And must speak to the issues our generation knows it must confront.

The focus groups will tell you that there's no votes in green issues.

Maybe not.

But taking the difficult steps to protect our planet for future generations is the greatest challenge our generation faces.

When I think about my son, I think what he will be asking me in twenty years' time is whether I was part of the last generation not to get climate change or the first generation to get it.

And climate change, just like the aging society, can't be tackled by the politics we have.

They don't lend themselves to the politics of now: instant results, instant votes, instant popularity. *X-Factor* politics.

So we can't be imprisoned by the focus groups.

Politics has to be about leadership or it is about nothing.

I also know something else. Wisdom is not the preserve of any one party. Some of the political figures in history who I admire most are [John Maynard] Keynes, [David] Lloyd George, [William] Beveridge, who were not members of the Labour Party.

Frankly, the political establishment too often conducts debate in a way that insults the intelligence of the public.

We must change this for the good of the country.

I will be a responsible Leader of the Opposition.

What does that mean?

When I disagree with the government, as on the deficit, I will say so loud and clear and I will take the argument to them.

But when Ken Clarke says we need to look at short sentences in prison because of high re-offending rates, I'm not going to say he's soft on crime.

When Theresa May says we should review stop and search laws to prevent excessive use of state power, I'm not going to say she is soft on terrorism.

I tell you this, conference, this new generation must find a new way of conducting politics.

And that brings me to some of the names I've been called...

Wallace out of Wallace and Gromit ... I can see the resemblance.

Forrest Gump ... Not so much.

And what about Red Ed?

Come off it.

Let's start to have a grown-up debate in this country about who we are and where we want to go and what kind of country we want to leave for our kids.

A few days ago our contest came to an end and now the real contest has begun.

I relish the chance to take on David Cameron.

We may be of a similar age, but in my values and ideals I am of a different and new generation.

The new generation is not simply defined by age, but by attitudes and ideals.

And there is a defining difference between us and David Cameron ... and that is optimism.

We are the heirs to an extraordinary tradition, to great leaders who were above all the optimists of history.

The optimism of 1945 which built the National Health Service and the welfare state.

The optimism of Harold Wilson and the white heat of technology and the great social reforms of that government.

The optimism of Tony and Gordon who took on the established thinking and reshaped our country.

We are the optimists in politics today.

So let's be humble about our past.

Let's understand the need to change.

Let's inspire people with our vision of the good society.

Let the message go out, a new generation has taken charge of Labour.

Optimistic about our country.

Optimistic about our world.

Optimistic about the power of politics.

We are the optimists and together we will change Britain.

NELSON MANDELA

'MASSIVE POVERTY AND OBSCENE INEQUALITY ARE THE TERRIBLE SCOURGES OF OUR TIME'

—

REMARKS AT THE CAMPAIGN TO END POVERTY IN THE DEVELOPING WORLD

LONDON, UNITED KINGDOM, 3 MARCH 2005

Born in Mvezo, a small village in Umtata, South Africa, Nelson Mandela was among the most revered of twentieth-century political leaders. He became active in the anti-apartheid African National Congress (ANC) in the 1950s, and later co-founded its paramilitary wing, 'Umkhonto We Swize' (Spear of the Nation). He was arrested in 1963 on charges of sabotage and treason, and served twenty-seven years in prison, including eighteen years on the notorious Robben Island, where he studied for a Bachelor of Laws degree via the University of London's exchange programme. In 1985, he was offered his freedom in exchange for renouncing violent resistance to apartheid, but refused, arguing that ANC violence had been and remained a legitimate response to the regime's brutality.

Upon his unconditional release in 1990 he negotiated an end to apartheid with then-President of South Africa F. W. de Klerk, and the two were jointly awarded the 1993 Nobel Peace Prize. In 1994, Mandela contested the first multi-racial, fully democratic election in South Africa as leader of the ANC, winning 62 per cent of the national vote and the Presidency. He served until 1999, declining to seek a second term. Like Václav Havel, Mandela became a figure of global moral authority.

In this speech he continues his post-presidential advocacy for the world's poor and disenfranchised. President Mandela has been talking about some of the issues advanced by the Occupy Movement and other groups for many years. Please notice his use of inclusive language. Global poverty is our problem, requiring all of us to work to end it. Such an effort can be successful. There is hope, even though the *complexity and scope of poverty is staggering. Mandela is not a divider. He is a visionary who believes we can do better. He uses speech to heal, to motivate us, and to help us unite. He knows how to turn positive speech into action.*

———

I am privileged to be here today at the invitation of the Campaign to Make Poverty History.

As you know, I recently formally announced my retirement from public life and should really not be here.

However, as long as poverty, injustice and gross inequality persist in our world, none of us can truly rest. Moreover, the Global Campaign for Action Against Poverty represents such a noble cause that we could not decline the invitation.

Massive poverty and obscene inequality are such terrible scourges of our times – times in which the world boasts breathtaking advances in science, technology, industry and wealth accumulation – that they have to rank alongside slavery and apartheid as social evils.

The Global Campaign for Action Against Poverty can take its place as a public movement alongside the movement to abolish slavery and the international solidarity against apartheid.

And I can never thank the people of Britain enough for their support through those days of the struggle against apartheid. Many stood in solidarity with us, just a few yards from this spot.

Through your will and passion, you assisted in consigning that evil system forever to history. But in this new century, millions of people in the world's poorest countries remain imprisoned, enslaved, and in chains.

They are trapped in the prison of poverty. It is time to set them free.

Like slavery and apartheid, poverty is not natural. It is man-made and it can be overcome and eradicated by the actions of human beings.

And overcoming poverty is not a gesture of charity. It is an act of justice. It is the protection of a fundamental human right, the right to dignity and a decent life.

While poverty persists, there is no true freedom.

The steps that are needed from the developed nations are clear. The first is ensuring trade justice.

I have said before that trade justice is a truly meaningful way for the developed countries to show commitment to bringing about an end to global poverty.

The second is an end to the debt crisis for the poorest countries.

The third is to deliver much more aid and make sure it is of the highest quality.

In 2005, there is a unique opportunity for making an impact.

In September, world leaders will gather in New York to measure progress since they made the Millennium Declaration in the year 2000.

That declaration promised to halve extreme poverty.

But at the moment, the promise is falling tragically behind. Those leaders must now honour their promises to the world's poorest citizens.

Tomorrow, here in London, the G7 finance ministers can make a significant beginning. I am happy to have been invited to meet with them.

The G8 leaders, when they meet in Scotland in July, have already promised to focus on the issue of poverty, especially in Africa.

I say to all those leaders: do not look the other way; do not hesitate. Recognise that the world is hungry for action, not words. Act with courage and vision.

I am proud to wear the symbol of this global call to action in 2005. This white band is from my country.

In a moment, I want to give this band to you – young people of Britain – and ask you to take it forward along with millions of others to the G8 summit in July.

I entrust it to you. I will be watching with anticipation.

We thank you for coming here today. Sometimes it falls upon a generation to be great. You can be that great generation. Let your greatness blossom.

Of course the task will not be easy. But not to do this would be a crime against humanity, against which I ask all humanity now to rise up.

Make Poverty History in 2005. Make History in 2005. Then we can all stand with our heads held high. Thank you.

ELLEN JOHNSON SIRLEAF

'THE RESILIENCE OF OUR PEOPLE'

—

INAUGURAL ADDRESS

MONROVIA, LIBERIA, 16 JANUARY 2006

President *Ellen Johnson Sirleaf of Liberia was the first democratically elected female head of state in Africa. Elected in 2005, she prioritised stabilising the country's economy, and prevailed upon the IMF, International Development Association, Paris Club and World Bank to write off billions of dollars in debt, attracting widespread international praise for her fiscal sobriety and campaign against corruption. She was re-elected in 2011, winning over 90 per cent of the vote in a second round run-off. That same year, she was awarded the Nobel Peace Prize, sharing it with Leyman Gbowee of Liberia and Tawakel Karman of Yemen. The following remarks are from her 2006 inaugural address. This speech provides great insight into how Liberians and West Africans see themselves. It also offers hope, dignity and a better future to Liberians. President Johnson Sirleaf offers a commanding, confident speech: words of history that make history. She discusses the problems that have plagued Liberia, especially civil war and violence, and outlines a future in which Liberians end strife and work for peaceful governance.*

—

Let us first praise Almighty God, the Arbiter of all affairs of humankind whose omnipotent Hand guides and steers our nation.

Before I begin this address, which signifies the high noon of this historic occasion, I ask that we bow our heads for a moment of silent prayer in memory of the thousands of our compatriots who have died as a result of the many conflicts.

Thank you!

I also ask your indulgence as I reflect on the memory of my two rural illiterate grandmothers and my mother and father who taught me to be what I am today, and the families who took them in and gave them the opportunity of a better life.

Let us also remember in prayers during his affliction, His Grace Archbishop Michael K. Francis, the conscience of our nation.

Vice President Boakai and I have just participated in the time-honoured constitutional ritual of oath-taking as we embark upon our responsibilities to lead this Republic. This ritual is symbolically and politically significant and substantive. It reflects the enduring character of the democratic tradition of the peaceful and orderly transfer of political power and authority. It also confirms the culmination of a commitment to our nation's collective search for a purposeful and responsive national leadership.

We applaud the resilience of our people who, weighed down and dehumanised by poverty and rendered immobile by the shackles of fourteen years of civil war, went courageously to the polls, to vote – not once but twice – to elect Vice President Joseph Boakai and me to serve them. We express to you, our people, our deep sense of appreciation and gratitude for the opportunity to serve you and our common Republic. We pledge to live up to your expectations of creating a government that is attentive and responsive to your needs, concerns, and the development and progress of our country.

We know that your vote was a vote for change; a vote for peace, security and stability; a vote for individual and national prosperity; a vote for healing and leadership. We have heard you loudly, and we humbly accept your vote of confidence and your mandate.

This occasion, held under the cloudy skies, marks a celebration of change and a dedication to an agenda for a socio-economic and political reordering; indeed, a national renewal.

Today, we wholeheartedly embrace this change. We recognise that this change is not change for change's sake, but a fundamental break with the past, thereby requiring that we take bold and decisive steps to address the problems that for decades have stunted our progress, undermined national unity, and kept old and new cleavages in ferment.

As we embrace this new commitment to change, it is befitting that, for the first time, the inauguration is being held on the Capitol Grounds, one of the three seats of government. We pledge anew our commitment to transparency, open government, and participatory democracy for all of our citizens.

Fellow Liberians: as I speak to you today, I am most gratified by the calibre of the delegations of our own African governments, foreign governments, partners and local partners as well, who have come to join us to celebrate this triumph of democracy in our country. I am particularly touched by those you see – our dear brothers, the delegation from the United States, headed by the wife of President Bush and my friend, our mediator, who has been with us so long and brought us to this day. We pay homage to all of you. We respect you. We welcome you.

Bienvenu à tous.

My dear brothers and sisters of West Africa: You have died for us; you have given refuge to thousands of our citizens; you have denied yourselves by utilising your scarce resources to assist us; you have agonised for us, and you have prayed for us. We thank you, and may God bless you for your support to Liberia as well as for your continuing commitment to promote peace, security, stability, and bilateral cooperation within our sub-region – and beyond.

I wish to acknowledge the stewardship of the National Transitional Government under the leadership of its former Chairman, Mr Gyude Bryant, for their contribution to peace and to the successful electoral process. I also recognise and thank the former National Transitional Legislative Assembly for their service to the nation. And I welcome the members of the 52nd Legislature who were sworn in a few moments ago. Distinguished ladies and gentlemen, I congratulate you as you assume your individual responsibilities of representing our people. I look forward to working with each of you as we strive to build a better nation.

I thank and applaud our gallant men and women of the armed forces of Liberia who have rendered sacrificial service to our nation and are now being willingly retired to facilitate the training and restructuring of the new armed forces of Liberia.

I also thank the leadership and gallant men and women of the United Nations Military Mission in Liberia who daily labour with us to keep the peace that we enjoy.

Fellow Liberians, ladies and gentlemen: no one who has lived in or visited this country in the past fifteen years will deny the physical destruction and the moral decadence that the civil war has left in its wake here in Monrovia and in other cities, towns, and villages across the nation.

We have all suffered. The individual sense of deprivation is immense. It is therefore understandable that our people will have high expectations and will demand aggressive solutions to the socio-economic and societal difficulties that we face.

Our record shows that we are a strong and resilient people, able to survive; able to rise from the ashes of civil strife and to start anew; able to forge a new beginning, forgiving if not forgetting the past. We are a good and friendly people, braced for hope even as we wipe away the tears of past suffering and despair. Our challenge, therefore, is to transform adversity into opportunity, to renew the promises upon which our nation was founded: freedom, equality, unity and individual progress.

In the history of our nation, in the history of every nation, each generation, each administration is summoned to define its nation's purpose and character. Now, it is our time to state clearly and unequivocally who we are, as Liberians, as your leaders – and where we plan to take this country in the next six years.

First, let me declare in our pursuit of political renewal, that the political campaign is over. It is time for us, regardless of our political affiliations and persuasions, to come together to heal and rebuild our nation. For my part, as President of the Republic of Liberia, my government extends a hand of friendship and solidarity to the leadership and members of all political parties, many of them sitting right in front of me, which participated in our recent presidential and legislative elections. I call upon those who have been long in the struggle – and those who recently earned their stripes – to play important roles in the rebuilding of our nation.

Committed to advance the spirit of inclusion, I assure all Liberians and our international partners and friends that our government will recognise and support a strong democratic and loyal opposition in Liberia. This is important because we believe that our democratic culture and our nation are best served when the opposition is strong and actively engaged in the process of nation building.

Moreover, we call upon our colleagues of all political persuasions now in the Diaspora to return home and join us in meeting this exciting challenge of national renewal.

We make a similar appeal to the thousands of our citizens who continue to live in refugee camps throughout the sub-region and beyond. We recognise and sympathise with your plight and will explore with our development partners ways and means to facilitate your early return home as a national imperative for our renewal and development.

To those who are still internally displaced, we pledge to work with our partners to get you back to your communities to enable you to start the process of rebuilding your lives.

We must have a new understanding. Your job, as citizens, is to work for your family and your country. Your country's only job is to work for you. That is the compact that I offer you today.

My fellow Liberians, ladies and gentlemen: ours has certainly not been an easy journey to where we are today. Indeed, the road has been tortuous and chequered. The tendencies of intolerance of each other's opinion rooted in parochial and selfish considerations – and greed – have driven us into our descent into recent tragedies and paralysis as a nation and as a people. These negative national tendencies have, in the past, bred ethnic suspicion and hatred, led to injustice, social and political exclusion. They have also weakened our capacity to peacefully co-exist as a people with diverse socio-cultural, economic, and political backgrounds. Consequently, we have witnessed needless generalised conflicts that have profoundly affected the Liberian family, the foundation of our society.

I know of this struggle because I have been a part of it. Without bitterness, or anger, or vindictiveness, I recall the inhumanity of confinement, the terror of attempted rape, the ostracism of exile. But I also recall the goodness and the kindness of the many who defied orders and instruction and saved my life, and gave food to the hungry and ... water to the thirsty. I recall their humanity – and thank them.

And so, my fellow Liberians, let us acknowledge and honour the sacrifices and the contributions of all as we put the past behind us. Let us rejoice that our recent democratic exercise has been a redemptive act of faith and an expression of renewed confidence in ourselves. Let us be proud that we were able to ultimately rise above our intense political and other differences in a renewed determination as a people to foster dialogue instead of violence, promote unity rather than disharmony, and engender hope rather than disillusionment and despair.

My administration therefore commits itself to the creation of a democracy in which the constitutional and civil liberties and rights of all of our people will be respected.

In a similar quest for economic renewal, we start on the premise that we are a wealthy people. Our nation is blessed with an endowment, rich in natural and human resources. Yet our economy has collapsed due to several civil conflicts and economic mismanagement by successive governments. The task of reconstructing our devastated economy is awesome, for which there will be no quick fix.

Yet we have the potential to promote a healthy economy in which Liberians and international investors can prosper. We can create an investment climate that gives confidence to Liberian and foreign investors. We can promote those activities that add value in the exploitation of our natural resources. We can recognise and give support to our small farmers and marketers who, through their own efforts over the years, have provided buoyancy and self-sufficiency in economic activity. We can revisit our land tenure system to promote more ownership and freeholding for communities.

This will call for a transformation of our economic vision into economic goals that are consistent with our national endowment and regional and global dynamics. We will ensure that allocation of our own resources reflect those priorities formulated on the basis of sequential measures of structural change that need to provide this transformation. And we will call upon our development partners to likewise recognise that although they have made significant investment to bring peace to our country, this peace can only be consolidated and sustained if we bring development to our people.

With this in mind, we are working with our partners to identify key objectives and deliverables in the first 150 days of our administration, which coincides with the remaining budgetary period of the former government. We must meet our commitment to restore some measure of electricity to our capital city. We must put Liberians back to work again. We must put our economic and financial house in order. Most of all, we must revive our mindset of courage, hard work, honesty, and a can-do spirit.

Our strategy is to achieve quick and visible progress that reaches a significant number of our people, to gain momentum, consolidate support, and establish the foundation for sustained economic development.

For the long term, more will be required from us and our partners. We will formulate a multi-year economic reconstruction plan tied to a Poverty Reduction Strategy Program that relieves our country from a staggering US$3.5bn debt and paves the way for acceleration in our national effort to make progress in the achievement of the Millennium Development Goals. We will also tackle the HIV/AIDS problem, thereby ensuring that this threat to our human capital and growth and prosperity is addressed.

We know that our desire for an environment for private sector-driven sustainable growth and development cannot be achieved without the political will and a civil service that is efficient, effective and honest. The workforce in our ministries and agencies is seriously bloated. Our administration will therefore embark on a process of rationalising our agencies of government to make them lean, efficient, and responsive to public service delivery. This will require the creation of a meritocracy that places premium on qualification, professionalism, and performance.

Fellow Liberians, ladies and gentlemen: across this country, from Cape Mount in the west to Cape Palmas in the east, from Mount Nimba in the north to Cape Monsterrado in the south, from Mount Wologizi in northcentral to Mount Gedeh in the southeast, our citizens at this very moment are listening by radio – some are watching by television. I want to talk to you!

As you know, in our various communities and towns, our children have a way of greeting their fathers when they come home after a long, tiring day of trying to find the means to feed the family that night and send the children to school in the morning. They say, 'Papa na come.'

For too many times, for too many families, Papa comes home with nothing, having failed to find a job or to get the help to feed the hungry children. Imagine the disappointment and the hurt in the mother and the children; the frustration and the loss of self-confidence in the father.

Through the message of this story, I want you to know that I understand what you ordinary citizens go through each day to make ends meet for yourselves and for your families.

Times were hard before. Times are even harder today. But I make this pledge to you: Under my administration, we will work to change that situation. We will work to ensure that when our children say 'papa na come', papa will come home joyfully with something, no matter how meagre, to sustain his family. In other words, we will create the jobs for our mothers and fathers to be gainfully employed. We will create the social and economic opportunities that will restore our people's dignity and self-worth.

We will make the children smile again. The thousands of children who could not present their voting cards, but repeatedly told me whenever I met and shook their hands that they voted for me. Indeed, they voted with their hearts. To those children and other Liberian children across this nation, I say to you: I love you very, very much. I shall work to give you hope and a better future.

Now, I would like to speak in particular to our youth. You are out there. You can believe my word that our administration will do its utmost to respond to your needs. We will build your capacity and empower you to enable you meaningfully to participate in the reconstruction of your country. We will give you the education that you asked for, and the skills training that we know you desire. We shall actively pursue the Kakata Declaration resulting from the National Youth Conference held in 2005 and the implementation of a National Youth Policy and Program.

Fellow Liberians, we know that if we are to achieve our economic and income distribution goals, we must take on forcibly and effectively the debilitating cancer of corruption. Throughout the campaign, I assured our people that, if elected, we would wage war against corruption regardless of where it exists, or by whom it is practised.

Today, I renew this pledge. Corruption, under my administration, will be the major public enemy. We will confront it. We will fight it. Any member of my administration who sees this affirmation as mere posturing or yet another attempt by another Liberian leader to play to the gallery on this grave issue should think twice.

In this respect, I will lead by example. I will expect and demand that everyone serving in my administration leads by example. The first testament of how my administration will tackle public service corruption will be that everyone appointed to high positions of public trust, such as in the Cabinet and heads of public corporations, will be required to declare their assets. I will be the first to comply, and I will call upon the Honourable Speaker and President Pro-Temps to say that they comply.

My administration will also accord high priority to the formulation and passage into law of a National Code of Conduct, to which all public servants will be subjected.

My fellow Liberians: if we are to achieve our development and anti-corruption goals, we must welcome and embrace the Governance and Economic Management Program, which the National Transitional Government of Liberia, working with our international partners, has formulated to deal with the serious economic and financial management deficiencies in our country.

We accept and enforce the terms of GEMAP, recognising the important assistance which it is expected to provide during the early years of our government. More importantly, we will ensure competence and integrity in the management of our own resources and insist on an integrated capacity building dimension initiative so as to render GEMAP non-applicable in a reasonable period of time.

My fellow Liberians: our nation's foreign policy has historically been rooted in our core values as a nation and people in the practices of good neighbourliness, non-interference in the affairs of other nations and peoples, peaceful co-existence, regional cooperation and integration. These values will continue to guide the conduct of our foreign policy under my administration. Our foreign policy will take due cognizance of the sacrifices and contributions that have been made by our brothers and sisters to restore peace, security, and stability to our country. We will therefore work to be a responsible member of sub-regional, regional, and international organisations, including the Mano River Union, Economic Community of West African States, African Union, and the United Nations. We will do all that we can to honour our obligations, past and current, and enforce all international treaties to which our country has subscribed.

To our sister republics west, east, and north of our borders, we make this pledge: under my administration, no inch of Liberian soil will be used to conspire to perpetrate aggression against your countries. In making this commitment, we will work for a new regional security that is based upon economic partnership aimed at enhancing the prospects for regional cooperation and integration.

My fellow citizens: let me assure you that my Presidency shall remain committed to serve all Liberians without fear or favour. I am President for all of the people of the country. I therefore want to assure all of our people that neither I, nor any person serving my administration, will pursue any vendetta. There will be no vindictiveness. There will be no policies of political, social, and economic exclusion. We will be inclusive and tolerant, ever sensitive to the anxieties, fears, hopes, and aspirations of all of our people irrespective of ethnic, political, religious affiliation, and social status.

By their votes, the Liberian people have sent a clear message! They want peace; they want to move on with their lives. My charge as President is to work to assure the wishes of our people. We will therefore encourage our citizens to utilise our system of due process for settling differences. We will make sure that we work together as a people, knowing, however, that we will forcefully and decisively respond to any acts of lawlessness, threats to our hard-earned peace, or destabilising actions that could return us to conflict.

As we savour the new dawn of hope and expectation, I pledge to bring the government closer to the people. The days of the imperial presidency, of a domineering and threatening chief executive are over. This was my campaign promise, which I intend to keep.

And now, before I close, I would like to talk to the women – the women of Liberia, the women of Africa, and the women of the world. Until a few decades ago, Liberian women endured the injustice of being treated as second-class citizens. During the years of our civil war, they bore the brunt of inhumanity and terror. They were conscripted into war, gang raped at will, forced into domestic slavery. Yet, it is the women who laboured and advocated for peace throughout our region.

It is therefore not surprising that during the period of our elections, Liberian women were galvanised – and demonstrated unmatched passion, enthusiasm, and support for my candidacy. They stood with me; they defended me; they worked with me; they prayed for me. The same can be said for the women throughout Africa. I want to here and now, gratefully acknowledge the powerful voice of women of all walks of life.

My administration shall thus endeavour to give Liberian women prominence in all affairs of our country. My administration shall empower Liberian women in all areas of our national life. We will support and increase the writ of laws that restore their dignity and deal drastically with crimes that dehumanise them. We will enforce without fear or favour the law against rape recently passed by the National Transitional Legislature. We shall encourage families to educate all children, particularly the girl child. We will also try to provide economic programmes that enable Liberian women – particularly our market women – to assume their proper place in our economic process.

My fellow Liberians: we are moving forward. The best days are coming. The future belongs to us because we have taken charge of it. We have the resources, and we have the resourcefulness. We now have the right government. And we have good friends, good brothers and sisters who will work with us. Our people are already building our roads, cleaning up our environment, creating jobs, rebuilding schools, bringing back water and electricity.

We are a good people; we are a kind people. We are a forgiving people – and we are a God-fearing people.

So, let us begin anew, moving forward into a future that is filled with promise, filled with hope!

'In Union Strong, Success is Sure! We cannot fail. We must not fail. We will not fail.'

God bless you all – and save the Republic.

I thank you.

EVO MORALES

'THE CONFRONTATION OF TWO CULTURES'

—

REMARKS AT THE 'IN DEFENCE
OF HUMANITY' CONFERENCE

MEXICO CITY, MEXICO, 24 OCTOBER 2003

Born into poverty, the child of subsistence farmers, Juan Evo Morales Ayma *(affectionately known as 'Evo, the Wrath of God'), is the incumbent President of Bolivia, leader of the Movement for Socialism Party and the Cocalero trade union, representing the interests of coca farmers. A former coca farmer himself, Morales has been a prominent opponent of attempts to eradicate coca led by the US Government, spearheading the 'coca is not cocaine' campaign, differentiating between the mildly stimulating coca leaf and the far more potent extracted alkaloid, cocaine hydrochloride. First elected President in 2005, he was a vocal critic of the 'War on Terror' and war in Iraq, while promoting domestic policies of land reform, the rights and welfare of indigenous peoples, nationalisation and resistance to both the dominance of Bolivia's traditional elites and perceived US interference in Latin America. Forced to contest a recall election in 2008, he won over two thirds of the vote, before again winning re-election in the scheduled 2009 Presidential contest with the support of 63 per cent of the electorate. In October 2009, the UN General Assembly named Morales 'World Hero of Mother Earth'. He is closely allied to both the new and old socialist leaders of Latin America, notably Hugo Chavez of Venezuela, Raoul Castro of Cuba, and former President Luiz Inácio Lula da Silva of Brazil.*

This speech was given in Mexico before his election, although some websites date it much later and place it at a different location. The events referenced here were not those of the 2005 election. Rather, they refer to the use of gas on protestors (the so-called 'gas war') and the flight from Bolivia of President Sánchez de Lozada on 17 October 2003. In this speech, Morales discusses the problems faced by indigenous peoples and the path toward greater political and economic freedom. There is an authenticity to this language that is unmistakable, even groundbreaking. It is a view of indigenous people who are fighting for social justice and political power. This is a view of minority rights that is familiar in other parts of the world. Now, through people like Morales it is voiced in international forums and has become part of our common awareness. Morales symbolises his movement and channels its language. There are some who would say that he is inventing a language of expression in his speeches.

—

What happened these past days in Bolivia was a great revolt by those who have been oppressed for more than 500 years. The will of the people was imposed this September and October, and has begun to overcome the empire's cannons. We have lived for so many years through the confrontation of two cultures: the culture of life represented by the indigenous people, and the culture of death represented by the West. When we the indigenous people – together with the workers and even the businessmen of our country – fight for life and justice, the State responds with its 'democratic rule of law'.

What does the 'rule of law' mean for indigenous people? For the poor, the marginalised, the excluded, the 'rule of law' means the targeted assassinations and collective massacres that we have endured. Not just this September and October, but for many years, in which they have tried to impose policies of hunger and poverty on the Bolivian people. Above all, the 'rule of law' means the accusations that we, the Quechuas, Aymaras and Guaranties of Bolivia, keep hearing from our governments: that we are narcos, that we are anarchists. This uprising of the Bolivian people has been not only about gas and hydrocarbons, but an intersection of many issues: discrimination, marginalisation, and most importantly, the failure of neo-liberalism.

The cause of all these acts of bloodshed, and for the uprising of the Bolivian people, has a name: neo-liberalism. With courage and defiance, we brought down Gonzalo Sánchez de Lozada – the symbol of neo-liberalism in our country – on October 17th, the Bolivians' day of dignity and identity. We began to bring down the symbol of corruption and the political mafia.

And I want to tell you, *compañeras* and *compañeros*, how we have built the consciousness of the Bolivian people from the bottom up. How quickly the Bolivian people have reacted, have said – as Subcomandate Marcos says – *ya basta!*, enough policies of hunger and misery.

For us, October 17th is the beginning of a new phase of construction. Most importantly, we face the task of ending selfishness and individualism, and creating – from the rural *campesino* and indigenous communities to the urban slums

– other forms of living, based on solidarity and mutual aid. We must think about how to redistribute the wealth that is concentrated among few hands. This is the great task we Bolivian people face after this great uprising.

It has been very important to organise and mobilise ourselves in a way based on transparency, honesty, and control over our own organisations. And it has been important not only to organise but also to unite. Here we are now, united intellectuals in defence of humanity – I think we must have not only unity among the social movements, but also that we must coordinate with the intellectual movements. Every gathering, every event of this nature for we labour leaders who come from the social struggle, is a great lesson that allows us to exchange experiences and to keep strengthening our people and our grassroots organisations.

Thus, in Bolivia, our social movements, our intellectuals, our workers – even those political parties which support the popular struggle joined together to drive out Gonzalo Sánchez de Lozada. Sadly, we paid the price with many of our lives, because the empire's arrogance and tyranny continue humiliating the Bolivian people.

It must be said, *compañeras* and *compañeros*, that we must serve the social and popular movements rather than the transnational corporations. I am new to politics; I had hated it and had been afraid of becoming a career politician. But I realised that politics had once been the science of serving the people, and that getting involved in politics is important if you want to help your people. By getting involved, I mean living for politics, rather than living off of politics. We have coordinated our struggles between the social movements and political parties, with the support of our academic institutions, in a way that has created a greater national consciousness. That is what made it possible for the people to rise up in these recent days.

When we speak of the 'defence of humanity', as we do at this event, I think that this only happens by eliminating neo-liberalism and imperialism. But I think that in this we are not so alone, because we see, every day, that anti-imperialist thinking is spreading, especially after Bush's bloody 'intervention' policy in Iraq. Our way of organising and uniting against the system, against the empire's aggression towards our people, is spreading, as are the strategies for creating and strengthening the power of the people.

I believe only in the power of the people. That was my experience in my own region, a single province – the importance of local power. And now, with all that has happened in Bolivia, I have seen the importance of the power of a whole people, of a whole nation. For those of us who believe it important to defend humanity, the best contribution we can make is to help create that popular power. This happens when we check our personal interests with those of the group. Sometimes, we commit to the social movements in order to win power. We need to be led by the people, not use or manipulate them.

We may have differences among our popular leaders – and it's true that we have them in Bolivia. But when the people are conscious, when the people know what needs to be done, any difference among the different local leaders ends. We've been making progress in this for a long time, so that our people are finally able to rise up, together.

What I want to tell you, *compañeras* and *compañeros* – what I dream of and what we as leaders from Bolivia dream of is that our task at this moment should be to strengthen anti-imperialist thinking. Some leaders are now talking about how we – the intellectuals, the social and political movements – can organise a great summit of people like Fidel, Chávez and Lula to say to everyone: 'We are here, taking a stand against the aggression of US imperialism.'

A summit at which we are joined by *compañera* Rigoberta Menchú, by other social and labour leaders, great personalities like Pérez Ezquivel. A great summit to say to our people that we are together, united, and defending humanity. We have no other choice, *compañeros* and *compañeras* – if we want to defend humanity we must change systems and this means overthrowing US imperialism.

LUIZ INÁCIO LULA DA SILVA

'HUNGER CANNOT WAIT'

—

REMARKS TO THE LEADERS OF THE G8 COUNTRIES

ÉVIAN-LES-BAINS, 2 JUNE 2003

Luiz Inácio Lula da Silva was a founding member of Brazil's Worker's Party (Patrido dos Trabalhadores) and ran for the presidency of Brazil unsuccessfully three times before his election in 2002. He was re-elected in 2006, serving until 2010. During his presidency he implemented a series of social programmes and implemented economic reforms, attaining a high level of popularity. He also played a visible role in international relations, taking a strong stance against US foreign policy and speaking urgently of the need for action to address climate change.

This speech is from early in his first administration. He discusses the rise of Brazil as an economic power. As an emerging economy Brazil has often been associated with other countries with growing gross domestic products, so-called 'emerging markets', such as Russia, India, Indonesia and China. There are other countries, like Mexico, Colombia or Vietnam, that have smaller gross national products. But they looked to President Lula to speak for them, too.

—

My first words are in appreciation for the initiative by President Jacques Chirac. The dialogue between the richest countries in the world with the developing countries is more necessary today than ever. We must work together. The solution for our problems necessarily includes respect for our differences. I come from a country that today is mobilised by an extraordinary ethical-political energy to confront not only our internal problems but also to establish new and more constructive international partnerships.

The poverty and misery that attacks millions of men and women in Brazil, in Latin America, in Africa, and in Asia, obligates us to construct a new alliance against social exclusion. I am convinced that there will not be economic development without social sustainability and that, without both, we will live in a world that is less secure each day. It is in the space of social inequality that resentments, criminality, and, especially, narco-trafficking and terrorism, prosper.

I would like to speak with you in a simple and direct manner: I come to propose collective and responsible actions of solidarity, in favour of surpassing the inhuman conditions in which a large part of the global population live. Hunger cannot wait. It is urgently necessary to confront it with emergency and structural measures. If we all accept our responsibilities, we will create a more equal environment of opportunity for all.

The world economy is showing worrisome signs of recession. Social problems like unemployment, including in the wealthy countries, are getting worse. I am sure that one of the goals of this meeting of the G8 is to seek paths so that the economy grows again. We need a new equation that permits the return to growth and that includes the developing countries. The incorporation of the developing countries into the global economy requires access without discrimination to the markets of the wealthy countries. We have made an enormous sacrifice to become competitive. But how do we compete freely in the middle of a war of subsidies and other mechanisms of protectionism that causes, in reality, commercial exclusion?

We're not here to lament or to simply join the chorus of recriminations. We know our responsibilities. We are doing our part, executing balanced economic policies, combating and defeating corruption, bettering institutions for the good function of our economies. We have demonstrated the political will to combat social inequality and poverty. We are doing this in Brazil with democracy and pluralism, without fundamentalism, with care and firmness. We are organising our finances and recovering the stability to grow in a sustained manner. But we know that organising and giving stability to our economy and work is necessary, but it is not enough. We need to forge a new paradigm of development that combines financial stability with economic growth and social justice. Today we want to grow with sustainable financing, distributing income, and strengthening democracy.

There is no theory, however sophisticated it may be, that can succeed by being indifferent to misery and exclusion. Looking at modern history, above all at those periods that survived serious economic and social crises, I see that development must begin with profound social reforms. These reforms will bring millions of men and women into production, consumption, and citizenship and will create a new and prolonged economic dynamism. That's what happened in the United States beginning in the 1930s. That's what happened after World War II in Europe.

Brazil and many developing countries, over the past decade, have made the effort demanded of us to join in the dominant economic strategies. But there have not been important advances in the combat against social exclusion. To the contrary, the fundamentalism that ruled did not comply with its promised economic stability. Unemployment, hunger, and misery increased. Our systems of production did not conquer spaces in world commerce in a manner that corresponds to our sacrifices. The lack of economic and social democracy threatens every part of democracy.

We don't want the rich countries to look upon us with pity. We need structural solutions that must begin together with changes in the global economy. We hope for coherence from our wealthier partners. I look with concern upon the resistance by the World Trade Organization to remove billionaire subsidies, principally to agriculture. Priority matters – like providing access to medicines – are put off to another day.

Such attitudes are not constructive and increase scepticism in relation to the good intentions and wisdom of the more prosperous. We have to define responsibilities, and this also implies new tasks for the developing countries. Those who have the better capacity can and must execute more generous policies of solidarity in favour of the most needy nations. And this is what Brazil is doing on the regional level. My government wants to strengthen the Mercosur alliance and promote a Latin American Union. As President Kirchner, of Argentina, said, these are strategic and political projects, aimed at bettering the conditions of life. Brazil is ready to deepen its partnerships with the countries of South America and to open more space in our markets for their exports. New financial mechanisms are helping this regional integration.

I know that here you are going to discuss the New Partnership for Africa's Development. Doing our part, regarding Africa, where I will visit in August, we are going to widen our cooperation especially in the areas of health, education, professional training, and infrastructure. The countries of Latin America and the Caribbean, who belong to the Rio Group, in the recent Cuzco Summit, sent President Vicente Fox of Mexico and me here as their spokesmen in Évian. There, we discussed innovative financing mechanisms to combat poverty and invest in infrastructure.

I recommend to my colleagues present here a careful reading of these proposals. Hunger is at an intolerable level. We know that there are plain conditions to surpass this epidemic. My proposal – made in Porto Alegre and in Davos – is that a world fund be created capable of giving food to whoever is hungry and, at the same time, creating conditions to end the structural causes of hunger. And this is what we have begun to do in Brazil. There are various ways to generate resources for a fund of this nature. I give you two examples. The first is taxation of the international arms trade – which would bring advantages from economic and ethical points of view. Another possibility is to create mechanisms to stimulate that the rich countries reinvest into this fund a percentage of the interest payments made by debtor countries. Some developing countries have presented proposals to confront this problem. They are valid initiatives that deserve to be considered.

Kind colleagues, multilateralism represents, on the level of international relations, an advance comparable to democracy in national terms. The obligation of every nation committed to the progress of civilisation must be valued independently of its economic size and its political and military strength. We have to maintain dialogue, widening it on firm bases, and not just from time to time. This applies to G8 and to the Security Council of the United Nations.

Brazil's hope is that the G8 countries will become true allies in the combat against hunger and social exclusion and that international cooperation for development will be assumed again as an indispensable condition for security and peace. My life and political trajectory cause me to believe that just causes become victorious when there is will, dialogue, and negotiation. In order for this unprecedented meeting in Évian to attend to the legitimate anxieties of our peoples – in the South and in the North – we must demonstrate, above all, determination to combat social inequality.

Thank you very much.

HUGO CHAVEZ

'YESTERDAY, THE DEVIL CAME HERE'

—

REMARKS AT THE UNITED NATIONS

NEW YORK CITY, NEW YORK, 20 SEPTEMBER 2006

A committed socialist, Hugo Chavez is the head of the United Socialist Party of Venezuela. Following a military career, he led a failed coup d'état in 1982 and was imprisoned for two years. He was elected President of Venezuela in 1998 and re-elected in 2000 and 2006, surviving a coup attempt in 2002. A controversial and persistent critic of the United States, Chavez has aligned himself with other anti-American leaders and regimes, including Cuba's and Iran's. Initially idolised by many Western leftists, troubling allegations of official anti-Semitism on the part of the Venezuelan government and Chavez's refusal to renew the license of audiovisual group Radio Caracas Televisión (RCTV) in 2007, have led many early admirers to question his democratic credentials. Recent insinuations by Chavez that his own colon cancer and cases of cancer afflicting other Latin American political leaders critical of the US may be the result of a covert plot have raised further questions, in some corners, about his fundamental credibility, even his sanity.

This speech was delivered the day after US President George W. Bush's remarks. He outlines his view of the international situation, particularly in reference to the actions of the United States. He begins the speech with a reference to American Noam Chomsky, a leftist academic, known for his landmark achievements in linguistics and his strident left-wing views. Chomsky, who has taught at the Massachusetts Institute of Technology, is a visible and persistent critic of his country's foreign policy. The language of the speech demonstrates the anti-Americanism that has become part of international dialogue. And this speech is memorable, instantly unforgettable, for its mention of 'sulphur'.

Madam President, Excellencies, heads of state, heads of government and other government's representatives, good morning.

First, and with all respect, I highly recommend this book by Noam Chomsky, one of the most prestigious intellectuals in America and the world, Chomsky. One of his most recent works: *Hegemony or Survival: America's Quest for Global Dominance (The American Empire Project)*. It's an excellent work to understand what's happened in the world in the twentieth century, what's currently happening, and the greatest threat on this planet; the hegemonic pretension of the North American imperialism endangers the human race's survival.

We continue warning about this danger and calling on the very same US people and the world to stop this threat, which resembles the Sword of Damocles over our heads. I had considered reading from this book, but for the sake of time, I shall just leave it as a recommendation. It reads easily. It's a very good book. I'm sure, Madam, you are familiar with it.

The book is in English, in Russian, in Arabic, in German.

I think that the first people who should read this book are our brothers and sisters in the United States, because their threat is in their own house. The devil is right at home. The devil – the devil, himself, is right in the house.

And the devil came here yesterday.

Yesterday, the devil came here. Right here. Right here. And it smells of sulphur still today, this table that I am now standing in front of.

Yesterday, ladies and gentlemen, from this rostrum, the President of the United States, the gentleman to whom I refer as the devil, came here, talking as if he owned the world. Truly. As the owner of the world.

I think we could call a psychiatrist to analyse yesterday's statement made by the President of the United States. As the spokesman of imperialism, he came to share his nostrums, to try to preserve the current pattern of domination, exploitation and pillage of the peoples of the world.

An Alfred Hitchcock movie could use it as a scenario. I would even propose a title: 'The Devil's Recipe'.

As Chomsky says here, clearly and in depth, the American empire is doing all it can to consolidate its system of domination. And we cannot allow them to do that. We cannot allow world dictatorship to be consolidated.

The world parent's statement – cynical, hypocritical, full of this imperial hypocrisy from the need they have to control everything.

They say they want to impose a democratic model. But that's their democratic model. It's the false democracy of elites, and, I would say, a very original democracy that's imposed by weapons and bombs and firing weapons.

What a strange democracy. Aristotle might not recognise it or others who are at the root of democracy.

What type of democracy do you impose with marines and bombs?

The President of the United States, yesterday, said to us, right here, in this room, and I'm quoting, 'Anywhere you look, you hear extremists telling you you can escape from poverty and recover your dignity through violence, terror and martyrdom.'

Wherever he looks, he sees extremists. And you, my brother – he looks at your colour, and he says, oh, there's an extremist. Evo Morales, the worthy President of Bolivia, looks like an extremist to him.

The imperialists see extremists everywhere. It's not that we are extremists. It's that the world is waking up. It's waking up all over. And people are standing up.

I have the feeling, dear world dictator, that you are going to live the rest of your days as a nightmare because the rest of us are standing up, all those who are rising up against American imperialism, who are shouting for equality, for respect, for the sovereignty of nations.

Yes, you can call us extremists, but we are rising up against the empire, against the model of domination.

The President then – and this he said himself, he said: 'I have come to speak directly to the populations in the Middle East, to tell them that my country wants peace.'

That's true. If we walk in the streets of the Bronx, if we walk around New York, Washington, San Diego, in any city, San Antonio, San Francisco, and we ask individuals, the citizens of the United States, what does this country want? Does it want peace? They'll say yes.

But the government doesn't want peace. The government of the United States doesn't want peace. It wants to exploit its system of exploitation, of pillage, of hegemony through war.

It wants peace. But what's happening in Iraq? What happened in Lebanon? In Palestine? What's happening? What's happened over the last 100 years in Latin America and in the world? And now threatening Venezuela – new threats against Venezuela, against Iran?

He spoke to the people of Lebanon. Many of you, he said, have seen how your homes and communities were caught in the crossfire. How cynical can you get? What a capacity to lie shamefacedly.

The bombs in Beirut with millimetric precision? Is this crossfire?

He's thinking of a western, when people would shoot from the hip and some-body would be caught in the crossfire.

This is imperialist, fascist, assassin, genocidal, the empire and Israel firing on the people of Palestine and Lebanon. That is what happened. And now we hear, 'We're suffering because we see homes destroyed.'

The President of the United States came to talk to the peoples – to the peoples of the world. He came to say – I brought some documents with me, because this morning I was reading some statements, and I see that he talked to the people of Afghanistan, the people of Lebanon, the people of Iran. And he addressed all these peoples directly.

And you can wonder, just as the President of the United States addresses those peoples of the world, what would those peoples of the world tell him if they were given the floor? What would they have to say?

And I think I have some inkling of what the peoples of the South, the oppressed people think. They would say, 'Yankee imperialist, go home.' I think that is what those people would say if they were given the microphone and if they could speak with one voice to the American imperialists.

And that is why, Madam President, my colleagues, my friends, last year we came here to this same hall as we have been doing for the past eight years, and we said something that has now been confirmed – fully, fully confirmed.

I don't think anybody in this room could defend the system. Let's accept – let's be honest. The UN system, born after the Second World War, collapsed. It's worthless.

Oh, yes, it's good to bring us together once a year, see each other, make statements and prepare all kinds of long documents, and listen to good speeches, like Evo's yesterday, or President Lula's. Yes, it's good for that.

And there are a lot of speeches, and we've heard lots from the President of Sri Lanka, for instance, and the President of Chile.

But we, the assembly, have been turned into a merely deliberative organ. We have no power, no power to make any impact on the terrible situation in the world. And that is why Venezuela once again proposes, here, today, 20 September, that we re-establish the United Nations.

Last year, Madam, we made four modest proposals that we felt to be crucially important. We have to assume the responsibility, our heads of state, our ambassadors, our representatives, and we have to discuss it.

The first is expansion, and Lula talked about this yesterday right here: The Security Council's expansion, both regarding its permanent and non-permanent categories. New developed and developing countries, the Third World, must be given access as new permanent members. That's step one.

Second, effective methods to address and resolve world conflicts, transparent decisions.

Point three, the immediate suppression – and that is something everyone's calling for – of the anti-democratic mechanism known as the veto, the veto on decisions of the Security Council.

Let me give you a recent example. The immoral veto of the United States allowed the Israelis, with impunity, to destroy Lebanon. Right in front of all of us as we stood there watching, a resolution in the council was prevented.

Fourthly, we have to strengthen, as we've always said, the role and the powers of the secretary general of the United Nations.

Yesterday, the secretary general practically gave us his speech of farewell. And he recognised that over the last ten years, things have just gotten more complicated; hunger, poverty, violence, human rights violations have just worsened. That is the tremendous consequence of the collapse of the United Nations system and American hegemonistic pretensions.

Madam, Venezuela a few years ago decided to wage this battle within the United Nations by recognising the United Nations, as members of it that we are, and lending it our voice, our thinking.

Our voice is an independent voice to represent the dignity and the search for peace and the reformulation of the international system; to denounce persecution and aggression of hegemonistic forces on the planet.

This is how Venezuela has presented itself. Bolivar's home has sought a non-permanent seat on the Security Council.

Let's see. Well, there's been an open attack by the US government, an immoral attack, to try and prevent Venezuela from being freely elected to a post in the Security Council.

The imperium is afraid of truth, is afraid of independent voices. It calls us extremists, but they are the extremists.

And I would like to thank all the countries that have kindly announced their support for Venezuela, even though the ballot is a secret one and there's no need to announce things.

But since the imperium has attacked, openly, they strengthened the convictions of many countries. And their support strengthens us.

Mercosur, as a bloc, has expressed its support, our brothers in Mercosur. Venezuela, with Brazil, Argentina, Paraguay, Uruguay, is a full member of Mercosur.

And many other Latin American countries, CARICOM, Bolivia have expressed their support for Venezuela. The Arab League, the full Arab League has voiced its support. And I am immensely grateful to the Arab world, to our Arab brothers, our Caribbean brothers, the African Union. Almost all of Africa has expressed its support for Venezuela and countries such as Russia or China and many others.

I thank you all warmly on behalf of Venezuela, on behalf of our people, and on behalf of the truth, because Venezuela, with a seat on the Security Council, will be expressing not only Venezuela's thoughts, but it will also be the voice of all the peoples of the world, and we will defend dignity and truth.

Over and above all of this, Madam President, I think there are reasons to be optimistic. A poet would have said 'helplessly optimistic', because over and above the wars and the bombs and the aggressive and the preventive war and the destruction of entire peoples, one can see that a new era is dawning.

As Silvio Rodriguez says, the era is giving birth to a heart. There are alternative ways of thinking. There are young people who think differently. And this has already been seen within the space of a mere decade. It was shown that the end of history was a totally false assumption, and the same was shown about *Pax Americana* and the establishment of the capitalist neo-liberal world. It has been shown, this system, to generate mere poverty. Who believes in it now?

What we now have to do is define the future of the world. Dawn is breaking out all over. You can see it in Africa and Europe and Latin America and Oceania. I want to emphasise that optimistic vision.

We have to strengthen ourselves, our will to do battle, our awareness. We have to build a new and better world.

Venezuela joins that struggle, and that's why we are threatened. The US has already planned, financed and set in motion a coup in Venezuela, and it continues to support coup attempts in Venezuela and elsewhere.

President Michelle Bachelet reminded us just a moment ago of the horrendous assassination of the former foreign minister, Orlando Letelier.

And I would just add one thing: Those who perpetrated this crime are free. And that other event where an American citizen also died were American themselves. They were CIA killers, terrorists.

And we must recall in this room that in just a few days there will be another anniversary. Thirty years will have passed from this other horrendous terrorist attack on the Cuban plane, where seventy-three innocents, in a Cubana de Aviacion airliner, died.

And where is the biggest terrorist of this continent who took the responsibility for blowing up the plane? He spent a few years in jail in Venezuela. Thanks to CIA and then government officials, he was allowed to escape, and he lives here in this country, protected by the government.

And he was convicted. He has confessed to his crime. But the US government has double standards. It protects terrorism when it wants to.

And this is to say that Venezuela is fully committed to combating terrorism and violence. And we are one of the people who are fighting for peace.

Luis Posada Carriles is the name of that terrorist who is protected here. And other tremendously corrupt people who escaped from Venezuela are also living here under protection: a group that bombed various embassies, that assassinated people during the coup. They kidnapped me and they were going to kill me, but I think God reached down and our people came out into the streets and the army was too, and so I'm here today.

But these people who led that coup are here today in this country protected by the American government. And I accuse the American government of protecting terrorists and of having a completely cynical discourse.

We mentioned Cuba. Yes, we were just there a few days ago. We just came from there happily.

And there you see another era born. The Summit of the Fifteen, the Summit of the Nonaligned, adopted a historic resolution. This is the outcome document. Don't worry, I'm not going to read it.

But you have a whole set of resolutions here that were adopted after open debate in a transparent matter – more than fifty heads of state. Havana was the capital of the South for a few weeks, and we have now launched, once again, the group of the nonaligned with new momentum.

And if there is anything I could ask all of you here, my companions, my brothers and sisters, it is to please lend your goodwill to lend momentum to the Nonaligned Movement for the birth of the new era, to prevent hegemony and prevent further advances of imperialism.

And as you know, Fidel Castro is the President of the Nonaligned for the next three years, and we can trust him to lead the charge very efficiently.

Unfortunately they thought, 'Oh, Fidel was going to die.' But they're going to be disappointed because he didn't. And he's not only alive, he's back in his green fatigues, and he's now presiding over the Nonaligned.

So, my dear colleagues, Madam President, a new, strong movement has been born, a movement of the South. We are men and women of the South.

With this document, with these ideas, with these criticisms, I'm now closing my file. I'm taking the book with me. And, don't forget, I'm recommending it very warmly and very humbly to all of you.

We want ideas to save our planet, to save the planet from the imperialist threat. And hopefully in this very century, in not too long a time, we will see this, we will see this new era, and for our children and our grandchildren a world of peace based on the fundamental principles of the United Nations, but a renewed United Nations.

And maybe we have to change location. Maybe we have to put the United Nations somewhere else; maybe a city of the South. We've proposed Venezuela.

You know that my personal doctor had to stay in the plane. The chief of security had to be left in a locked plane. Neither of these gentlemen was allowed to arrive and attend the UN meeting. This is another abuse and another abuse of power on the part of the devil. It smells of sulphur here, but God is with us and I embrace you all.

May God bless us all. Good day to you.

VLADIMIR PUTIN

'HISTORY HAS GIVEN RUSSIA
A UNIQUE OPPORTUNITY'

—

REMARKS AT THE WORLD ECONOMIC FORUM

DAVOS, SWITZERLAND, 28 JANUARY 2009

Vladimir Vladimirovich Putin, President-elect of Russia, began his career as a KGB officer in the 1970s. Appointed Prime Minister by President Boris Yeltsin, he became Acting President upon Yeltsin's resignation on 31 December 1999, and was subsequently elected President in 2000 and 2004. He engineered the growing economic strength of Gazprom and other Russian energy enterprises, but placed limits on Russia's fledgling democracy, replacing elective offices with presidential prerogatives of appointment. Prohibited by the Russian Constitution from seeking a third consecutive term, he supported Dmitri Medvedev as his successor, and was appointed Prime Minister by Medvedev in 2008. Many argued that Putin as Prime Minister remained the power behind the throne, and in March 2012, he was elected to a third term as President. Official results claim that Putin received 64 per cent of the vote against a divided and confused field of opponents: election monitors have reported widespread irregularities and fraud in the conduct of the poll, with allegations of voter intimidation, organised multiple voting, and the systemic suppression of credible opposition movements. An international consensus, at time of writing, seems to be developing that while Putin did in fact win a majority vote, his prior manipulation of electoral law and persecution of political opponents lends a distinctly Soviet flavour to his victory. The OSCE (Organisation for Security and Cooperation in Europe) has called for a thorough investigation of the 2012 election.

This speech outlines Putin's views on energy dependence in the industrialised world and the financial crisis that led to a global recession in 2008 and 2009. Please note

the value of this speech in comparison to those remarks in a later section of this book
devoted to the turbulence in the world financial markets. As an emerging economy,
Russia is now becoming a more prominent voice in global finance. The use of energy
for influence in Europe makes Russia's views important for many countries reliant
on Russian oil and gas. Putin's words show a confidence in the escalating relevance
of Russia.

—

Good afternoon, colleagues, ladies and gentlemen.

I would like to thank the forum's organisers for this opportunity to share my thoughts on global economic developments and to share our plans and proposals.

The world is now facing the first truly global economic crisis, which is continuing to develop at an unprecedented pace.

The current situation is often compared to the Great Depression of the late 1920s and the early 1930s. True, there are some similarities.

However, there are also some basic differences. The crisis has affected everyone at this time of globalisation. Regardless of their political or economic system, all nations have found themselves in the same boat.

There is a certain concept, called the perfect storm, which denotes a situation when Nature's forces converge in one point of the ocean and increase their destructive potential many times over. It appears that the present-day crisis resembles such a perfect storm.

Responsible and knowledgeable people must prepare for it. Nevertheless, it always flares up unexpectedly.

The current situation is no exception either. Although the crisis was simply hanging in the air, the majority strove to get their share of the pie, be it one dollar or a billion, and did not want to notice the rising wave.

In the last few months, virtually every speech on this subject started with criticism of the United States. But I will do nothing of the kind.

I just want to remind you that, just a year ago, American delegates speaking from this rostrum emphasised the US economy's fundamental stability and its cloudless prospects. Today, investment banks, the pride of Wall Street, have virtually ceased to exist. In just twelve months, they have posted losses exceeding the profits they made in the last twenty-five years. This example alone reflects the real situation better than any criticism.

The time for enlightenment has come. We must calmly, and without gloating, assess the root causes of this situation and try to peek into the future.

In our opinion, the crisis was brought about by a combination of several factors.

The existing financial system has failed. Substandard regulation has contributed to the crisis, failing to duly heed tremendous risks.

Add to this colossal disproportions that have accumulated over the last few years. This primarily concerns disproportions between the scale of financial operations and the fundamental value of assets, as well as those between the increased burden on international loans and the sources of their collateral.

The entire economic growth system, where one regional centre prints money without respite and consumes material wealth, while another regional centre manufactures inexpensive goods and saves money printed by other governments, has suffered a major setback.

I would like to add that this system has left entire regions, including Europe, on the outskirts of global economic processes and has prevented them from adopting key economic and financial decisions.

Moreover, generated prosperity was distributed extremely unevenly among various population strata. This applies to differences between social strata in certain countries, including highly developed ones. And it equally applies to gaps between countries and regions.

A considerable share of the world's population still cannot afford comfortable housing, education and quality health care. Even a global recovery posted in the last few years has failed to radically change this situation.

And, finally, this crisis was brought about by excessive expectations. Corporate appetites with regard to constantly growing demand swelled unjustifiably. The race between stock market indices and capitalisation began to overshadow rising labour productivity and real-life corporate effectiveness.

Unfortunately, excessive expectations were not only typical of the business community. They set the pace for rapidly growing personal consumption standards, primarily in the industrial world. We must openly admit that such growth was not backed by a real potential. This amounted to unearned wealth, a loan that will have to be repaid by future generations.

This pyramid of expectations would have collapsed sooner or later. In fact, this is happening right before our eyes.

Esteemed colleagues, one is sorely tempted to make simple and popular decisions in times of crisis. However, we could face far greater complications if we merely treat the symptoms of the disease.

Naturally, all national governments and business leaders must take resolute actions.

Nevertheless, it is important to avoid making decisions, even in such *force majeure* circumstances, that we will regret in the future.

This is why I would first like to mention specific measures which should be avoided and which will not be implemented by Russia.

We must not revert to isolationism and unrestrained economic egotism. The leaders of the world's largest economies agreed during the November 2008 G20 summit not to create barriers hindering global trade and capital flows. Russia shares these principles.

Although additional protectionism will prove inevitable during the crisis, all of us must display a sense of proportion.

Excessive intervention in economic activity and blind faith in the state's omnipotence is another possible mistake.

True, the state's increased role in times of crisis is a natural reaction to market setbacks. Instead of streamlining market mechanisms, some are tempted to expand state economic intervention to the greatest possible extent.

The concentration of surplus assets in the hands of the state is a negative aspect of anti-crisis measures in virtually every nation.

In the twentieth century, the Soviet Union made the state's role absolute. In the long run, this made the Soviet economy totally uncompetitive. This lesson cost us dearly. I am sure nobody wants to see it repeated.

Nor should we turn a blind eye to the fact that the spirit of free enterprise, including the principle of personal responsibility of businesspeople, investors and shareholders for their decisions, is being eroded in the last few months. There is no reason to believe that we can achieve better results by shifting responsibility onto the state.

And one more point: anti-crisis measures should not escalate into financial populism and a refusal to implement responsible macroeconomic policies. The unjustified swelling of the budgetary deficit and the accumulation of public debts are just as destructive as adventurous stock-jobbing.

Ladies and gentlemen, unfortunately, we have so far failed to comprehend the true scale of the ongoing crisis. But one thing is obvious: the extent of the recession and its scale will largely depend on specific high-precision measures, due to be charted by governments and business communities and on our coordinated and professional efforts.

In our opinion, we must first atone for the past and open our cards, so to speak. This means we must assess the real situation and write off all hopeless debts and 'bad' assets. True, this will be an extremely painful and unpleasant process. Far from everyone can accept such measures, fearing for their capitalisation, bonuses or reputation. However, we would 'conserve' and prolong the crisis, unless we clean up our balance sheets. I believe financial authorities must work out the required mechanism for writing off debts that corresponds to today's needs.

Second. Apart from cleaning up our balance sheets, it is high time we got rid of virtual money, exaggerated reports and dubious ratings. We must not harbour any illusions while assessing the state of the global economy and the real corporate standing, even if such assessments are made by major auditors and analysts.

In effect, our proposal implies that the audit, accounting and ratings system reform must be based on a reversion to the fundamental asset value concept. In other words, assessments of each individual business must be based on its ability to generate added value, rather than on subjective concepts. In our opinion, the economy of the future must become an economy of real values.

How to achieve this is not so clear-cut. Let us think about it together.

Third. Excessive dependence on a single reserve currency is dangerous for the global economy. Consequently, it would be sensible to encourage the objective process of creating several strong reserve currencies in the future. It is high time we launched a detailed discussion of methods to facilitate a smooth and irreversible switchover to the new model.

Fourth. Most nations convert their international reserves into foreign currencies and must therefore be convinced that they are reliable. Those issuing reserve and accounting currencies are objectively interested in their use by other states.

This highlights mutual interests and interdependence.

Consequently, it is important that reserve currency issuers must implement more open monetary policies. Moreover, these nations must pledge to abide by internationally recognised rules of macroeconomic and financial discipline. In our opinion, this demand is not excessive.

At the same time, the global financial system is not the only element in need of reforms. We are facing a much broader range of problems.

This means that a system based on cooperation between several major centres must replace the obsolete unipolar world concept.

We must strengthen the system of global regulators based on international law and a system of multilateral agreements in order to prevent chaos and unpredictability in such a multipolar world.

Consequently, it is very important that we reassess the role of leading international organisations and institutions.

I am convinced that we can build a more equitable and efficient global economic system. But it is impossible to create a detailed plan at this event today.

It is clear, however, that every nation must have guaranteed access to vital resources, new technology and development sources. What we need is guarantees that could minimise risks of recurring crises.

Naturally, we must continue to discuss all these issues, including at the G20 meeting in London, which will take place in April.

Our decisions should match the present-day situation and heed the requirements of a new post-crisis world.

The global economy could face energy-resource shortages and the threat of thwarted future growth while overcoming the crisis.

Three years ago, at a summit of the Group of Eight, we raised the issue of global energy security. We called for the shared responsibility of suppliers, consumers and transit countries. I think it is time to launch truly effective mechanisms ensuring such responsibility.

The only way to ensure truly global energy security is to form interdependence, including a swap of assets, without any discrimination or dual standards. It is such interdependence that generates real mutual responsibility.

Unfortunately, the existing Energy Charter has failed to become a working instrument able to regulate emerging problems.

I propose we start laying down a new international legal framework for energy security. Implementation of our initiative could play a political role comparable to the treaty establishing the European Coal and Steel Community. That is to say, consumers and producers would finally be bound into a real single energy partnership based on clear-cut legal foundations.

Every one of us realises that sharp and unpredictable fluctuations of energy prices are a colossal destabilising factor in the global economy. Today's landslide fall of prices will lead to a growth in the consumption of resources.

On the one hand, investments in energy saving and alternative sources of energy will be curtailed. On the other, less money will be invested in oil production, which will result in its inevitable downturn. Which, in the final analysis, will escalate into another fit of uncontrolled price growth and a new crisis.

It is necessary to return to a balanced price, based on an equilibrium between supply and demand, to strip pricing of a speculative element generated by many derivative financial instruments.

To guarantee the transit of energy resources remains a challenge. There are two ways of tackling it, and both must be used.

The first is to go over to generally recognised market principles of fixing tariffs on transit services. They can be recorded in international legal documents.

The second is to develop and diversify the routes of energy transportation. We have been working long and hard along these lines.

In the past few years alone, we have implemented such projects as the Yamal-Europe and Blue Stream gas pipelines. Experience has proved their urgency and relevance.

I am convinced that such projects as South Stream and North Stream are equally needed for Europe's energy security. Their total estimated capacity is something like 85 billion cubic metres of gas a year.

Gazprom, together with its partners – Shell, Mitsui and Mitsubishi – will soon launch capacities for liquefying and transporting natural gas produced in the Sakhalin area. And that is also Russia's contribution to global energy security.

We are developing the infrastructure of our oil pipelines. The first section of the Baltic Pipeline System [BPS] has already been completed. BPS-1 supplies up to 75 million tonnes of oil a year. It does this direct to consumers – via our ports on the Baltic Sea. Transit risks are completely eliminated in this way. Work is currently under way to design and build BPS-2 (its throughput capacity is 50 million tonnes of oil a year).

We intend to build transport infrastructure in all directions. The first stage of the pipeline system Eastern Siberia – Pacific Ocean is in the final stage. Its terminal point will be a new oil port in Kozmina Bay and an oil refinery in the Vladivostok area. In the future a gas pipeline will be laid parallel to the oil pipeline, towards the Pacific and China.

Addressing you here today, I cannot but mention the effects of the global crisis on the Russian economy. We have also been seriously affected.

However, unlike many other countries, we have accumulated large reserves. They expand our possibilities for confidently passing through the period of global instability.

The crisis has made the problems we had more evident. They concern the excessive emphasis on raw materials in exports and the economy in general and a weak financial market. The need to develop a number of fundamental market institutions, above all of a competitive environment, has become more acute.

We were aware of these problems and sought to address them gradually. The crisis is only making us move more actively towards the declared priorities, without changing the strategy itself, which is to effect a qualitative renewal of Russia in the next ten to twelve years.

Our anti-crisis policy is aimed at supporting domestic demand, providing social guarantees for the population, and creating new jobs. Like many countries, we have reduced production taxes, leaving money in the economy. We have optimised state spending.

But, I repeat, along with measures of prompt response, we are also working to create a platform for post-crisis development.

We are convinced that those who will create attractive conditions for global investment and will be able to preserve and strengthen sources of strategically meaningful resources will become leaders of the restoration of the global economy.

This is why among our priorities we have the creation of a favourable business environment and development of competition; the establishment of a stable loan system resting on sufficient internal resources; and implementation of transport and other infrastructure projects.

Russia is already one of the major exporters of a number of food commodities. And our contribution to ensuring global food security will only increase.

We are also going to actively develop the innovation sectors of the economy. Above all, those in which Russia has a competitive edge – space, nuclear energy, aviation. In these areas, we are already actively establishing cooperative ties with other countries. A promising area for joint efforts could be the sphere of energy saving. We see higher energy efficiency as one of the key factors for energy security and future development.

We will continue reforms in our energy industry. Adoption of a new system of internal pricing based on economically justified tariffs. This is important, including for encouraging energy saving. We will continue our policy of openness to foreign investments.

I believe that the twenty-first-century economy is an economy of people, not of factories. The intellectual factor has become increasingly important in the economy. That is why we are planning to focus on providing additional opportunities for people to realise their potential.

We are already a highly educated nation. But we need for Russian citizens to obtain the highest quality and most up-to-date education, and such professional skills that will be widely in demand in today's world. Therefore, we will be proactive in promoting educational programmes in leading specialities.

We will expand student exchange programmes, arrange training for our students at the leading foreign colleges and universities and with the most advanced companies. We will also create such conditions that the best researchers and professors – regardless of their citizenship – will want to come and work in Russia.

History has given Russia a unique chance. Events urgently require that we reorganise our economy and update our social sphere. We do not intend to pass up this chance. Our country must emerge from the crisis renewed, stronger and more competitive.

Separately, I would like to comment on problems that go beyond the purely economic agenda, but nevertheless are very topical in present-day conditions.

Unfortunately, we are increasingly hearing the argument that the build-up of military spending could solve today's social and economic problems. The logic is simple enough. Additional military allocations create new jobs.

At a glance, this sounds like a good way of fighting the crisis and unemployment. This policy might even be quite effective in the short term. But in the longer run, militarisation won't solve the problem but will rather quell it temporarily. What it will do is squeeze huge financial and other resources from the economy instead of finding better and wiser uses for them.

My conviction is that reasonable restraint in military spending, especially coupled with efforts to enhance global stability and security, will certainly bring significant economic dividends.

I hope that this viewpoint will eventually dominate globally. On our part, we are geared to intensive work on discussing further disarmament.

I would like to draw your attention to the fact that the economic crisis could aggravate the current negative trends in global politics.

The world has lately come to face an unheard-of surge of violence and other aggressive actions, such as Georgia's adventurous sortie in the Caucasus, recent terrorist attacks in India, and escalation of violence in the Gaza Strip. Although not apparently linked directly, these developments still have common features.

First of all, I am referring to the existing international organisations' inability to provide any constructive solutions to regional conflicts, or any effective proposals for interethnic and interstate settlement. Multilateral political mechanisms have proved as ineffective as global financial and economic regulators.

Frankly speaking, we all know that provoking military and political instability, regional and other conflicts is a helpful means of distracting the public from growing social and economic problems. Such attempts cannot be ruled out, unfortunately.

To prevent this scenario, we need to improve the system of international relations, making it more effective, safe and stable.

There are a lot of important issues on the global agenda in which most countries have shared interests. These include anti-crisis policies, joint efforts to reform international financial institutions, to improve regulatory mechanisms, ensure energy security and mitigate the global food crisis, which is an extremely pressing issue today.

Russia is willing to contribute to dealing with international priority issues. We expect all our partners in Europe, Asia and America, including the new US administration, to show interest in further constructive cooperation in dealing with all these issues and more. We wish the new team success.

Ladies and gentlemen, the international community is facing a host of extremely complicated problems, which might seem overpowering at times. But, a journey of a thousand miles begins with a single step, as the proverb goes.

We must seek a foothold relying on the moral values that have ensured the progress of our civilisation. Integrity and hard work, responsibility and self-confidence will eventually lead us to success.

We should not despair. This crisis can and must be fought, also by pooling our intellectual, moral and material resources.

This kind of consolidation of effort is impossible without mutual trust, not only between business operators, but primarily between nations.

Therefore, finding this mutual trust is a key goal we should concentrate on now.

Trust and solidarity are key to overcoming the current problems and avoiding more shocks, to reaching prosperity and welfare in this new century.

Thank you.

NICOLAS SARKOZY

'A CRISIS OF THE DENATURING OF CAPITALISM'

—

REMARKS AT THE WORLD ECONOMIC FORUM

DAVOS, SWITZERLAND, 27 JANUARY 2010

*C*alled *by some 'the hyper-president' for his energetic and at times combative style, Nicolas Sarkozy was elected President of France in 2007 as candidate of the Gaullist UMP (Union pour un Mouvement Populaire), defeating Socialist Party candidate Ségolène Royal. He had previously won election as Mayor of Neuilly-sur-Seine, Vice-President and President of the General Council of Hauts-de-Seine, a member of the European Parliament, and member of the National Assembly. Sarkozy – often referred to as 'Sarko' – served as Minister of the Interior in Prime Minister Jean-Pierre Raffarin's first two governments under President Jacques Chirac, later moving to the Ministry of Finance and returning to the Ministry of the Interior under Dominique de Villepin's premiership in the final years of Chirac's presidency. Upon winning the Élysée Palace, Sarkozy surprised many by appointing opposition politicians to his Cabinet, such as socialists Bernard Kouchner, founder of Médecins Sans Frontières, and Eric Besson, who had worked for Ségolène Royal's campaign. President Sarkozy went on to further surprise the world with his whirlwind courtship of former supermodel and chart-topping singer-songwriter Carla Bruni, leading some to complain that the President was overly focused on his personal life.*

A man of many nicknames, Sarkozy has also been called 'the American', reflecting his efforts to improve relations between Europe and the United States. He has been a strong advocate for the preservation of the Euro and addressing the economic problems in Greece, Ireland, Spain and Italy. Along with German Chancellor Angela Merkel he has emerged as a 'voice for Europe'. In this speech he discusses the world's financial crisis. His perspective reflects the importance of France in the global economy, a vision for saving the Eurozone, and the need for responsible policies to address the current EU and global financial crisis. Contrary to his reputation, this speech shows an attention to the need for unity, exploring considerable common ground with the countries represented in the audience. In a discussion policy, especially concerning the financial markets, words matter. The right words can build confidence and support, which may lead to successful solutions and financial stability. The global markets react favourably to the right words. The wrong words can destroy confidence, dooming policy and sending the markets downwards into an abyss. It is extremely difficult to inspire confidence. As one former journalist, Renée Lorraine, has said, 'It is easier to talk yourself into the crap.' That's right. Sometimes politicians or pundits, looking for headlines, make a trade with the devil and conjure up a brew of negative hyperbole and irresponsible over-reaction, leading to fear and failure. President Sarkozy seems mindful of that problem. He has to generate optimism and confidence. So he must be careful in how he states the financial problems and in stating the workability of the proposed solutions. One is mindful of the former Chancellor of the Exchequer, Alistair Darling, who told the British people in 2010 that Britain could 'dip' back into recession before the election. Is such language responsible or does it risk a double-dip recession, becoming self-fulfilling? Therein lies the danger of wording: the financial markets are sensitive to words.

In this speech, the problems we face now are not the fault of runaway capitalism as much as not allowing capitalism to work properly.

Ladies and gentlemen, heads of state and government:

May I begin by thanking Professor [Klaus] Schwab and all the organisational staff for inviting me to give the opening address to this 40th Annual Meeting of the World Economic Forum.

Ladies and gentlemen, let me make things perfectly clear: as a political leader, I have not come here to teach, but to learn together from the lessons of the crisis. We are all responsible for the crisis.

And we are all responsible for the world we are going to leave to our children.

We all know what would have occurred, without State intervention to maintain confidence and support industry: total collapse. Not to draw the conclusion that we must, therefore, change our ways would be, quite simply, irresponsible.

This crisis is not just a global crisis. It is not a crisis in globalisation. This crisis is a crisis of globalisation.

It is our vision of the world which, at a given moment, revealed its failings.

That is what we must correct.

There can be no prosperity without an efficient financial system, without the free circulation of goods and services, without situational revenues being called into question by competition. But finance, free trade and competition are only means, not ends.

From the moment we accepted the idea that the market was always right and that no other opposing factors need be taken into account, globalisation skidded out of control.

Let us look at the root of the problem: it was the imbalances in the world economy which fed the growth of global finance. Financial deregulation was introduced in order to be able to service the deficit of those who were consuming too much with the surplus of those who were not consuming enough. The perpetuation and accrual of these imbalances was both the driving force and the consequence of financial globalisation. In just the same way, the instability of financial markets was both the driving force and the consequence of the growth in financial trading.

Globalisation first took the form of globalisation of savings. It gave rise to a world in which everything was given to financial capital and almost nothing to labour, in which the entrepreneur gave way to the speculator, in which those who lived on unearned income left the workers far behind, in which the use of leverage, to an unreasonably disproportionate extent, created a form of capitalism in which taking risks with other people's money was the norm, allowing quick and easy profits but all too often without creating either prosperity or jobs.

One of the most striking characteristics of this type of economy is that, within it, the present was all that mattered and the future counted for nothing. The steady depreciation of the future could be inferred from the exorbitant demand for high yields in the present. Those yields, inflated by leverage and speculation, were the discount rate applied to future revenues: the higher they rose, the lower the value of the future fell.

The same depreciation of the future could be seen in accounting practices which valued assets at the prices set by a marketplace fluctuating constantly to keep up with the ups and downs in share values.

When the markets were on a high, balance sheets were reassessed, and the very same artificially boosted figures would feed a new high. When confidence fell, the balance sheets would suffer as a result and bring share prices down.

During the financial crisis we saw, up close, the damage done by that kind of accounting, when the collapse of the markets led to a collapse in the banks' capital reserves and further tightened the credit crunch.

Our entire system of representation had been falsified: the economic value of a company does not change from one second to another, nor every minute, nor every hour... To gain a clear idea of just how absurd that kind of accounting can be, we need only think of the fact that, in a market value system, a company in trouble can report a profit simply because its diminished credit rating has reduced the market value of its debts!

Our entire system of statistical assessment had been distorted, too.

In the statistics, we noted the increase in revenues.

In life, we saw a widening inequality gap.

In the statistics the standard of living was rising, but meanwhile the number of those feeling ever more keenly the hardships of life was also constantly increasing.

Let us read through the report from the commission led by Joseph Stiglitz, Amartya Sen and Jean-Paul Fitoussi on the measurement of economic perform-ance and social progress: to ask ourselves questions about how we measure these things is to ask ourselves what our goals are.

Such reflections must not be the exclusive province of experts and statisti-cians. We have to leave behind the culture of experts who talk only among themselves, each in their own field.

We have to learn to think things through together, to discuss together prob-lems which, whatever their technical specifics, are the concern of all.

We will not be able to change our set ways if we do not change the way we measure and represent things, our criteria. That is not an issue only for the experts. It concerns us all.

We will continue to make our economy run risks greater than it can bear, to encourage speculation and to sacrifice our long-term future, if we do not change the regulation of our banking system and the rules for accounting and prudential oversight. That is not an issue only for the experts. It concerns us all.

We will never put an end to hunger, poverty and misery in the world if we do not succeed in stabilising the prices of raw materials, which at present are completely erratic. That is not an issue only for the experts. It concerns us all.

We will not save the future of our planet if we do not pay the true price of scarcity. That is not an issue only for the experts. It concerns us all.

We will not reconcile our citizens to globalisation and to capitalism, if we are not capable of offsetting market forces with counterbalances and corrective measures. That, too, concerns us all.

By discarding all our responsibilities in the marketplace, we have created an economy which has ended up running counter to the values on which it was nominally based, and to its own objectives.

By over-mutualising ownership and risk, we have diluted responsibility.

By placing free trade above all else we have weakened democracy, because citizens expect from democracy that it should protect them.

By prioritising short-term logic, we have paved the way for our entry into a time of scarcity. We have exhausted non-renewable resources, devastated the environment, caused global warming. Sustainable development cannot be achieved if profits up front and dividends for shareholders are our sole criteria.

Through excessive deregulation, we have let dumping and unfair competition set in. We have let globalisation be based on external growth, with everybody trying to grow by taking the businesses, the jobs, the market shares of others, instead of by working harder, investing more, increasing productivity and capacity for innovation.

The globalisation we had dreamed of at the outset was of the kind where, instead of taking from others by means of monetary, social, fiscal or ecological dumping, each of us would found development on social progress, increased purchasing power, reduced inequality, improved standards of living, health and education.

Whether the venue is the International Labour Organization [ILO], the International Monetary Fund [IMF], the World Bank, the Food and Agriculture Organization [FAO] or the G20, at bottom we are always talking about the self-same thing, seen from different points of view: how can we return the economy to the service of mankind? How can we act to ensure that the economy no longer appears as an end itself, but as a means to an end? How can we move towards globalisation in which the development of each will assist the development of others? How can we build a more cooperative, less conflictual form of globalisation?

Let us be clear about this: we're not asking ourselves what we will replace capitalism with, but what kind of capitalism we want.

The crisis we are experiencing is not a crisis of capitalism. It is a crisis of the denaturing of capitalism – a crisis linked to loss of the values and references that have always been the foundation of capitalism.

Capitalism has always been inseparable from a system of values, a conception of civilisation, an idea of mankind.

Purely financial capitalism is a distortion, and we have seen the risks it involves for the world economy. But anti-capitalism is a dead end that is even worse.

We can only save capitalism by rebuilding it, by restoring its moral dimension. I know that this expression will call forth many questions.

What do we need, in the end, if it is not rules, principles, a governance that reflects shared values, a common morality?

We cannot govern the world of the twenty-first century with the rules and principles of the twentieth century.

We cannot govern globalisation while relegating half of humanity to the sidelines, without India, Africa or Latin America.

We cannot look at the post-crisis world in the same way as the world before the crisis.

Each of us must hold the conviction that the world of tomorrow cannot be the same as the world of yesterday.

There are indecent behaviours that will no longer be tolerated by public opinion in any country in the world.

There are excessive profits that will no longer be accepted because they are without common measure to the capacity to create wealth and jobs.

There are remuneration packages that will no longer be tolerated because they bear no relationship to merit. That those who create jobs and wealth may earn a lot of money is not shocking. But that those who contribute to destroying jobs and wealth also earn a lot of money is morally indefensible.

In the future, there will be a much greater demand for income to better reflect social utility and merit. There will be a much greater demand for justice. There will be a much greater demand for protection.

And no one can escape this.

Either we change of our own accord, or change will be imposed on us by economic, social and political crises.

Either we are capable of responding to the demand for protection, justice and fairness through cooperation, regulation and governance, or we will have isolation and protectionism.

The G20 foreshadows the planetary governance of the twenty-first century. It symbolises the return of politics whose legitimacy was denied by unregulated globalisation.

In just one year, we have seen a genuine revolution in mentalities. For the first time in history, the heads of state and government of the world's twenty largest economic powers decided together on the measures that must be taken to combat a world crisis. They committed themselves, together, to adopting common rules that will radically change the way the world economy operates.

Without the G20, trust could not have been restored.

Without the G20, we would have had the triumph of 'every man for himself'.

Without the G20, it would not have been possible to envisage regulating bonuses, closing down tax havens and changing the rules of accounting and prudential standards.

These decisions will not solve every problem, but just one year ago, would anyone have thought they were possible?

Now, however, they must be implemented!

I would like to seize the opportunity to say this: the signs of recovery that seem to herald the end of the global recession should not encourage us to be less daring; rather, we must be even bolder. If we do nothing to change world governance, nothing to regulate the economy, if we do not reform our systems of social protection, pensions, education and research, if we do not clean up our public finances, if we do not stringently prosecute the war against tax fraud, if we do not invest to prepare for the future, this recovery will be only a respite. The same causes will produce the same effects. Look at the new bubbles that are already starting to form. Here, we cannot be certain that the states will still have the means to guarantee trust.

And how can we hope that people will continue to trust the word of states if the commitments made are not kept?

If the absolutely crucial debate on accounting standards gets bogged down, if the private agencies to which we have delegated regulatory power deliberately flout the mandate given them by heads of state and government, and we let them get away with it, what will be left of the credibility of the G20 and the prospect of world governance?

If competition is skewed by prudential rules that remain very different from one country to another, from one continent to another, whereas we had decided to implement the opposite; if we cannot coordinate our efforts, if we cannot even come to an understanding around a common definition of capital when we had promised to do so – how can we be surprised that so many players consider it normal to return to the habits they had before the crisis?

How can we conceive that in a competitive world, we can insist that European banks have three times more capital to cover the risks of their market activities, without demanding the same of American or Asian banks?

How can we accept the obligation for banks to retain in their balance sheets a portion of their securitised loans if this obligation is not included in the regulation of G20 member countries, given that the principle was adopted by unanimous agreement?

If we devise standards that do not draw the lessons of the crisis and that lead long-term investors to scale down their equity portfolios, then we must not be surprised that market prices become even more unstable and that a large number of companies find themselves even more threatened by speculative pressure.

Failing to do what we decided would be an economic error, a political error, a moral error.

Giving in to unilateralism, to 'every man for himself', would also be an economic, political and moral error.

We must build our common future on the gains of multilateralism, on the gains of the G20, on the gains of Copenhagen.

Basically, we all know very well what we have to do together. We must do away with a system without rules that drags everyone down and replace it with rules that draw everyone up. But what is the point of agreeing on the rules if they are not applied? This doesn't mean having the same labour legislation everywhere. It doesn't mean imposing on poor countries the same standards as the rich countries.

But how can we accept that some fifty member states of the ILO have not yet ratified the eight conventions defining the fundamental rights of labour? And how can we ensure these conventions are respected? In Copenhagen, quanti-fied commitments on climate change were made by all the big countries. How can we ensure these commitments are respected without a World Environment Organisation to monitor their implementation? How can we not see that the possibility of adopting a carbon tax at borders against environmental dump-ing would, without any doubt, constitute a strong incentive to respect the common rule?

The crucial advance would be to put environment law, labour law and health law on the same footing as the law of trade. This revolution in world regulation would imply that specialised institutions can intervene in international – and notably commercial – disputes through prejudicial questions to be decided before an action can be brought. As I said before the General Meeting of the ILO in June last year: the international community cannot continue to be schizophrenic by disowning at the WTO or the IMF what it decided at the ILO or the WHO, what it proclaimed in Copenhagen. Establishment of such prejudicial jurisdiction would put an end to this schizophrenia.

But how can we conceive of implementing these social and environmen-tal standards without helping the poor countries to achieve the capacity to respect them?

How can we demand such a huge effort from them, given their many difficul-ties, if we do not support them in their efforts?

The question of innovative financing is central. We cannot avoid the debate on a tax on speculation.

Whether we wish to restrain the frenzy of the financial markets, finance devel-opment aid or bring the poor countries into the fight against climate change, it all comes back to taxing financial transactions.

Taxing the exorbitant profits of finance to combat poverty: who cannot see how such a decision – even if I am well aware of the complexity of implement-ing it – would contribute to putting us on the path of a moralisation of financial capitalism? I support without reservation the commitment of Gordon Brown, who was one of the first to defend this idea.

The other question we can no longer avoid is that of the role banks must play in the economy. The banker's job is not to speculate, it is to analyse credit risk, assess the capacity of borrowers to repay their loans and finance growth of the economy. If financial capitalism went so wrong, it was, first and foremost, because many banks were no longer doing their job. Why take the risk of lend-ing to entrepreneurs when it is so easy to earn money by speculating on the markets? Why lend only to those who can repay the loan when it is so easy to shift the risks off the balance sheet?

President Obama is right when he says that banks must be dissuaded from engaging in proprietary speculation or financing speculative funds. But this debate cannot be confined to a single country, whatever its weight in global finance. This debate must be settled within the G20.

But I also wanted to say that it will not be possible to emerge from the crisis and protect ourselves against future crises, if we perpetuate the imbalances that are the root of the problem. Countries with trade surpluses must consume more and improve the living standards and social protection of their citizens. Countries with deficits must make an effort to consume a little less and repay their debts.

Currency is central to these imbalances. It is the principal instrument of the policies that perpetuate them. We cannot put finance and the economy back in order if we allow the disorder of currencies to persist. Exchange rate instability and the under-valuation of certain currencies militate against fair trade and honest competition. Employment and purchasing power constitute the adjustment variable for correcting monetary manipulations. The prosperity of the post-war era owed a great deal to Bretton Woods, to its rules and its institutions.

Today, we need a new Bretton Woods. We cannot have, on the one hand, a multipolar world and, on the other, a single benchmark currency across the globe. We cannot, on the one hand, preach free trade and, on the other, tolerate monetary dumping. France, which will chair the G8 and the G20 in 2011, will place the reform of the international monetary system on the agenda.

Until then, we must manage, prudently, the adoption of measures to support activity and the withdrawal of the surplus liquidities injected during the crisis. We must take care to prevent too abrupt a tightening that would result in a global collapse.

So, what remains to be done is to bring into being a new growth model, invent a new linkage between public action and private initiative, invest massively in the technologies of the future that will drive the digital revolution and the ecological revolution. We must now invent the state, the company and the city of the twenty-first century.

A few years ago, people were predicting the end of nations, the advent of nomadism. But in the crisis, even the most globalised companies and the most global banks rediscovered that they had a nationality.

A few years ago, people were announcing the decline of organisations, the end of companies. We wanted to apply to companies the principles of portfolio management. We are rediscovering the fact that they are, first and foremost, human communities and living organisations.

A few years ago, people were predicting that the city would spread, break up, and with it social cohesion, human relations and community relations. We are rediscovering the need for community, for urban cohesion.

Basically, it looked as if citizenship would dissolve in the global market. But it has found new springs in the ordeal of the crisis. In the world of tomorrow, we must again reckon with citizens.

Citizen is not a separate category, it is each one of us. The company head, the shareholder, the employee, the trade unionist, the non-profit activist, the policy maker – they are all citizens who have responsibilities towards others, towards their country, towards future generations, towards the planet.

Yes, in the world of tomorrow, we must again reckon with citizens, with the demands of morality, the demands of responsibility, the demands of dignity for citizens. We must see this not as yet another problem, but as part of the solution; not as an additional difficulty, but as something healthy and virtuous, that may, perhaps, allow us to feel happier with what we are, happier with what we accomplish.

BENAZIR BHUTTO

'THE MOVING FINGER OF HISTORY'

—

REMARKS AT THE WORLD POLITICAL FORUM

TURIN, ITALY, 19 MAY 2003

The daughter of a former Prime Minister of Pakistan, Benazir Bhutto distinguished herself at the University of Oxford in 1976 by winning election as the first female Asian President of the Oxford Union Society. In 1982 she became leader of the democratic socialist Pakistan People's Party. She was elected Prime Minister of Pakistan in 1988, becoming the first woman to serve as head of government in a Muslim state. Her administration was dismissed in 1990 by President Ghulam Ishaq Khan, a long-term political rival who Bhutto had successfully marginalised from the decision-making process, on charges of nepotism and corruption. Bhutto was re-elected in 1993 and served as Prime Minister until 1996, surviving a coup attempt in 1995. After losing the 1997 election she went into self-imposed exile in London. She returned to Pakistan on 18 October 2007, to contest the 2008 elections. Shortly after touching down at Jinnah International Airport, two explosions killed 136 people, injuring a further 450 in what was soon discovered to have been a suicide bomb attack on Bhutto. Well aware of the risk she faced in returning to Pakistan, Bhutto had spoken on CNN of possible assassination attempts, and on 27 December 2007, she was killed by injuries sustained in an attack on her motorcade combining gunfire and explosives. The attack came after giving a speech in Rawalpindi two weeks before the Pakistani general election in 2008.

In this speech Bhutto discusses the war in Iraq and the possibility of democracy in Islamic countries. This speech could be viewed as a road map to a possible future in Pakistan and the region, where the international community finds Pakistan to be a partner in the war on terrorism and a voice for peace. Benazir Bhutto is singularly positioned to offer a dual perspective, the view from the West and a regional view from Central and Southern Asia.

—

With Iraq divided into American-, British- and Polish-controlled zones, we gather together in Turin at an extraordinary and difficult time. Whatever our own views on the path leading to the recent Iraq War, it is time to look forward.

It is time to assess the new world reality.

The post-Iraq international situation gives an opportunity to look for ways to promote the cause of democratisation, human rights and the global community to which we are all committed.

Many in the international community felt uncomfortable with a war without United Nations sanction.

Demonstrations for peace broke out in the heart of Europe, at times larger than demonstrations within the Muslim world.

No one likes war.

No one likes repression either.

Western societies absorb dissent.

Non-Western societies are yet to deal with the challenge of those victimised, persecuted, imprisoned, tortured and exiled because of their political views.

This community of the disaffected and the disenfranchised played a pivotal role both in Afghanistan and Iraq.

In Kabul and Baghdad, popular voices of the people were denied political space. They formed the political front for a war to reclaim their own land.

Countries descend into the darkness of international terrorism and state terrorism when pluralism is disrupted, when diversity is suppressed, when one man directs the destiny of millions be it a Mullah Omar or Saddam Hussein or other dictators.

America's President George Bush justified war claiming: 'Men and women in every culture need liberty like they need food and water and air. Everywhere that freedom arrives, humanity rejoices; and everywhere that freedom stirs, let tyrants fear.'

Post-Iraq, tyrants should fear.

It is troubling that some of those tyrants still feel little fear. Sadly, some of them are still close allies of Washington. In the case of Pakistan, a repressive regime exiles the popular opposition, imprisons dissidents and rigs elections.

In the post-Iraq world that dawned this April, the words rationalising the Iraq war can be used to press all nations, and especially Washington, to make consistent application of democratic principles the essence of internationalism in this new millennium.

There were moments in recent history where historic moments were squandered.

When the moving finger of history writes of the end of the twentieth century, it will write of the international community's failure to reinforce the democratic breakthrough that the end of communism brought as the era's greatest missed opportunity.

I recall speaking to European Parliaments, to the Congress of the United States, proclaiming that the era of the dictator was over, that militaries all over the world had finally returned to their barracks, that democracy was blooming on every continent.

In retrospect, I fear it was merely a mirage. The forces of realpolitik were waiting to collide with the ideology of democracy.

We proclaimed a new moral era, but actually constructed an era of moral relativity. And ladies and gentlemen, selective morality is by its very definition, immoral.

Our standards are inconsistent and our policies selective. Those that decry dictatorship in Burma are silent about tyranny elsewhere. Those decrying dictatorship in Iraq, stay close to dictators in Pakistan. Many in this room rightfully demand self-determination in Palestine, but are less vocal about the rights of the Kashmiri people.

In this age of moral relativism, political standards vary according to political expediency and economic imperatives. Democracy for Iraq, but dictatorship just miles away. Iraqi violations of UN resolutions bring a strong response. Violations of UN resolutions in the Middle East or in South Asia draw a less vocal reaction.

We evaluate national security by hardened borders and tanks and missiles. But true security is linked to the fight for economic justice that will liberate nations; true security is linked to the fight against famine and AIDs; true security means protecting the environment from pollution and desecration.

No matter how great and powerful a nation may be, true leadership is more than military action. It is leading the fight against AIDS, against hunger, against poverty, against racism, and for women, the fight for justice.

Ladies and gentlemen, the post-Iraq world situation allows us to focus once again on the principle of freedom. This time it must be more than rhetoric that is exploited in pursuit of limited, foreign policy objectives.

I remember a time when the world walked from Afghanistan after the defeat of the Soviets in 1989. The fundamental mistake was that we were not consistently committed to the values of freedom, democracy and self-determination that ultimately undermine terrorism. The result was Taliban dictatorship, al Qaeda and terrorism.

Dictatorship doesn't constrain fundamentalism or terrorism. It provokes it. The goal of rational foreign policy must always be to simultaneously promote stability and to strengthen democratic values.

The stakes are high. Every war in the South Asian subcontinent from where I come started when my country was under a military dictator or one of its civilian surrogates.

I do not know of a single case when a democratic country has gone to war against another democratic country.

Dictators are not accountable and do not need a popular mandate behind their policies.

The tragedy of Iraq is that Saddam Hussein spurned all offers of a peaceful transition from his regime to a democratic one. None dared tell him that he could not win a military war against American technology.

None dared criticise his flawed strategy of a prolonged guerrilla conflict with house-to-house fighting in Iraq's cities to force Washington into a ceasefire while he remained in control.

Dictators are cut off from reality by sycophants too scared to tell them the truth, allowing for miscalculations that innocent people pay for in lives.

Democracies are different. Democratic leaders are accountable before the Parliament, the press and the people. Democratic governments must provide for the public welfare, must provide schools and hospitals, health and housing. Dictatorships need not. They rely on unaccountable secret services and are free to divert resources to schemes that parliamentary scrutiny simply would not permit.

History has taught us the very hard lesson that when democratic states turn against democracy, they turn against themselves.

Ladies and gentlemen: the international press has speculated about Islamabad's support for North Korea's nuclear programme. Islamabad denies the charges. Even though Islamabad is a key ally of the US in the war against terrorism, Pakistani citizens are fingerprinted and photographed when they visit America. Military dictator General [Pervez] Musharaf promised the world community he would seal the borders with Afghanistan to prevent fleeing al Qaeda from slipping into Pakistan. Yet scores made their way into the country, as the recent arrests by the FBI demonstrate.

Ladies and gentlemen: I believe a democratic Pakistan is the best guarantee of respect and dignity for the people of Pakistan. I believe that a democratic Pakistan living by the rule of law within and without is the best guarantee of the triumph of moderation and modernity among one billion Muslims at the crossroads of our history.

These are difficult times. We stand at the crossroads of a new world order. We witness the dawn of a unipolar world environment where wars can take place with the coalition of the willing. We witness disunity in the United Nations Security Council, in NATO, in Europe and in the Muslim world.

We can remember that the future is in our hands. As the European philosopher Goethe once wrote, 'Freedom must be reinvented in every generation.'

Unipolarism can lead to unilateralism. As power shifts to new paradigms the challenge is to find ways where the voices of the rest of the world community can also be heard effectively.

This is our turn to reinvent freedom.

And we shall prevail.

Thank you, ladies and gentlemen.

MANMOHAN SINGH

'WE ARE BUILDING A NEW INDIA'

—

INDEPENDENCE DAY

RED FORT, INDIA, 15 AUGUST 2010

H ead of the Indian National Congress party and the United Progressive Alliance, Manmohan Singh became Prime Minister of India in 2004 and was re-elected in 2009. As a Sikh, he is the first non-Hindi Prime Minister of India. He was first elected to the upper house of India's Congress in 1991, representing Assam. He served as finance minister of India from 1991–1996. This speech is given on Indian Independence Day. He explains his country's rise as a global power and the problems faced by an emerging India.

The 'Naxalism' to which he makes repeated reference, below, is an umbrella term for a range of communist, often specifically Maoist, insurgent groups that mostly developed out of the Communist Party of India. Although some Naxalite factions have abandoned their traditional revolutionary techniques, disavowing violence and entering the political process (including communist members of India's Parliament), others have continued a campaign of guerrilla actions and terrorism. In April 2010, Naxalite militants killed seventy-six police officers and wounded fifty others in a well-planned ambush that was followed by attacks in May and June killing a further fifteen policemen, twenty civilians and twenty-six army reservists. More recently, a policy of negotiation and reconciliation appears to be having some success in reducing Naxalite violence, a success generally attributed to government investment in the development of remote rural areas that have long been the Naxalite power bases.

—

Dear citizens,

I greet you on the sixty-third anniversary of our independence. When Pandit Jawaharlal Nehru unfurled the Tricolour on this historic Red Fort, on 15 August, 1947, he called himself the first servant of India. I address you today in the same spirit of service.

A few days back, many precious lives were lost in Ladakh due to a cloudburst. I convey my heartfelt condolences to the family members and other near and dear ones of those who have perished. In this hour of grief, the whole country stands with the people of Ladakh. It is my assurance that the central government will do everything possible for rehabilitation of the affected people.

When I addressed you last year on Independence Day, our country was facing a number of difficulties. There was a drought-like situation in many parts of the country. We were also affected by the global economic slowdown. I am happy to say that we have acquitted ourselves well in these difficult circumstances. Despite many problems, the rate of our economic growth has been better than most other countries in the world. This shows the strength of our economy.

This strength has been evident not only in the last one year but also in our economic progress in the last many years. Today, India stands among the fastest growing economies of the world. As the world's largest democracy, we have become an example for many other countries to emulate. Our citizens have the right to make their voice heard. Our country is viewed with respect all over the world. Our views command attention in international forums.

All of you have contributed to India's success. The hard work of our workers, our artisans, our farmers has brought our country to where it stands today. I especially salute our soldiers whose bravery ensures the safety of our borders. I pay tribute to all those martyrs who have sacrificed their lives for our country.

We are building a new India in which every citizen would have a stake, an India which would be prosperous and in which all citizens would be able to live a life of honour and dignity in an environment of peace and good-will. An India in which all problems could be solved through democratic means. An India in which the basic rights of every citizen would be protected. In the last few years, we have taken many significant steps in this direction. Every person living in rural areas now has the assurance of 100 days of employment through the Mahatma Gandhi National Rural Employment Guarantee Act. The Right to Information Act is helping our citizens to become more aware. This year our government has enacted the Right to Education which will help every Indian to share in the benefits of the country's economic progress and also to contribute to it. To ensure equal partnership of women in our progress, we have taken initiative reserving seats for women in Parliament and in state legislatures. Apart from this, reservation for women has been increased to 50 per cent in local bodies.

Despite our many strengths, we face some serious challenges. We should resolve today that we will meet these challenges as one people. Our society often gets divided in the name of religion, state, caste or language. We should resolve that we will not allow divisions in our society under any circumstance. Tolerance and generosity have been a part of our traditions. We should strengthen these traditions. As we progress economically our society should also become more sensitive. We should be modern and progressive in our outlook.

Our government has laid special emphasis on the welfare of our farmers and on increasing agricultural production. After we came to power in 2004, we realised that the state of Indian agriculture in the preceding seven to eight years was not satisfactory. Our government increased public investment in agriculture. We started new schemes for increasing production. We encouraged agricultural planning at the district level. I am happy that the growth rate of our agriculture has increased substantially in the last few years. But we are still far from achieving our goal. We need to work harder so that we can increase the agricultural growth rate to 4 per cent per annum.

Our government wants a food safety net in which no citizen of ours would go hungry. This requires enhanced agricultural production which is possible only by increasing productivity. Our country has not witnessed any big technological breakthrough in agriculture after the Green Revolution. We need technology which would address the needs of dry land agriculture. In addition, our agriculture should also be able to deal with new challenges like climate change, falling levels of ground water and deteriorating quality of soil. In the history of Indian agriculture, Norman Borlaug commands a special place. About forty to fifty years back he developed new and more productive seeds of wheat. Under the leadership of Smt [Mrs] Indira Gandhi, India achieved the Green Revolution by adopting these seeds. I am happy to announce that the Borlaug Institute of South Asia is being established in India. This institute would facilitate availability of new and improved seeds and new technology to the farmers of India and other countries of South Asia.

We have always taken care to provide remunerative prices to farmers so that they are encouraged to increase production. Support prices have been increased every year in the last six years. The support price for wheat was enhanced to Rs.1,100 per quintal last year from Rs.630 per quintal in 2003–04. In paddy, this increase was from Rs.550 per quintal to Rs.1,000 per quintal. But one effect of providing higher prices to farmers is that food prices in the open market also increase.

I know that in the last few months high inflation has caused you difficulties. It is the poor who are the worst affected by rising prices, especially when the prices of commodities of everyday use like food grains, pulses, vegetables increase. It is for this reason that we have endeavoured to minimise the burden of increased prices on the poor. Today, I do not want to go into the detailed reasons for high inflation. But, I would certainly like to say that we are making every possible effort to tackle this problem. I am also confident that we will succeed in these efforts.

It is obvious that any person or institution cannot spend more than his income over a long period of time, even if it is the government. It is our responsibility that we manage our economy with prudence so that our development is not affected adversely in the future because of high debt. We import about 80 per cent of our requirement of petroleum products. After 2004, we have increased the prices of petroleum products much less compared to the increase in the price of crude oil in the international market. The subsidy on petroleum products has been increasing every year. It had become necessary therefore to increase the prices of petroleum products. If this had not been done, it would not have been possible for our budget to bear the burden of subsidy and our programmes for education, health and employment of the poor would have been adversely affected.

In the sixty-three years after independence, India has covered a long distance on the path of development. But our destination is still far away. A large part of our population still suffers from persistent poverty, hunger and disease. When our government came to power in 2004, we resolved to build a new India under a progressive social agenda. We wanted the fruits of development to reach the common man. We initiated programmes especially targeted to the welfare of the socially and economically backward sections of our society. We still stand committed to the welfare of the poor, the Scheduled Castes and Scheduled Tribes, minorities, women and other backward sections of our society. But today we do not need many new programmes to achieve our goals. However, we do need to implement the schemes we have already started more effectively, minimising the chances of corruption and misuse of public money. We want to achieve this in partnership with the state governments, Panchayat Raj Institutions and civil society groups.

Secularism is one of the pillars of our democracy. It has been the tradition of our country and society to treat all religions with equal respect. For centuries India has welcomed new religions and all have flourished here. Secularism is also our constitutional obligation. Our government is committed to maintaining communal peace and harmony. We also consider it our duty to protect the minorities and provide for their special needs. This is why we have started many new programmes in the last four years for the welfare of our brothers and sisters belonging to the minority communities. These include scholarships for minority students and special programmes for the development of districts which have a high concentration of minorities. These schemes have shown good results. We will vigorously take this work forward.

We have been giving special attention to education and health in the last six years. Improvement in these two areas is an important component of our strategy for inclusive growth. It is also necessary for higher economic growth in the years to come. After independence, these two areas could not get the importance they deserved. We tried to change this state of affairs in the Eleventh Plan. Today, almost every child in our country has access to primary education. Now, we need to pay more attention to secondary and higher education. We also need to improve the quality of education at all levels. It is our endeavour that every child, irrespective of whether he is rich or poor and which section of the society he belongs to, should be given an education that enables him to realise his potential and makes him a responsible citizen of our country. We will continue to implement the new schemes that we have started in the last six years in the areas of education and health with sincerity and hard work and in partnership with the state governments. We will soon bring a Bill to Parliament for the constitution of two separate councils in higher education and health respectively so that reforms in these two areas can be accelerated.

Nutritious food and good health services are necessary but not enough for ensuring the good health of our citizens. We also need cleanliness and good sanitation in our villages, towns and cities. There are many diseases which would be difficult to prevent otherwise. The truth is that our country lags behind in this area. I consider it a primary responsibility of all our citizens to maintain cleanliness and hygiene around them. I would like our children to be taught the importance of cleanliness and hygiene in schools from the very beginning under a campaign for a Clean India. I appeal to the state governments, Panchayat Raj Institutions, civil society groups and common citizens to make this campaign successful.

Mahatma Gandhi said that our earth has enough for everyone's need but not for everyone's greed. Imprudent use of the earth's natural resources has resulted in the problem of climate change. We need to use our natural resources with care and prudence. It is our responsibility towards the coming generations to protect and preserve our forests, rivers and mountains. Our government will endeavour to take care of environmental concerns in our projects for economic development.

There is a large deficit in our physical infrastructure which affects our economic development adversely. There is a shortfall in the supply of electricity to industries. Our roads, ports and airports are not of world standards. We have been trying to increase electricity production and improve our roads, ports and airports. The resources required to create good physical infrastructure are difficult for the government alone to mobilise. Therefore, we have endeavoured to involve the private sector in our efforts. The steps that we have taken after 2004 to improve our physical infrastructure have started bearing fruit now. About one and a half months back, I dedicated a new terminal of the Delhi airport to the nation. This is an excellent terminal which has been completed in record time. We will continue to make such efforts to improve our physical infrastructure.

There has been much discussion recently on the issue of internal security.

If law and order in any part of India deteriorates or peace and harmony gets disturbed, the common man is adversely affected. Therefore, it is one of the primary responsibilities of any government to maintain law and order so that the citizens can live and earn their livelihood in an atmosphere of peace and harmony. Naxalism is a serious challenge to our internal security. I pay tribute to the men and officers of our security forces who have become martyrs in the attacks by Naxalites in the last few months. I have stated this before and I say it again – our government will fully discharge its responsibility to protect each and every citizen of our country. We will deal firmly with those who resort to violence. We will provide all possible help to state governments to maintain the rule of law in areas affected by Naxalism. I once again appeal to Naxalites to abjure violence, come for talks with the government and join hands with us to accelerate social and economic development. A few days back I took a meeting with the Chief Ministers of states affected by Naxalism. We will fully implement the consensus that emerged in that meeting. I would like to repeat here a point that I made in that meeting. It is imperative that centre and states work together to meet the challenge of Naxalism. It would be very difficult for any state to tackle this problem without cooperation from the centre and coordination between states. We all need to rise above our personal and political interests to meet this challenge.

As I have stated earlier, most Naxalite-affected areas lag behind in development. Many such areas also have a large concentration of our Adivasi [aboriginal] brothers and sisters. We want to end the neglect of these areas. I have asked the Planning Commission to formulate a comprehensive scheme towards this end, which we would implement fully. It is also our endeavour that our Adivasi brothers and sisters join the mainstream of development. They have been dependent on forest produce for centuries and this dependence should not end without the creation of new sources of livelihood. Apart from adequate compensation for land which is acquired from them, we should also ensure that our Adivasi brothers and sisters have a stake in the developmental project being undertaken.

I would like to state one more thing in this context. It is very necessary to make the administrative machinery more sensitive in areas affected by Naxalism. The government officials who work there should not only be sincere but should also be alive to the special needs of our Adivasi brothers and sisters. It is my hope that the state governments will pay adequate attention to these requirements.

We have a special responsibility towards the states of the North East. We are trying to live up to that responsibility. The North Eastern part of our country has been witness to some unpleasant incidents in the recent months. I would like to convey to all political parties and groups of the North East that disputes in the name of state or tribe can only harm all of us. Discussion and dialogue are the only options to resolve complex issues. As far as the central government is concerned, we are ready to take forward every process of talks which could lead to progress in resolution of problems.

In Jammu and Kashmir, we are ready to talk to every person or group which abjures violence. Kashmir is an integral part of India. Within this framework, we are ready to move forward in any talks which would increase the partnership of the common man in governance and also enhance their welfare. Recently, some young men have lost their lives in violence in Jammu and Kashmir. We deeply regret this. The years of violence should now end. Such violence would not benefit anyone. I believe that India's democracy has the generosity and flexibility to be able to address the concerns of any area or group in the country. I recently participated in a meeting with political parties from Jammu and Kashmir. We will endeavour to take this process forward. I would like to convey to our countrymen, especially our citizens in Jammu and Kashmir and in the North East, that they should adopt democratic means to join hands with us for their country's welfare.

We want prosperity, peace and harmony in our neighbouring countries. Whatever differences we have with our neighbouring countries, we want to resolve them through discussions. As far as Pakistan is concerned, we expect from them that they would not let their territory be used for acts of terrorism against India. We have been emphasising this in all our discussions with the Pakistan government. If this is not done, we cannot progress far in our dialogue with Pakistan.

I would also like to say something which is related to our glorious cultural traditions. The use of harsh and unpleasant words in our political discourse has increased in recent days. This is against our traditions of generosity, humility and tolerance. Criticism has a place of its own in a democracy and in a progressive society. However, criticism should not be undignified. We should have the capacity to reconcile opposite points of view on important issues through debate and discussion. I would request all political parties to consider this issue.

The Commonwealth Games will start in Delhi after about one and a half months. This will be a proud moment for the whole country and especially for Delhi. I am convinced that all our countrymen will treat the Games as a national festival and will leave no stone unturned to make them a success. The successful organisation of Commonwealth Games would be another signal to the world that India is rapidly marching ahead with confidence.

Our future is bright. The day when our dreams will come true is not far off. Let us all resolve on this anniversary of our independence that we will keep the flag of our nation flying high. Let us march ahead together on the path of progress and prosperity.

Dear children, please say Jai Hind with me.

HENRY M. PAULSON, JR

'CHINA'S EMERGENCE AS A GLOBAL LEADER'

—

REMARKS TO THE NATIONAL COMMITTEE ON US—CHINA RELATIONS

NEW YORK CITY, NEW YORK, 21 OCTOBER 2008

*H*enry Paulson was CEO of Goldman Sachs from 1999–2006 and served in President George W. Bush's Cabinet as Treasury Secretary from 2006–2009. Paulson was a visible frontline voice for US financial and economic policy during the global financial crisis. He is also a recognised expert on China. Knowing that a Chinese panic would turn a recession into a depression, Paulson's speech explains the causes of the American recession and reassures Chinese investors, especially those who have purchased government-backed securities, that their money is safe.

In this speech, Paulson deploys some of the language that has entered common usage in policy circles since the emergence of the financial crisis. There are some words that are essential to any discussion of the world markets: 'transparency', 'responsibility', 'trust', 'fiduciary duty', 'stewardship', 'stability', 'security', and other terms that send signals of care and concern with mortgage lending practices. There are some new terms, like 'sub-prime loans' (variable rate loans that were often given to potential homeowners who did not quality for traditional, fixed-rate loans), 'underwater' (a situation where the value of the mortgage exceeds the value of the property upon which the mortgage is based), and 'moral hazard' (a practice in which one takes undue risks because the cost is not borne by the party taking the risks, such as the practice of a lender or a borrower making irresponsible loans because they will not bear the costs of that financially risky behaviour). In this speech, Secretary Paulson must calm the American markets, the banking industry, the global markets, and the Chinese government which fears that they will suffer from the mortgage practices and financial difficulties in the United States. Because China holds more than one trillion *dollars in government-backed securities, and holds the single largest investment in United States government debt, there must be a delicate balancing of language and policy necessary to acknowledge financial problems in the United States, while continuing to attract Chinese investment. At a minimum, Paulson is trying to make sure that China does not withdraw significant funds from its American investments.*

—

Good evening. Thank you, Carla, and thanks to all of you at the National Committee for the exceptional work that you do for US–China relations. As we approach the thirty-year anniversary of a turning point in US and Chinese history, we also recall the strategic vision of the National Committee and its role in the historic 1971 ping-pong exchange that helped make resumption of normalised relations possible. Through visions such as yours, the American and Chinese people began to understand one another and to see the benefits – indeed, the necessity – of normalisation.

My remarks will focus on the future of our economic relationship with China. We will soon have a new US President who will face the continuing challenge and opportunity of responding to China's emergence as a global economic leader.

The world's financial markets are undergoing the most serious stresses in recent memory and this financial crisis has begun to negatively impact real economies here and around the world. China is feeling this stress as well, but fortunately its economy is expected to continue to be an important engine for global growth during this period. In the United States, recent collaborative actions by the Federal Reserve, the Federal Deposit Insurance Corporation and the Treasury clearly demonstrate that our government will do what is necessary to significantly strengthen our banks and financial institutions, enabling them to increase financing for the consumption and business investments that drive US economic growth. Through a multitude of powerful actions we have and will demonstrate our commitment to unlocking our credit markets and minimising the impact of the current instability on the rest of the US economy.

Addressing the effects of financial market turmoil around the world requires the dramatic steps we are taking here in the United States, and it requires close international corroboration and cooperation. We have been in close contact with Chinese leaders, as well as with leaders of many other nations. And we welcome Premier Wen's statement that China will play a constructive and cooperative role in global efforts to deal with the current financial market turmoil. Throughout this turbulent time, I have stayed in close touch with Vice Premier Wang Qishan, who has now been appointed to lead China's newly established international financial crisis committee. Our conversations have been useful and constructive. It is clear that China accepts its responsibility as a major world economy that will work with the United States and other partners to ensure global economic stability.

Governments must continue to take individual and collective actions to provide much-needed liquidity, strengthen financial institutions through the provision of capital and the disposition of troubled assets, prevent market abuse, and protect the savings of their citizens. We must also take care to ensure that our actions are closely coordinated and communicated so that the action of one country does not come at the expense of others or the stability of the system as a whole.

Ten days ago leaders from the world's twenty largest economies met in Washington and found ways to further enhance our collective efforts to lessen the effects of global market turmoil. Those meetings brought concrete actions that have supported world markets. I am heartened that the international community is working together for stability and to regain a footing of confidence. As confidence returns to the system, normal financial activities will resume. And we are all grateful for President Bush's leadership during this time. As the President said on Friday, 'The American people … can have confidence that this economy will recover. We're a country where all people have the freedom to realise their potential and chase their dreams.' As the President knows, Americans are a strong and optimistic people. Although we expect current challenges to continue for a number of months, we will overcome them as we have overcome every challenge our nation has ever faced.

We will elect a new President two weeks from today, and our new President should start from the perspective that China will continue to play a key role in the world economy. As a matter of fact, today more than ever the world is looking to China to be a big contributor to global economic growth. While some see China as a threat that must be countered or contained, I believe that the only path to success with China is through engagement. We must recognise that China's growth is an opportunity for US companies and consumers, for our producers, exporters and investors. A stable, prosperous and peaceful China is in the best interest of the Chinese people, the American people and the rest of the world.

US–China relations are more productive today than ever before, largely because we have engaged China as it is, not as we might wish or imagine it to be. We have acted to lessen misperceptions and miscommunication between our countries.

An important part of the engagement has been through the Strategic Economic Dialogue established in 2006 by President Bush and President Hu. We have worked from the understanding that robust and sustained economic growth is a social imperative for China and that Beijing views its international interactions primarily through an economic lens. We have worked with Beijing on economic issues that are of mutual interest, and we have found that we can produce tangible results in both economic and noneconomic areas. Our recent close and frequent communication and cooperation as we address the challenges in the financial markets is a tangible example of the power and utility of a Strategic Economic Dialogue [SED] based on mutual trust.

Over the past two years we have built a strong foundation for this dialogue by focusing on policy areas in which China's reform agenda and US interests intersect. The SED has found new and constructive ways to address some of the most important matters in our economic relationship – including growth imbalances, energy security and environmental sustainability, trade and investment issues, product safety, and China's position in the world economy. Addressing these questions serves China's interests, and is also vital to the US and global economic future.

One of the SED's major achievements is the Ten Year Energy and Environment Cooperation Framework. This framework is a bilateral mechanism to create a new energy-efficient model for sustainable economic development and to address the factors that cause climate change. Greater breakthroughs can be expected in the years ahead, and this framework provides the next administration a critically important platform for US economic engagement with China.

Trade and investment, once the glue of US–Chinese relations, now also represent a source of increased tension. Any dynamic economy that is constantly creating new, higher-value jobs faces factory closings and job losses that are real and painful. The benefits of free trade are often spread across an entire country, while the lost jobs are more immediately visible. But succumbing to the temptation to make trade and foreign investment a scapegoat only breeds support for isolationist policies that will make us worse off, sacrificing future job opportunities and higher standards of living.

American investors in China, and Chinese investors in America, question whether the other country is truly open to investment and provides adequate legal protections. To answer this question, we sent a powerful and clear signal at the June SED meeting by launching negotiations of a US–China bilateral investment treaty. Through these negotiations, we seek to assure our people and the world that our two nations welcome investment and will treat each other's investors in a fair and transparent manner. And we will work even harder to resolve a critical issue for American companies working in China, better enforcement of intellectual property laws, to help China on its path to become an innovation society, while accelerating the development and competitiveness of its economy.

In the area of product safety, we have made real progress but need to intensify our work together to enhance China's regulatory and legal infrastructure, to help them build quality into each stage of the manufacturing and distribution process.

In the financial sector, we have worked steadily to help China develop and open up its institutions. Some in China look at the recent failures in our financial markets and conclude that they should slow down their reforms. But there is a great opportunity for China to learn from our significant mistakes and move forward with reforms that have the potential to produce important gains for China and its people.

For example, a capital markets reform agenda will advance China's economic goals in four important ways. It will rebalance the sources of China's growth to ensure that it is more harmonious, more energy and environmentally efficient, and provides greater welfare for Chinese households. It will create effective macroeconomic policy tools to ensure stable, non-inflationary growth. It will support China's transition to a market-driven and innovation-based economy; and, finally, it will assist China in dealing with its demographic challenges.

The SED has also provided an excellent forum for discussing the value of the RMB [Renminbi, China's currency]; I am pleased that China has appreciated the RMB by over 20 per cent since July of 2005.

The SED has shown that active economic engagement between the highest levels of US and Chinese leadership can keep our relationship on an even keel even as we tackle our most challenging issues and manage short-term tensions.

Chinese leaders understand that if the SED is to be sustained, it must be more than talk; it must continue to yield specific, tangible results, what I call signposts along the path toward transformational reform. We look forward to further progress in the ongoing discussions with Chinese officials and at our next SED meeting in Beijing in December.

The successes of the SED in the past two years have created a foundation of mutual understanding and trust and a platform for further progress. And perhaps most importantly the SED has established a new model for communication, enabling us to address urgent issues such as turmoil in our financial markets, energy security and climate change. I hope that the next US President will expand on the SED to take US–Chinese relations to the next level.

Thank you.

ALPHONSO JACKSON

'HOUSING IS CENTRAL TO THE HUMAN CONDITION'

—

REMARKS TO THE ASIAN REAL ESTATE SOCIETY

MACAU, CHINA, 10 JULY 2007

A long with Paulson, Alphonso Jackson took a leading role in explaining the American financial turbulence. After heading the housing authorities in St Louis, Washington, DC, and Dallas, Jackson became President of American Electric Power-Texas. In 2001 he was confirmed as Deputy Secretary of the Department of Housing and Urban Development. He was promoted to the Cabinet as Secretary of the Department in 2004 and served until 2008. Jackson is now a Distinguished University Professor and Director of the Center for Public Policy at HamptonUniversity, Hampton, Virginia.

In this speech he explains the role played by the housing market in the American financial crisis, reassuring Asian investors that the market remains sound. Like the previous speech, this one covers much of the language and argumentation used in the financial crisis. This speech is particularly notable for an argument about Chinese home ownership, which is severely restricted except in Hong Kong and Macau. Jackson predicts that Chinese wealth will increase even faster through home owner-ship. Given the role of predatory lending and mortgage defaults in conditioning the global financial crisis this seems, at first glance, to be a somewhat fanciful proposi-tion. But it holds an important kernel of truth, as China has untapped areas of potential wealth creation. Home equity could provide an enormous source of wealth, while running the risks that accompany widespread homeownership. Jackson's speech was notable at the time. It may prove to have been prophetic.

Also, note the use of Confucius. Since Mao is no longer a credible source of wisdom and inspiration, Chinese leaders have turned to Confucius. Once the ancient philos-opher had been discredited by Chinese communists. Now he is viewed as a safe source

of guidance, linking modern China with its ancient past. I have repeatedly heard
Chinese officials thank American and Western politicians for quoting Confucius.
For example, in a later speech at this conference, Jackson was complimented by his
Chinese counterpart for citing Confucius in this speech.

The audience is the Asian Real Estate Society. The version of this speech on the web
claims it is the 'American Real Estate Society'. That is a mistake made by those who
uploaded the speech. The mistake has not been corrected to date.

———

Housing represents an important, vast area of common ground between countries and peoples. Each of us, and each of our nations, confront many similar
problems. These issues often transcend history, ideology, circumstance, and
economics. People need to be housed, and that is true in the developing world
and the developed world, in Africa as well as Asia. True, each country faces
a unique set of challenges. But there is so much overlap and commonality. I
believe we have much to learn from each other.

And, believe me, I am here to learn. The problems of housing are complex
and defiant. They are intertwined in problems related to economic development,
population growth, the environment, infrastructure, transportation, health,
water, what we call urban sprawl, and property ownership, just to mention a
few issues that accompany our discussions.

And housing is about personal finance, government expenditures, and international investment. We know that homeownership can be a personal source of
wealth and financial security, as equity builds over the years. You see that right
here in Macau, where property prices are booming and the value of homes and
buildings is increasing rapidly. And, as you know, Hong Kong is a financial force
of nature, with property values among the highest in the world.

We know that domestic investment in housing is now a major part of any
country's gross domestic product. We have seen a rapid rise of housing values in
the United States. Home equity has grown from $6.6 trillion in 2000 to $10.9
trillion in 2006, a 66 per cent increase over six years. In the United States, home
equity is about 7 per cent of GDP, 20 per cent if you include housing services.

And provision of housing is increasingly challenging. We know that affordable housing is in short supply in many countries. As property values increase,
many people are simply priced out of the market. We see our service providers
– teachers, firemen, policemen, restaurant workers, and transportation workers
– pushed out of some communities, and then forced to spend more time and
money commuting to their jobs from farther and farther distances.

Add to that another problem – the migration to cities, which started in the
late 1700s and early 1800s in Europe and the United States, as a product of the

Industrial Revolution. Now it is a global phenomenon. More and more people come to the cities, looking for opportunity and employment. Despite efforts by many countries to regulate and control this flow of people, they still come, cities continue to grow, overwhelming our resources, our planning, and even our projections. They come in larger and larger numbers, a powerful flow of people magnetically drawn to the cities.

We cannot ignore this problem. People need to be properly housed, they should not be forced into slums or poverty-ridden enclaves. We must find a way to integrate more and more people into the city, to make them a part of the city, and to give them a stake in the city.

And increasingly, the world will turn to Asia for solutions. You will help lead the way into the future. More than 60 per cent of the increase in the world's urban population over the next three decades will be in Asia. The world will be learning from your experiences in Tokyo, Seoul, Beijing, Shanghai, Ho Chi Minh City, Bangkok, Singapore, Jakarta, Kuala Lumpur, Manila, and elsewhere.

Growth management is not easy – it may seem impossible – it may be impossible. But we must do our very best. Housing is central to the human condition. It is vital for everyone. And we must provide solutions that are equitable, just, fair, and comprehensive.

I know there are many ways to do this. And I am very interested in this region's efforts to address housing and urban growth. I noted with interest the eleventh Five Year Plan released by the Chinese government last year. There was an entire chapter dedicated to urban growth. China is now committed to, and I quote, 'coordinated development of large, medium and small cities and towns' and 'actively and safely (promoting) urbanisation according to the principles of steady and orderly progression, land conservation, concentrated and efficient growth, and rational distribution of cities.' China's landmark Property Law, passed this March, coupled with broad changes to the Constitution, will better define what it means to own and use property.

In the United States and many other countries there has been an emphasis on homeownership. In fact, President Bush has asked that America become an 'ownership society'. As a result, approximately 70 per cent of American families now own a home. However, this result has not been evenly distributed between minority peoples and majority whites. Only about 50 per cent of Black American and Hispanic Americans own a home, and about 60 per cent of Asian Americans are homeowners. So the President has emphasised minority ownership, and in 2002 dedicated our country to 5.5 million more minority homeowners by the end of the decade. Because of this emphasis, we have already increased minority ownership by almost 3.5 million people, so we are more than half way to the goal.

We know that homeownership rates as a whole can rise even higher. Some countries, like Ireland, have a rate approaching 80 per cent homeownership.

There does not seem to be a fixed ceiling. So, in the United States, we are hopeful that the rates can reach higher and higher.

As we encourage homeownership, we must beware of potential dangers. In the United States, we have witnessed the economic push of sub-prime loans, which helped democratise credit and opened up homeownership for millions of people in my country. But there was a risk. And for about 20 per cent of those loans made over the last few years, the risk was realised. But for the other 80 per cent, the loans are secure. We witnessed the economic pull of the failed sub-prime loans, which often came about through predatory lending and poor consumer preparation. Many of those in failed sub-prime loans didn't read the contracts; about half didn't even call their lenders and tell them of the difficulties.

The sub-prime problems hit as our housing market was making a cyclical adjustment after several years of historic growth. The lower rates of home construction and higher rates of foreclosure were accelerated by the sub-prime problem, giving rise to some headlines screaming of doom. But I want to assure you that those with oversight of the American housing market all agree on this – that the vast majority of sub-prime loans are sound. Fed Chief Bernanke has been vocal with his views, and I certainly agree with him.

We have aggressively taken steps to address difficult sub-prime loans. We have refinanced many of them through public institutions like our Federal Housing Administration. We have also promoted much wider housing counselling, with 2,300 housing counsellors in the United States.

I am very thankful the President has increased funding for housing counselling by over 200 per cent since coming into office. And we have used equity to solve payment problems for seniors through reverse mortgages, which are guaranteed by my government.

Overall, I am of the belief that the sub-prime market can actually be a good thing. It allowed for the creation of a new class of homeowners, as long as people act responsibly. I agree with Confucius, who counselled that 'the cautious rarely make a mistake'. As we explore new credit options for potential homeowners, we must be vigilant in educating them. We must make certain that the loans are affordable. Nationally and internationally, we must be on guard against predatory lending. It is nothing more than a scam, a crime, a lie. The loan process must be transparent and understandable. I see much merit in programmes that help poor and middle-class buyers with help on down payments or the cost of purchase.

The sub-prime market helped contribute to an historic boom in American housing. I think we can learn from this experience, find out what worked, and use that information, while minimising the exotic, unaffordable aspects of the sub-prime revolution.

Worldwide, the wind is blowing toward homeownership. You see it blowing in Thailand, the Philippines, South Korea, Japan, and elsewhere, even here in

Macau and Hong Kong. In the future, we could even see it blow across China, from the coast to the Himalayas, to the west, and to the Mongolian deserts. And it would be a powerful wind, generating unprecedented wealth and opportunity.

Of course, part of our success in the United States is due to investments by your countries in mortgage-backed securities. We know that international investment in housing has become a positive, powerful part of the United States economy. By tapping the global capital market to provide financing for home-owners, the mortgage-backed securities market contributes to lower mortgage rates in the United States.

And it's been a good investment for Asian countries, too. A true win-win situation.

Much of this investment has come from Asia. Most of this investment has been in US Treasury Securities. But now there is a growing investment in mort-gage-backed securities. Let me give you an example. In June of 2003, Chinese investors held less than $3 billion in Agency Mortgage-Based Securities. But in June 2006, just three years later, that number had risen to $107 billion. Chinese investors hold more Agency Mortgage-Backed Securities than investors from any other country.

They are a sound, solid investment, a win-win situation for the investors and for the American people. These securities are attractive because they have no credit risk and are backed by the full faith and credit of the US Government. Also, most Agency Mortgage-Backed Securities have an even higher yield than the Treasury Securities.

The positive benefits from these arrangements are recognised by all involved. I know that one agency, called 'Ginnie Mae', which is a United States government-owned corporation within my department, has made increased investment by other countries a top priority. We are talking to investors about increasing their portfolios. We welcome new investment.

In your countries and mine, citizens are restless consumers. They want to find ways to increase wealth and expand purchasing power. One scholar has said that, globally, our citizens are leading us into an age of 'post-modern govern-ment', where people want government to give them more information, more choices, and more economic power.

I know from my own experience that citizens expect cities that function properly and competently. They want vibrant, inclusive, crime-free, and economically-thriving cities, which will become places of art, culture, educa-tion, and compassion. Our citizens even want more than that – they want us to get ahead of the curve, to become proactive, to anticipate problems and prevent them. In an age of technology, the Internet, and a wired global village, our citizens are increasingly impatient. They want solutions now, and the best solu-tion is one that removes problems from the horizon, long before they happen.

Our citizens expect good governance, transparency, competence, and vision. And they want it now. In this century, we must be committed to meeting the needs of our citizens as never before, and to do this by involving the entire community. We must include advocacy groups and community organisations in our planning, deliberations, and implementation. We must construct workable and inclusive partnerships that help us best meet the needs of our citizens.

And I believe homeownership is an important part of the future. Homeownership gives people a stake in the community, a piece of the community. It is their home to maintain and develop. It is their place to live, a place of relaxation, recreation, and solitude. It is the place of privacy and tranquillity.

And homeownership is a place for wealth creation, for most of us our most important and successful investment. I have often wondered what would happen if 70 or 80 per cent of families in Asian countries owned their own homes. I personally believe the wealth creation would be staggering, shocking – off the charts.

So I am very interested in efforts to promote homeownership in countries like China. I know some steps have been taken which are very promising. I personally believe that these efforts will generate further large rates of economic growth in China and lead to even greater social stability.

And as this happens, as the future unfolds, we will continue to meet in forums like the Asian Real Estate Society. For here we will share our common goals and needs, and glimpse the future. We will help make the future better for citizens in our own countries and around the world.

Thank you again for inviting me.

DAVID CAMERON

'BRITAIN REMAINS A GREAT ECONOMIC POWER'

—

REMARKS ON BRITISH FOREIGN RELATIONS
AT THE LORD MAYOR'S BANQUET

LONDON, UNITED KINGDOM, 15 NOVEMBER 2010

David Cameron is the Prime Minister of the United Kingdom. The Lord Mayor's Banquet is an annual event to commemorate the election and installation of the Lord Mayor of London. Traditionally, at this dinner, the Prime Minister outlines his country's foreign policy.

This speech made headlines by announcing deep defence cuts and limitations on international commitments, especially in Afghanistan, necessitated by austerity measures introduced by Cameron's coalition government. It set a benchmark for the work of the coalition government. The language is straightforward and often surprising. I sat in the audience and listened to some people gasp during this speech. There is also a compelling argument for reaching out to emerging markets. The Prime Minister believes that emerging markets can be an answer to Great Britain's financial difficulties, that growth may be one way out of austerity. The speech was broadcast to the nation. The paragraph arrangement is mine.

—

My Lord Mayor, My Late Lord Mayor, Your Grace, My Lord Chancellor, Mr Speaker, Your Excellencies, My Lords, Alderman, Sheriffs, Chief Commissioner, Ladies and Gentlemen.

I've just come back from visiting two of the fastest growing economies in the world. China, with average growth of nearly 10 per cent a year for the last three decades and set to return as the biggest economy in the world later this century, and Korea, which in 1960 had a GDP only twice that of Zambia but which today has a GDP forty times higher.

In Seoul I was at the G20, forged at the height of the financial crisis, it's now the main forum for global economic decision-making, bringing together not only the United States and China, but also Brazil, South Africa, India, Russia.

Beijing and Seoul provide good vantage points to reflect on the huge changes sweeping our world: the rise of new great powers, the shifting balance of economic power and the tensions of globalisation.

This interconnected world, the world of restless markets so well represented in this room here tonight, is creating huge new opportunities for the countries that are able to seize them.

But this very same interconnectedness is creating new and more diverse threats to our security. The device found on a plane at the East Midlands airport, which we now know was a viable and dangerous bomb, originated in Yemen and was carried to the UAE, to Germany and to Britain en route to America.

Today threats originating in one part of the world become threats in all parts of the world.

As you are all too aware in the City, the threat from cyber attacks has increased exponentially over the last decade with last year alone accounting for more than half of all malicious software threats that have ever been identified.

All of this shows how fast our world is changing, how much Britain's interests depend on the interests of others and why we need to maintain a global foreign policy, because our national interests are affected more than ever by events well beyond our shores.

Our national interest is easily defined. It is to ensure our future prosperity and keep our country safe in the years ahead. The key question is how do we best advance this national interest when the threats and opportunities are evolving so fast before our very eyes?

Now there are some who say that Britain is embarked on an inevitable path of decline. That the rise of new economic powers is the end of Britain's influence in the world. That we are in some vast zero-sum game in which we are bound to lose out. That our claim to the status of a major military power is now a sham and that we should be pulling back from our military engagements.

I want to take this argument head on. Britain remains a great economic power. Show me a City in the world with stronger credentials than the City of London. Show me another gathering with the same line-up of financial, legal, accounting, communications and other professional expertise.

You know even better than me, Britain is a great trading force in the world.

Yes, our economy has needed urgent attention. The coalition government inherited the largest deficit in our peacetime history and no credible plan to get a grip of it. But whenever I meet foreign leaders, they do not see a Britain shuffling apologetically off the world stage.

On the contrary, they respect our determination to get our economic house in order so that we can remain masters of our nation's destiny. They can see the immense advantages of doing business with Britain.

We're already ranked first in Europe for ease of doing business. And we intend to become first in the world. We are cutting our corporation tax to 24 per cent, the lowest in the G7, creating one of the most competitive corporate tax regimes in the G20, cutting the time it takes to set up a new business, and scrapping the needless red tape and excessive regulation that has held us back for too long.

There is no reason why the rise of new economic powers should lead to a loss of British influence in the world. And neither is there any reason why our military power should be diminished.

We have the fourth largest defence budget in the world and remain one of only a handful of countries with the military, technological and logistical means to deploy serious military force around the world. Our armed forces are respected around the world as among the most effective and professional in the business and on the day after Remembrance Sunday, I know everyone in this room will want to pay tribute to all those who have served and continue to serve our country.

In terms of our role in the world, the truth is that many other countries would envy the cards we hold. Not only the hard power of our military, but our unique inventory of other assets, all of which contribute to our political weight in the world.

Our global language, the intercontinental reach of our time zone, our world-class universities, the cultural impact around the world of the BBC, the British Council and our great museums. A civil service and a diplomatic service which are admired the world over for their professionalism and impartiality.

And there's also the cosmopolitan breadth of our vibrant and tolerant society, and the buccaneering spirit of our expatriate community abroad. One in ten of our citizens live permanently overseas, reflecting our long tradition as an outward-facing nation, with a history of deep engagement around the world, whose instinct to be self-confident and active well beyond our shores is in our DNA.

We sit at the heart of the world's most powerful institutions from the G8 and the G20 to the Commonwealth, NATO and the UN Security Council.

Our centuries-long engagement with all parts of the world has left a rich legacy in the strong communities which add so much to this country. We have a deep and close relationship with America. We are a strong and active member of the EU and gateway to the world's largest single market.

Few countries on earth have this powerful combination of assets, and even fewer have the ability to make the best use of them. What I have seen in my first six months as Prime Minister is a Britain at the centre of all the big discussions.

So I reject the thesis of decline. I firmly believe that this open, networked world plays to Britain's strengths.

But these vast changes in the world mean we constantly have to adapt.

Let me turn to how.

We need to sort out the economy if we are to carry weight in the world. Economic weakness at home translates into political weakness abroad. Economic strength will restore our respect in the world and our national self-confidence. So the faster we can get our domestic house in order, the more substantial and credible our international impact is going to be.

But we also have to be more strategic and hard-headed about how we go about advancing our national interests.

In recent years, we've made too many commitments without the resources to back them up. And we failed to think properly, across government, about what we were getting ourselves into and how we would see it through to success. So in Iraq there was no plan for winning the peace. In Afghanistan we failed to think through properly the implications of the decision to deploy into Helmand Province in the summer of 2006.

As a new government, we should learn the lessons and make changes.

I am not suggesting that we turn the country's entire foreign policy on its head. As Leader of the Opposition, I always made clear to foreign leaders that there was a great deal of common ground between the policies of the government and the opposition.

We have an active foreign policy that is staunch in its support for democracy and human rights – as we have been, for example, in arguing for the release of Aung San Suu Kyi and the rights of the Burmese people. Wasn't it a fantastic sight on our television screens over the weekend to see that wonderful woman free? We want a foreign policy that is vigorous in its efforts to address climate change, which poses such a threat to humanity and which can only be dealt with by nations coming together.

We will continue to build on our special relationship with America. It is not just special, it is crucial, because it is based on solid practical foundations such as our cooperation on defence, counter-terrorism and intelligence.

In other areas, where we believe that Britain's interests require a change of course, we should lose no time in adjusting the national tiller accordingly.

I want to highlight three areas this evening.

First, we must link our economy up with the fastest growing parts of the world, placing our commercial interest at the heart of our foreign policy.

Second, we're taking a more strategic and hard-headed approach to our national security and applying that to our mission in Afghanistan.

Third, we must focus more of our aid budget on building security and preventing conflict.

Let me take these in turn.

First, a more commercial foreign policy. This is not just about making Britain an attractive place to invest, it's about selling Britain to the world, too. Some people think it is somehow grubby to mix money and diplomacy. I say: when it is harder than ever for this country to earn a living, we need to mobilise all the resources we can.

Today we trade more with the Netherlands than with Brazil, Russia, India, China and Turkey combined. Of course our ties with the Netherlands are important – indeed the Deputy Prime Minister has been there today to promote new UK–Dutch business partnerships.

But this statistic just shows we are not making nearly enough of the opportunities out there.

That's why one of the first visits I made as Prime Minister was to India. It's the second fastest growing major economy in the world. We already have unique ties of history, culture, people and language. And extending and deepening our relations with that country is a huge foreign policy priority for us.

I have also been to Turkey, which is growing at 11 per cent this year, and just last week I took one of the biggest and most high-powered delegations in our country's history to China.

Next year I plan to visit Brazil and Russia.

We are also rebuilding our relationships with countries in the Gulf. They feel strong links with Britain but have also felt sidelined in recent years. I'm delighted that Her Majesty the Queen will visit the UAE and Oman next week. And I will be making my own visit early next year.

But this isn't just about what the monarch, ministers or I do. It's about what our ambassadors, diplomats and hard-working staff at UKTI [UK Trade and Investment] do, day in and day out, in every country of the world. I have told them: every time anyone representing Britain meets a foreign counterpart, I want them walking into that room armed with a list of things they are there to deliver for our country.

When it comes to the European Union, we've shown in recent months how we are constructive and firm partners, using our membership of the EU to defend and advance UK interests. This needs to start with the Budget, which is why I led efforts to block the European Parliament's call for a 6 per cent rise and I have got the European Union, for the first time, to accept that its Budget should reflect what member states are having to do to their own budgets.

Britain will be a cheerleader for the continued enlargement of the EU, which has already brought huge benefits to Britain. And I can promise you this: we will stand up, at each and every turn, for our financial services industry and the City of London. London is Europe's pre-eminent financial centre. With this government, I am determined it will remain so.

Second, bringing a more strategic approach to defending our national security.

We set up for the first time a National Security Council which met on the first day of the government. And it has met on a weekly basis since then. Foreign policy, defence policy, domestic policy, development policy – all the decision-makers not off pursuing disparate missions in different departments but sitting round a table together asking what is best for Britain and working out how we can gear up the government machine to deliver it.

Our first priority was to set a clear direction for our military and civilian mission in Afghanistan. The fact remains that we're still the second largest contributor to the NATO-led force, with 10,000 troops there, most of them in the most difficult part of the country.

We are not there to build a perfect democracy, still less a model society. We are there to help Afghans take control of their security and ensure that al Qaeda can never again pose a threat to us from Afghan soil. A hard-headed, time-limited approach based squarely on the national interest.

In August, we transferred British Forces out of Sangin to enable them to concentrate in greater numbers in Central Helmand where the bulk of the population live and share the burden more sensibly with US Forces across the province as a whole.

I have said that our combat forces will be out of Afghanistan by 2015. And this week's NATO Summit in Lisbon is set to mark the starting point for passing responsibility for security progressively to Afghan forces.

We've also concluded a truly strategic review of all aspects of security and defence. This was long overdue: it has been twelve years and four wars since the last defence review.

We started with a detailed audit of our national security. We took a clear view of the risks we faced and we set priorities including a new focus on meeting unconventional threats from terrorism and cyber attack. We then took a detailed look at the capabilities we will need to deal with tomorrow's threats.

Yes we made tough choices. We had to, given the budgetary mess we inherited.

But we have ensured that our magnificent armed forces will always have the kit they need for the threats they face, whether today in Afghanistan or in the world of 2020. We will be one of the few countries able to deploy a fully-equipped brigade-sized force anywhere in the world.

With the Joint Strike Fighter and Typhoon, the Royal Air Force will have the most capable combat aircraft money can buy, backed by a new fleet of tankers and transport aircraft.

The Royal Navy will have a new operational aircraft carrier, new Type 45 destroyers and seven new nuclear-powered hunter killer submarines, the most advanced in the world. And we will renew Trident, our ultimate insurance policy in an age of uncertainty.

My determination is that Britain will have some of the most modern and most flexible armed forces in the world. And our historic defence treaty with France will ensure that both nations can make the most of their military assets and save precious resources.

But our security does not depend on our military forces alone. That's why we have also given priority to investment in our counter-terrorism capacity, new programmes to improve our resilience against cyber attack, and ensuring that our world-leading intelligence agencies are able to maintain their brilliant work in disrupting threats and keeping our country safe, in accordance with the guidelines the government has recently published.

Britain's moral authority in the world depends on showing that we uphold our values.

And there's one more area where, despite the economic pressures we face, this new government has been determined to hold firm: our commitment to spend 0.7 per cent of our GDP on aid by 2013. We will meet that target and we will do so for good reasons.

Our aid programme, like the activities of the myriad of charitable aid organisations, literally saves lives. It helps prevent conflict, which is why we have doubled the amount of our aid budget that is spent on security programmes in countries like Pakistan and Somalia.

And for millions of people our aid programme is the most visible example of Britain's global reach. It is a powerful instrument of our foreign policy and profoundly in our national interest.

That theme – pursuit of our national interest – has been at the heart of everything I have said this evening.

Our foreign policy is one of hard-headed internationalism. More commercial in enabling Britain to earn its way in the world, more strategic in its focus on meeting the new and emerging threats to our national security, and firmly committed to upholding our values and defending Britain's moral authority even in the most difficult of circumstances.

Above all, our foreign policy is more hard-headed in this respect: it will focus like a laser on defending and advancing Britain's national interest.

That concept of national interest is of course as old as our nation itself and I am conscious of the many Prime Ministers who have stood here before me and set out Britain's national interest as they saw it.

Many of them have confronted circumstances more perilous than those which face Britain today. But perhaps few will have dealt with a world which is changing so fast. From Beijing to Seoul, from Washington to San Paolo, leaders must work out what it all means for their countries and where their national interest lies.

When some people look at the world today they are quick to prophesy dark times ahead; difficulties for Britain.

Our foreign policy runs counter to that pessimism.

We have the resources – commercial, military and cultural – to remain a major player in the world. We have the relationships – with the most established powers and the fastest-growing nations – that will benefit our economy. And we have the values – national values that swept slavery from the seas, that stood up to both fascism and communism and that helped to spread democracy and human rights around the planet – that will drive us to do good around the world.

With these strengths in our armoury we can drive our prosperity, we can increase our security, we can maintain our integrity.

We are choosing ambition. Far from shrinking back, Britain is reaching out. And far from looking back starry-eyed on a glorious past, this country can look forward clear-eyed to a great future.

MICHAEL BEAR

'WE NOW LIVE IN A NEW WORLD'

—

REMARKS AT THE LORD MAYOR'S DINNER FOR BANKERS AND MERCHANTS

LONDON, UNITED KINGDOM, 15 JUNE 2011

K*nown for his leadership in the revitalisation and development of Spitalfields Market in London, Michael Bear was the 683rd Lord Mayor of London from 2010–2011. In this speech, given in the presence of the Chancellor of the Exchequer and the Governor of the Bank of England, the Lord Mayor outlines the need for the British government to protect and promote the City of London in this new age of austerity. Bear reminds the audience that the City is the source of much taxation revenue and employment in the UK, as well as a financial centre for the European Union and the world. He warns that efforts to over-regulate or over-tax the City will be counter-productive, thwarting plans to address debt or curb government spending. Rather, the City should become more attractive to emerging markets. For Bear, as for the Prime Minister, growth is the way out of the UK's financial troubles. The Lord Mayor also argues that the financial market must act responsibly, self-regulating before the coalition government or the European Union are forced to act to prevent further financial difficulties. There is a vision of London as the world's premier financial centre. The City can provide national and global leadership. It must have the courage and boldness to create the wealth necessary to pay for government services and reduce debt in the UK and abroad.*

Michael Bear was knighted in the New Year's Honours List in 2012 for his work as Lord Mayor, his efforts at urban revitalisation, and for his charitable activities.

—

I want to welcome all of you to Mansion House this evening, a house of history in a city of history. Sir Peter Hall, in his monumental study of *Cities in Civilisation* called London the 'quintessential city', the city by which all others are measured.

For over 2,000 years, London, in his words, has been a place where 'the flames of creativity burn bright'. In other words, cities are created and maintained by choices and visions.

London's greatness is a product of choices made over two millennia.

Although his book was published in 1998, Sir Peter predicted the stunning growth of banking in the last thirteen years, and the risks, and temptations, inherent in that growth.

He foresaw that the City's banking would become increasingly international.

That the strength of wealth generation in London would act as a gravitational pull for investment from other countries.

And that the wealth creation in London would ripple out to the entire United Kingdom and the European Union.

But he also saw that the very structure of the banking environment would allow risk-taking that might exceed prudential practices.

Well, he was right. And we have witnessed the results: London is the premier financial centre of the world.

The wealth generated since 1998 has been epic. The good years were great.

But the international nature of banking and finance, coupled with risk-taking here and abroad, also contributed to the recent recession.

Decisions and choices made here, and elsewhere, are not contained by borders or boundaries. Banking has become the lifeblood of our global village, transcending nations or regional unions.

So, because of choices made here and around the world, recession became inevitable.

Now we live in an age of austerity.

We know what that means. For some, it is a blame-game. There is in some quarters a determination for punitive regulation, retribution, and revenge. And part of our contemporary dialogue is unfortunate: bank bashing, finger-pointing, demonisation, threats of crippling legislation, and predictions of shocking changes in the financial landscape.

For others, the recession has been a wake-up call. We now live in a new world.

Economic turbulence created new ways of financing projects, better ways of doing business.

We know that there are numerous ways to fund growth, including venture capital and equity markets. There are new opportunities, new goals, a new tone, new visions, and new ideas.

A restart. A look to the future.

Chancellor, I want to thank you for helping to change the tenor of the discussion on banking reform.

I also want to thank the coalition government for its careful and measured approach in tackling the recession.

In particular, I want to praise the reduction in the corporate tax rate. This was a sound move to make London even more competitive than its rivals.

And we have to do more. In my view, this is a decisive moment in our economic history right now. The choices we make will shape our future.

This is a time for choice … choices that are wise and prudential. And these choices must be made with vision, a vision of a future that offers strong stability and steady growth, where the markets are less volatile and the foundations secure.

Fear and uncertainty are major reasons why liquidity remains on the sidelines. And that fear comes from uncertainty about the future regulatory climate.

Perspective is necessary. There have been lean years. But the City has weathered them better than most financial centres.

For our generation, this was a moment of truth. We learned again the value of responsibility, prudent decision-making, accountability, transparency, and due diligence. And we have re-affirmed the importance of best practices.

We have witnessed the short-sightedness of excessive risk.

Economic stewardship has been re-enforced. Fiduciary duties have been re-emphasised.

And we can see the City taking self-corrective actions. There has also been profound cooperation between the banks and the government, such as Project Merlin, which will help generate liquidity, especially for small businesses with sound business plans. We all know that the City must remain competitive internationally. That is important to everyone in the United Kingdom … citizens, investors, shareholders, and the coalition government.

The City makes a huge contribution to the United Kingdom: 10 per cent of GDP, £53.4 billion into the Exchequer, 300,000 jobs in the City of London, and another three quarters of a million across the country.

Globally, foreign direct investment in the United Kingdom was valued at over £1 trillion in 2010. And the investment and business that comes here arrives and thrives at perhaps the safest and most prosperous destination in the world.

And we must not forget that European firms operating in the City employ thousands of people. Fund managers have billions of Euros under management for major European public and private sector utilities.

So pensioners and savers right across the continent benefit from a strong, successful and profitable City.

The City is a profound economic asset for the European Union.

Chancellor, like all of us, I know you have read the interim report from the Vickers Commission very carefully.

And we look forward to hearing your views on retail banking, capital rates and ringfencing, trailed somewhat in the media.

It is in all our interests to help banks stay competitive. And operate in a globally equivalent – not super-equivalent – regulatory environment.

Keeping costs down is also imperative.

Because increased costs for the banking industry will ripple out to harm the UK economy in countless ways, eliminating jobs and opportunities.

And we must also seize the enormous opportunities available right now. The Prime Minister has asked the City to engage with emerging markets. I agree.

Over the next five years, emerging economies are expected to account for over 50 per cent of global growth, but only 13 per cent of the increase in net global public debt.

Here at home, investment in emerging markets will raise revenues and create jobs … possibly even enable the UK to balance our national budget and move from an age of austerity to one of prosperity.

But there is more that will happen. Our investment in emerging markets will lift millions of people … possibly billions … out of poverty.

In the past decade, Africa's real GDP growth was just under 5 per cent. Its total GDP puts it on par with Brazil or Russia.

And we have witnessed stunning growth in China. Between 2008 and 2015, 75 million urban households will be joining the ranks of the middle class. China has become the world's second biggest economy.

And we need to work with countries experiencing a mass migration to cities. Already more than half of the world's population lives in cities. By 2050, that figure will rise to more than 70 per cent.

This isn't just about megacities like Mexico City or Mumbai. Four hundred midsize cities – places like Chennai and Hangzhou – will produce 40 per cent of the world's growth over the next fifteen years.

Chancellor, I agree with the Prime Minister and the Foreign Secretary … we must be involved in these markets. Britain's future may depend on it. The City's banks have to be at the forefront of this global growth. And there is enormous competition. Even banks in emerging markets are often moving forward with lightning speed to become more efficient, innovative, and cutting-edge.

London has always been known as a city that reaches out to the world. That must be as true now as never before.

I began by talking about choices. Our choices have defined us.

One choice, perhaps the major reason for London's influence for the past four centuries, has been to create a powerful, positive climate for the banking industry.

Although the City is far more than just banking, banking and the City are inextricably linked.

Britain's future will be determined by the choices we make about Britain's banks. Banks that in the long run will do best in the private sector.

And, Chancellor, we – the City and the City's banks – want to work with you for a more prosperous Great Britain.

GEORGE OSBORNE

'THE BRITISH DILEMMA'

—

REMARKS AT THE LORD MAYOR'S DINNER
FOR BANKERS AND MERCHANTS

LONDON, UNITED KINGDOM, 15 JUNE 2011

George Osborne was elected to Parliament in 2001, representing Tatton for the Conservative Party. David Cameron appointed him as Chancellor of the Exchequer in 2010. Traditionally, the Lord Mayor's Dinner for Bankers and Merchants has been the occasion for the Chancellor to explain the government's economic policies.

This speech was given the same night as the previous set of remarks. Osborne outlines the coalition government's approach to the financial crisis in the United Kingdom and in Europe. This speech delivered startling, unmistakable wording on policy, as well as the announcement that Northern Rock, a bank placed under government control as part of the preceding Labour government's financial bailout, would return to the private sector.

The speech generated massive press coverage and was reproduced in full in several newspapers and Internet sites. It sent out powerful ripple effects throughout the economy and the financial markets. Sir Mervyn King, Governor of the Bank of England, also spoke at the dinner. The combined speeches by the Lord Mayor, the Chancellor of the Exchequer, and the Governor of the Bank of England made for a memorable evening. The speeches were analysed and parsed for weeks. The structure of the paragraphs is my own, linking stand-alone lines together.

—

Lord Mayor, a year ago, standing here just five weeks after the government had come to office, I spoke about the financial crisis and I quoted what Winston Churchill had said in this very room in the middle of the war.

'Now this is not the end. It is not even the beginning of the end. But it is, perhaps, the end of the beginning.'

I believe that sentiment of cautious optimism has been borne out by events in the twelve months since then. The British economy is recovering. Output is growing. The necessary rebalancing of the economy, away from debt-fuelled consumption towards investment and exports, has gained momentum. Half a million new private sector jobs have been created, the second highest rate of net job creation in the whole G7. Today's unemployment figures showed a fall of 88,000 – the fastest pace for more than a decade. Our budget deficit is now falling from its record highs. Stability has returned. Britain is on the mend.

But it is taking time. External shocks have made that recovery more difficult.

- The dramatic and debilitating rise in the world's oil price – up almost 60 per cent since last June.
- The terrible Japanese earthquake and the impact on the supply chain.
- The ongoing crisis in the Eurozone, our largest market for British goods and services.
- The softness in the US economy.

Across the world, choppy economic waters have become choppier still.

But the truth is this. Even without these substantial headwinds, the journey the British economy has to travel would be a hard one. As I said at the time of the Autumn Forecast last November: 'recovery was always going to be more challenging than after previous recessions'. For we are seeing the unwinding of debts built up over an entire decade. Of all the major economies in the world, Britain's was the most over-borrowed. Our families were more in debt than any other in the G7. Our house price bubble was bigger than America's. Our government deficit higher than that of Greece. And the balance sheets of our banks went from around 300 per cent of GDP in 1998 to a staggering 550 per cent just a decade later. Now those bank balance sheets are shrinking. Not just because of new rules from regulators. But because the markets themselves demand it. So money and credit growth remain weak. And that acts as a powerful drag anchor on recovery.

Here is a striking fact about the British economy over the last six quarters since the recession ended – a fact little understood but crucial to understanding our challenge. For five out of those six quarters, the financial sector has continued to contract. While our economy as a whole has grown by 2.5 per cent, the financial sector has shrunk by 4 per cent. Take the financial sector out of the equation, and economic growth in the rest of the economy during the recovery has actually been above its average rate of the last two decades. Put the financial sector into the equation, and economic growth has been below trend. Our banking system fuelled the boom. Now it is slowing the recovery from the bust.

That might surprise you. Look around the City today, and activity is growing. The investment banks are hiring again – and they're hiring here in London. There are some 25,000 more jobs in the Square Mile than a year ago. I've seen it – I've been at the openings of new headquarters and new buildings. Funds are out there investing. Law firms, accountants and insurance are busy. And this year, for all the doomsayers who warn of decline, London has topped the global league table of financial centres.

We're officially the number one place to do business – so instead of talking ourselves down, let's agree to go around the world and say so.

Of course, we've got to stay in pole position. That's why, even in these straitened times, we've committed to the multi-billion-pound Crossrail link – the greatest urban infrastructure investment in the Western world today. We've changed our taxation of overseas earnings, so that multinationals are moving back to Britain instead of leaving it. I've made it clear that the 50 pence tax rate I inherited must only be temporary – not permanent, as some politicians now propose. And this week we're publishing plans that end the uncertainty over tax residence rules and the treatment of non-domiciles, and set out new plans to encourage their investments.

All the activity and wealth creation you see in the City today is very welcome. But sadly it does not compensate for the many billions of pounds being shed from the balance sheets of our banks.

Economists like Ken Rogoff and Carmen Reinhart warned us that this would be the case – that recoveries from recessions with a financial crisis are always slower than recoveries from other less severe recessions.

How can government respond? For a start, we have to avoid that now well-trodden path from banking crisis to sovereign debt crisis. Unsustainable borrowing in our banks must not lead to unsustainable borrowing by the government. I promised you a year ago that we would take conscious and determined action. And we have. The benefits are there to see. In a world where so many countries are seeing their credit ratings put on negative outlook or downgraded, our country's triple-A rating has come off negative outlook and been affirmed. We have a deficit larger than Portugal, but virtually the same interest rates as Germany. That is the huge stimulus our plan delivers to our economy. And abandoning our deficit reduction plan would take that stimulus away. That was the IMF's verdict last week. In the recovery from a banking crisis, stability and low market rates are precious, hard-won achievements. And we will do nothing to undermine them. Instead, we should try to manage the nature and pace of the deleveraging. A large part of the rapid build-up of borrowing within our banking sector consisted of lending from one part of the financial system to another. That can be reduced without directly impacting the real economy, even if it reduces the measured contribution of banking to GDP.

What is crucial is that this inevitable process of deleveraging does not strangle the supply of credit to businesses and families who need it. We are taking action to ensure this doesn't happen. We are resolving regulatory uncertainty and encouraging new capital investment in our banking system, so that deleveraging is not only achieved through smaller balance sheets. In the G20 and the Basel Committee, Britain has successfully argued for higher capital and liquidity standards, but crucially for standards that are phased in over long time periods. And the new Financial Policy Committee has been mandated to take an overview of our financial system, and watch that our own regulators do not act in a pro-cyclical way. We have struck the Merlin deal with the banks to prevent small and medium-sized businesses becoming the innocent victims of shrinking balance sheets. I very much welcome the commitments from the BBA's [British Bankers' Association] taskforce and the new Business Growth Fund that is now investing in Britain's businesses. But the banks should also be in no doubt that I will use every tool available to me to hold them to the published lending commitments they made.

Lord Mayor, the government can also actively help to rebalance our economy by being unequivocally pro-business and pro-enterprise. Our Plan for Growth set out a new wave of supply-side reforms to restore Britain's competitiveness. We're investing in apprenticeships, cutting employment tribunal costs, reforming pensions and anti-growth planning rules, reducing regulation, creating a Green Investment Bank, reforming the welfare system and taking low paid people out of tax. And we're actively pursuing the lowest business tax rates of any major Western economy – a 5 per cent reduction in the rate of corporation tax in the space of just four years.

From Shanghai to Seattle, investors can see that Britain is open for business. So while the gradual unwinding of the debts built up in the boom creates powerful headwinds, all of this demonstrates that we are not powerless to respond.

But the legacy of the financial crisis does confront us with a very simple dilemma – what you might call 'the British Dilemma'. As a global financial centre that generates hundreds of thousands of jobs, a successful banking and financial services industry is clearly in our national economic interests. But we cannot afford to let it pose a risk to the stability and prosperity of the nation's entire economy. We should strive for global success in financial services, but that success should not come at an unacceptably high price. We should be clear that we want Britain to be the home of some of the world's leading banks, but those banks cannot be underwritten by the British taxpayer.

I said here last year that the uncertainty hanging over your industry was causing real damage; that it couldn't be resolved overnight, but that I owed you a process that would lead to a conclusion. And one year on, I believe we are much closer to a consensus on how we can achieve both successful, competitive financial services and a healthy, balanced economy.

That consensus is about:

- What is the right culture of regulation;
- How the international rules apply;
- And where successful banks fit in.

First, the culture of regulation. The failure of the tripartite system was not a series of unfortunate accidents – it was hard-wired into its design. The decision to divide the responsibility for assessing systemic financial risks from the responsibility for applying that assessment to particular financial institutions created a world in which no one was in charge. Yet at the same time the system required endless box ticking and costly processes. We had the worst of both worlds.

This new government proposes, therefore, a completely new culture of regulation. Tomorrow we publish our White Paper and the detailed draft legislation. A permanent Financial Policy Committee [FPC] will be established inside the Bank of England. Its remit will be set by Parliament and refined by the Chancellor on an annual basis. And its job will be to monitor overall risks in the financial system, identify bubbles as they develop, spot dangerous inter-connections and deploy new tools to deal with excessive levels of leverage before it is too late. This has never been done before. The Committee will work alongside a new Prudential Regulation Authority that will also sit in the Bank of England. This will assess the safety and soundness of individual firms.

I've heard your argument that insurance companies face different risks, so I can announce that we will set a specific statutory objective for them. The operation of markets, and the protection of consumers, will be the responsibility of a new Financial Conduct Authority. I am delighted that Martin Wheatley, who brings valuable experience as Hong Kong's market regulator, will be the new CEO. Here too we've listened to representations, and I confirm tonight that as well as protecting consumer interests, the Financial Conduct Authority will have a new primary duty to promote competition.

If the result of all these changes is simply that some brass plates on some doors have changed, then we will have failed. We don't undertake the institutional change for the sake of it. We do it to change the culture. We want to move away from the tick-box mentality of the current system, where there's no shortage of costly regulation but too little room for invaluable judgement. In its place we will have clear lines of accountability and the space for regulators to exercise judgement. You will have the freedom to innovate, grow your businesses, and compete in the world. You will be constrained if you put taxpayers or consumers at undue risk. A new culture of regulation is the first step towards solving the British Dilemma.

But getting supervision right in one country is not enough. As the world's leading financial centre, we are particularly exposed to financial instability elsewhere in the world. And you are all exposed to fierce overseas competition. For both these reasons, global standards are strongly in our national interest. So we want to see the full implementation of the new Basel standards, right around the world, including here in the European Union. It's vital that those European rules give national regulators the discretion to add to the Basel requirements when national circumstances require it. This is what the de Larosière Committee themselves recommended. It would help the FPC do their job. We need European coordination, to enforce common rules in a single market, and it's good news that the headquarters of the new European Banking Authority is here in London. We support their efforts to make this year's stress tests more credible than last year's.

But we will always fight hard against badly thought-through European regulation that undermines Europe as a location for wholesale finance, or London's role as this continent's pre-eminent global centre for it. That's a fight we won on the regulation of hedge funds, and we're still fighting on EMIR, the new derivatives regulation. Pay in the financial services sector should also be regulated internationally, to avoid a race to excess. Britain now has world-beating standards of transparency. The Financial Stability Board have come up with good principles and must now focus on their consistent implementation.

So, Lord Mayor, these are the first two steps towards solving the British Dilemma: A new culture of regulation that judges unacceptable risks, while creating the space for innovation and commercial success. And an agreed set of international rules that makes the global financial system safer and protects us from competitive arbitrage by other financial centres.

But history teaches us that that risk can never be reduced to zero. We cannot hope to abolish boom and bust. So the British Dilemma will remain as long as taxpayers are first on the hook if things do go wrong.

When this government came to office there was no agreement in Britain about how this 'too-big-to-fail' problem should be addressed. Indeed, I've sat as a guest at this very dinner in years past listening as one speech from this lectern was completely contradicted by the speech that followed. That's why when I first spoke here, I announced the names of five highly respected individuals whose job it would be to listen to all sides of the argument, propose a solution and help bring an end to the uncertainty. The Independent Commission on Banking has now published its Interim Report and I would like to pay tribute to Sir John Vickers and his fellow commissioners for the excellent job they have done. It has commanded respect at home and huge interest abroad. The Independent Commission on Banking has put forward two particularly important proposals. Bail-in instead of bail-out – so that private investors, not taxpayers, bear the losses if things go wrong. And a ring-fence around better capitalised high street banks to make them safer, and to protect their vital services to the economy if things go wrong.

Today I have told the Commission that the Government endorses both these proposals in principle.

Of course, the commissioners are still consulting and preparing their final report – and I won't pre-empt their conclusions. We will judge their final proposals in practice against the following conditions:

- All banks should be allowed to fail safely without affecting vital banking services;
- Without imposing costs on the taxpayer;
- In a manner applicable across our diverse sector;
- And consistent with EU and international law.

In line with the interim report, we agree with the need for further capital requirements on systemically important banks, but I agree with the Commission that outside the ring-fence this is best done internationally. I also strongly welcome the Commission's proposal on increasing competition in retail banking. For healthy competition is a powerful defender of consumers' interests.

Lord Mayor, we will make these changes to banking to protect taxpayers in the future. But we still have to clear up the mess of the past. Taxpayers today own a large part of the banking system, and underwrite guarantees to parts of the rest. It's time we started to plan our exit. So I've opened the Credit Guarantee Scheme to early redemption. I'm pleased that banks are taking up the opportunity and they are ahead of schedule in repaying the Bank of England's special liquidity support. This is a sign of confidence in our banking system. And I remind everyone with deposits that we have increased the level of deposit insurance to 100 per cent for sums up to £85,000 and we have made clear that there is no implicit taxpayer guarantee for sums above that level.

Once all these other forms of subsidy are removed, our direct shareholdings in banks still remain. It will take some time – possibly several years – before we can sell them all.

But we can start that process. I can announce tonight that on behalf of you the British taxpayer, I have decided to put Northern Rock up for sale. Images of the queues outside Northern Rock branches were a symbol of all that went wrong, and its chaotic collapse did great damage to Britain's international reputation. Its return now to the private sector would help to rebuild that reputation. It would be a sign of confidence and could increase competition in high street banking. We could start to get at least some of our money back. The sale process will be open and transparent and in line with state aid rules. Any interested parties can bid for it, including mutuals, which this government is actively committed to promoting. We will continue to own Northern Rock Asset Management, the separate 'bad bank', whose assets are being run down over time. This does not mean that other options to return Northern Rock to the private sector have been ruled out. But the independent advice I have received is that a sale process is likely to generate substantially the best value for the taxpayer and should be explored as a first option. And it would be a very important first step in getting the British taxpayer out of the business of owning banks – and a sign of confidence in the industry.

Lord Mayor, last year I came here with debates raging about all these questions of regulation and the future of banking. I was not the cause of them – but I told you that it was my job to resolve them. And I said that our goal should be a new settlement between our financial system and the British people. A new settlement where the City is able to be the leading financial centre in the world, without putting at risk the entire economy. I believe we are now within touching distance of that new settlement. If we achieve it, then we will have answered the British Dilemma – and put our country on the path to prosperity. I want the City of London to be a thriving centre of enterprise, more interested in serving its customers than in what government might do to it next. Resolving the British Dilemma is the way to do that.

Thank you.

BEN BERNANKE

'THIS ECONOMIC HEALING WILL TAKE A WHILE'

—

REMARKS AT THE FEDERAL RESERVE
BANK OF KANSAS CITY, ECONOMIC SYMPOSIUM

JACKSON HOLE, WYOMING, 26 AUGUST 2011

Ben Bernanke is currently the Chairman of the United States Federal Reserve Board, a position held since 2006. Prior to that he was Chairman of the President's Council of Economic Advisors from 2005–2006. Earlier he was a member of the Board of Governors of the Federal Reserve System from 2002–2005. Bernanke's post is non-partisan. He directs the banking system in the United States. The Board also sets interest rates and monetary policy, with the intention of stabilising prices and controlling inflation, allowing for maximum employment. Without exaggeration, Bernanke is the leading voice in American economics and finance. His may be the most powerful financial voice in the world.

In this speech he addresses the American and global financial crisis, offering short- and long-term perspectives on the scope and direction of its resolution. This speech is a comprehensive statement, a summary of where we are and where the world financial markets may be going. It should be viewed in conjunction with other speeches in this volume by Putin, Jackson, Paulson, Cameron, Bear, Sarkozy and Osborne.

—

Good morning. As always, thanks are due to the Federal Reserve Bank of Kansas City for organising this conference. This year's topic, long-term economic growth, is indeed pertinent – as has so often been the case at this symposium in past years. In particular, the financial crisis and the subsequent slow recovery have caused some to question whether the United States, notwithstanding its long-term record of vigorous economic growth, might not now be facing a prolonged period of stagnation, regardless of its public policy choices. Might not the very slow pace of economic expansion of the past few years, not only in the United States but also in a number of other advanced economies, morph into something far more long-lasting?

I can certainly appreciate these concerns and am fully aware of the challenges that we face in restoring economic and financial conditions conducive to healthy growth, some of which I will comment on today. With respect to longer-run prospects, however, my own view is more optimistic. As I will discuss, although important problems certainly exist, the growth fundamentals of the United States do not appear to have been permanently altered by the shocks of the past four years. It may take some time, but we can reasonably expect to see a return to growth rates and employment levels consistent with those underlying fundamentals. In the interim, however, the challenges for US economic policy-makers are twofold: first, to help our economy further recover from the crisis and the ensuing recession, and second, to do so in a way that will allow the economy to realise its longer-term growth potential. Economic policies should be evaluated in light of both of those objectives.

This morning I will offer some thoughts on why the pace of recovery in the United States has, for the most part, proved disappointing thus far, and I will discuss the Federal Reserve's policy response. I will then turn briefly to the longer-term prospects of our economy and the need for our country's economic policies to be effective from both a shorter-term and longer-term perspective.

In discussing the prospects for the economy and for policy in the near term, it bears recalling briefly how we got here. The financial crisis that gripped global markets in 2008 and 2009 was more severe than any since the Great Depression. Economic policy-makers around the world saw the mounting risks of a global financial meltdown in the fall of 2008 and understood the extraordinarily dire economic consequences that such an event could have. As I have described in previous remarks at this forum, governments and central banks worked forcefully and in close coordination to avert the looming collapse. The actions to stabilise the financial system were accompanied, both in the United States and abroad, by substantial monetary and fiscal stimulus. But notwithstanding these strong and concerted efforts, severe damage to the global economy could not be avoided. The freezing of credit, the sharp drops in asset prices, dysfunction in financial markets, and the resulting blows to confidence sent global production and trade into free fall in late 2008 and early 2009.

We meet here today almost exactly three years since the beginning of the most intense phase of the financial crisis and a bit more than two years since the National Bureau of Economic Research's date for the start of the economic recovery. Where do we stand?

There have been some positive developments over the past few years, particularly when considered in the light of economic prospects as viewed at the depth of the crisis. Overall, the global economy has seen significant growth, led by the emerging-market economies. In the United States, a cyclical recovery, though a modest one by historical standards, is in its ninth quarter. In the financial sphere, the US banking system is generally much healthier now, with banks holding substantially more capital. Credit availability from banks has improved, though it remains tight in categories – such as small business lending – in which the balance sheets of potential borrowers remain impaired. Companies with access to the public bond markets have had no difficulty obtaining credit on favourable terms. Importantly, structural reform is moving forward in the financial sector, with ambitious domestic and international efforts under way to enhance the capital and liquidity of banks, especially the most systemically important banks; to improve risk management and transparency; to strengthen market infrastructure; and to introduce a more systemic, or macroprudential, approach to financial regulation and supervision.

In the broader economy, manufacturing production in the United States has risen nearly 15 per cent since its trough, driven substantially by growth in exports. Indeed, the US trade deficit has been notably lower recently than it was before the crisis, reflecting in part the improved competitiveness of US goods and services. Business investment in equipment and software has continued to expand, and productivity gains in some industries have been impressive, though new data have reduced estimates of overall productivity improvement in recent years. Households also have made some progress in repairing their balance sheets – saving more, borrowing less, and reducing their burdens of interest payments and debt. Commodity prices have come off their highs, which will reduce the cost pressures facing businesses and help increase household purchasing power.

Notwithstanding these more positive developments, however, it is clear that the recovery from the crisis has been much less robust than we had hoped. From the latest comprehensive revisions to the national accounts as well as the most recent estimates of growth in the first half of this year, we have learned that the recession was even deeper and the recovery even weaker than we had thought; indeed, aggregate output in the United States still has not returned to the level that it attained before the crisis. Importantly, economic growth has for the most part been at rates insufficient to achieve sustained reductions in unemployment, which has recently been fluctuating a bit above 9 per cent. Temporary factors, including the effects of the run-up in commodity prices on consumer and business budgets and the effect of the Japanese disaster on global supply chains and production, were part of the reason for the weak performance of the economy in the first half of 2011; accordingly, growth in the second half looks likely to improve as their influence recedes. However, the incoming data suggest that other, more persistent factors also have been at work.

Why has the recovery from the crisis been so slow and erratic? Historically, recessions have typically sowed the seeds of their own recoveries as reduced spending on investment, housing, and consumer durables generates pent-up demand. As the business cycle bottoms out and confidence returns, this pent-up demand, often augmented by the effects of stimulative monetary and fiscal policies, is met through increased production and hiring. Increased production in turn boosts business revenues and household incomes and provides further impetus to business and household spending. Improving income prospects and balance sheets also make households and businesses more creditworthy, and financial institutions become more willing to lend. Normally, these develop-ments create a virtuous circle of rising incomes and profits, more supportive financial and credit conditions, and lower uncertainty, allowing the process of recovery to develop momentum.

These restorative forces are at work today, and they will continue to promote recovery over time. Unfortunately, the recession, besides being extraordinarily severe as well as global in scope, was also unusual in being associated with both a very deep slump in the housing market and a historic financial crisis. These two features of the downturn, individually and in combination, have acted to slow the natural recovery process.

Notably, the housing sector has been a significant driver of recovery from most recessions in the United States since World War II, but this time – with an overhang of distressed and foreclosed properties, tight credit conditions for builders and potential homebuyers, and ongoing concerns by both potential borrowers and lenders about continued house price declines – the rate of new home construction has remained at less than one-third of its pre-crisis level. The low level of construction has implications not only for builders but for providers of a wide range of goods and services related to housing and homebuilding. Moreover, even as tight credit for some borrowers has been one of the factors restraining housing recovery, the weakness of the housing sector has in turn had adverse effects on financial markets and on the flow of credit. For example, the sharp declines in house prices in some areas have left many homeowners 'underwater' on their mortgages, creating financial hardship for households and, through their effects on rates of mortgage delinquency and default, stress for financial institutions as well. Financial pressures on financial institutions and households have contributed, in turn, to greater caution in the extension of credit and to slower growth in consumer spending.

I have already noted the central role of the financial crisis of 2008 and 2009 in sparking the recession. As I also noted, a great deal has been done and is being done to address the causes and effects of the crisis, including a substantial programme of financial reform, and conditions in the US banking system and financial markets have improved significantly overall. Nevertheless, financial stress has been and continues to be a significant drag on the recovery, both here and abroad. Bouts of sharp volatility and risk aversion in markets have recently re-emerged in reaction to concerns about both European sovereign debts and developments related to the US fiscal situation, including the recent downgrade of the US long-term credit rating by one of the major rating agencies and the controversy concerning the raising of the US federal debt ceiling. It is difficult to judge by how much these developments have affected economic activity thus far, but there seems little doubt that they have hurt household and business confidence and that they pose ongoing risks to growth. The Federal Reserve continues to monitor developments in financial markets and institutions closely and is in frequent contact with policy-makers in Europe and elsewhere.

Monetary policy must be responsive to changes in the economy and, in particular, to the outlook for growth and inflation. As I mentioned earlier, the recent data have indicated that economic growth during the first half of this year was considerably slower than the Federal Open Market Committee had been expecting, and that temporary factors can account for only a portion of the economic weakness that we have observed. Consequently, although we expect a moderate recovery to continue and indeed to strengthen over time, the Committee has marked down its outlook for the likely pace of growth over coming quarters. With commodity prices and other import prices moderating and with longer-term inflation expectations remaining stable, we expect inflation to settle, over coming quarters, at levels at or below the rate of 2 per cent, or a bit less, that most Committee participants view as being consistent with our dual mandate.

In light of its current outlook, the Committee recently decided to provide more specific forward guidance about its expectations for the future path of the federal funds rate. In particular, in the statement following our meeting earlier this month, we indicated that economic conditions – including low rates of resource utilisation and a subdued outlook for inflation over the medium run – are likely to warrant exceptionally low levels for the federal funds rate at least through mid-2013. That is, in what the Committee judges to be the most likely scenarios for resource utilisation and inflation in the medium term, the target for the federal funds rate would be held at its current low levels for at least two more years.

In addition to refining our forward guidance, the Federal Reserve has a range of tools that could be used to provide additional monetary stimulus. We discussed the relative merits and costs of such tools at our August meeting. We will continue to consider those and other pertinent issues, including of course economic and financial developments, at our meeting in September, which has been scheduled for two days (the 20th and the 21st) instead of one to allow a fuller discussion. The Committee will continue to assess the economic outlook in light of incoming information and is prepared to employ its tools as appropriate to promote a stronger economic recovery in a context of price stability.

The financial crisis and its aftermath have posed severe challenges around the globe, particularly in the advanced industrial economies. Thus far I have reviewed some of those challenges, offered some diagnoses for the slow economic recovery in the United States, and briefly discussed the policy response by the Federal Reserve. However, this conference is focused on longer-run economic growth, and appropriately so, given the fundamental importance of long-term growth rates in the determination of living standards. In that spirit, let me turn now to a brief discussion of the longer-run prospects for the US economy and the role of economic policy in shaping those prospects.

Notwithstanding the severe difficulties we currently face, I do not expect the long-run growth potential of the US economy to be materially affected by the crisis and the recession if – and I stress if – our country takes the neces-sary steps to secure that outcome. Over the medium term, housing activity will stabilise and begin to grow again, if for no other reason than that ongoing population growth and household formation will ultimately demand it. Good, proactive housing policies could help speed that process. Financial markets and institutions have already made considerable progress toward normalisation, and I anticipate that the financial sector will continue to adapt to ongoing reforms while still performing its vital intermediation functions. Households will continue to strengthen their balance sheets, a process that will be sped up considerably if the recovery accelerates but that will move forward in any case. Businesses will continue to invest in new capital, adopt new technologies, and build on the productivity gains of the past several years. I have confidence that our European colleagues fully appreciate what is at stake in the difficult issues they are now confronting and that, over time, they will take all necessary and appropriate steps to address those issues effectively and comprehensively.

This economic healing will take a while, and there may be setbacks along the way. Moreover, we will need to remain alert to risks to the recovery, including financial risks. However, with one possible exception on which I will elaborate in a moment, the healing process should not leave major scars. Notwithstanding the trauma of the crisis and the recession, the US economy remains the largest in the world, with a highly diverse mix of industries and a degree of inter-national competitiveness that, if anything, has improved in recent years. Our economy retains its traditional advantages of a strong market orientation, a robust entrepreneurial culture, and flexible capital and labour markets. And our country remains a technological leader, with many of the world's leading research universities and the highest spending on research and development of any nation.

Of course, the United States faces many growth challenges. Our population is aging, like those of many other advanced economies, and our society will have to adapt over time to an older workforce. Our K-12 educational system, despite considerable strengths, poorly serves a substantial portion of our population. The costs of health care in the United States are the highest in the world, without fully commensurate results in terms of health outcomes. But all of these long-term issues were well known before the crisis; efforts to address these problems have been ongoing, and these efforts will continue and, I hope, intensify.

The quality of economic policy-making in the United States will heavily influence the nation's longer-term prospects. To allow the economy to grow at its full potential, policy-makers must work to promote macroeconomic and financial stability; adopt effective tax, trade, and regulatory policies; foster the development of a skilled workforce; encourage productive investment, both private and public; and provide appropriate support for research and development and for the adoption of new technologies.

The Federal Reserve has a role in promoting the longer-term performance of the economy. Most importantly, monetary policy that ensures that inflation remains low and stable over time contributes to long-run macroeconomic and financial stability. Low and stable inflation improves the functioning of markets, making them more effective at allocating resources; and it allows households and businesses to plan for the future without having to be unduly concerned with unpredictable movements in the general level of prices. The Federal Reserve also fosters macroeconomic and financial stability in its role as a financial regulator, a monitor of overall financial stability, and a liquidity provider of last resort.

Normally, monetary or fiscal policies aimed primarily at promoting a faster pace of economic recovery in the near term would not be expected to significantly affect the longer-term performance of the economy. However, current circumstances may be an exception to that standard view – the exception to which I alluded earlier. Our economy is suffering today from an extraordinarily high level of long-term unemployment, with nearly half of the unemployed having been out of work for more than six months. Under these unusual circumstances, policies that promote a stronger recovery in the near term may serve longer-term objectives as well. In the short term, putting people back to work reduces the hardships inflicted by difficult economic times and helps ensure that our economy is producing at its full potential rather than leaving productive resources fallow. In the longer term, minimising the duration of unemployment supports a healthy economy by avoiding some of the erosion of skills and loss of attachment to the labour force that is often associated with long-term unemployment.

Notwithstanding this observation, which adds urgency to the need to achieve a cyclical recovery in employment, most of the economic policies that support robust economic growth in the long run are outside the province of the central bank. We have heard a great deal lately about federal fiscal policy in the United States, so I will close with some thoughts on that topic, focusing on the role of fiscal policy in promoting stability and growth.

To achieve economic and financial stability, US fiscal policy must be placed on a sustainable path that ensures that debt relative to national income is at least stable or, preferably, declining over time. As I have emphasised on previous occasions, without significant policy changes, the finances of the federal government will inevitably spiral out of control, risking severe economic and financial damage. The increasing fiscal burden that will be associated with the aging of the population and the ongoing rise in the costs of health care make prompt and decisive action in this area all the more critical.

Although the issue of fiscal sustainability must urgently be addressed, fiscal policy-makers should not, as a consequence, disregard the fragility of the current economic recovery. Fortunately, the two goals of achieving fiscal sustainability – which is the result of responsible policies set in place for the longer term – and avoiding the creation of fiscal headwinds for the current recovery are not incompatible. Acting now to put in place a credible plan for reducing future deficits over the longer term, while being attentive to the implications of fiscal choices for the recovery in the near term, can help serve both objectives.

Fiscal policy-makers can also promote stronger economic performance through the design of tax policies and spending programmes. To the fullest extent possible, our nation's tax and spending policies should increase incentives to work and to save, encourage investments in the skills of our workforce, stimulate private capital formation, promote research and development, and provide necessary public infrastructure. We cannot expect our economy to grow its way out of our fiscal imbalances, but a more productive economy will ease the trade-offs that we face.

Finally, and perhaps most challenging, the country would be well served by a better process for making fiscal decisions. The negotiations that took place over the summer disrupted financial markets and probably the economy as well, and similar events in the future could, over time, seriously jeopardise the willingness of investors around the world to hold US financial assets or to make direct investments in job-creating US businesses. Although details would have to be negotiated, fiscal policy-makers could consider developing a more effective process that sets clear and transparent budget goals, together with budget mechanisms to establish the credibility of those goals. Of course, formal budget goals and mechanisms do not replace the need for fiscal policy-makers to make the difficult choices that are needed to put the country's fiscal house in order, which means that public understanding of and support for the goals of fiscal policy are crucial. Economic policy-makers face a range of difficult decisions, relating to both the short-run and long-run challenges we face. I have no doubt, however, that those challenges can be met, and that the fundamental strengths of our economy will ultimately reassert themselves. The Federal Reserve will certainly do all that it can to help restore high rates of growth and employment in a context of price stability.

DAVID CAMERON

'TO PROTECT BRITAIN'S NATIONAL INTERESTS'

—

STATEMENT ON THE EUROPEAN COUNCIL

HOUSE OF COMMONS, LONDON, UNITED KINGDOM, 12 DECEMBER 2011

David Cameron has been the Prime Minister of the United Kingdom since 2010. During that time, the European Union has confronted a disastrous financial crisis, involving possible default by the governments of Greece and Italy. This crisis comes after earlier problems in Ireland, Spain and Greece, resulting in the creation of a bailout fund and efforts to prop up failing businesses, plunging housing markets with record foreclosures, and debt-ridden governments. The continued existence of the Euro itself is now in question.

Cameron was asked to approve a bailout plan for European countries in trouble, primarily Greece. He vetoed the plan, which would proceed without Great Britain's participation. He explains his actions to the House of Commons. I have structured the paragraphs.

—

With permission, Mr Speaker, I would like to make a statement on last week's European Council.

I went to Brussels with one objective: to protect Britain's national interest. And that is what I did.

Let me refer back to what I said to this House last Wednesday. I made it clear that if the Eurozone countries wanted a treaty involving all twenty-seven members of the European Union we would insist on some safeguards for Britain to protect our own national interests. Some thought what I was asking for was relatively modest. Nevertheless, satisfactory safeguards were not forthcoming and so I didn't agree to the treaty.

Mr Speaker, let me be clear about exactly what happened, what it means for Britain and what I see happening next.

Mr Speaker, let me take the House through the events of last week. At this Council, the Eurozone economies agreed that there should be much tighter fiscal discipline in the Eurozone as part of restoring market confidence.

Mr Speaker, that is something Britain recognises is necessary in a single currency. We want the Eurozone to sort out its problems. This is in Britain's national interest because the crisis in the Eurozone is having a chilling effect on Britain's economy too. So the question at the Council was not whether there should be greater fiscal discipline in the Eurozone, but rather how it should be achieved. There were two possible outcomes. Either a treaty of all twenty-seven countries with proper safeguards for Britain. Or a separate treaty in which Eurozone countries and others would pool their sovereignty on an intergovernmental basis ... with Britain maintaining its position in the Single Market, and in the European Union of twenty-seven members. We went seeking a deal at twenty-seven and I responded to the German and French proposal for treaty change in good faith, genuinely looking to reach an agreement at the level of the whole European Union, with the necessary safeguards for Britain. Those safeguards – on the Single Market and on financial services – were modest, reasonable and relevant.

We were not trying to create an unfair advantage for Britain. London is the leading centre for financial services in the world. And this sector employs 100,000 in Birmingham, and a further 150,000 in Scotland. It supports the rest of the economy in Britain and more widely in Europe. We were not asking for a UK opt-out, special exemption or generalised emergency brake on financial services legislation. They were safeguards sought for the EU as a whole. We were simply asking for a level playing field for open competition for financial services companies in all EU countries ... with arrangements that would enable every EU member state to regulate its financial sector properly.

To those who say we were trying to go soft on the banks, nothing can be further from the truth. We have said that we are going to respond positively to the tough measures set out in the Vickers Report. There are issues about whether this can be done under current European regulations. So one of the things we wanted was to make sure we could go further than European rules in regulating the banks. The Financial Services Authority report on RBS [Royal Bank of Scotland] today demonstrates how necessary that is. We have problems in this country that this government inherited and needs to sort out.

And those who say that this proposed treaty change was all about safeguarding the Eurozone – and so Britain shouldn't have tried to interfere or to insist on safeguards – are also fundamentally wrong. The EU Treaty is the treaty of those outside the Euro as much as those inside. Creating a new Eurozone Treaty within the existing EU Treaty without proper safeguards would have changed the EU profoundly for us too. It's not just that it would have meant a whole new bureaucracy, with rules and competences for the Eurozone countries being incorporated directly into the EU Treaty … it would have changed the nature of the EU – strengthening the Eurozone without balancing measures to strengthen the Single Market. Of course an intergovernmental arrangement is not without risks, but we did not want to see that imbalance hard-wired into the treaty.

And to those who believe this wasn't a real risk, France and Germany said in their letter last week that the Eurozone should work on Single Market issues like financial regulation and competitiveness. That is why we required safeguards and I make no apologies for it. Of course I wish those safeguards had been accepted. But frankly I have to tell the House the choice was a treaty without proper safeguards or no treaty. And the right answer was no treaty.

It was not an easy thing to do, but it was the right thing to do.

As a result, Eurozone countries and others are now making separate arrangements for co-ordinating their budgets and making sure there is more surveillance of what they do and the fiscal integration they need to solve the problems in the Eurozone. They recognise this approach will be less attractive, more complex and more difficult to enforce and they would prefer to incorporate the new treaty into the EU treaties in the future. Our position remains the same.

Let me turn to what this means for Britain.

Mr Speaker, Britain remains a full member of the European Union. And the events of the last week do nothing to change that. Our membership of the EU is vital to our national interest.

We are a trading nation and we need the Single Market for trade, investment and jobs. The EU makes Britain a gateway to the largest single market in the world for investors. It secures more than half of our exports and millions of British jobs. And membership of the EU strengthens our ability to progress our foreign policy objectives too … giving us a strong voice on the global stage in issues such as trade, and as we have seen in Durban this weekend, climate change.

So we are in the European Union and we want to be. This week there will be meetings of the councils on Transport, Telecommunications and Energy, and Agriculture and Fisheries. Britain will be there as a full member at each one. But I believe in an EU with the flexibility of a network, not the rigidity of a bloc. We're not in the Schengen no-borders agreement and neither should we be …because it is right that we should use our natural geographical advantage as an island to protect us against illegal immigration, guns and drugs. We're not in the Single Currency and while I am Prime Minister we will never join. We are not in the new Euro area bailout funds, even though we had to negotiate our way out it. And we are not in this year's Euro-Plus pact. When the Euro was created, the previous government agreed there would need to be separate meetings of Eurozone ministers. It is hardly surprising that those countries required by treaty to join the Euro chose to join the existing Eurozone members in developing future arrangements for the Eurozone. Those countries are going to be negotiating a treaty that passes unprecedented powers from their nation states to Brussels. Some will have budgets effectively checked and re-written by the European Commission.

None of this will happen in Britain.

But just as we wanted safeguards for Britain's interests if we changed the EU Treaty, so we will continue to be vigilant in protecting our national interests. An intergovernmental treaty, while it doesn't carry with it the same dangers for Britain, nonetheless is not without risks. The decision of the new Eurozone-led arrangement is a discussion that is just beginning. We want the new treaty to work in stabilising the Euro and putting it on a firm foundation. And I understand why they would want to use the institutions. But this is new territory and does raise important issues which we will need to explore with the Euro-Plus countries.

So in the months to come we will be vigorously engaged in the debate about how institutions built for twenty-seven should continue to operate fairly for all member states, and in particular for Britain. The UK is very supportive of the role the institutions – and the Commission in particular – play in safeguarding the Single Market. So we will look constructively at any proposals with an open mind.

But let's be clear about one thing: if Britain had agreed treaty change without safeguards, there would be no discussion. Britain would have no protection.

Mr Speaker, let me turn to the next steps. The most pressing need is to fix the problems of the Euro. As I have said, that involves far more than simply greater medium-term fiscal integration, important though that is. Above all, the Eurozone needs to focus at the very least on implementing its October agreement. The markets want to be assured that the Eurozone firewall is big enough, that Europe's banks are being adequately recapitalised and that the problems in countries like Greece have been properly dealt with.

There was some progress at the Council. The Eurozone countries noted the possibility of additional IMF assistance. Our position on IMF resources remains the one I set out at the Cannes G20 summit. Alongside non-European G20 countries, we are ready to look positively at strengthening the IMF's capacity to help countries in difficulty across the world. But IMF resources are for countries not currencies, and can't be used specifically to support the Euro. There also needs to be greater competitiveness between the countries of the Eurozone.

But let's be frank – the whole of Europe needs to become more competitive.

That is the way to more jobs and growth. Many Eurozone countries have substantial trade deficits as well as budget deficits. If they are not to be reliant on massive transfers of capital they need to become more competitive and trade out of those deficits. The British agenda has always been about improving Europe's competitiveness. And at recent councils we have achieved substantial progress on completing the Single Market in services, opening up our energy markets and exempting microbusinesses from future regulations. This has been done by working in partnership with a combination of countries that are in the Eurozone and outside it. We will continue to work with like-minded countries to push forward this agenda. Those countries such as Holland, Sweden and Germany want these issues discussed as a full twenty-seven – as they will be – because they want our support in the debate against some other members who don't share these views. Similarly on this year's EU budget it was Britain in partnership with France, Germany and Holland among others that successfully insisted on no real increase in resources – for the first time in many years.

On defence, Britain is an absolutely key European player, whether leading the NATO Rapid Reaction Force ... or tackling piracy in the Indian Ocean. And our partnership with France was crucial in taking action in Libya.

Britain will continue to form alliances on the things we want to get done. We've always had a leading role in advocating the policy of enlargement. And at this Council, we all celebrated the signing of Croatia's accession treaty. That's one European Treaty I was happy to sign.

Mr Speaker, let me conclude with this point. I do not believe there is a binary choice for Britain: that we can either sacrifice the national interest on issue after issue ... or lose our influence at the heart of Europe's decision-making processes. I am absolutely clear that it is possible both to be a full, committed and influential member of the European Union ... and to stay out of arrangements where we cannot protect our interests.

That is what I have done at this Council. That is what I will continue to do as long as I am Prime Minister. It is the right course for this country.

And I commend this statement to the House.

GEORGE W. BUSH

'EITHER YOU ARE WITH US OR YOU ARE WITH THE TERRORISTS'

—

REMARKS BEFORE A JOINT SESSION OF CONGRESS

WASHINGTON, DC, 20 SEPTEMBER 2001

T*he son of a former President, George W. Bush was Governor of Texas from 1995–2000. He was elected President and served two terms from 2001–2009. In response to the terrorist attacks on the United States on 11 September 2001, Bush addressed the US Congress and the world, explaining the nature of the attack and the American response. With a global stage and the later wars in Afghanistan and Iraq, this speech was the most important policy statement of the last decade. Almost every policy announcement in the speech was newsworthy. The Congressional audience visibly and audibly reacted to the pronouncements and scope of the speech. This speech became part of American thinking and language, instantly becoming a document of history.*

This speech was delivered flawlessly, with no audible verbal mistakes. That is an amazing result, given his public-speaking reputation and the quick construction of this major speech within days, reacting to an unprecedented and shocking situation. The whole world was watching and listening.

This speech is one of the great speechwriting achievements of our time.

—

Mr Speaker, Mr President Pro Tempore, members of Congress, and fellow Americans:

In the normal course of events, Presidents come to this chamber to report on the state of the Union. Tonight, no such report is needed. It has already been delivered by the American people.

We have seen it in the courage of passengers, who rushed terrorists to save others on the ground – passengers like an exceptional man named Todd Beamer. And would you please help me to welcome his wife, Lisa Beamer, here tonight. We have seen the state of our Union in the endurance of rescuers, working past exhaustion. We've seen the unfurling of flags, the lighting of candles, the giving of blood, the saying of prayers – in English, Hebrew, and Arabic. We have seen the decency of a loving and giving people who have made the grief of strangers their own. My fellow citizens, for the last nine days, the entire world has seen for itself the state of our Union – and it is strong.

Tonight we are a country awakened to danger and called to defend freedom. Our grief has turned to anger, and anger to resolution. Whether we bring our enemies to justice, or bring justice to our enemies, justice will be done. I thank the Congress for its leadership at such an important time. All of America was touched on the evening of the tragedy to see Republicans and Democrats joined together on the steps of this Capitol, singing 'God Bless America'. And you did more than sing; you acted, by delivering 40 billion dollars to rebuild our communities and meet the needs of our military. Speaker [Dennis] Hastert, Minority Leader [Dick] Gephardt, Majority Leader [Tom] Daschle, and Senator [Trent] Lott, I thank you for your friendship, for your leadership, and for your service to our country. And on behalf of the American people, I thank the world for its outpouring of support. America will never forget the sounds of our National Anthem playing at Buckingham Palace, on the streets of Paris, and at Berlin's Brandenburg Gate.

We will not forget South Korean children gathering to pray outside our embassy in Seoul, or the prayers of sympathy offered at a mosque in Cairo. We will not forget moments of silence and days of mourning in Australia and Africa and Latin America. Nor will we forget the citizens of eighty other nations who died with our own: dozens of Pakistanis; more than 130 Israelis; more than 250 citizens of India; men and women from El Salvador, Iran, Mexico, and Japan; and hundreds of British citizens. America has no truer friend than Great Britain. Once again, we are joined together in a great cause – so honoured the British Prime Minister [Tony Blair] has crossed an ocean to show his unity with America. Thank you for coming, friend.

On September the 11th, enemies of freedom committed an act of war against our country. Americans have known wars – but for the past 136 years, they have been wars on foreign soil, except for one Sunday in 1941. Americans have known the casualties of war – but not at the centre of a great city on a peaceful morning. Americans have known surprise attacks – but never before on thousands of civilians. All of this was brought upon us in a single day – and night fell on a different world, a world where freedom itself is under attack.

Americans have many questions tonight. Americans are asking: Who attacked our country? The evidence we have gathered all points to a collection of loosely affiliated terrorist organisations known as al Qaeda. They are some of the murderers indicted for bombing American embassies in Tanzania and Kenya, and responsible for bombing the USS *Cole*. Al Qaeda is to terror what the mafia is to crime. But its goal is not making money; its goal is remaking the world – and imposing its radical beliefs on people everywhere.

The terrorists practise a fringe form of Islamic extremism that has been rejected by Muslim scholars and the vast majority of Muslim clerics, a fringe movement that perverts the peaceful teachings of Islam. The terrorists' directive commands them to kill Christians and Jews, to kill all Americans, and make no distinctions among military and civilians, including women and children. This group and its leader – a person named Usama bin Laden – are linked to many other organisations in different countries, including the Egyptian Islamic Jihad and the Islamic Movement of Uzbekistan. There are thousands of these terrorists in more than sixty countries. They are recruited from their own nations and neighbourhoods and brought to camps in places like Afghanistan, where they are trained in the tactics of terror. They are sent back to their homes or sent to hide in countries around the world to plot evil and destruction.

The leadership of al Qaeda has great influence in Afghanistan and supports the Taliban regime in controlling most of that country. In Afghanistan, we see al Qaeda's vision for the world. Afghanistan's people have been brutalised; many are starving and many have fled. Women are not allowed to attend school. You can be jailed for owning a television. Religion can be practised only as their leaders dictate. A man can be jailed in Afghanistan if his beard is not long enough.

The United States respects the people of Afghanistan. After all, we are currently its largest source of humanitarian aid; but we condemn the Taliban regime. It is not only repressing its own people, it is threatening people everywhere by sponsoring and sheltering and supplying terrorists. By aiding and abetting murder, the Taliban regime is committing murder.

And tonight, the United States of America makes the following demands on the Taliban: Deliver to United States authorities all the leaders of al Qaeda who hide in your land. Release all foreign nationals, including American citizens, you have unjustly imprisoned. Protect foreign journalists, diplomats, and aid workers in your country. Close immediately and permanently every terrorist training camp in Afghanistan, and hand over every terrorist, and every person in their support structure, to appropriate authorities. Give the United States full access to terrorist training camps, so we can make sure they are no longer operating. These demands are not open to negotiation or discussion. The Taliban must act, and act immediately. They will hand over the terrorists, or they will share in their fate.

I also want to speak tonight directly to Muslims throughout the world. We respect your faith. It's practised freely by many millions of Americans, and by millions more in countries that America counts as friends. Its teachings are good and peaceful, and those who commit evil in the name of Allah blaspheme the name of Allah. The terrorists are traitors to their own faith, trying, in effect, to hijack Islam itself. The enemy of America is not our many Muslim friends; it is not our many Arab friends. Our enemy is a radical network of terrorists, and every government that supports them. Our war on terror begins with al Qaeda, but it does not end there. It will not end until every terrorist group of global reach has been found, stopped, and defeated.

Americans are asking, why do they hate us? They hate what they see right here in this chamber – a democratically elected government. Their leaders are self-appointed. They hate our freedoms – our freedom of religion, our freedom of speech, our freedom to vote and assemble and disagree with each other. They want to overthrow existing governments in many Muslim countries, such as Egypt, Saudi Arabia, and Jordan. They want to drive Israel out of the Middle East. They want to drive Christians and Jews out of vast regions of Asia and Africa. These terrorists kill not merely to end lives, but to disrupt and end a way of life. With every atrocity, they hope that America grows fearful, retreating from the world and forsaking our friends. They stand against us, because we stand in their way.

We are not deceived by their pretences to piety. We have seen their kind before. They are the heirs of all the murderous ideologies of the twentieth century. By sacrificing human life to serve their radical visions – by abandoning every value except the will to power – they follow in the path of fascism, Nazism, and totalitarianism. And they will follow that path all the way, to where it ends: in history's unmarked grave of discarded lies.

Americans are asking: How will we fight and win this war? We will direct every resource at our command – every means of diplomacy, every tool of intelligence, every instrument of law enforcement, every financial influence, and every necessary weapon of war – to the disruption and to the defeat of the global terror network.

Now this war will not be like the war against Iraq a decade ago, with a decisive liberation of territory and a swift conclusion. It will not look like the air war above Kosovo two years ago, where no ground troops were used and not a single American was lost in combat. Our response involves far more than instant retaliation and isolated strikes. Americans should not expect one battle, but a lengthy campaign, unlike any other we have ever seen. It may include dramatic strikes, visible on TV, and covert operations, secret even in success. We will starve terrorists of funding, turn them one against another, drive them from place to place, until there is no refuge and no rest. And we will pursue nations that provide aid or safe haven to terrorism. Every nation, in every region, now has a decision to make. Either you are with us, or you are with the terrorists. From this day forward, any nation that continues to harbour or support terrorism will be regarded by the United States as a hostile regime.

Our nation has been put on notice: We're not immune from attack. We will take defensive measures against terrorism to protect Americans. Today, dozens of federal departments and agencies, as well as state and local governments, have responsibilities affecting homeland security. These efforts must be coordinated at the highest level. So tonight I announce the creation of a Cabinet-level position reporting directly to me – the Office of Homeland Security. And tonight I also announce a distinguished American to lead this effort, to strengthen American security: a military veteran, an effective governor, a true patriot, a trusted friend – Pennsylvania's Tom Ridge. He will lead, oversee, and coordinate a comprehensive national strategy to safeguard our country against terrorism, and respond to any attacks that may come. These measures are essential. But the only way to defeat terrorism as a threat to our way of life is to stop it, eliminate it, and destroy it where it grows. Many will be involved in this effort, from FBI agents to intelligence operatives to the reservists we have called to active duty. All deserve our thanks, and all have our prayers. And tonight, a few miles from the damaged Pentagon, I have a message for our military: Be ready. I've called the armed forces to alert, and there is a reason. The hour is coming when America will act, and you will make us proud. This is not, however, just America's fight. And what is at stake is not just America's freedom. This is the world's fight. This is civilisation's fight. This is the fight of all who believe in progress and pluralism, tolerance and freedom.

We ask every nation to join us. We will ask, and we will need, the help of police forces, intelligence services, and banking systems around the world. The United States is grateful that many nations and many international organisations have already responded – with sympathy and with support. Nations from Latin America, to Asia, to Africa, to Europe, to the Islamic world. Perhaps the NATO Charter reflects best the attitude of the world: An attack on one is an attack on all. The civilised world is rallying to America's side. They understand that if this terror goes unpunished, their own cities, their own citizens may be next. Terror, unanswered, can not only bring down buildings, it can threaten the stability of legitimate governments. And you know what? We're not going to allow it.

Americans are asking: What is expected of us? I ask you to live your lives, and hug your children. I know many citizens have fears tonight, and I ask you to be calm and resolute, even in the face of a continuing threat. I ask you to uphold the values of America, and remember why so many have come here. We are in a fight for our principles, and our first responsibility is to live by them. No one should be singled out for unfair treatment or unkind words because of their ethnic background or religious faith. I ask you to continue to support the victims of this tragedy with your contributions. Those who want to give can go to a central source of information, libertyunites.org, to find the names of groups providing direct help in New York, Pennsylvania, and Virginia.

The thousands of FBI agents who are now at work in this investigation may need your cooperation, and I ask you to give it. I ask for your patience, with the delays and inconveniences that may accompany tighter security; and for your patience in what will be a long struggle. I ask your continued participation and confidence in the American economy. Terrorists attacked a symbol of American prosperity. They did not touch its source. America is successful because of the hard work, and creativity, and enterprise of our people. These were the true strengths of our economy before September 11th, and they are our strengths today. And, finally, please continue praying for the victims of terror and their families, for those in uniform, and for our great country. Prayer has comforted us in sorrow, and will help strengthen us for the journey ahead.

Tonight I thank my fellow Americans for what you have already done and for what you will do. And ladies and gentlemen of the Congress, I thank you, their representatives, for what you have already done and for what we will do together. Tonight, we face new and sudden national challenges. We will come together to improve air safety, to dramatically expand the number of air marshals on domestic flights, and take new measures to prevent hijacking. We will come together to promote stability and keep our airlines flying, with direct assistance during this emergency. We will come together to give law enforcement the additional tools it needs to track down terror here at home. We will come together to strengthen our intelligence capabilities to know the plans of terrorists before they act, and to find them before they strike.

We will come together to take active steps that strengthen America's economy, and put our people back to work. Tonight we welcome two leaders who embody the extraordinary spirit of all New Yorkers: [New York State] Governor George Pataki, and [New York City] Mayor Rudolph Giuliani. As a symbol of America's resolve, my administration will work with Congress, and these two leaders, to show the world that we will rebuild New York City.

After all that has just passed – all the lives taken, and all the possibilities and hopes that died with them – it is natural to wonder if America's future is one of fear. Some speak of an age of terror. I know there are struggles ahead, and dangers to face. But this country will define our times, not be defined by them. As long as the United States of America is determined and strong, this will not be an age of terror; this will be an age of liberty, here and across the world.

Great harm has been done to us. We have suffered great loss. And in our grief and anger we have found our mission and our moment. Freedom and fear are at war. The advance of human freedom – the great achievement of our time, and the great hope of every time – now depends on us. Our nation, this generation will lift a dark threat of violence from our people and our future. We will rally the world to this cause by our efforts, by our courage. We will not tire, we will not falter, and we will not fail.

It is my hope that in the months and years ahead, life will return almost to normal. We'll go back to our lives and routines, and that is good. Even grief recedes with time and grace. But our resolve must not pass. Each of us will remember what happened that day, and to whom it happened. We'll remember the moment the news came – where we were and what we were doing. Some will remember an image of a fire, or a story of rescue. Some will carry memories of a face and a voice gone forever.

And I will carry this: it is the police shield of a man named George Howard, who died at the World Trade Centre trying to save others. It was given to me by his mom, Arlene, as a proud memorial to her son. This is my reminder of lives that ended, and a task that does not end. I will not forget this wound to our country or those who inflicted it. I will not yield; I will not rest; I will not relent in waging this struggle for freedom and security for the American people. The course of this conflict is not known, yet its outcome is certain. Freedom and fear, justice and cruelty, have always been at war, and we know that God is not neutral between them.

Fellow citizens, we'll meet violence with patient justice – assured of the rightness of our cause, and confident of the victories to come. In all that lies before us, may God grant us wisdom, and may He watch over the United States of America. Thank you.

TONY BLAIR

'THE KALEIDOSCOPE HAS BEEN SHAKEN'

—

REMARKS TO THE LABOUR PARTY CONFERENCE

BRIGHTON, UNITED KINGDOM, 2 OCTOBER 2001

Tony Blair was Prime Minister from 1997–2007. He went to the United States right after the September 11th attacks, attending President Bush's speech to Congress (see previous speech). He returned to the United Kingdom and addressed his Party Conference less than three weeks later, explaining Britain's role in the war on terror, urging responsible action and a calming perspective. This speech was widely reproduced at the time, becoming his defining statement on the need to combat terrorism without damaging the multicultural harmony necessary for democratic states to survive. Domestic issues are discussed. But this is primarily a speech about international terrorism. The paragraph formation is mine, similar to that used by others who reprinted this speech. In this speech the casualties from 9/11 were said to number about 7,000 people. The final death toll was eventually determined to be about 3,000. The conclusion of this speech is noted for its language of urgency.

—

In retrospect the Millennium marked only a moment in time. It was the events of 11 September that marked a turning point in history, where we confront the dangers of the future and assess the choices facing humankind.

It was a tragedy. An act of evil. From this nation, goes our deepest sympathy and prayers for the victims and our profound solidarity with the American people. We were with you at the first. We will stay with you to the last. Just two weeks ago, in New York, after the church service I met some of the families of the British victims. It was in many ways a very British occasion. Tea and biscuits.

It was raining outside. Around the edge of the room, strangers making small talk, trying to be normal people in an abnormal situation. And as you crossed the room, you felt the longing and sadness; hands clutching photos of sons and daughters, wives and husbands; imploring you to believe them when they said there was still an outside chance of their loved ones being found alive, when you knew in truth that all hope was gone.

And then a middle-aged mother looks you in the eyes and tells you her only son has died, and asks you: why?

I tell you: you do not feel like the most powerful person in the country at times like that. Because there is no answer. There is no justification for their pain. Their son did nothing wrong. The woman, seven months pregnant, whose child will never know its father, did nothing wrong.

They don't want revenge. They want something better in memory of their loved ones.

I believe their memorial can and should be greater than simply the punishment of the guilty. It is that out of the shadow of this evil, should emerge lasting good: destruction of the machinery of terrorism wherever it is found; hope among all nations of a new beginning where we seek to resolve differences in a calm and ordered way; greater understanding between nations and between faiths; and above all justice and prosperity for the poor and dispossessed, so that people everywhere can see the chance of a better future through the hard work and creative power of the free citizen, not the violence and savagery of the fanatic.

I know that here in Britain people are anxious, even a little frightened. I understand that. People know we must act but they worry what might follow. They worry about the economy and talk of recession. And, of course there are dangers; it is a new situation.

But the fundamentals of the US, British and European economies are strong. Every reasonable measure of internal security is being undertaken. Our way of life is a great deal stronger and will last a great deal longer than the actions of fanatics, small in number and now facing a unified world against them.

People should have confidence. This is a battle with only one outcome: our victory not theirs.

What happened on 11 September was without parallel in the bloody history of terrorism. Within a few hours, up to 7,000 people were annihilated, the commercial centre of New York was reduced to rubble and in Washington and Pennsylvania further death and horror on an unimaginable scale. Let no one say this was a blow for Islam when the blood of innocent Muslims was shed along with those of the Christian, Jewish and other faiths around the world.

We know those responsible. In Afghanistan are scores of training camps for the export of terror. Chief among the sponsors and organisers is Usama Bin

Laden. He is supported, shielded and given succour by the Taliban regime. Two days before the 11 September attacks, [Ahmad Shah] Masood, the Leader of the Opposition Northern Alliance, was assassinated by two suicide bombers. Both were linked to Bin Laden. Some may call that coincidence. I call it payment – payment in the currency these people deal in: blood. Be in no doubt: Bin Laden and his people organised this atrocity. The Taliban aid and abet him. He will not desist from further acts of terror. They will not stop helping him.

Whatever the dangers of the action we take, the dangers of inaction are far, far greater. Look for a moment at the Taliban regime. It is undemocratic. That goes without saying. There is no sport allowed, or television or photography. No art or culture is permitted. All other faiths, all other interpretations of Islam are ruthlessly suppressed. Those who practise their faith are imprisoned. Women are treated in a way almost too revolting to be credible. First driven out of university; girls not allowed to go to school; no legal rights; unable to go out of doors without a man. Those that disobey are stoned. There is now no contact permitted with Western agencies, even those delivering food. The people live in abject poverty. It is a regime founded on fear and funded on the drugs trade. The biggest drugs hoard in the world is in Afghanistan, controlled by the Taliban. Ninety per cent of the heroin on British streets originates in Afghanistan. The arms the Taliban are buying today are paid for with the lives of young British people buying their drugs on British streets. That is another part of their regime that we should seek to destroy.

So what do we do? 'Don't overreact', some say. We aren't. We haven't lashed out. No missiles on the first night just for effect. 'Don't kill innocent people.' We are not the ones who waged war on the innocent. We seek the guilty. 'Look for a diplomatic solution.' There is no diplomacy with Bin Laden or the Taliban regime. 'State an ultimatum and get their response.' We stated the ultimatum; they haven't responded. 'Understand the causes of terror.' Yes, we should try, but let there be no moral ambiguity about this: nothing could ever justify the events of 11 September, and it is to turn justice on its head to pretend it could.

The action we take will be proportionate; targeted; we will do all we humanly can to avoid civilian casualties. But understand what we are dealing with. Listen to the calls of those passengers on the planes. Think of the children on them, told they were going to die. Think of the cruelty beyond our comprehension as among the screams and the anguish of the innocent, those hijackers drove at full throttle planes laden with fuel into buildings where tens of thousands worked. They have no moral inhibition on the slaughter of the innocent. If they could have murdered not 7,000 but 70,000 does anyone doubt they would have done so and rejoiced in it? There is no compromise possible with such people, no meeting of minds, no point of understanding with such terror.

Just a choice: defeat it or be defeated by it. And defeat it we must.

Any action taken will be against the terrorist network of Bin Laden. As for the Taliban, they can surrender the terrorists; or face the consequences and again in any action the aim will be to eliminate their military hardware, cut off their finances, disrupt their supplies, target their troops, not civilians. We will put a trap around the regime.

I say to the Taliban: surrender the terrorists; or surrender power. It's your choice.

We will take action at every level, national and international, in the UN, in G8, in the EU, in NATO, in every regional grouping in the world, to strike at international terrorism wherever it exists.

For the first time, the UN Security Council has imposed mandatory obligations on all UN members to cut off terrorist financing and end safe havens for terrorists. Those that finance terror, those who launder their money, those that cover their tracks are every bit as guilty as the fanatic who commits the final act. Here in this country and in other nations round the world, laws will be changed, not to deny basic liberties but to prevent their abuse and protect the most basic liberty of all: freedom from terror. New extradition laws will be introduced; new rules to ensure asylum is not a front for terrorist entry. This country is proud of its tradition in giving asylum to those fleeing tyranny. We will always do so. But we have a duty to protect the system from abuse. It must be overhauled radically so that from now on, those who abide by the rules get help and those that don't can no longer play the system to gain unfair advantage over others.

Round the world, 11 September is bringing governments and people to reflect, consider and change. And in this process, amid all the talk of war and action, there is another dimension appearing. There is a coming together. The power of community is asserting itself. We are realising how fragile are our frontiers in the face of the world's new challenges. Today conflicts rarely stay within national boundaries. Today a tremor in one financial market is repeated in the markets of the world. Today confidence is global; either its presence or its absence. Today the threat is chaos; because for people with work to do, family life to balance, mortgages to pay, careers to further, pensions to provide, the yearning is for order and stability and if it doesn't exist elsewhere, it is unlikely to exist here.

I have long believed this interdependence defines the new world we live in. People say: we are only acting because it's the USA that was attacked. Double standards, they say. But when [Slobodon] Milošević embarked on the ethnic cleansing of Muslims in Kosovo, we acted. The sceptics said it was pointless, we'd make matters worse, we'd make Milosovic stronger and look what happened, we won, the refugees went home, the policies of ethnic cleansing were reversed and one of the great dictators of the last century will see justice in this century. And I tell you if Rwanda happened again today as it did in 1993, when a million people were slaughtered in cold blood, we would have a moral duty to act there also. We were there in Sierra Leone when a murderous group of gangsters threatened its democratically elected government and people.

And we as a country should, and I as Prime Minister do, give thanks for the brilliance, dedication and sheer professionalism of the British Armed Forces.

We can't do it all. Neither can the Americans. But the power of the international community could, together, if it chose to.

It could, with our help, sort out the blight that is the continuing conflict in the Democratic Republic of the Congo, where three million people have died through war or famine in the last decade. A Partnership for Africa, between the developed and developing world based around the New African Initiative, is there to be done if we find the will. On our side: provide more aid, untied to trade; write off debt; help with good governance and infrastructure; training to the soldiers, with UN blessing, in conflict resolution; encouraging investment; and access to our markets so that we practise the free trade we are so fond of preaching. But it's a deal: on the African side: true democracy, no more excuses for dictatorship, abuses of human rights; no tolerance of bad governance, from the endemic corruption of some states, to the activities of Mr Mugabe's henchmen in Zimbabwe. Proper commercial, legal and financial systems. The will, with our help, to broker agreements for peace and provide troops to police them. The state of Africa is a scar on the conscience of the world. But if the world as a community focused on it, we could heal it. And if we don't, it will become deeper and angrier.

We could defeat climate change if we chose to. Kyoto is right. We will implement it and call upon all other nations to do so. But it's only a start. With imagination, we could use or find the technologies that create energy without destroying our planet; we could provide work and trade without deforestation. If humankind was able, finally, to make industrial progress without the factory conditions of the 19th century; surely we have the wit and will to develop economically without despoiling the very environment we depend upon.

And if we wanted to, we could breathe new life into the Middle East Peace Process and we must. The state of Israel must be given recognition by all; freed from terror; know that it is accepted as part of the future of the Middle East not its very existence under threat. The Palestinians must have justice, the chance to prosper and in their own land, as equal partners with Israel in that future.

We know that. It is the only way, just as we know in our own peace process, in Northern Ireland, there will be no unification of Ireland except by consent – and there will be no return to the days of Unionist or Protestant supremacy because those days have no place in the modern world. So the Unionists must accept justice and equality for Nationalists. The Republicans must show they have given up violence – not just a ceasefire but weapons put beyond use. And not only the Republicans, but those people who call themselves Loyalists, but who by acts of terrorism, sully the name of the United Kingdom.

We know this also. The values we believe in should shine through what we do in Afghanistan.

To the Afghan people we make this commitment. The conflict will not be the end. We will not walk away, as the outside world has done so many times before. If the Taliban regime changes, we will work with you to make sure its successor is one that is broad-based, that unites all ethnic groups, and that offers some way out of the miserable poverty that is your present existence. And, more than ever now, with every bit as much thought and planning, we will assemble a humanitarian coalition alongside the military coalition so that inside and outside Afghanistan, the refugees, four and a half million on the move even before 11 September, are given shelter, food and help during the winter months.

The world community must show as much its capacity for compassion as for force.

The critics will say: but how can the world be a community? Nations act in their own self-interest. Of course they do. But what is the lesson of the financial markets, climate change, international terrorism, nuclear proliferation or world trade? It is that our self-interest and our mutual interests are today inextricably woven together.

This is the politics of globalisation.

I realise why people protest against globalisation. We watch aspects of it with trepidation. We feel powerless, as if we were now pushed to and fro by forces far beyond our control.

But there's a risk that political leaders, faced with street demonstrations, pander to the argument rather than answer it. The demonstrators are right to say there's injustice, poverty, environmental degradation.

But globalisation is a fact and, by and large, it is driven by people. Not just in finance, but in communication, in technology, increasingly in culture, in recreation. In the world of the Internet, information technology and TV, there will be globalisation. And in trade, the problem is not there's too much of it; on the contrary there's too little of it.

The issue is not how to stop globalisation. The issue is how we use the power of community to combine it with justice. If globalisation works only for the benefit of the few, then it will fail and will deserve to fail. But if we follow the principles that have served us so well at home – that power, wealth and opportunity must be in the hands of the many, not the few – if we make that our guiding light for the global economy, then it will be a force for good and an international movement that we should take pride in leading.

Because the alternative to globalisation is isolation.

Confronted by this reality, round the world, nations are instinctively drawing together. In Quebec, all the countries of North and South America deciding to make one huge free trade area, rivalling Europe. In Asia, ASEAN. In Europe, the most integrated grouping of all, we are now fifteen nations. Another twelve countries negotiating to join, and more beyond that. A new relationship between Russia and Europe is beginning. And will not India and China, each with three times as many citizens as the whole of the EU put together, once their economies have developed sufficiently as they will do, not reconfigure entirely the geopolitics of the world and in our lifetime? That is why, with 60 per cent of our trade dependent on Europe, three million jobs tied up with Europe, much of our political weight engaged in Europe, it would be a fundamental denial of our true national interest to turn our backs on Europe.

We will never let that happen. For fifty years, Britain has, uncharacteristically, followed not led in Europe. At each and every step. There are debates central to our future coming up: how we reform European economic policy; how we take forward European defence; how we fight organised crime and terrorism.

Britain needs its voice strong in Europe and bluntly Europe needs a strong Britain, rock solid in our alliance with the USA, yet determined to play its full part in shaping Europe's destiny. We should only be part of the single currency if the economic conditions are met. They are not window-dressing for a political decision. They are fundamental. But if they are met, we should join, and if met in this Parliament, we should have the courage of our argument, to ask the British people for their consent in this Parliament.

Europe is not a threat to Britain. Europe is an opportunity. It is in taking the best of the Anglo-Saxon and European models of development that Britain's hope of a prosperous future lies. The American spirit of enterprise; the European spirit of solidarity. We have, here also, an opportunity. Not just to build bridges politically, but economically.

What is the answer to the current crisis? Not isolationism but the world coming together with America as a community.

What is the answer to Britain's relations with Europe? Not opting out, but being leading members of a community in which, in alliance with others, we gain strength.

What is the answer to Britain's future? Not each person for themselves, but working together as a community to ensure that everyone, not just the privileged few, get the chance to succeed.

This is an extraordinary moment for progressive politics. Our values are the right ones for this age: the power of community, solidarity, the collective ability to further the individual's interests.

People ask me if I think ideology is dead. My answer is: In the sense of rigid forms of economic and social theory, yes. The twentieth century killed those ideologies and their passing causes little regret. But, in the sense of a governing idea in politics, based on values, no. The governing idea of modern social democracy is community. Founded on the principles of social justice. That people should rise according to merit not birth; that the test of any decent society is not the contentment of the wealthy and strong, but the commitment to the poor and weak.

But values aren't enough. The mantle of leadership comes at a price: the courage to learn and change; to show how values that stand for all ages can be applied in a way relevant to each age. Our politics only succeed when the realism is as clear as the idealism.

This party's strength today comes from the journey of change and learning we have made.

We learned that however much we strive for peace, we need strong defence capability when a peaceful approach fails. We learned that equality is about equal worth, not equal outcomes.

Today our idea of society is shaped around mutual responsibility; a deal, an agreement between citizens, not a one-way gift from the well-off to the dependent. Our economic and social policy today owes as much to the liberal social democratic tradition of [David] Lloyd George, [John Maynard] Keynes and [William Henry] Beveridge as to the socialist principles of the 1945 government.

Just over a decade ago, people asked if Labour could ever win again. Today they ask the same question of the opposition. Painful though that journey of change has been, it has been worth it, every stage of the way. On this journey, the values have never changed. The aims haven't. Our aims would be instantly recognisable to every Labour leader from Keir Hardie onwards. But the means do change. The journey hasn't ended. It never ends. The next stage for New Labour is not backwards; it is renewing ourselves again. Just after the election, an old colleague of mine said: 'Come on Tony, now we've won again, can't we drop all this New Labour and do what we believe in?' I said: 'It's worse than you think. I really do believe in it.' We didn't revolutionise British economic policy – Bank of England independence, tough spending rules – for some managerial reason or as a clever wheeze to steal Tory clothes. We did it because the victims of economic incompetence – 15 per cent interest rates, 3 million unemployed – are hard-working families. They are the ones – and even more so, now – with tough times ahead – that the economy should be run for, not speculators, or currency dealers or senior executives whose pay packets don't seem to bear any resemblance to the performance of their companies. Economic competence is the pre-condition of social justice. We have legislated for fairness at work, like the minimum wage which people struggled a century for. But we won't give up the essential flexibility of our economy or our commitment to enterprise. Why? Because in a world leaving behind mass production, where technology revolutionises not just companies but whole industries, almost overnight, enterprise creates the jobs people depend on. We have boosted pensions, child benefit, family incomes. We will do more. But our number one priority for spending is and will remain education. Why? Because in the new markets countries like Britain can only create wealth by brain power, not low wages and sweatshop labour. We have cut youth unemployment by 75 per cent. By more than any government before us. But we refuse to pay benefit to those who refuse to work. Why? Because the welfare that works is welfare that helps people to help themselves. The graffiti, the vandalism, the burned-out cars, the street corner drug dealers, the teenage mugger just graduating from the minor school of crime: we're not old-fashioned or right-wing to take action against this social menace. We're standing up for the people we represent, who play by the rules and have a right to expect others to do the same.

And especially at this time let us say: we celebrate the diversity in our country, get strength from the cultures and races that go to make up Britain today; and racist abuse and racist attacks have no place in the Britain we believe in.

All these policies are linked by a common thread of principle. Now with this second term, our duty is not to sit back and bask in it. It is across the board, in competition policy, enterprise, pensions, criminal justice, the civil service and of course public services, to go still further in the journey of change. All for the same reason: to allow us to deliver social justice in the modern world.

Public services are the power of community in action. They are social justice made real. The child with a good education flourishes. The child given a poor education lives with it for the rest of their life. How much talent and ability and potential do we waste? How many children never know not just the earning power of a good education but the joy of art and culture and the stretching of imagination and horizons which true education brings? Poor education is a personal tragedy and national scandal. Yet even now, with all the progress of recent years, a quarter of eleven-year-olds fail their basic tests and almost a half of sixteen-year-olds don't get five decent GCSEs.

The NHS meant that for succeeding generations, anxiety was lifted from their shoulders. For millions who get superb treatment still, the NHS remains the ultimate symbol of social justice.

But for every patient waiting in pain, that can't get treatment for cancer or a heart condition or in desperation ends up paying for their operation, that patient's suffering is the ultimate social injustice. And the demands on the system are ever greater. Children need to be better and better educated. People live longer. There is a vast array of new treatment available. And expectations are higher. This is a consumer age. People don't take what they're given. They demand more. We're not alone in this. All round the world governments are struggling with the same problems. So what is the solution? Yes, public services need more money. We are putting in the largest ever increases in NHS, education and transport spending in the next few years; and on the police too. We will keep to those spending plans.

And I say in all honesty to the country: if we want that to continue and the choice is between investment and tax cuts, then investment must come first. There is a simple truth we all know. For decades there has been chronic under-investment in British public services. Our historic mission is to put that right; and the historic shift represented by the election of June 7 was that investment to provide quality public services for all comprehensively defeated short-term tax cuts for the few. We need better pay and conditions for the staff; better incentives for recruitment; and for retention. We're getting them and recruitment is rising. This year, for the first time in nearly a decade, public sector pay will rise faster than private sector pay. And we are the only major government in Europe this year to be increasing public spending on health and education as a percentage of our national income.

This party believes in public services; believes in the ethos of public service; and believes in the dedication the vast majority of public servants show; and the proof of it is that we're spending more, hiring more and paying more than ever before. Public servants don't do it for money or glory. They do it because they find fulfilment in a child well taught or a patient well cared for or a community made safer; and we salute them for it. All that is true. But this is also true. That often they work in systems and structures that are hopelessly old-fashioned or even worse, work against the very goals they aim for. There are schools, with exactly the same social intake. One does well; the other badly. There are hospitals with exactly the same patient mix. One performs well; the other badly.

Without reform, more money and pay won't succeed. First, we need a national framework of accountability, inspection; and minimum standards of delivery. Second, within that framework, we need to free up local leaders to be able to innovate, develop and be creative. Third, there should be far greater flexibility in the terms and conditions of employment of public servants. Fourth, there has to be choice for the user of public services and the ability, where provision of the service fails, to have an alternative provider. If schools want to develop or specialise in a particular area or hire classroom assistants or computer profes-sionals as well as teachers, let them. If in a Primary Care Trust, doctors can provide minor surgery or physiotherapists see patients otherwise referred to a consultant, let them. There are too many old demarcations, especially between nurses, doctors and consultants; too little use of the potential of new technology; too much bureaucracy, too many outdated practices, too great an adherence to the way we've always done it rather than the way public servants would like to do it if they got the time to think and the freedom to act.

It's not reform that is the enemy of public services. It's the status quo. Part of that reform programme is partnership with the private or voluntary sector. Let's get one thing clear. Nobody is talking about privatising the NHS or schools. Nobody believes the private sector is a panacea.

There are great examples of public service and poor examples. There are excellent private sector companies and poor ones. There are areas where the private sector has worked well; and areas where, as with parts of the railways, it's been a disaster. Where the private sector is used, it should not make a profit simply by cutting the wages and conditions of its staff. But where the private sector can help lever in vital capital investment, where it helps raise standards, where it improves the public service as a public service, then to set up some dogmatic barrier to using it, is to let down the very people who most need our public services to improve. This programme of reform is huge: in the NHS, education, including student finance – we have to find a better way to combine state funding and student contributions – criminal justice; and transport.

I regard it as being as important for the country as Clause IV's reform was for the party, and obviously far more important for the lives of the people we serve. And it is a vital test for the modern Labour Party.

If people lose faith in public services, be under no illusion as to what will happen. There is a different approach waiting in the wings. Cut public spending drastically; let those that can afford to, buy their own services; and those that can't, will depend on a demoralised, sink public service. That would be a denial of social justice on a massive scale. It would be contrary to the very basis of community.

So this is a battle of values. Let's have that battle but not among ourselves. The real fight is between those who believe in strong public services and those who don't. That's the fight worth having.

In all of this, at home and abroad, the same beliefs throughout: that we are a community of people, whose self-interest and mutual interest at crucial points merge, and that it is through a sense of justice that community is born and nurtured. And what does this concept of justice consist of? Fairness, people all of equal worth, of course. But also reason and tolerance. Justice has no favourites; not among nations, peoples or faiths.

When we act to bring to account those that committed the atrocity of 11 September, we do so, not out of bloodlust. We do so because it is just. We do not act against Islam. The true followers of Islam are our brothers and sisters in this struggle. Bin Laden is no more obedient to the proper teaching of the Koran than those Crusaders of the twelfth century who pillaged and murdered, represented the teaching of the Gospel. It is time the West confronted its ignorance of Islam. Jews, Muslims and Christians are all children of Abraham. This is the moment to bring the faiths closer together in understanding of our common values and heritage, a source of unity and strength. It is time also for parts of Islam to confront prejudice against America, and not only Islam but parts of Western societies too. America has its faults as a society, as we have ours. But I think of the Union of America born out of the defeat of slavery. I think of its Constitution, with its inalienable rights granted to every citizen, still a model for the world. I think of a black man, born in poverty, who became Chief of their Armed Forces and is now Secretary of State, Colin Powell, and I wonder, frankly, whether such a thing could have happened here. I think of the Statue of Liberty and how many refugees, migrants and the impoverished passed its light and felt that if not for them, for their children, a new world could indeed be theirs. I think of a country where people who do well, don't have questions asked about their accent, their class, their beginnings but have admiration for what they have done and the success they've achieved.

I think of those New Yorkers I met, still in shock, but resolute; the fire fighters and police, mourning their comrades but still heads held high. I think of all this and I reflect: yes, America has its faults, but it is a free country, a democracy, it is our ally and some of the reaction to 11 September betrays a hatred of America that shames those that feel it.

So I believe this is a fight for freedom. And I want to make it a fight for justice too. Justice not only to punish the guilty. But justice to bring those same values of democracy and freedom to people round the world. And I mean freedom, not only in the narrow sense of personal liberty but in the broader sense of each individual having the economic and social freedom to develop their potential to the full. That is what community means, founded on the equal worth of all. The starving, the wretched, the dispossessed, the ignorant, those living in want and squalor from the deserts of Northern Africa to the slums of Gaza, to the mountain ranges of Afghanistan: they too are our cause.

This is a moment to seize. The kaleidoscope has been shaken. The pieces are in flux. Soon they will settle again. Before they do, let us re-order this world around us. Today, humankind has the science and technology to destroy itself or to provide prosperity to all. Yet science can't make that choice for us. Only the moral power of a world acting as a community can. 'By the strength of our common endeavour we achieve more together than we can alone.' For those people who lost their lives on 11 September and those that mourn them; now is the time for the strength to build that community. Let that be their memorial.

GEORGE W. BUSH

'THE THREAT COMES FROM IRAQ'

—

REMARKS ON THE THREAT OF IRAQ

CINCINNATI, OHIO, 7 OCTOBER 2002

*G*eorge W. Bush was President of the United States from 2001–2009.
After the terrorist attacks and the invasion of Afghanistan by coalition forces, there was a growing appeal for an invasion of Iraq to remove the threats posed by Saddam Hussein. In this speech Bush explains his reasoning for an invasion of Iraq. Oddly, Bush presents a wide range of evidence, but later places most of his justification on Iraq's development of weapons of mass destruction. At the time, there was conflicting evidence about the existence of these weapons. Hussein did little to dispel this confusion, perhaps believing that the possibility of the weapons' existence provided a deterrent to invasion. Iraq was invaded by a US-led coalition of international forces on 20 March 2003. Hussein was overthrown in 2003 and later executed by the Iraqi government in 2006.

—

Thank you all. Thank you for that very gracious and warm Cincinnati welcome. I'm honoured to be here tonight; I appreciate you all coming.

Tonight I want to take a few minutes to discuss a grave threat to peace, and America's determination to lead the world in confronting that threat.

The threat comes from Iraq. It arises directly from the Iraqi regime's own actions – its history of aggression, and its drive toward an arsenal of terror. Eleven years ago, as a condition for ending the Persian Gulf War, the Iraqi regime was required to destroy its weapons of mass destruction, to cease all development of such weapons, and to stop all support for terrorist groups. The Iraqi regime has violated all of those obligations. It possesses and produces chemical and biological weapons. It is seeking nuclear weapons. It has given shelter and support to terrorism, and practises terror against its own people. The entire world has witnessed Iraq's eleven-year history of defiance, deception and bad faith.

We also must never forget the most vivid events of recent history. On September the 11th, 2001, America felt its vulnerability – even to threats that gather on the other side of the earth. We resolved then, and we are resolved today, to confront every threat, from any source, that could bring sudden terror and suffering to America.

Members of the Congress of both political parties, and members of the United Nations Security Council, agree that Saddam Hussein is a threat to peace and must disarm. We agree that the Iraqi dictator must not be permitted to threaten America and the world with horrible poisons and diseases and gases and atomic weapons. Since we all agree on this goal, the issue is: how can we best achieve it?

Many Americans have raised legitimate questions: about the nature of the threat; about the urgency of action – why be concerned now; about the link between Iraq developing weapons of terror, and the wider war on terror. These are all issues we've discussed broadly and fully within my administration. And tonight, I want to share those discussions with you.

First, some ask why Iraq is different from other countries or regimes that also have terrible weapons. While there are many dangers in the world, the threat from Iraq stands alone – because it gathers the most serious dangers of our age in one place. Iraq's weapons of mass destruction are controlled by a murderous tyrant who has already used chemical weapons to kill thousands of people. This same tyrant has tried to dominate the Middle East, has invaded and brutally occupied a small neighbour, has struck other nations without warning, and holds an unrelenting hostility toward the United States.

By its past and present actions, by its technological capabilities, by the merciless nature of its regime, Iraq is unique. As a former chief weapons inspector of the UN has said, 'The fundamental problem with Iraq remains the nature of the regime, itself. Saddam Hussein is a homicidal dictator who is addicted to weapons of mass destruction.'

Some ask how urgent this danger is to America and the world. The danger is already significant, and it only grows worse with time. If we know Saddam Hussein has dangerous weapons today – and we do – does it make any sense for the world to wait to confront him as he grows even stronger and develops even more dangerous weapons?

In 1995, after several years of deceit by the Iraqi regime, the head of Iraq's military industries defected. It was then that the regime was forced to admit that it had produced more than 30,000 litres of anthrax and other deadly biological agents. The inspectors, however, concluded that Iraq had likely produced two to four times that amount. This is a massive stockpile of biological weapons that has never been accounted for, and capable of killing millions.

We know that the regime has produced thousands of tons of chemical agents, including mustard gas, sarin nerve gas, VX nerve gas. Saddam Hussein also has experience in using chemical weapons. He has ordered chemical attacks on Iran, and on more than forty villages in his own country. These actions killed or injured at least 20,000 people, more than six times the number of people who died in the attacks of September the 11th.

And surveillance photos reveal that the regime is rebuilding facilities that it had used to produce chemical and biological weapons. Every chemical and biological weapon that Iraq has or makes is a direct violation of the truce that ended the Persian Gulf War in 1991. Yet Saddam Hussein has chosen to build and keep these weapons despite international sanctions, UN demands, and isolation from the civilised world.

Iraq possesses ballistic missiles with a likely range of hundreds of miles – far enough to strike Saudi Arabia, Israel, Turkey, and other nations – in a region where more than 135,000 American civilians and service members live and work. We've also discovered through intelligence that Iraq has a growing fleet of manned and unmanned aerial vehicles that could be used to disperse chemical or biological weapons across broad areas. We're concerned that Iraq is exploring ways of using these UAVS for missions targeting the United States. And, of course, sophisticated delivery systems aren't required for a chemical or biological attack; all that might be required are a small container and one terrorist or Iraqi intelligence operative to deliver it.

And that is the source of our urgent concern about Saddam Hussein's links to international terrorist groups. Over the years, Iraq has provided safe haven to terrorists such as Abu Nidal, whose terror organisation carried out more than ninety terrorist attacks in twenty countries that killed or injured nearly 900 people, including twelve Americans. Iraq has also provided safe haven to Abu Abbas, who was responsible for seizing the *Achille Lauro* and killing an American passenger. And we know that Iraq is continuing to finance terror and gives assistance to groups that use terrorism to undermine Middle East peace.

We know that Iraq and the al Qaeda terrorist network share a common enemy – the United States of America. We know that Iraq and al Qaeda have had high-level contacts that go back a decade. Some al Qaeda leaders who fled Afghanistan went to Iraq. These include one very senior al Qaeda leader who received medical treatment in Baghdad this year, and who has been associated with planning for chemical and biological attacks. We've learned that Iraq has trained al Qaeda members in bomb-making and poisons and deadly gases. And we know that after September the 11th, Saddam Hussein's regime gleefully celebrated the terrorist attacks on America.

Iraq could decide on any given day to provide a biological or chemical weapon to a terrorist group or individual terrorists. Alliance with terrorists could allow the Iraqi regime to attack America without leaving any fingerprints.

Some have argued that confronting the threat from Iraq could detract from the war against terror. To the contrary; confronting the threat posed by Iraq is crucial to winning the war on terror. When I spoke to Congress more than a year ago, I said that those who harbour terrorists are as guilty as the terrorists themselves. Saddam Hussein is harbouring terrorists and the instruments of terror, the instruments of mass death and destruction. And he cannot be trusted. The risk is simply too great that he will use them, or provide them to a terror network.

Terror cells and outlaw regimes building weapons of mass destruction are different faces of the same evil. Our security requires that we confront both. And the United States military is capable of confronting both.

Many people have asked how close Saddam Hussein is to developing a nuclear weapon. Well, we don't know exactly, and that's the problem. Before the Gulf War, the best intelligence indicated that Iraq was eight to ten years away from developing a nuclear weapon. After the war, international inspectors learned that the regime has been much closer – the regime in Iraq would likely have possessed a nuclear weapon no later than 1993. The inspectors discovered that Iraq had an advanced nuclear weapons development programme, had a design for a workable nuclear weapon, and was pursuing several different methods of enriching uranium for a bomb.

Before being barred from Iraq in 1998, the International Atomic Energy Agency dismantled extensive nuclear weapons-related facilities, including three uranium enrichment sites. That same year, information from a high-ranking Iraqi nuclear engineer who had defected revealed that despite his public promises, Saddam Hussein had ordered his nuclear programme to continue.

The evidence indicates that Iraq is reconstituting its nuclear weapons programme. Saddam Hussein has held numerous meetings with Iraqi nuclear scientists, a group he calls his 'nuclear mujahideen' – his nuclear holy warriors. Satellite photographs reveal that Iraq is rebuilding facilities at sites that have been part of its nuclear programme in the past. Iraq has attempted to purchase high-strength aluminum tubes and other equipment needed for gas centrifuges, which are used to enrich uranium for nuclear weapons.

If the Iraqi regime is able to produce, buy, or steal an amount of highly enriched uranium a little larger than a single softball, it could have a nuclear weapon in less than a year. And if we allow that to happen, a terrible line would be crossed. Saddam Hussein would be in a position to blackmail anyone who opposes his aggression. He would be in a position to dominate the Middle East.

He would be in a position to threaten America. And Saddam Hussein would be in a position to pass nuclear technology to terrorists.

Some citizens wonder, after eleven years of living with this problem, why do we need to confront it now? And there's a reason. We've experienced the horror of September the 11th. We have seen that those who hate America are willing to crash airplanes into buildings full of innocent people. Our enemies would be no less willing, in fact, they would be eager, to use biological or chemical, or nuclear weapons.

Knowing these realities, America must not ignore the threat gathering against us. Facing clear evidence of peril, we cannot wait for the final proof – the smoking gun – that could come in the form of a mushroom cloud. As President Kennedy said in October of 1962, 'Neither the United States of America, nor the world community of nations can tolerate deliberate deception and offensive threats on the part of any nation, large or small. We no longer live in a world,' he said, 'where only the actual firing of weapons represents a sufficient challenge to a nation's security to constitute maximum peril.'

Understanding the threats of our time, knowing the designs and deceptions of the Iraqi regime, we have every reason to assume the worst, and we have an urgent duty to prevent the worst from occurring.

Some believe we can address this danger by simply resuming the old approach to inspections, and applying diplomatic and economic pressure. Yet this is precisely what the world has tried to do since 1991. The UN inspections programme was met with systematic deception. The Iraqi regime bugged hotel rooms and offices of inspectors to find where they were going next; they forged documents, destroyed evidence, and developed mobile weapons facilities to keep a step ahead of inspectors. Eight so-called presidential palaces were declared off-limits to unfettered inspections. These sites actually encompass twelve square miles, with hundreds of structures, both above and below the ground, where sensitive materials could be hidden.

The world has also tried economic sanctions – and watched Iraq use billions of dollars in illegal oil revenues to fund more weapons purchases, rather than providing for the needs of the Iraqi people.

The world has tried limited military strikes to destroy Iraq's weapons of mass destruction capabilities – only to see them openly rebuilt, while the regime again denies they even exist.

The world has tried no-fly zones to keep Saddam from terrorising his own people – and in the last year alone, the Iraqi military has fired upon American and British pilots more than 750 times.

After eleven years during which we have tried containment, sanctions, inspections, even selected military action, the end result is that Saddam Hussein still has chemical and biological weapons and is increasing his capabilities to make more. And he is moving ever closer to developing a nuclear weapon.

Clearly, to actually work, any new inspections, sanctions or enforcement mechanisms will have to be very different. America wants the UN to be an effective organisation that helps keep the peace. And that is why we are urging the Security Council to adopt a new resolution setting out tough, immediate requirements. Among those requirements: the Iraqi regime must reveal and destroy, under UN supervision, all existing weapons of mass destruction. To ensure that we learn the truth, the regime must allow witnesses to its illegal activities to be interviewed outside the country – and these witnesses must be free to bring their families with them so they are all beyond the reach of Saddam Hussein's terror and murder. And inspectors must have access to any site, at any time, without pre-clearance, without delay, without exceptions.

The time for denying, deceiving, and delaying has come to an end. Saddam Hussein must disarm himself – or, for the sake of peace, we will lead a coalition to disarm him.

Many nations are joining us in insisting that Saddam Hussein's regime be held accountable. They are committed to defending the international security that protects the lives of both our citizens and theirs. And that's why America is challenging all nations to take the resolutions of the UN Security Council seriously.

And these resolutions are clear. In addition to declaring and destroying all of its weapons of mass destruction, Iraq must end its support for terrorism. It must cease the persecution of its civilian population. It must stop all illicit trade outside the Oil For Food programme. It must release or account for all Gulf War personnel, including an American pilot, whose fate is still unknown.

By taking these steps, and by only taking these steps, the Iraqi regime has an opportunity to avoid conflict. Taking these steps would also change the nature of the Iraqi regime itself. America hopes the regime will make that choice. Unfortunately, at least so far, we have little reason to expect it. And that's why two administrations – mine and President Clinton's – have stated that regime change in Iraq is the only certain means of removing a great danger to our nation.

I hope this will not require military action, but it may. And military conflict could be difficult. An Iraqi regime faced with its own demise may attempt cruel and desperate measures. If Saddam Hussein orders such measures, his generals would be well advised to refuse those orders. If they do not refuse, they must understand that all war criminals will be pursued and punished. If we have to act, we will take every precaution that is possible. We will plan carefully; we will act with the full power of the United States military; we will act with allies at our side, and we will prevail.

There is no easy or risk-free course of action. Some have argued we should wait – and that's an option. In my view, it's the riskiest of all options, because the longer we wait, the stronger and bolder Saddam Hussein will become. We could wait and hope that Saddam does not give weapons to terrorists, or develop a nuclear weapon to blackmail the world. But I'm convinced that is a hope against all evidence. As Americans, we want peace – we work and sacrifice for peace. But there can be no peace if our security depends on the will and whims of a ruthless and aggressive dictator. I'm not willing to stake one American life on trusting Saddam Hussein.

Failure to act would embolden other tyrants, allow terrorists access to new weapons and new resources, and make blackmail a permanent feature of world events. The United Nations would betray the purpose of its founding, and prove irrelevant to the problems of our time. And through its inaction, the United States would resign itself to a future of fear.

That is not the America I know. That is not the America I serve. We refuse to live in fear. This nation, in world war and in Cold War, has never permitted the brutal and lawless to set history's course. Now, as before, we will secure our nation, protect our freedom, and help others to find freedom of their own.

Some worry that a change of leadership in Iraq could create instability and make the situation worse. The situation could hardly get worse, for world security and for the people of Iraq. The lives of Iraqi citizens would improve dramatically if Saddam Hussein were no longer in power, just as the lives of Afghanistan's citizens improved after the Taliban. The dictator of Iraq is a student of Stalin, using murder as a tool of terror and control, within his own Cabinet, within his own army, and even within his own family.

On Saddam Hussein's orders, opponents have been decapitated, wives and mothers of political opponents have been systematically raped as a method of intimidation, and political prisoners have been forced to watch their own children being tortured.

America believes that all people are entitled to hope and human rights, to the non-negotiable demands of human dignity. People everywhere prefer freedom to slavery; prosperity to squalor; self-government to the rule of terror and torture. America is a friend to the people of Iraq. Our demands are directed only at the regime that enslaves them and threatens us. When these demands are met, the first and greatest benefit will come to Iraqi men, women and children. The oppression of Kurds, Assyrians, Turkomans, Shi'a, Sunnis and others will be lifted. The long captivity of Iraq will end, and an era of new hope will begin.

Iraq is a land rich in culture, resources, and talent. Freed from the weight of oppression, Iraq's people will be able to share in the progress and prosperity of our time. If military action is necessary, the United States and our allies will help the Iraqi people rebuild their economy, and create the institutions of liberty in a unified Iraq at peace with its neighbours.

Later this week, the United States Congress will vote on this matter. I have asked Congress to authorise the use of America's military, if it proves necessary, to enforce UN Security Council demands. Approving this resolution does not mean that military action is imminent or unavoidable. The resolution will tell the United Nations, and all nations, that America speaks with one voice and is determined to make the demands of the civilised world mean something.

Congress will also be sending a message to the dictator in Iraq: that his only chance – his only choice – is full compliance, and the time remaining for that choice is limited.

Members of Congress are nearing an historic vote. I'm confident they will fully consider the facts, and their duties.

The attacks of September the 11th showed our country that vast oceans no longer protect us from danger. Before that tragic date, we had only hints of al Qaeda's plans and designs. Today in Iraq, we see a threat whose outlines are far more clearly defined, and whose consequences could be far more deadly. Saddam Hussein's actions have put us on notice, and there is no refuge from our responsibilities.

We did not ask for this present challenge, but we accept it. Like other generations of Americans, we will meet the responsibility of defending human liberty against violence and aggression. By our resolve, we will give strength to others. By our courage, we will give hope to others. And by our actions, we will secure the peace, and lead the world to a better day.

May God bless America.

ROBIN COOK

'THE RIGHT OF THIS PLACE TO VOTE'

—

RESIGNATION SPEECH, REMARKS BEFORE THE HOUSE OF COMMONS

LONDON, UNITED KINGDOM, 17 MARCH 2003

Widely regarded as among the leading intellectuals of his generation of Labour politicians, Robin Cook was elected to Parliament in 1983 representing Livingston, a constituency he served until his untimely death. He was Foreign Secretary of the United Kingdom from 1997–2001, and Leader of the House of Commons from 2001 until his resignation from the Cabinet with this speech in 2003.

Cook offers as his reason for resigning from government the invasion of Iraq. He argues that the House of Commons should have voted on the war. He cannot support the war on principle. He believes there are constitutional issues at stake.

This was a painful resignation for the Labour Party and the Prime Minister. Cook himself explains his own difficulties with resignation. The language in the speech reveals the controversy in the government itself with the invasion of Iraq and continued concerns about the conduct of the war.

Robin Cook died of a sudden heart attack in 2005 while descending Ben Stack mountain in Northern Scotland. He was widely expected to return to the Cabinet under Gordon Brown and many supporters of Labour and the Liberal Democrats longed to see Cook as Prime Minister at the head of a Labour–Liberal Democrat coalition.

—

This is the first time for twenty years that I have addressed the House from the backbenches. I must confess that I had forgotten how much better the view is from here. None of those twenty years were more enjoyable or more rewarding than the past two, in which I have had the immense privilege of serving this House as Leader of the House, which were made all the more enjoyable, Mr Speaker, by the opportunity of working closely with you.

It was frequently the necessity for me as Leader of the House to talk my way out of accusations that a statement had been preceded by a press interview. On this occasion I can say with complete confidence that no press interview has been given before this statement. I have chosen to address the House first on why I cannot support a war without international agreement or domestic support.

The present Prime Minister is the most successful leader of the Labour Party in my lifetime. I hope that he will continue to be the leader of our party, and I hope that he will continue to be successful. I have no sympathy with, and I will give no comfort to, those who want to use this crisis to displace him.

I applaud the heroic efforts that the Prime Minister has made in trying to secure a second resolution. I do not think that anybody could have done better than the Foreign Secretary in working to get support for a second resolution within the Security Council. But the very intensity of those attempts underlines how important it was to succeed. Now that those attempts have failed, we cannot pretend that getting a second resolution was of no importance. France has been at the receiving end of bucketloads of commentary in recent days. It is not France alone that wants more time for inspections. Germany wants more time for inspections; Russia wants more time for inspections; indeed, at no time have we signed up even the minimum necessary to carry a second resolution. We delude ourselves if we think that the degree of international hostility is all the result of President Chirac. The reality is that Britain is being asked to embark on a war without agreement in any of the international bodies of which we are a leading partner – not NATO, not the European Union and, now, not the Security Council.

To end up in such diplomatic weakness is a serious reverse. Only a year ago, we and the United States were part of a coalition against terrorism that was wider and more diverse than I would ever have imagined possible. History will be astonished at the diplomatic miscalculations that led so quickly to the disintegration of that powerful coalition. The US can afford to go it alone, but Britain is not a superpower. Our interests are best protected not by unilateral action but by multilateral agreement and a world order governed by rules. Yet tonight the international partnerships most important to us are weakened: the European Union is divided; the Security Council is in stalemate. Those are heavy casualties of a war in which a shot has yet to be fired.

I have heard some parallels between military action in these circumstances and the military action that we took in Kosovo. There was no doubt about the multilateral support that we had for the action that we took in Kosovo. It was supported by NATO; it was supported by the European Union; it was supported by every single one of the seven neighbours in the region. France and Germany were our active allies. It is precisely because we have none of that support in this case that it was all the more important to get agreement in the Security Council as the last hope of demonstrating international agreement.

The legal basis for our action in Kosovo was the need to respond to an urgent and compelling humanitarian crisis. Our difficulty in getting support this time is that neither the international community nor the British public is persuaded that there is an urgent and compelling reason for this military action in Iraq.

The threshold for war should always be high. None of us can predict the death toll of civilians from the forthcoming bombardment of Iraq, but the US warning of a bombing campaign that will 'shock and awe' makes it likely that casualties will be numbered at least in the thousands. I am confident that British servicemen and women will acquit themselves with professionalism and with courage. I hope that they all come back. I hope that Saddam, even now, will quit Baghdad and avert war, but it is false to argue that only those who support war support our troops. It is entirely legitimate to support our troops while seeking an alternative to the conflict that will put those troops at risk.

Nor is it fair to accuse those of us who want longer for inspections of not having an alternative strategy. For four years as Foreign Secretary I was partly responsible for the Western strategy of containment. Over the past decade that strategy destroyed more weapons than in the Gulf War, dismantled Iraq's nuclear weapons programme and halted Saddam's medium and long-range missiles programmes. Iraq's military strength is now less than half its size than at the time of the last Gulf War.

Ironically, it is only because Iraq's military forces are so weak that we can even contemplate its invasion. Some advocates of conflict claim that Saddam's forces are so weak, so demoralised and so badly equipped that the war will be over in a few days. We cannot base our military strategy on the assumption that Saddam is weak and at the same time justify pre-emptive action on the claim that he is a threat.

Iraq probably has no weapons of mass destruction in the commonly understood sense of the term – namely a credible device capable of being delivered against a strategic city target. It probably still has biological toxins and battlefield chemical munitions, but it has had them since the 1980s when US companies sold Saddam anthrax agents and the then British government approved chemical and munitions factories. Why is it now so urgent that we should take military action to disarm a military capacity that has been there for twenty years, and which we helped to create? Why is it necessary to resort to war this week, while Saddam's ambition to complete his weapons programme is blocked by the presence of UN inspectors?

Only a couple of weeks ago, Hans Blix told the Security Council that the key remaining disarmament tasks could be completed within months. I have heard it said that Iraq has had not months but twelve years in which to complete disarmament, and that our patience is exhausted. Yet it is more than thirty years since resolution 242 called on Israel to withdraw from the occupied territories. We do not express the same impatience with the persistent refusal of Israel to comply. I welcome the strong personal commitment that the Prime Minister has given to Middle East peace, but Britain's positive role in the Middle East does not redress the strong sense of injustice throughout the Muslim world at what it sees as one rule for the allies of the US and another rule for the rest.

Nor is our credibility helped by the appearance that our partners in Washington are less interested in disarmament than they are in regime change in Iraq. That explains why any evidence that inspections may be showing progress is greeted in Washington not with satisfaction but with consternation: it reduces the case for war.

What has come to trouble me most over past weeks is the suspicion that if the hanging chads in Florida had gone the other way and Al Gore had been elected, we would not now be about to commit British troops.

The longer that I have served in this place, the greater the respect I have for the good sense and collective wisdom of the British people. On Iraq, I believe that the prevailing mood of the British people is sound. They do not doubt that Saddam is a brutal dictator, but they are not persuaded that he is a clear and present danger to Britain. They want inspections to be given a chance, and they suspect that they are being pushed too quickly into conflict by a US administration with an agenda of its own. Above all, they are uneasy at Britain going out on a limb on a military adventure without a broader international coalition and against the hostility of many of our traditional allies.

From the start of the present crisis, I have insisted, as Leader of the House, on the right of this place to vote on whether Britain should go to war. It has been a favourite theme of commentators that this House no longer occupies a central role in British politics. Nothing could better demonstrate that they are wrong than for this House to stop the commitment of troops in a war that has neither international agreement nor domestic support. I intend to join those tomorrow night who will vote against military action now. It is for that reason, and for that reason alone, and with a heavy heart, that I resign from the government.

POPE BENEDICT XVI

'FAITH AND REASON'

—

LECTURE AT A MEETING WITH REPRESENTATIVES OF SCIENCE

UNIVERSITY OF REGENSBURG, REGENSBURG, GERMANY, 12 SEPTEMBER 2006

After serving as the Vatican's Prefect of the Sacred Congregation for the Doctrine of the Faith from 1981–2005, Joseph Cardinal Ratzinger became Pope after the death of his predecessor, John Paul II, and election by the College of Cardinals on 19 April 2005. Earlier in his career, from 1969–1977, he had been a professor of theology at Regensburg.

This speech marked his return. Despite his intention to promote multicultural and ecumenical dialogue, the lecture generated an intense and hostile backlash because it cited historical language denigrating the contributions of Islam. The debate continues as to whether or not those remarks were taken out of context. They certainly were an indicator of the ability, or lack of it, to discuss the history of Islam and its interactions with the Christian West. At the very least, the lecture and its reception raised the issue, yet again, of freedom to criticise Islamic beliefs or practices, as well as the self-censorship that anticipates violent reactions. Perhaps this lecture is best remembered as a benchmark of freedom of speech vs. respect for religion, measuring the boundaries of language and the chilling effect of self-restraint. Below is the lecture given by Pope Benedict, complete with his footnotes.

—

Your Eminences, Your Magnificences, Your Excellencies, Distinguished Ladies and Gentlemen:

It is a moving experience for me to be back again in the university and to be able once again to give a lecture at this podium. I think back to those years when, after a pleasant period at the Freisinger Hochschule, I began teaching at the University of Bonn. That was in 1959, in the days of the old university made up of ordinary professors. The various chairs had neither assistants nor secretaries, but in recompense there was much direct contact with students and in particular among the professors themselves. We would meet before and after lessons in the rooms of the teaching staff. There was a lively exchange with historians, philosophers, philologists and, naturally, between the two theological faculties. Once a semester there was a *dies academicus*, when professors from every faculty appeared before the students of the entire university, making possible a genuine experience of *universitas* – something that you too, Magnificent Rector, just mentioned – the experience, in other words, of the fact that despite our specialisations, which at times make it difficult to communicate with each other, we made up a whole, working in everything on the basis of a single rationality with its various aspects and sharing responsibility for the right use of reason – this reality became a lived experience. The university was also very proud of its two theological faculties. It was clear that, by inquiring about the reasonableness of faith, they too carried out a work which is necessarily part of the 'whole' of the *universitas scientiarum*, even if not everyone could share the faith which theologians seek to correlate with reason as a whole. This profound sense of coherence within the universe of reason was not troubled, even when it was once reported that a colleague had said there was something odd about our university: it had two faculties devoted to something that did not exist: God. That even in the face of such radical scepticism it is still necessary and reasonable to raise the question of God through the use of reason, and to do so in the context of the tradition of the Christian faith: this, within the university as a whole, was accepted without question.

I was reminded of all this recently, when I read the edition by Professor Theodore Khoury [Münster] of part of the dialogue carried on – perhaps in 1391 in the winter barracks near Ankara – by the erudite Byzantine emperor Manuel II Paleologus and an educated Persian on the subject of Christianity and Islam, and the truth of both.[1] It was presumably the emperor himself who set down

---

1   Of the total number of 26 conversations (διάλεξις – Khoury translates this as 'controversy') in the dialogue ('Entretien'), T. Khoury published the seventh 'controversy' with footnotes and an extensive introduction on the origin of the text, on the manuscript tradition and on the structure of the dialogue, together with brief summaries of the 'controversies' not included in the edition; the Greek text is accompanied by a French translation: 'Manuel II Paléologue, Entretiens avec un Musulman. 7ᵉ Controverse', *Sources Chrétiennes* n. 115, Paris 1966. In the meantime, Karl Förstel published in *Corpus Islamico-Christianum* (*Series Graeca* ed. A. T. Khoury and R. Glei) an edition of the text in Greek and German with commentary: 'Manuel

this dialogue, during the siege of Constantinople between 1394 and 1402; and this would explain why his arguments are given in greater detail than those of his Persian interlocutor.[2] The dialogue ranges widely over the structures of faith contained in the Bible and in the Qur'an, and deals especially with the image of God and of man, while necessarily returning repeatedly to the relationship between – as they were called – three 'Laws' or 'rules of life': the Old Testament, the New Testament and the Qur'an. It is not my intention to discuss this question in the present lecture; here I would like to discuss only one point – itself rather marginal to the dialogue as a whole – which, in the context of the issue of 'faith and reason', I found interesting and which can serve as the starting-point for my reflections on this issue.

In the seventh conversation (διάλεξις – controversy) edited by Professor Khoury, the emperor touches on the theme of the holy war. The emperor must have known that surah 2, 256 reads: 'There is no compulsion in religion'. According to some of the experts, this is probably one of the suras of the early period, when Mohammed was still powerless and under threat. But naturally the emperor also knew the instructions, developed later and recorded in the Qur'an, concerning holy war. Without descending to details, such as the difference in treatment accorded to those who have the 'Book' and the 'infidels', he addresses his interlocutor with a startling brusqueness, a brusqueness that we find unacceptable, on the central question about the relationship between religion and violence in general, saying: 'Show me just what Mohammed brought that was new, and there you will find things only evil and inhuman, such as his command to spread by the sword the faith he preached.'[3] The emperor, after having expressed himself so forcefully, goes on to explain in detail the reasons why spreading the faith through violence is something unreasonable. Violence is incompatible with the nature of God and the nature of the soul. 'God,' he says, 'is not pleased by blood – and not acting reasonably (σὺν λόγῳ) is contrary to God's nature. Faith is born of the soul, not the body. Whoever would lead

---

II. Palaiologus, Dialoge mit einem Muslim', 3 vols., Würzburg-Altenberge 1993–1996. As early as 1966, E. Trapp had published the Greek text with an introduction as vol. II of *Wiener byzantinische Studien*. I shall be quoting from Khoury's edition.

2   On the origin and redaction of the dialogue, cf. Khoury, pp. 22–29; extensive comments in this regard can also be found in the editions of Förstel and Trapp.

3   Controversy VII, 2 c: Khoury, pp. 142–143; Förstel, vol. I, VII. Dialog 1.5, pp. 240–241. In the Muslim world, this quotation has unfortunately been taken as an expression of my personal position, thus arousing understandable indignation. I hope that the reader of my text can see immediately that this sentence does not express my personal view of the Qur'an, for which I have the respect due to the holy book of a great religion. In quoting the text of the Emperor Manuel II, I intended solely to draw out the essential relationship between faith and reason. On this point I am in agreement with Manuel II, but without endorsing his polemic.

someone to faith needs the ability to speak well and to reason properly, without violence and threats... To convince a reasonable soul, one does not need a strong arm, or weapons of any kind, or any other means of threatening a person with death...'[4]

The decisive statement in this argument against violent conversion is this: not to act in accordance with reason is contrary to God's nature.[5] The editor, Theodore Khoury, observes: For the emperor, as a Byzantine shaped by Greek philosophy, this statement is self-evident. But for Muslim teaching, God is absolutely transcendent. His will is not bound up with any of our categories, even that of rationality.[6] Here Khoury quotes a work of the noted French Islamist R. Arnaldez, who points out that Ibn Hazm went so far as to state that God is not bound even by his own word, and that nothing would oblige him to reveal the truth to us. Were it God's will, we would even have to practise idolatry.[7]

At this point, as far as understanding of God and thus the concrete practice of religion is concerned, we are faced with an unavoidable dilemma. Is the conviction that acting unreasonably contradicts God's nature merely a Greek idea, or is it always and intrinsically true? I believe that here we can see the profound harmony between what is Greek in the best sense of the word and the biblical understanding of faith in God. Modifying the first verse of the Book of Genesis, the first verse of the whole Bible, John began the prologue of his Gospel with the words: 'In the beginning was the λόγος'. This is the very word used by the emperor: God acts, σὺν λόγῳ, with *logos*. *Logos* means both reason and word – a reason which is creative and capable of self-communication, precisely as reason. John thus spoke the final word on the biblical concept of God, and in this word all the often toilsome and tortuous threads of biblical faith find their culmination and synthesis. In the beginning was the *logos*, and the *logos* is God, says the Evangelist. The encounter between the Biblical message and Greek thought did not happen by chance. The vision of Saint Paul, who saw the roads to Asia barred and in a dream saw a Macedonian man plead with him: 'Come over to Macedonia and help us!' (cf. Acts 16:6–10) – this vision can be interpreted as a 'distillation' of the intrinsic necessity of a rapprochement between Biblical faith and Greek inquiry.

In point of fact, this rapprochement had been going on for some time. The mysterious name of God, revealed from the burning bush, a name which

---

4   Controversy VII, 3 b–c: Khoury, pp. 144–145; Förstel vol. I,VII. Dialog 1.6, pp. 240–243.

5   It was purely for the sake of this statement that I quoted the dialogue between Manuel and his Persian interlocutor. In this statement the theme of my subsequent reflections emerges.

6   Cf. Khoury, p. 144, n. 1.

7   R. Arnaldez, *Grammaire et théologie chez Ibn Hazm de Cordoue*, Paris 1956, p. 13; cf. Khoury, p. 144. The fact that comparable positions exist in the theology of the late Middle Ages will appear later in my discourse.

separates this God from all other divinities with their many names and simply asserts being, 'I am', already presents a challenge to the notion of myth, to which Socrates's attempt to vanquish and transcend myth stands in close analogy.[8] Within the Old Testament, the process which started at the burning bush came to new maturity at the time of the Exile, when the God of Israel, an Israel now deprived of its land and worship, was proclaimed as the God of heaven and earth and described in a simple formula which echoes the words uttered at the burning bush: 'I am'. This new understanding of God is accompanied by a kind of enlightenment, which finds stark expression in the mockery of gods who are merely the work of human hands (cf. Psalms 115). Thus, despite the bitter conflict with those Hellenistic rulers who sought to accommodate it forcibly to the customs and idolatrous cult of the Greeks, biblical faith, in the Hellenistic period, encountered the best of Greek thought at a deep level, resulting in a mutual enrichment evident especially in the later wisdom literature. Today we know that the Greek translation of the Old Testament produced at Alexandria – the Septuagint – is more than a simple (and in that sense really less than satisfactory) translation of the Hebrew text: it is an independent textual witness and a distinct and important step in the history of revelation, one which brought about this encounter in a way that was decisive for the birth and spread of Christianity.[9] A profound encounter of faith and reason is taking place here, an encounter between genuine enlightenment and religion. From the very heart of Christian faith and, at the same time, the heart of Greek thought now joined to faith, Manuel II was able to say: Not to act 'with *logos*' is contrary to God's nature.

In all honesty, one must observe that in the late Middle Ages we find trends in theology which would sunder this synthesis between the Greek spirit and the Christian spirit. In contrast with the so-called intellectualism of Augustine and Thomas, there arose with Duns Scotus a voluntarism which, in its later developments, led to the claim that we can only know God's *voluntas ordinata*. Beyond this is the realm of God's freedom, in virtue of which he could have done the opposite of everything he has actually done. This gives rise to positions which clearly approach those of Ibn Hazm and might even lead to the image of a capricious God, who is not even bound to truth and goodness. God's transcendence

---

8 Regarding the widely discussed interpretation of the episode of the burning bush, I refer to my book *Introduction to Christianity*, London 1969, pp. 77–93 (originally published in German as *Einführung in das Christentum*, Munich 1968; N.B. the pages quoted refer to the entire chapter entitled 'The Biblical Belief in God'). I think that my statements in that book, despite later developments in the discussion, remain valid today.

9 Cf. A. Schenker, 'L'Écriture sainte subsiste en plusieurs formes canoniques simultanées', in *L'Interpretazione della Bibbia nella Chiesa. Atti del Simposio promosso dalla Congregazione per la Dottrina della Fede*, Vatican City 2001, pp. 178–186.

and otherness are so exalted that our reason, our sense of the true and good, are no longer an authentic mirror of God, whose deepest possibilities remain eternally unattainable and hidden behind his actual decisions. As opposed to this, the faith of the Church has always insisted that between God and us, between his eternal Creator Spirit and our created reason there exists a real analogy, in which – as the Fourth Lateran Council in 1215 stated – unlikeness remains infinitely greater than likeness, yet not to the point of abolishing analogy and its language. God does not become more divine when we push him away from us in a sheer, impenetrable voluntarism; rather, the truly divine God is the God who has revealed himself as *logos* and, as *logos*, has acted and continues to act lovingly on our behalf. Certainly, love, as Saint Paul says, 'transcends' knowledge and is thereby capable of perceiving more than thought alone (cf. Ephesians 3:19); nonetheless it continues to be love of the God who is *Logos*. Consequently, Christian worship is, again to quote Paul – 'λογικη λατρεία', worship in harmony with the eternal Word and with our reason (cf. Romans 12:1).[10]

This inner rapprochement between Biblical faith and Greek philosophical inquiry was an event of decisive importance not only from the standpoint of the history of religions, but also from that of world history – it is an event which concerns us even today. Given this convergence, it is not surprising that Christianity, despite its origins and some significant developments in the East, finally took on its historically decisive character in Europe. We can also express this the other way around: this convergence, with the subsequent addition of the Roman heritage, created Europe and remains the foundation of what can rightly be called Europe.

The thesis that the critically purified Greek heritage forms an integral part of Christian faith has been countered by the call for a dehellenisation of Christianity – a call which has more and more dominated theological discussions since the beginning of the modern age. Viewed more closely, three stages can be observed in the programme of dehellenisation: although interconnected, they are clearly distinct from one another in their motivations and objective.[11]

Dehellenisation first emerges in connection with the postulates of the Reformation in the sixteenth century. Looking at the tradition of scholastic theology, the Reformers thought they were confronted with a faith system totally conditioned by philosophy, that is to say an articulation of the faith based on an

---

10 On this matter I expressed myself in greater detail in my book *The Spirit of the Liturgy*, San Francisco 2000, pp. 44–50.

11 Of the vast literature on the theme of dehellenisation, I would like to mention above all: A. Grillmeier, 'Hellenisierung-Judaisierung des Christentums als Deuteprinzipien der Geschichte des kirchlichen Dogmas', in idem, *Mit ihm und in ihm. Christologische Forschungen und Perspektiven*, Freiburg 1975, pp. 423–488.

alien system of thought. As a result, faith no longer appeared as a living historical Word but as one element of an overarching philosophical system. The principle of *sola scriptura*, on the other hand, sought faith in its pure, primordial form, as originally found in the biblical Word. Metaphysics appeared as a premise derived from another source, from which faith had to be liberated in order to become once more fully itself. When Kant stated that he needed to set thinking aside in order to make room for faith, he carried this programme forward with a radicalism that the Reformers could never have foreseen. He thus anchored faith exclusively in practical reason, denying it access to reality as a whole.

The liberal theology of the nineteenth and twentieth centuries ushered in a second stage in the process of dehellenisation, with Adolf von Harnack as its outstanding representative. When I was a student, and in the early years of my teaching, this programme was highly influential in Catholic theology too. It took as its point of departure Pascal's distinction between the God of the philosophers and the God of Abraham, Isaac and Jacob. In my inaugural lecture at Bonn in 1959, I tried to address the issue,[12] and I do not intend to repeat here what I said on that occasion, but I would like to describe at least briefly what was new about this second stage of dehellenisation. Harnack's central idea was to return simply to the man Jesus and to his simple message, underneath the accretions of theology and indeed of hellenisation: this simple message was seen as the culmination of the religious development of humanity. Jesus was said to have put an end to worship in favour of morality. In the end he was presented as the father of a humanitarian moral message. Fundamentally, Harnack's goal was to bring Christianity back into harmony with modern reason, liberating it, that is to say, from seemingly philosophical and theological elements, such as faith in Christ's divinity and the triune God. In this sense, historical-critical exegesis of the New Testament, as he saw it, restored to theology its place within the university: theology, for Harnack, is something essentially historical and therefore strictly scientific. What it is able to say critically about Jesus is, so to speak, an expression of practical reason and consequently it can take its rightful place within the university. Behind this thinking lies the modern self-limitation of reason, classically expressed in Kant's 'Critiques', but in the meantime further radicalised by the impact of the natural sciences. This modern concept of reason is based, to put it briefly, on a synthesis between Platonism (Cartesianism) and empiricism, a synthesis confirmed by the success of technology. On the one hand it presupposes the mathematical structure of matter, its intrinsic rationality, which makes it possible to understand how matter works

---

12   Newly published with commentary by Heino Sonnemans (ed.): Joseph Ratzinger-Benedikt XVI, Der Gott des Glaubens und der Gott der Philosophen. Ein Beitrag zum Problem der theologia naturalis, Johannes-Verlag Leutesdorf, 2nd revised edition, 2005

and use it efficiently: this basic premise is, so to speak, the Platonic element in the modern understanding of nature. On the other hand, there is nature's capacity to be exploited for our purposes, and here only the possibility of verification or falsification through experimentation can yield decisive certainty. The weight between the two poles can, depending on the circumstances, shift from one side to the other. As strongly positivistic a thinker as J. Monod has declared himself a convinced Platonist/Cartesian.

This gives rise to two principles which are crucial for the issue we have raised. First, only the kind of certainty resulting from the interplay of mathematical and empirical elements can be considered scientific. Anything that would claim to be science must be measured against this criterion. Hence the human sciences, such as history, psychology, sociology and philosophy, attempt to conform themselves to this canon of scientificity. A second point, which is important for our reflections, is that by its very nature this method excludes the question of God, making it appear an unscientific or pre-scientific question. Consequently, we are faced with a reduction of the radius of science and reason, one which needs to be questioned.

I will return to this problem later. In the meantime, it must be observed that from this standpoint any attempt to maintain theology's claim to be 'scientific' would end up reducing Christianity to a mere fragment of its former self. But we must say more: if science as a whole is this and this alone, then it is man himself who ends up being reduced, for the specifically human questions about our origin and destiny, the questions raised by religion and ethics, then have no place within the purview of collective reason as defined by 'science', so understood, and must thus be relegated to the realm of the subjective. The subject then decides, on the basis of his experiences, what he considers tenable in matters of religion, and the subjective 'conscience' becomes the sole arbiter of what is ethical. In this way, though, ethics and religion lose their power to create a community and become a completely personal matter. This is a dangerous state of affairs for humanity, as we see from the disturbing pathologies of religion and reason which necessarily erupt when reason is so reduced that questions of religion and ethics no longer concern it. Attempts to construct an ethic from the rules of evolution or from psychology and sociology, end up being simply inadequate.

Before I draw the conclusions to which all this has been leading, I must briefly refer to the third stage of dehellenisation, which is now in progress. In the light of our experience with cultural pluralism, it is often said nowadays that the synthesis with Hellenism achieved in the early Church was an initial inculturation which ought not to be binding on other cultures. The latter are said to have the right to return to the simple message of the New Testament prior to that inculturation, in order to inculturate it anew in their own particular milieux.

This thesis is not simply false, but it is coarse and lacking in precision. The New Testament was written in Greek and bears the imprint of the Greek spirit, which had already come to maturity as the Old Testament developed. True, there are elements in the evolution of the early Church which do not have to be integrated into all cultures. Nonetheless, the fundamental decisions made about the relationship between faith and the use of human reason are part of the faith itself; they are developments consonant with the nature of faith itself.

And so I come to my conclusion. This attempt, painted with broad strokes, at a critique of modern reason from within has nothing to do with putting the clock back to the time before the Enlightenment and rejecting the insights of the modern age. The positive aspects of modernity are to be acknowledged unreservedly: we are all grateful for the marvellous possibilities that it has opened up for mankind and for the progress in humanity that has been granted to us. The scientific ethos, moreover, is – as you yourself mentioned, Magnificent Rector – the will to be obedient to the truth, and, as such, it embodies an attitude which belongs to the essential decisions of the Christian spirit. The intention here is not one of retrenchment or negative criticism, but of broadening our concept of reason and its application. While we rejoice in the new possibilities open to humanity, we also see the dangers arising from these possibilities and we must ask ourselves how we can overcome them. We will succeed in doing so only if reason and faith come together in a new way, if we overcome the self-imposed limitation of reason to the empirically falsifiable, and if we once more disclose its vast horizons. In this sense theology rightly belongs in the university and within the wide-ranging dialogue of sciences, not merely as a historical discipline and one of the human sciences, but precisely as theology, as inquiry into the rationality of faith.

Only thus do we become capable of that genuine dialogue of cultures and religions so urgently needed today. In the Western world it is widely held that only positivistic reason and the forms of philosophy based on it are universally valid. Yet the world's profoundly religious cultures see this exclusion of the divine from the universality of reason as an attack on their most profound convictions. A reason which is deaf to the divine and which relegates religion into the realm of subcultures is incapable of entering into the dialogue of cultures. At the same time, as I have attempted to show, modern scientific reason with its intrinsically Platonic element bears within itself a question which points beyond itself and beyond the possibilities of its methodology. Modern scientific reason quite simply has to accept the rational structure of matter and the correspondence between our spirit and the prevailing rational structures of nature as a given, on which its methodology has to be based. Yet the question why this has to be so is a real question, and one which has to be remanded by the natural sciences to other modes and planes of thought – to philosophy and theology. For philosophy and, albeit in a different way, for theology, listening to the great experiences and insights of the religious traditions of humanity, and those of the Christian faith in particular, is a source of knowledge, and to ignore it would be an unacceptable restriction of our listening and responding. Here I am reminded of something Socrates said to Phaedo. In their earlier conversations, many false philosophical opinions had been raised, and so Socrates says: 'It would be easily understandable if someone became so annoyed at all these false notions that for the rest of his life he despised and mocked all talk about being – but in this way he would be deprived of the truth of existence and would suffer a great loss.'[13] The West has long been endangered by this aversion to the questions which underlie its rationality, and can only suffer great harm thereby. The courage to engage the whole breadth of reason, and not the denial of its grandeur – this is the programme with which a theology grounded in Biblical faith enters into the debates of our time. 'Not to act reasonably, not to act with *logos*, is contrary to the nature of God,' said Manuel II, according to his Christian understanding of God, in response to his Persian interlocutor. It is to this great *logos*, to this breadth of reason, that we invite our partners in the dialogue of cultures. To rediscover it constantly is the great task of the university.

---

13 Cf. 90 c-d. For this text, cf. also R. Guardini, *Der Tod des Sokrates*, 5th edition, Mainz-Paderborn 1987, pp. 218–221.

BARACK OBAMA

'A NEW BEGINNING'

—

REMARKS AT THE UNIVERSITY OF CAIRO

CAIRO, EGYPT, 4 JUNE 2009

*B*arack Obama was sworn in as President of the United States in 2009.
In this speech he explains the common ground between Islamic believers and the citizens of the United States. Given his own background, as an African-American who had lived in Indonesia in his early childhood, Obama provides a bridge between two cultures with his personal history. In this speech, given at the prestigious University of Cairo, Obama challenges the audience to find constructive ways to work with the United States and European countries. He asks for a new beginning in Muslim-Western relations. This is a remarkable speech by a United States President. In the history of American speechwriting this is a singular effort, a speech that takes the speaker and the audience into uncharted territory. Subsequently, Obama ended the United States involvement in the war in Iraq in 2011. He was awarded the Nobel Peace Prize in 2010.

—

I am honoured to be in the timeless city of Cairo, and to be hosted by two remarkable institutions. For over a thousand years, Al-Azhar has stood as a beacon of Islamic learning, and for over a century, Cairo University has been a source of Egypt's advancement. Together, you represent the harmony between tradition and progress. I am grateful for your hospitality, and the hospitality of the people of Egypt. I am also proud to carry with me the goodwill of the American people, and a greeting of peace from Muslim communities in my country: *assalaamu alaykum*.

We meet at a time of tension between the United States and Muslims around the world – tension rooted in historical forces that go beyond any current policy debate. The relationship between Islam and the West includes centuries of co-existence and cooperation, but also conflict and religious wars. More recently, tension has been fed by colonialism that denied rights and opportunities to many Muslims, and a Cold War in which Muslim-majority countries were too often treated as proxies without regard to their own aspirations. Moreover, the sweeping change brought by modernity and globalisation led many Muslims to view the West as hostile to the traditions of Islam.

Violent extremists have exploited these tensions in a small but potent minority of Muslims. The attacks of September 11th, 2001, and the continued efforts of these extremists to engage in violence against civilians has led some in my country to view Islam as inevitably hostile not only to America and Western countries, but also to human rights. This has bred more fear and mistrust.

So long as our relationship is defined by our differences, we will empower those who sow hatred rather than peace, and who promote conflict rather than the cooperation that can help all of our people achieve justice and prosperity. This cycle of suspicion and discord must end.

I have come here to seek a new beginning between the United States and Muslims around the world; one based upon mutual interest and mutual respect; and one based upon the truth that America and Islam are not exclusive, and need not be in competition. Instead, they overlap, and share common principles – principles of justice and progress; tolerance and the dignity of all human beings.

I do so recognising that change cannot happen overnight. No single speech can eradicate years of mistrust, nor can I answer in the time that I have all the complex questions that brought us to this point. But I am convinced that in order to move forward, we must say openly the things we hold in our hearts, and that too often are said only behind closed doors. There must be a sustained effort to listen to each other; to learn from each other; to respect one another; and to seek common ground. As the Holy Koran tells us, 'Be conscious of God and speak always the truth.'

That is what I will try to do – to speak the truth as best I can, humbled by the task before us, and firm in my belief that the interests we share as human beings are far more powerful than the forces that drive us apart.

Part of this conviction is rooted in my own experience. I am a Christian, but my father came from a Kenyan family that includes generations of Muslims. As a boy, I spent several years in Indonesia and heard the call of the azaan at the break of dawn and the fall of dusk. As a young man, I worked in Chicago communities where many found dignity and peace in their Muslim faith.

As a student of history, I also know civilisation's debt to Islam. It was Islam –
at places like Al-Azhar University – that carried the light of learning through so
many centuries, paving the way for Europe's Renaissance and Enlightenment.
It was innovation in Muslim communities that developed the order of alge-
bra; our magnetic compass and tools of navigation; our mastery of pens and
printing; our understanding of how disease spreads and how it can be healed.
Islamic culture has given us majestic arches and soaring spires; timeless poetry
and cherished music; elegant calligraphy and places of peaceful contemplation.
And throughout history, Islam has demonstrated through words and deeds the
possibilities of religious tolerance and racial equality.

I know, too, that Islam has always been a part of America's story. The first
nation to recognise my country was Morocco. In signing the Treaty of Tripoli in
1796, our second President John Adams wrote, 'The United States has in itself
no character of enmity against the laws, religion or tranquility of Muslims.' And
since our founding, American Muslims have enriched the United States. They
have fought in our wars, served in government, stood for civil rights, started
businesses, taught at our universities, excelled in our sports arenas, won Nobel
Prizes, built our tallest building, and lit the Olympic Torch. And when the first
Muslim-American was recently elected to Congress, he took the oath to defend
our Constitution using the same Holy Koran that one of our Founding Fathers
– Thomas Jefferson – kept in his personal library.

So I have known Islam on three continents before coming to the region
where it was first revealed. That experience guides my conviction that partnership between America and Islam must be based on what Islam is, not what it
isn't. And I consider it part of my responsibility as President of the United States
to fight against negative stereotypes of Islam wherever they appear.

But that same principle must apply to Muslim perceptions of America. Just
as Muslims do not fit a crude stereotype, America is not the crude stereotype of
a self-interested empire. The United States has been one of the greatest sources
of progress that the world has ever known. We were born out of revolution
against an empire. We were founded upon the ideal that all are created equal,
and we have shed blood and struggled for centuries to give meaning to those
words – within our borders, and around the world. We are shaped by every
culture, drawn from every end of the Earth, and dedicated to a simple concept:
E pluribus unum: 'Out of many, one.'

Much has been made of the fact that an African-American with the name
Barack Hussein Obama could be elected President. But my personal story is
not so unique. The dream of opportunity for all people has not come true for
everyone in America, but its promise exists for all who come to our shores –
that includes nearly seven million American Muslims in our country today who
enjoy incomes and education that are higher than average.

Moreover, freedom in America is indivisible from the freedom to practise one's religion. That is why there is a mosque in every state of our union, and over 1,200 mosques within our borders. That is why the US government has gone to court to protect the right of women and girls to wear the hijab, and to punish those who would deny it.

So let there be no doubt: Islam is a part of America. And I believe that America holds within her the truth that regardless of race, religion, or station in life, all of us share common aspirations – to live in peace and security; to get an education and to work with dignity; to love our families, our communities, and our God. These things we share. This is the hope of all humanity.

Of course, recognising our common humanity is only the beginning of our task. Words alone cannot meet the needs of our people. These needs will be met only if we act boldly in the years ahead; and if we understand that the challenges we face are shared, and our failure to meet them will hurt us all.

For we have learned from recent experience that when a financial system weakens in one country, prosperity is hurt everywhere. When a new flu infects one human being, all are at risk. When one nation pursues a nuclear weapon, the risk of nuclear attack rises for all nations. When violent extremists operate in one stretch of mountains, people are endangered across an ocean. And when innocents in Bosnia and Darfur are slaughtered, that is a stain on our collective conscience. That is what it means to share this world in the twenty-first century. That is the responsibility we have to one another as human beings.

This is a difficult responsibility to embrace. For human history has often been a record of nations and tribes subjugating one another to serve their own interests. Yet in this new age, such attitudes are self-defeating. Given our inter-dependence, any world order that elevates one nation or group of people over another will inevitably fail. So whatever we think of the past, we must not be prisoners of it. Our problems must be dealt with through partnership; progress must be shared.

That does not mean we should ignore sources of tension. Indeed, it suggests the opposite: we must face these tensions squarely. And so in that spirit, let me speak as clearly and plainly as I can about some specific issues that I believe we must finally confront together.

The first issue that we have to confront is violent extremism in all of its forms.

In Ankara, I made clear that America is not – and never will be – at war with Islam. We will, however, relentlessly confront violent extremists who pose a grave threat to our security. Because we reject the same thing that people of all faiths reject: the killing of innocent men, women, and children. And it is my first duty as President to protect the American people.

The situation in Afghanistan demonstrates America's goals, and our need to work together. Over seven years ago, the United States pursued al Qaeda and the Taliban with broad international support. We did not go by choice, we went because of necessity. I am aware that some question or justify the events of 9/11. But let us be clear: al Qaeda killed nearly 3,000 people on that day. The victims were innocent men, women and children from America and many other nations who had done nothing to harm anybody. And yet al Qaeda chose to ruthlessly murder these people, claimed credit for the attack, and even now states their determination to kill on a massive scale. They have affiliates in many countries and are trying to expand their reach. These are not opinions to be debated; these are facts to be dealt with.

Make no mistake: we do not want to keep our troops in Afghanistan. We seek no military bases there. It is agonising for America to lose our young men and women. It is costly and politically difficult to continue this conflict. We would gladly bring every single one of our troops home if we could be confident that there were not violent extremists in Afghanistan and Pakistan determined to kill as many Americans as they possibly can. But that is not yet the case. That's why we're partnering with a coalition of forty-six countries. And despite the costs involved, America's commitment will not weaken. Indeed, none of us should tolerate these extremists. They have killed in many countries. They have killed people of different faiths – more than any other, they have killed Muslims. Their actions are irreconcilable with the rights of human beings, the progress of nations, and with Islam. The Holy Koran teaches that whoever kills an innocent, it is as if he has killed all mankind; and whoever saves a person, it is as if he has saved all mankind. The enduring faith of over a billion people is so much bigger than the narrow hatred of a few. Islam is not part of the problem in combating violent extremism – it is an important part of promoting peace.

We also know that military power alone is not going to solve the problems in Afghanistan and Pakistan. That is why we plan to invest $1.5 billion each year over the next five years to partner with Pakistanis to build schools and hospitals, roads and businesses, and hundreds of millions to help those who have been displaced. And that is why we are providing more than $2.8 billion to help Afghans develop their economy and deliver services that people depend upon.

Let me also address the issue of Iraq. Unlike Afghanistan, Iraq was a war of choice that provoked strong differences in my country and around the world. Although I believe that the Iraqi people are ultimately better off without the tyranny of Saddam Hussein, I also believe that events in Iraq have reminded America of the need to use diplomacy and build international consensus to resolve our problems whenever possible. Indeed, we can recall the words of Thomas Jefferson, who said: 'I hope that our wisdom will grow with our power, and teach us that the less we use our power the greater it will be.'

Today, America has a dual responsibility: to help Iraq forge a better future – and to leave Iraq to Iraqis. I have made it clear to the Iraqi people that we pursue no bases, and no claim on their territory or resources. Iraq's sovereignty is its own. That is why I ordered the removal of our combat brigades by next August. That is why we will honour our agreement with Iraq's democratically elected government to remove combat troops from Iraqi cities by July, and to remove all our troops from Iraq by 2012. We will help Iraq train its security forces and develop its economy. But we will support a secure and united Iraq as a partner, and never as a patron.

And finally, just as America can never tolerate violence by extremists, we must never alter our principles. 9/11 was an enormous trauma to our country. The fear and anger that it provoked was understandable, but in some cases, it led us to act contrary to our ideals. We are taking concrete actions to change course. I have unequivocally prohibited the use of torture by the United States, and I have ordered the prison at Guantanamo Bay closed by early next year.

So America will defend itself respectful of the sovereignty of nations and the rule of law. And we will do so in partnership with Muslim communities which are also threatened. The sooner the extremists are isolated and unwelcome in Muslim communities, the sooner we will all be safer.

The second major source of tension that we need to discuss is the situation between Israelis, Palestinians and the Arab world.

America's strong bonds with Israel are well known. This bond is unbreakable. It is based upon cultural and historical ties, and the recognition that the aspiration for a Jewish homeland is rooted in a tragic history that cannot be denied.

Around the world, the Jewish people were persecuted for centuries, and anti-Semitism in Europe culminated in an unprecedented Holocaust. Tomorrow, I will visit Buchenwald, which was part of a network of camps where Jews were enslaved, tortured, shot and gassed to death by the Third Reich. Six million Jews were killed – more than the entire Jewish population of Israel today. Denying that fact is baseless, ignorant, and hateful. Threatening Israel with destruction – or repeating vile stereotypes about Jews – is deeply wrong, and only serves to evoke in the minds of Israelis this most painful of memories while preventing the peace that the people of this region deserve.

On the other hand, it is also undeniable that the Palestinian people – Muslims and Christians – have suffered in pursuit of a homeland. For more than sixty years they have endured the pain of dislocation. Many wait in refugee camps in the West Bank, Gaza, and neighbouring lands for a life of peace and security that they have never been able to lead. They endure the daily humiliations – large and small – that come with occupation. So let there be no doubt: the situation for the Palestinian people is intolerable. America will not turn our backs on the legitimate Palestinian aspiration for dignity, opportunity, and a state of their own.

For decades, there has been a stalemate: two peoples with legitimate aspirations, each with a painful history that makes compromise elusive. It is easy to point fingers – for Palestinians to point to the displacement brought by Israel's founding, and for Israelis to point to the constant hostility and attacks throughout its history from within its borders as well as beyond. But if we see this conflict only from one side or the other, then we will be blind to the truth: the only resolution is for the aspirations of both sides to be met through two states, where Israelis and Palestinians each live in peace and security.

That is in Israel's interest, Palestine's interest, America's interest, and the world's interest. That is why I intend to personally pursue this outcome with all the patience that the task requires. The obligations that the parties have agreed to under the Road Map are clear. For peace to come, it is time for them – and all of us – to live up to our responsibilities.

Palestinians must abandon violence. Resistance through violence and killing is wrong and does not succeed. For centuries, black people in America suffered the lash of the whip as slaves and the humiliation of segregation. But it was not violence that won full and equal rights. It was a peaceful and determined insistence upon the ideals at the centre of America's founding. This same story can be told by people from South Africa to South Asia; from Eastern Europe to Indonesia. It's a story with a simple truth: that violence is a dead end. It is a sign of neither courage nor power to shoot rockets at sleeping children, or to blow up old women on a bus. That is not how moral authority is claimed; that is how it is surrendered.

Now is the time for Palestinians to focus on what they can build. The Palestinian Authority must develop its capacity to govern, with institutions that serve the needs of its people. Hamas does have support among some Palestinians, but they also have responsibilities. To play a role in fulfilling Palestinian aspirations, and to unify the Palestinian people, Hamas must put an end to violence, recognise past agreements, and recognise Israel's right to exist.

At the same time, Israelis must acknowledge that just as Israel's right to exist cannot be denied, neither can Palestine's. The United States does not accept the legitimacy of continued Israeli settlements. This construction violates previous agreements and undermines efforts to achieve peace. It is time for these settlements to stop.

Israel must also live up to its obligations to ensure that Palestinians can live, and work, and develop their society. And just as it devastates Palestinian families, the continuing humanitarian crisis in Gaza does not serve Israel's security; neither does the continuing lack of opportunity in the West Bank. Progress in the daily lives of the Palestinian people must be part of a road to peace, and Israel must take concrete steps to enable such progress.

Finally, the Arab states must recognise that the Arab Peace Initiative was an important beginning, but not the end of their responsibilities. The Arab–Israeli conflict should no longer be used to distract the people of Arab nations from other problems. Instead, it must be a cause for action to help the Palestinian people develop the institutions that will sustain their state; to recognise Israel's legitimacy; and to choose progress over a self-defeating focus on the past.

America will align our policies with those who pursue peace, and say in public what we say in private to Israelis and Palestinians and Arabs. We cannot impose peace. But privately, many Muslims recognise that Israel will not go away. Likewise, many Israelis recognise the need for a Palestinian state. It is time for us to act on what everyone knows to be true.

Too many tears have flowed. Too much blood has been shed. All of us have a responsibility to work for the day when the mothers of Israelis and Palestinians can see their children grow up without fear; when the Holy Land of three great faiths is the place of peace that God intended it to be; when Jerusalem is a secure and lasting home for Jews and Christians and Muslims, and a place for all of the children of Abraham to mingle peacefully together as in the story of Isra, when Moses, Jesus, and Mohammed (peace be upon them) joined in prayer.

The third source of tension is our shared interest in the rights and responsibilities of nations on nuclear weapons.

This issue has been a source of tension between the United States and the Islamic Republic of Iran. For many years, Iran has defined itself in part by its opposition to my country, and there is indeed a tumultuous history between us. In the middle of the Cold War, the United States played a role in the overthrow of a democratically elected Iranian government. Since the Islamic Revolution, Iran has played a role in acts of hostage-taking and violence against US troops and civilians. This history is well known. Rather than remain trapped in the past, I have made it clear to Iran's leaders and people that my country is prepared to move forward. The question, now, is not what Iran is against, but rather what future it wants to build.

It will be hard to overcome decades of mistrust, but we will proceed with courage, rectitude and resolve. There will be many issues to discuss between our two countries, and we are willing to move forward without preconditions on the basis of mutual respect. But it is clear to all concerned that when it comes to nuclear weapons, we have reached a decisive point. This is not simply about America's interests. It is about preventing a nuclear arms race in the Middle East that could lead this region and the world down a hugely dangerous path.

I understand those who protest that some countries have weapons that others do not. No single nation should pick and choose which nations hold nuclear weapons. That is why I strongly reaffirmed America's commitment to seek a world in which no nations hold nuclear weapons. And any nation – including Iran – should have the right to access peaceful nuclear power if it complies with its responsibilities under the nuclear Non-Proliferation Treaty. That commitment is at the core of the Treaty, and it must be kept for all who fully abide by it. And I am hopeful that all countries in the region can share in this goal.

The fourth issue that I will address is democracy.

I know there has been controversy about the promotion of democracy in recent years, and much of this controversy is connected to the war in Iraq. So let me be clear: no system of government can or should be imposed upon one nation by any other.

That does not lessen my commitment, however, to governments that reflect the will of the people. Each nation gives life to this principle in its own way, grounded in the traditions of its own people. America does not presume to know what is best for everyone, just as we would not presume to pick the outcome of a peaceful election. But I do have an unyielding belief that all people yearn for certain things: the ability to speak your mind and have a say in how you are governed; confidence in the rule of law and the equal administration of justice; government that is transparent and doesn't steal from the people; the freedom to live as you choose. Those are not just American ideas, they are human rights, and that is why we will support them everywhere.

There is no straight line to realise this promise. But this much is clear: governments that protect these rights are ultimately more stable, successful and secure. Suppressing ideas never succeeds in making them go away. America respects the right of all peaceful and law-abiding voices to be heard around the world, even if we disagree with them. And we will welcome all elected, peaceful governments – provided they govern with respect for all their people.

This last point is important because there are some who advocate for democracy only when they are out of power; once in power, they are ruthless in suppressing the rights of others. No matter where it takes hold, government of the people and by the people sets a single standard for all who hold power: you must maintain your power through consent, not coercion; you must respect the rights of minorities, and participate with a spirit of tolerance and compromise; you must place the interests of your people and the legitimate workings of the political process above your party. Without these ingredients, elections alone do not make true democracy.

The fifth issue that we must address together is religious freedom.

Islam has a proud tradition of tolerance. We see it in the history of Andalusia and Cordoba during the Inquisition. I saw it first-hand as a child in Indonesia, where devout Christians worshipped freely in an overwhelmingly Muslim country. That is the spirit we need today. People in every country should be free to choose and live their faith based upon the persuasion of the mind, heart, and soul. This tolerance is essential for religion to thrive, but it is being challenged in many different ways.

Among some Muslims, there is a disturbing tendency to measure one's own faith by the rejection of another's. The richness of religious diversity must be upheld – whether it is for Maronites in Lebanon or the Copts in Egypt. And fault lines must be closed among Muslims as well, as the divisions between Sunni and Shia have led to tragic violence, particularly in Iraq.

Freedom of religion is central to the ability of peoples to live together. We must always examine the ways in which we protect it. For instance, in the United States, rules on charitable giving have made it harder for Muslims to fulfil their religious obligation. That is why I am committed to working with American Muslims to ensure that they can fulfill zakat.

Likewise, it is important for Western countries to avoid impeding Muslim citizens from practising religion as they see fit – for instance, by dictating what clothes a Muslim woman should wear. We cannot disguise hostility towards any religion behind the pretence of liberalism.

Indeed, faith should bring us together. That is why we are forging service projects in America that bring together Christians, Muslims, and Jews. That is why we welcome efforts like Saudi Arabian King Abdullah's Interfaith dialogue and Turkey's leadership in the Alliance of Civilizations. Around the world, we can turn dialogue into Interfaith service, so bridges between peoples lead to action – whether it is combating malaria in Africa, or providing relief after a natural disaster.

The sixth issue that I want to address is women's rights.

I know there is debate about this issue. I reject the view of some in the West that a woman who chooses to cover her hair is somehow less equal, but I do believe that a woman who is denied an education is denied equality. And it is no coincidence that countries where women are well-educated are far more likely to be prosperous.

Now let me be clear: issues of women's equality are by no means simply an issue for Islam. In Turkey, Pakistan, Bangladesh and Indonesia, we have seen Muslim-majority countries elect a woman to lead. Meanwhile, the struggle for women's equality continues in many aspects of American life, and in countries around the world.

Our daughters can contribute just as much to society as our sons, and our common prosperity will be advanced by allowing all humanity – men and women – to reach their full potential. I do not believe that women must make the same choices as men in order to be equal, and I respect those women who choose to live their lives in traditional roles. But it should be their choice. That is why the United States will partner with any Muslim-majority country to support expanded literacy for girls, and to help young women pursue employment through micro-financing that helps people live their dreams.

Finally, I want to discuss economic development and opportunity.

I know that for many, the face of globalisation is contradictory. The Internet and television can bring knowledge and information, but also offensive sexuality and mindless violence. Trade can bring new wealth and opportunities, but also huge disruptions and changing communities. In all nations – including my own – this change can bring fear. Fear that because of modernity we will lose control over our economic choices, our politics, and most importantly our identities – those things we most cherish about our communities, our families, our traditions, and our faith.

But I also know that human progress cannot be denied. There need not be contradiction between development and tradition. Countries like Japan and South Korea grew their economies while maintaining distinct cultures. The same is true for the astonishing progress within Muslim-majority countries from Kuala Lumpur to Dubai. In ancient times and in our times, Muslim communities have been at the forefront of innovation and education.

This is important because no development strategy can be based only upon what comes out of the ground, nor can it be sustained while young people are out of work. Many Gulf states have enjoyed great wealth as a consequence of oil, and some are beginning to focus it on broader development. But all of us must recognise that education and innovation will be the currency of the twenty-first century, and in too many Muslim communities there remains underinvestment in these areas. I am emphasising such investments within my country. And while America in the past has focused on oil and gas in this part of the world, we now seek a broader engagement.

On education, we will expand exchange programmes, and increase scholarships, like the one that brought my father to America, while encouraging more Americans to study in Muslim communities. And we will match promising Muslim students with internships in America; invest in online learning for teachers and children around the world; and create a new online network, so a teenager in Kansas can communicate instantly with a teenager in Cairo.

On economic development, we will create a new corps of business volunteers to partner with counterparts in Muslim-majority countries. And I will host a Summit on Entrepreneurship this year to identify how we can deepen ties between business leaders, foundations and social entrepreneurs in the United States and Muslim communities around the world.

On science and technology, we will launch a new fund to support technological development in Muslim-majority countries, and to help transfer ideas to the marketplace so they can create jobs. We will open centres of scientific excellence in Africa, the Middle East and Southeast Asia, and appoint new Science Envoys to collaborate on programmes that develop new sources of energy, create green jobs, digitise records, clean water, and grow new crops. And today I am announcing a new global effort with the Organization of the Islamic Conference to eradicate polio. And we will also expand partnerships with Muslim communities to promote child and maternal health.

All these things must be done in partnership. Americans are ready to join with citizens and governments, community organisations, religious leaders, and businesses in Muslim communities around the world to help our people pursue a better life.

The issues that I have described will not be easy to address. But we have a responsibility to join together on behalf of the world we seek – a world where extremists no longer threaten our people, and American troops have come home; a world where Israelis and Palestinians are each secure in a state of their own, and nuclear energy is used for peaceful purposes; a world where governments serve their citizens, and the rights of all God's children are respected. Those are mutual interests. That is the world we seek. But we can only achieve it together.

I know there are many – Muslim and non-Muslim – who question whether we can forge this new beginning. Some are eager to stoke the flames of division, and to stand in the way of progress. Some suggest that it isn't worth the effort – that we are fated to disagree, and civilisations are doomed to clash. Many more are simply sceptical that real change can occur. There is so much fear, so much mistrust. But if we choose to be bound by the past, we will never move forward. And I want to particularly say this to young people of every faith, in every country – you, more than anyone, have the ability to remake this world.

All of us share this world for but a brief moment in time. The question is whether we spend that time focused on what pushes us apart, or whether we commit ourselves to an effort – a sustained effort – to find common ground, to focus on the future we seek for our children, and to respect the dignity of all human beings.

It is easier to start wars than to end them. It is easier to blame others than to look inward; to see what is different about someone than to find the things we share. But we should choose the right path, not just the easy path. There is also one rule that lies at the heart of every religion – that we do unto others as we would have them do unto us. This truth transcends nations and peoples – a belief that isn't new; that isn't black or white or brown; that isn't Christian, or Muslim or Jew. It's a belief that pulsed in the cradle of civilisation, and that still beats in the heart of billions. It's a faith in other people, and it's what brought me here today.

We have the power to make the world we seek, but only if we have the courage to make a new beginning, keeping in mind what has been written.

The Holy Koran tells us, 'O mankind! We have created you male and a female; and we have made you into nations and tribes so that you may know one another.'

The Talmud tells us, 'The whole of the Torah is for the purpose of promoting peace.'

The Holy Bible tells us, 'Blessed are the peacemakers, for they shall be called sons of God.'

The people of the world can live together in peace. We know that is God's vision. Now, that must be our work here on Earth. Thank you. And may God's peace be upon you.

DAVID CAMERON

'WE MUST BUILD STRONGER SOCIETIES'

—

REMARKS AT THE MUNICH SECURITY CONFERENCE

MUNICH, GERMANY, 5 FEBRUARY 2011

avid Cameron became Prime Minister of the United Kingdom in 2010. This speech may be an echo. On 17 October 2010, German Chancellor Angela Merkel told members of the Christian Democratic Union Party that multiculturalism had 'utterly failed' in her country. In these remarks Cameron discusses the lack of racial harmony in Great Britain and much of Europe. He argues that multiculturalism is not working and that new efforts at racial harmony are needed to create functional, peaceful communities. In August 2011 there were several days of rioting in London and other cities, sparked, in part, by reaction to the fatal shooting by police of Mark Duggan, a young black man. While many rioters were confronted by people from minority communities bent on restoring law and order, drawing praise from police and Members of Parliament, there are some who argue race relations have deteriorated since the riots. Some even blame minority communities for starting the riots, despite considerable evidence to the contrary. The August riots, whatever their initial cause, soon became an orgy of looting.

—

Today I want to focus my remarks on terrorism, but first let me address one point. Some have suggested that by holding a strategic defence and security review, Britain is somehow retreating from an activist role in the world. That is the opposite of the truth. Yes, we are dealing with our budget deficit, but we are also making sure our defences are strong. Britain will continue to meet the NATO 2 per cent target for defence spending. We will still have the fourth largest military defence budget in the world. At the same time, we are putting that money to better use, focusing on conflict prevention and building a much more flexible army. That is not retreat; it is hard-headed.

Every decision we take has three aims in mind. First, to continue to support the NATO mission in Afghanistan. Second, to reinforce our actual military capability. As Chancellor Merkel's government is showing right here in Germany, what matters is not bureaucracy, which frankly Europe needs a lot less of, but the political will to build military capability that we need as nations and allies, that we can deliver in the field. Third, we want to make sure that Britain is protected from the new and various threats that we face. That is why we are investing in a national cyber security programme that I know William Hague talked about yesterday, and we are sharpening our readiness to act on counter-proliferation.

But the biggest threat that we face comes from terrorist attacks, some of which are, sadly, carried out by our own citizens. It is important to stress that terrorism is not linked exclusively to any one religion or ethnic group. My country, the United Kingdom, still faces threats from dissident Republicans in Northern Ireland. Anarchist attacks have occurred recently in Greece and in Italy, and of course, yourselves in Germany were long scarred by terrorism from the Red Army Faction. Nevertheless, we should acknowledge that this threat comes in Europe overwhelmingly from young men who follow a completely perverse, warped interpretation of Islam, and who are prepared to blow themselves up and kill their fellow citizens. Last week at Davos I rang the alarm bell for the urgent need for Europe to recover its economic dynamism, and today, though the subject is complex, my message on security is equally stark. We will not defeat terrorism simply by the action we take outside our borders. Europe needs to wake up to what is happening in our own countries. Of course, that means strengthening, as Angela has said, the security aspects of our response, on tracing plots, on stopping them, on counter-surveillance and intelligence gathering.

But this is just part of the answer. We have got to get to the root of the problem, and we need to be absolutely clear on where the origins of these terrorist attacks lie. That is the existence of an ideology, Islamist extremism. We should be equally clear what we mean by this term, and we must distinguish it from Islam. Islam is a religion observed peacefully and devoutly by over a billion people. Islamist extremism is a political ideology supported by a minority. At the furthest end are those who back terrorism to promote their ultimate goal: an entire Islamist realm, governed by an interpretation of Sharia. Move along the spectrum, and you find people who may reject violence, but who accept various parts of the extremist worldview, including real hostility towards Western democracy and liberal values. It is vital that we make this distinction between religion on the one hand, and political ideology on the other. Time and again, people equate the two. They think whether someone is an extremist is dependent on how much they observe their religion. So, they talk about moderate Muslims as if all devout Muslims must be extremist. This is profoundly wrong. Someone can be a devout Muslim and not be an extremist. We need to be clear: Islamist extremism and Islam are not the same thing.

This highlights, I think, a significant problem when discussing the terrorist threat that we face. There is so much muddled thinking about this whole issue. On the one hand, those on the hard right ignore this distinction between Islam and Islamist extremism, and just say that Islam and the West are irreconcilable – that there is a clash of civilisations. So, it follows: we should cut ourselves off from this religion, whether that is through forced repatriation, favoured by some fascists, or the banning of new mosques, as is suggested in some parts of Europe. These people fuel Islamophobia, and I completely reject their argument. If they want an example of how Western values and Islam can be entirely compatible, they should look at what's happened in the past few weeks on the streets of Tunis and Cairo : hundreds of thousands of people demanding the universal right to free elections and democracy.

The point is this: the ideology of extremism is the problem; Islam emphatically is not. Picking a fight with the latter will do nothing to help us to confront the former. On the other hand, there are those on the soft left who also ignore this distinction. They lump all Muslims together, compiling a list of grievances, and argue that if only governments addressed these grievances, the terrorism would stop. So, they point to the poverty that so many Muslims live in and say, 'Get rid of this injustice and the terrorism will end.' But this ignores the fact that many of those found guilty of terrorist offences in the UK and elsewhere have been graduates and often middle class. They point to grievances about Western foreign policy and say, 'Stop riding roughshod over Muslim countries and the terrorism will end.' But there are many people, Muslim and non-Muslim alike, who are angry about Western foreign policy, but who don't resort to acts of terrorism. They also point to the profusion of unelected leaders across the Middle East and say, 'Stop propping these people up and you will stop creating the conditions for extremism to flourish.' But this raises the question: if it's the lack of democracy that is the problem, why are there so many extremists in free and open societies?

Now, I'm not saying that these issues of poverty and grievance about foreign policy are not important. Yes, of course we must tackle them. Of course we must tackle poverty. Yes, we must resolve the sources of tension, not least in Palestine, and yes, we should be on the side of openness and political reform in the Middle East. On Egypt, our position should be clear. We want to see the transition to a more broadly based government, with the proper building blocks of a free and democratic society. I simply don't accept that there is somehow a dead-end choice between a security state on the one hand, and an Islamist one on the other. But let us not fool ourselves. These are just contributory factors. Even if we sorted out all of the problems that I have mentioned, there would still be this terrorism. I believe the root lies in the existence of this extremist ideology. I would argue an important reason so many young Muslims are drawn to it comes down to a question of identity.

What I am about to say is drawn from the British experience, but I believe there are general lessons for us all. In the UK, some young men find it hard to identify with the traditional Islam practised at home by their parents, whose customs can seem staid when transplanted to modern Western countries. But these young men also find it hard to identify with Britain too, because we have allowed the weakening of our collective identity. Under the doctrine of state multiculturalism, we have encouraged different cultures to live separate lives, apart from each other and apart from the mainstream. We've failed to provide a vision of society to which they feel they want to belong. We've even tolerated these segregated communities behaving in ways that run completely counter to our values.

So, when a white person holds objectionable views, racist views for instance, we rightly condemn them. But when equally unacceptable views or practices come from someone who isn't white, we've been too cautious frankly – frankly, even fearful – to stand up to them. The failure, for instance, of some to confront the horrors of forced marriage, the practice where some young girls are bullied and sometimes taken abroad to marry someone when they don't want to, is a case in point. This hands-off tolerance has only served to reinforce the sense that not enough is shared. And this all leaves some young Muslims feeling rootless. And the search for something to belong to and something to believe in can lead them to this extremist ideology. Now for sure, they don't turn into terrorists overnight, but what we see – and what we see in so many European countries – is a process of radicalisation.

Internet chatrooms are virtual meeting places where attitudes are shared, strengthened and validated. In some mosques, preachers of hate can sow misinformation about the plight of Muslims elsewhere. In our communities, groups and organisations led by young, dynamic leaders promote separatism by encouraging Muslims to define themselves solely in terms of their religion. All these interactions can engender a sense of community, a substitute for what the wider society has failed to supply. Now, you might say, as long as they're not hurting anyone, what is the problem with all this?

Well, I'll tell you why. As evidence emerges about the backgrounds of those convicted of terrorist offences, it is clear that many of them were initially influenced by what some have called 'non-violent extremists', and they then took those radical beliefs to the next level by embracing violence. And I say this is an indictment of our approach to these issues in the past. And if we are to defeat this threat, I believe it is time to turn the page on the failed policies of the past. So first, instead of ignoring this extremist ideology, we – as governments and as societies – have got to confront it, in all its forms. And second, instead of encouraging people to live apart, we need a clear sense of shared national identity that is open to everyone.

Let me briefly take each in turn. First, confronting and undermining this ideology. Whether they are violent in their means or not, we must make it impossible for the extremists to succeed. Now, for governments, there are some obvious ways we can do this. We must ban preachers of hate from coming to our countries. We must also proscribe organisations that incite terrorism against people at home and abroad. Governments must also be shrewder in dealing with those that, while not violent, are in some cases part of the problem. We need to think much harder about who it's in the public interest to work with. Some organisations that seek to present themselves as a gateway to the Muslim community are showered with public money despite doing little to combat extremism. As others have observed, this is like turning to a right-wing fascist party to fight a violent white supremacist movement. So we should properly judge these organisations: do they believe in universal human rights – including for women and people of other faiths? Do they believe in equality of all before the law? Do they believe in democracy and the right of people to elect their own government? Do they encourage integration or separation? These are the sorts of questions we need to ask. Fail these tests and the presumption should be not to engage with organisations – so, no public money, no sharing of platforms with ministers at home.

At the same time, we must stop these groups from reaching people in publicly funded institutions like universities or even, in the British case, prisons. Now, some say, this is not compatible with free speech and intellectual inquiry. Well, I say, would you take the same view if these were right-wing extremists recruiting on our campuses? Would you advocate inaction if Christian fundamentalists who believed that Muslims are the enemy were leading prayer groups in our prisons? And to those who say these non-violent extremists are actually helping to keep young, vulnerable men away from violence, I say nonsense. Would you allow the far-right groups a share of public funds if they promise to help you lure young white men away from fascist terrorism? Of course not. But, at root, challenging this ideology means exposing its ideas for what they are, and that is completely unjustifiable. We need to argue that terrorism is wrong in all circumstances. We need to argue that prophecies of a global war of religion pitting Muslims against the rest of the world are nonsense.

Now, governments cannot do this alone. The extremism we face is a distortion of Islam, so these arguments, in part, must be made by those within Islam. So let us give voice to those followers of Islam in our own countries – the vast, often unheard majority – who despise the extremists and their worldview. Let us engage groups that share our aspirations.

Now, second, we must build stronger societies and stronger identities at home. Frankly, we need a lot less of the passive tolerance of recent years and a much more active, muscular liberalism. A passively tolerant society says to its citizens, as long as you obey the law we will just leave you alone. It stands neutral between different values. But I believe a genuinely liberal country does much more; it believes in certain values and actively promotes them. Freedom of speech, freedom of worship, democracy, the rule of law, equal rights regardless of race, sex or sexuality. It says to its citizens, this is what defines us as a society: to belong here is to believe in these things. Now, each of us in our own countries, I believe, must be unambiguous and hard-nosed about this defence of our liberty.

There are practical things that we can do as well. That includes making sure that immigrants speak the language of their new home and ensuring that people are educated in the elements of a common culture and curriculum. Back home, we're introducing National Citizen Service: a two-month programme for sixteen-year-olds from different backgrounds to live and work together. I also believe we should encourage meaningful and active participation in society, by shifting the balance of power away from the state and towards the people. That way, common purpose can be formed as people come together and work together in their neighbourhoods. It will also help build stronger pride in local identity, so people feel free to say, 'Yes, I am a Muslim, I am a Hindu, I am Christian, but I am also a Londoner or a Berliner too.' It's that identity, that feeling of belonging in our countries, that I believe is the key to achieving true cohesion.

So, let me end with this. This terrorism is completely indiscriminate and has been thrust upon us. It cannot be ignored or contained; we have to confront it with confidence – confront the ideology that drives it by defeating the ideas that warp so many young minds at their root, and confront the issues of identity that sustain it by standing for a much broader and generous vision of citizenship in our countries. Now, none of this will be easy. We will need stamina, patience and endurance, and it won't happen at all if we act alone. This ideology crosses not just our continent but all continents, and we are all in this together. At stake are not just lives, it is our way of life. That is why this is a challenge we cannot avoid; it is one we must rise to and overcome. Thank you.

MAHMUD ABBAS

'WORTHY OF A GENUINE STATE'

—

REMARKS TO THE PALESTINIAN LEGISLATIVE COUNCIL

RIMAL, GAZA, 29 APRIL 2003

Born in Safed, Galilee, Mahmud Abbas was named Chairman of the Palestinian Liberation Organisation in 2005. He was elected President of the Palestinian National Authority in 2005 and extended his term after it expired in 2009, claiming that the Palestinian Authorities' Basic Law empowered him to do so. This claim was rejected by the rival Hamas faction, exacerbating hostility between the two groups that would later explode into violence in Gaza. Abbas was named President of the State of Palestine by the Palestinian Liberation Organization's Central Committee in 2008, a position he had held unofficially since 2005.

In this speech he makes a case for the creation of a Palestinian State, and, in his allusions to the immorality and inefficiency of violence in pursuing the cause of statehood, is clearly criticising his militant Hamas opponents. In the conflict in the Middle East, words matter more than in most places in the world. The words in a speech may convey policy, make diplomatic suggestions or start a war. Speeches by key figures draw particular attention. The words are examined, parsed, debated, stretched and probed. The following four speeches, two by President Abbas and two by Israeli Prime Minister Binyamin (Benjamin) Netanyahu, help give the world examples of the current rhetorical landscape. Hopefully, somewhere within these words, there exists common ground for conflict resolution.

—

In the name of Allah the most Merciful, the Compassionate (And He says: Do. For Allah will see the results of your work and so will his Prophet and believers.)

Brother and life-long comrade, President Yasser Arafat, President of the State of Palestine, Chairman of the Palestine Liberation Organization, President of the National Authority, Brother Saleem Al-Za'noun, Chair of the National Council, Brother Ahmad Qurei', Speaker of the Legislative Council, ladies and gentlemen, members of the Council, brothers and sisters, members of the diplomatic community and distinguished guests, may peace and the Mercy of Allah be upon you.

I am filled with confidence and pride as I stand here before our elected Legislative Council, one of the expressions of the sovereignty of our people, and the constitutional reference for the government, and whose elected members are an integral part of our National Council that guards our political organisation, the Palestine Liberation Organization.

I begin my speech by expressing all respect and esteem to the Palestinian people in every city, village and refugee camp in our homeland and in the Diaspora, to our resilient and struggling people of whom we are proud. We cherish this unlimited pride that has extended across several generations. This pride is exemplified in the hundreds of thousands of martyrs, injured and detainees who protect our national identity in spite of all attempts to destroy and annul our rights. We have preserved our inalienable rights and established our National Authority as an imperative step towards the establishment of our forthcoming independent state, with Jerusalem as its capital.

Our people, who have been steadfast throughout the past two and a half years during the courageous uprising against Israel's aggression, despite the killing and destruction in Jenin and its heroic camp, in Nablus, Tulkarm, Qalqilya, Hebron and all of our resistant cities, villages and camps in the West Bank and in Rafah, Khan Yunis, Dayr al-Balah, Gaza City, Beit Hanoun, Jabalya and in every part of our steadfast Strip. I specifically want to honour the families who have lost their loved ones, those who have suffered injuries, Palestinian political prisoners and those who have personally suffered. Palestinian accomplishments will always be indebted to the sacrifices of these heroes and to their families, people and homeland.

We are a highly distinguished people and our energy has grown – in the eyes of the whole world – to be worthy of a genuine state that enjoys sovereignty like all other peoples and states: a modern and democratic state that will constitute a safe home to all Palestinians and an effective partner in building and supporting security and stability in the region. I believe that part of the responsibilities of the government should be to build the pillars of this state including the preparation for presidential, parliamentary and municipal elections, based on the Elections Law which we hope will be passed soon by your distinguished council.

Mr President, brothers and sisters, the root of our suffering and the source of our pain is the occupation and its detestable oppressive policies. We all commit to ending the occupation in all of its shapes and forms. This requires that we direct our main efforts to internal housekeeping while being committed to the provisions of the Basic Law adopted by the Palestinian Legislative Council and ratified by President Yasser Arafat. The government commits itself to abiding by the law and enforcing it on all Palestinian institutions in order to ensure that in a short time there will be no violations of the law and no signs of chaos or ambiguity in society. We will implement our Basic Law in a manner proving that we merit a state and will abide by its constitution. Our government will not allow for any violation of this law.

The government is certain that internal organisation cannot be achieved without a collective commitment to the principle of the rule of law. The rule of law will be meaningless without an independent, effective and impartial judiciary, and efficient legal institutions with a Ministry of Justice that supports the independence of the judiciary and an enforcement mechanism capable of implementing such provisions. The government promises to work side by side with the President and the Legislative Council [PLC] to restructure the Higher Judiciary Council in accordance with the provisions of the law and the independence of the judiciary. It also promises to improve the courts. It is committed to helping the courts overcome their gaps and perform their duties in the best manner. The government commits itself to work on the preparation of draft laws and regulations to complete the National Authority's body of laws. The judicial system is the real face of any society and the most accurate indicator of its civilisation, progress and development. Accordingly, the government shall pay special attention to the judiciary.

Mr President, ladies and gentlemen, the government will concentrate on the question of security. Our understanding of security is the security of Palestinian citizens in their homeland. We seek the security of the homeland for all sectors of society. Based on this understanding, the government endeavours to develop the security organs and apparatuses according to law. It will allocate special attention to the professional qualifications of the leaders and members of such security organs. It will tolerate no breach of discipline or violations of the law. The government will not allow – to the contrary it will strictly prevent – interference by the security forces in the lives, affairs and business of citizens unless within the limits permitted by the law. In this respect, the government will build upon the achievements of the previous government regarding the organisation and responsibilities of the security apparatuses. These security arrangements give the Minister of the Interior wide jurisdiction, and provide him with the ability to control the internal situation and improve security performance.

The government understands that citizens' feeling of safety and security is the most important pillar of national resistance and is the most important requirement for growth and progress in all aspects of life for both individuals and the community. Therefore, the unauthorised possession of weapons, with its direct threat to the security of the population, is a major concern that will be relentlessly addressed. We aim to ensure that only legitimate weapons are used to preserve public order and implement the law. There will be no other decision-making authority except for the legitimate one – the Palestinian Authority. On this land and for this people, there is only one authority, one law, and one democratic and national decision that applies to us all.

It should be understood here that the rights of citizens to freely express themselves will not be jeopardised by any person or under any pretence or justification. Palestinians may hold any political views, and exercise such rights and freedoms in accordance with the law.

The government is aware of the importance of political opposition and is fully aware of the right of the opposition to strive to achieve power. In order to foster this, we call upon the opposition factions and forces to develop their institutions, frameworks and dialogues and to halt any incitement and negative campaigning. We call upon the opposition to make use of both the free press and the law to exercise its voice and to present its viewpoints. We also call on all sectors of Palestinian society to utilise the Political Party Law to revive internal political debate and enhance its effectiveness. I reconfirm here that our government will stand for pluralism within the framework of national unity in accordance with the law, but pluralism does not extend to security.

Within this framework, we will develop the most effective means of reaching an internal understanding aimed at ensuring the rights of all forces, parties and factions to exist and work. Here, I call upon all of you to partake in the election of representative institutions, particularly given that we have chosen elections as a non-revocable means to formulate and activate these organs.

Mr President, ladies and gentlemen, members of the PLC, the government understands the magnitude of our suffering and economic difficulties as a result of the continuation and escalation of Israeli measures. This suffering has led to an increase in poverty and unemployment rates with a major deterioration in economic indicators. This is a result of the enormous destruction of our infrastructure, our private property and sources of livelihood caused by the occupation. Palestinian citizens seek a glimmer of hope to eradicate their suffering and its destructive impact on their lives. The government pledges to address this economic situation by taking timely measures, within its capacities, to improve the living conditions mainly of the unemployed and other people living in extreme hardship until passage of the Social Security Law. The government will also work to restore the infrastructure that has been destroyed by the occupation. Within this framework, the government promises to launch an international effort to seek rehabilitation for the economic destruction caused by Israel's oppression, invasions, and killings.

The government will work to prepare a comprehensive national development plan (that includes Jerusalem) in which we will devote sufficient attention to the service and economic sectors and will provide necessary health, educational, cultural, media and agricultural services to citizens. The plan will be carried out in a professional and transparent manner. In this context, the government is keen to continue working with the private sector in order to enact and enforce legislation and regulations that will strengthen the market economy and develop the national economy and provide protection to investments and investors.

Moreover, the government will devote itself to the situation of Palestinian women, who constitute half of our population, and who play a major and effective role in our lives. We will also continue to work on the protection of the rights of children and families and develop the youth sector to ensure a better future for our people.

As regards the financial issue, the government will continue its efforts to implement the new fiscal policy and all the measures and arrangements as they were submitted to you by the Minister of Finance through the Budget Law. The fiscal policy reasserts our commitment to regulate the investments of the Palestinian Authority. These investments will be fully placed under the government's supervision and control so that all resources of the Palestinian Authority will be unified in the Ministry of Finance in accordance with international best practices in the administration of public funds.

The government will not allow – and will devise strict regulations to combat – abuse of personal positions in the exercise of trade and investment.

Public funds belong to the citizens and to the nation. Preserving public funds is a national and moral duty that will be exercised through institutions, laws, transparency and continuous supervision. In this context, the government will prosecute persons accused of corruption and embezzlement based on concrete evidence and pursuant to due process. The government is fully prepared to receive any complaints and supporting evidence in this regard, and to refer these to the competent authorities.

The government is fully aware of the problems facing our administrative structure and understands that it is necessary to quickly remedy this problem. It will continue to implement and develop its reform plan – in particular the reform plan adopted by the Legislative Council through a joint committee between the council, the government and in cooperation with all relevant parties, including civil society. The government will build the Ministerial Cabinet with professionalism and work ethics that will improve the work of all Executive Authority institutions in order to serve the public interest. One of the most important steps in this regard is the implementation of the financial and administrative components of the Civil Service Law. We will ensure that all civil servants (who number more than 120,000) are given guarantees for their present and future so that they have sufficient pension salaries upon the termination of their employment, in accordance with a comprehensive pension system that we hope to finalise in the coming few months.

The government will not allow for any sign of chaos, waste or duplication in our administrative structure and will therefore continue our efforts to restructure government ministries, institutions and agencies by merging and abolishing such organs as needed to allow them to best perform their tasks in serving the state and its citizens. All of this will be framed within a modern and comprehensive administrative law that the government will work to formulate in order to organise all aspects of the Executive Authority.

Mr President, ladies and gentlemen, members of the PLC, you may have noticed that I intentionally began this statement with the government's vision of the internal situation and the areas of major concern.

This is a message that we are conveying to Palestinian citizens who seek wide-scale reforms in all aspects of their lives and related to their rights.

However, the internal situation cannot be separated from the painful and political reality in which we live and encounter: the deplorable occupation and its accompanying colonisation and oppressive policies that have caused us tremendous pain and suffering.

Once again, I reiterate that the military and colonising occupation with its practices that include assassinations, detentions, checkpoints, sieges, demolition of homes and properties, is the root of our suffering, has deepened our suffering and is the main source of our problems. The occupation impedes our growth and therefore ending the occupation in all of its forms and from all of the territories occupied since 1967, including our eternal capital Jerusalem, is our national priority that requires solidarity and unity among all Palestinian forces under the leadership of the Palestine Liberation Organization, the sole representative of our people authorised by the major Palestinian institutions, foremost among which are the National and Central Council, to negotiate and conclude agreements on behalf of the Palestinian people.

The government, which is part of our national political system, the PLO, is fully committed to the programmes and decisions of our National and Central Councils on political and strategic levels.

We should translate our decades and generations of popular and revolutionary struggles into political achievements that will bring us closer to our goal of establishing our independent state (with Jerusalem as its capital) and resolving the question of our refugees on the basis of international law.

Based on our realistic and practical understanding of the contents, mechanisms and goals of our national struggle, our people fought with honour and undertook political initiatives with consciousness and seriousness.

Every means of struggle has its time, mechanisms and calculated return. Based on this, our people, through its legitimate leadership, has presented successive serious peace initiatives and has not hesitated to adopt peace as our strategic, irrevocable choice. The peace process has gone through essential failings and major deteriorations, to the point that we have now reached the most difficult stage of this bloody and escalating conflict. While we should learn from the lessons of the past, what we are living under does not cause us to lose hope in the benefits of peace, or to turn our backs on Arab and international initiatives that aim to achieve peace.

Before us, we have the Arab peace initiative that came out of the summit in Beirut. This has formed a national consensus on the need to end the Arab–Israeli conflict peacefully and in accordance with international law. This initiative will ensure that our region goes from one of conflict to that of stability and normalised relations between all states. We also have before us the Road Map as an international blueprint to aims to reach a permanent solution to the Palestinian question. The government is committed to the Palestinian leadership's official approval of this plan reached after an in-depth and thorough review of it. Nonetheless, I would like to mention a few points in this regard:

Israel is attempting to alter the Road Map as we know it by entering into complicated negotiations and by outlining its own understanding of the clauses of this plan and its means of engaging in the plan.

Our engagement in this Road Map will not be affected by Israel's attempts and we will not negotiate the Road Map. The Road Map must be implemented not negotiated. Therefore, the government supports the Palestinian leadership in asserting its refusal of the so-called Israeli amendments and calls upon the Quartet – author of this plan – to announce the Road Map as we know it as soon as possible, and to guarantee and verify the implementation of each phase with an effective and guaranteed enforcement and monitoring mechanisms.

In this context, the government reconfirms the Palestinian commitment to the implementation of all of our obligations within the framework of this plan, whether it be on political or security levels. It is quite natural that we require Israel to fulfil its mutual obligations.

Yet, what we have outlined will be meaningless if Israel's policy of imposing facts on the ground continues. Settlements, which violate international law, continue to be the major threat to the creation of a Palestinian state with genuine sovereignty. Thus, settlements are the primary obstacle to any peace process.

Settlement expansion in and around Jerusalem, with its accompanying house demolitions, confiscation of land and property (in addition to the economic, social, administrative and cultural strangulation in the lives of Palestinians and Israel's attempt to impose a permanent solution for this Holy City by means other than negotiations) will only lead to inflaming the conflict and destroying any chance for peace.

The construction of the so-called 'separation' wall is a dangerous continuation of the colonisation project. In addition to the confiscation of Palestinian citizens' lands and the cutting off of their sources of livelihood, the wall is an Israeli measure that is designed to annex large areas of land, to confiscate underground water, isolate our cities and villages and to encircle the city of Jerusalem. This is another attempt to destroy any chance for peace and destroy any possibility to reach a permanent and accepted solution to the Palestinian–Israeli conflict. The removal of the wall will be among the first issues that our government will address because, without its removal, Israel will effectively destroy the Road Map and any other peace initiative.

Here, I would like to address the Israeli people and the Israeli government frankly and directly.

We want a lasting peace with you achieved through negotiations and on the basis of international law, to implement Security Council Resolutions 242 and 338, as well as signed agreements.

We denounce terrorism by any party and in all its shapes and forms both because of our religious and moral traditions and because we are convinced that such methods do not lend support to a just cause like ours, but rather destroy it. These methods do not achieve peace, to which we aspire.

We understand peace as a message of conscience and behaviour based on mutual desire and recognition of rights with the goal of living in peace and security on the basis of equality.

As we extend our hand to you in peace, we reiterate that peace cannot be possible with the continuation of settlement activity. Peace will not be possible with the expropriation and annexation of land. The choice is yours: peace without settlements or a continuation of the occupation, subjugation, hatred and conflict.

To be clear, the Palestinian people will not accept anything less than the exercise of our right to self-determination and the establishment of our independent, sovereign state with Jerusalem as its capital; a genuine, contiguous state without any settlements, on all of the territories occupied in 1967.

I am quite certain that you realise the importance of the question of refugees, not only in the Palestinian–Israeli conflict, but also on Arab and regional levels as we are speaking of millions of Palestinian refugees around the world. Because you realise the importance of this issue, you placed it on the timetable of the permanent status negotiations.

Thus, a just, agreed-upon, fair and acceptable solution to the refugee problem consistent with international law (particularly UN Resolution 194) will be the basis of peace and coexistence.

These are the fundamentals of any solution to the Palestinian–Israeli conflict and this will not be changed.

To the Arab population inside Israel, our people and our loved ones: I extend to you appreciation and respect for your continuous support to us in the Occupied Territories. I am certain that you will continue to play a positive role in Israeli politics, media and popular civic organisation to strengthen and establish an Israeli public opinion that shares our commitment to a just political solution to the Palestinian–Israeli conflict and to the establishment of an independent Palestinian state.

We do not ignore the sufferings of Jews throughout history. And in exchange, we hope that the Israelis will not turn their back to the sufferings of the Palestinians, which include displacement, occupation, colonisation and continuous oppression of the Palestinians.

To the Israeli government, which advised us that we learn the lessons of Iraq, I say.

The Palestinian people are the ones who choose their leadership. The leadership decides its politics according to independent Palestinian choice. Our legitimacy is derived from the will of the people, which is embodied in national organisations.

Those who need to learn the lessons of war and its calamities are those who still believe that military might is capable of imposing political solutions and that implicit and explicit threats are capable of dissuading people from demanding their rights. I repeat, there is no military solution to our conflict. Our people do not accept threats and will not succumb to them. On the contrary, there is no alternative to a just and comprehensive political solution. Our people welcome peace, security and prosperity to all. We welcome a peace that guarantees Israel's withdrawal from all occupied Palestinian and Arab territories in accordance with international law.

We have heard a lot of your desire for peace, but what we have witnessed from you is siege, assassinations, invasions, destruction and a continuation of settlements. We hope that your desire for peace will be translated into action.

Mr President, ladies and gentlemen, our hearts are filled with grief and pain because of what happened to our people in Iraq who throughout history have sacrificed for the Palestinian people. We hope for stability for our brothers and sisters in Iraq. We hope that the foreign occupation of their land will end. We hope that the reconstruction of their land will begin in the near future under an Iraqi government that represents the will of the Iraqi people and speaks on its behalf.

We understand what happened in Iraq is an expression of a new and straightforward policy vis-à-vis the Middle East, led unilaterally, to redraw the borders of the political map of the whole region. It is naive to assume that Palestine will not be affected by these turbulent developments, as it is only natural to feel concern for the impact and repercussions of the situation in Iraq on the Palestinian people and our cause.

We do not want to address this serious shift in policy with slogans and ardent mottos, but rather with sound logic and an understanding of our national aspirations in order to avoid losses or reduce the amount of such loss and to provide practical and realistic methods to achieve our goals.

Sisters and brothers, the path of negotiations is our choice and the resumption of negotiations with Israel – under the much-appreciated auspices and sponsorship of the Quartet, and in close coordination with our brothers in Egypt, Jordan and Saudi Arabia – is a constant Palestinian demand.

All through the long negotiation process, there were criticisms of our performance in negotiations. However such criticisms do not nullify the fact that we have a rich accumulated experience from which we should benefit.

Therefore, our government will work side by side with the PLO Executive Committee and its Higher Negotiations Committee, under the direction of President Yasser Arafat, President of State and Palestinian Authority, Chairman of the PLO, in order to restructure our negotiations framework and to allow the negotiations team to dedicate itself to this important, sensitive and vital task.

I thank our Arab brothers for their continued and constant support to our people and cause and confirm the government's commitment to the concerns of the Arab states and to the Charter of the Arab League and its decisions. We will continue to coordinate and cooperate with our brothers to consolidate Arab consensus.

The government will remain keen on developing our strategic relations with the rest of our friends in the world whom we thank for their support and who share our commitment to balanced international relations based on compliance with international law and UN resolutions. We also call upon the Security Council to fulfil its obligations in maintaining security and peace in our region and to ensuring the implementation of its resolutions in a fair and consistent manner, while also working to protect our people and to help us achieve independence and freedom.

Mr President, sisters and brothers, I am embarking on a new mission in my political career by fulfilling a newly created role in Palestine. I heard and read much speculation about the aim of this position. Allow me to clarify.

The post of the Prime Minister (and regardless of the person in the post), along with the Ministerial Cabinet, the Legislative Council and all of the institutions of the National Authority are an integral part of the Palestinian political system, the framework of which is the PLO. It is a constitutional position approved by all of our national institutions. In its essence, it is a serious attempt to improve the performance of our National Authority and prepare for the construction of our state including the preparation for upcoming elections – after the removal of obstacles put forth by the occupation – to establish a democratic political system. It is a position from which I will implement my government's programme using all the constitutional powers vested in this post.

I wish to end my speech with a word to my brother and companion, elected President Yasser Arafat.

The government, Mr President, is your government and the siege on you is symbolic of the resistance, pride and esteem of our great people. We will not, from this moment forth, cease our serious and assiduous work to end this unacceptable situation. The President of this people, leader of its struggle and maker of peace on its behalf, has the right to regain his natural right to freedom and mobility without restrictions.

We know, Mr President, that you have always prided yourself on sharing your people's suffering. Thus, the government, under your leadership, will not spare any effort to work to release all of our detainees, honourable heroes detained by the occupation – whose number has exceeded 10,000 – including members of the Executive Committee of the PLO, Tayseer Khaled and Abdul Rahim Malowah, as well as member of the Central Council Rakad Salem and members of the Legislative Council Marwan Barghouti and Hussam Khader and the longest-detained Palestinian, Ahmad Jubarah [Abu Sukkar].

All of us in Palestine and everywhere, regardless of our positions, do not have different stances. If we have different titles, we do not have different commitments and if we have different missions, we do not have different goals.

Sisters and brothers, members of the Council, before I present to you the members of my Cabinet, I would like to share with you frankly the considerations that were in my mind as I was forming the government.

The formation before you is a result of the Palestinian political reality, with all its positive and negative aspects. I know that there are many objections regarding names and portfolios, and regarding political representation, professional abilities, and so on and so forth. However, this formation is what I believe in after my extensive consultations and after taking into account our domestic politics which are known to you all.

I seek your confidence, support and cooperation because this plan requires all of our efforts. The credibility of the government will be based on the effectiveness of its performance. Therefore, just as I ask for your confidence, I call upon you to use your powers in monitoring and holding the government accountable to the fullest extent. These are tenets of the parliamentary life we have chosen. Let us move forward on these bases.

May Peace and the Mercy of Allah be upon you.

BINYAMIN NETANYAHU

'WE WANT TO SEE A PARALLEL COMMITMENT'

—

REMARKS BEFORE THE GENERAL ASSEMBLY OF THE
JEWISH FEDERATIONS OF NORTH AMERICA

NEW ORLEANS, LOUISIANA, 11 AUGUST 2010

Born in Tel Aviv in 1949, Binyamin Netanyahu fought in the Six-Day War of 1967, rising to the rank of captain. In the 1970s, he studied at the Massachusetts Institute of Technology, attaining an M.S. degree from the Sloan School of Management. His older brother, Yonatan, commander of the elite Israeli army commando unit Sayeret Matka, was killed in the famous Operation Entebbe in Idi Amin's Uganda. Binyamin (often referred to as 'Bibi' by Israelis) founded the Yonatan Netanyahu Anti-Terror Institute, devoted to the study of terrorism and counter-terror measures. This led to his making a series of political connections, and his eventual appointment by Foreign Minister Moshe Arens as Deputy Chief of Mission at the Israeli Embassy in Washington, DC. He went on to serve as Israel's Ambassador to the United Nations from 1984–1988.

Netanyahu returned to Israel in 1988 and was elected to fifth place on the Likud Party list, ensuring his election to Israel's parliament, the Knesset, in that year's election. He served as Deputy Minister in the Prime Minister's Office under Yitzhak Shamir, and participated in the Madrid Conference of 1991, a joint US–Soviet attempt to promote a peaceful settlement to the Israeli-Palestinian conflict. After the Likud lost the 1992 general elections, Netanyahu contested the Likud Party leadership, defeating Benny Begin, son of former Prime Minister Menachem Begin. He was elected Prime Minister in 1994, following the assassination of Yitzhak Rabin, in a close race with Shimon Peres (this was one of three Israeli elections in which direct balloting for the post of Prime Minister took place alongside the party list election to the Knesset, in an attempt to strengthen executive authority). Netanyahu embarked on a series of *neo-liberal economic reforms and took a hard line on security. In 1997, the police proposed that Netanyahu face prosecution on corruption charges, but no case was ever filed. Netanyahu lost the premiership to Ehud Barak in 1999, and claimed he was retiring from politics. However, when the Likud defeated Barak under Ariel Sharon, he served as Finance Minister. Netanyahu returned to the party leadership when Ariel Sharon left the Likud to found Kadima, and was leader of the opposition from 2005–2009.*

Although his party came second to Kadima in the 2009 election, Netanyahu was able to piece together a coalition government, becoming Prime Minister once again.

In this speech he provides a justification for the state of Israel's existence. He also provides perspectives on the war in Iraq and the strength of the Israeli economy. He indicates his disagreement with Hamas and argues that Israel will continue to seek peaceful settlement with its neighbours, even if it has to do so without international support.

The story of the Jewish people is that of great destruction followed by miraculous redemption. That same resilient spirit is exemplified by your collective efforts to help this great city rebuild itself after Hurricane Katrina. Just as you have rallied time after time to help Israel weather the storms it has faced, you rallied to help New Orleans to get back on its feet.

You should be proud of what you have been doing for the Jewish people and the Jewish state, and for others. I am doubly proud to be with you here today. Thank you.

On the eve of the twentieth century, Theodore Herzl, the founder of modern Zionism, foresaw the great challenges that stood before the dispersed Jewish people. He charted a clear path to direct the Jewish destiny to the safer shores of a Jewish state. Herzl's vision was guided by three principles: recognise perils, seize opportunities, forge unity.

These same three principles should guide us at the dawn of the twenty-first century. We must recognise the dangers facing us and work to thwart them. We must seize the opportunity for prosperity and for peace with those of our neighbours who want peace. And we must forge unity among our people to shoulder these monumental tasks.

The greatest danger facing Israel and the world is the prospect of a nuclear-armed Iran. Iran threatens to annihilate Israel. It denies the Holocaust. It sponsors terror. It confronts America in Afghanistan and Iraq. It dominates Lebanon and Gaza. It establishes beachheads in Arabia and in Africa. It even spreads its influence into this hemisphere, into South America.

Now, this is what Iran is doing without nuclear weapons. Imagine what it would do with them. Imagine the devastation that its terror proxies, Hezbollah and Hamas and others, would wreak under an Iranian nuclear umbrella.

This is why Israel appreciates President Obama's successful efforts to have the UN Security Council adopt new sanctions against Iran. It values American efforts to successfully mobilise other countries to pass tough sanctions of their own. There is no doubt that these sanctions are putting strong economic pressures on the Iranian regime.

But we have yet to see any signs that the tyrants of Tehran are reconsidering their pursuit of nuclear weapons. The only time that Iran suspended its nuclear programme was for a brief period in 2003 when the regime believed it faced a credible threat of military action against it. And the simple paradox is this: if the international community, led by the United States, hopes to stop Iran's nuclear programme without resorting to military action, it will have to convince Iran that it is prepared to take such action. Containment will not work against Iran. It won't work with a brazen regime that accuses America of bombing its own cities on 9/11, openly calls for Israel's annihilation, and is the world's leading sponsor of terrorism.

When faced with such a regime, the only responsible policy is to prevent it from developing atomic bombs in the first place. The bottom line is this: Iran's nuclear programme must be stopped. Iran's nuclear programme is the greatest danger we face. The assault on Israel's legitimacy is another.

We know from our history that attacks on the Jews were often preceded by attempts to dehumanise the Jewish people – to paint them as vile criminals, as the scourge of humanity. This is why the attempts by our enemies and their misguided fellow travellers to delegitimise the Jewish state must be countered.

Herzl was right about many things. He was right about the conflagration that would soon engulf Europe. He was right about the need for a Jewish state and for a Jewish army to defend that state.

Yet Herzl was too optimistic in believing that the rebirth of the Jewish state would gradually put an end to anti-Semitism.

The establishment of Israel did not end the hatred towards the Jews. It merely redirected it. The old hatred against the Jewish people is now focused against the Jewish state. If in the past Jews were demonised, singled out or denied the rights that were automatically granted to others, today in many quarters Israel is demonised, singled out and denied the rights automatically granted to other nations, first and foremost the right of self-defence.

For too many, Israel is guilty until proven guilty. The greatest success of our detractors is when Jews start believing that too – we've seen that today.

Last year, at the UN General Assembly, I spoke out against the travesty of the Goldstone Report, which falsely accused Israel of war crimes in Gaza two years ago. The United States, led by President Obama, and Canada, led by Prime Minister Stephen Harper, stood by Israel's side against this blood libel. Many countries didn't.

Well, last week, Hamas finally admitted that over 700 of its fighters in Gaza were killed by the IDF during that war. This is precisely what the Israeli army said all along – that roughly 50 per cent of the casualties of the war were Hamas terrorists. Such a high percentage of enemy combatants and such a low percentage of unintended civilian casualties is remarkable in modern urban warfare. It is even more remarkable when fighting an enemy that deliberately and shamelessly embeds itself next to schools and inside mosques and hospitals.

The authors of the Goldstone Report owe the Israeli army an apology. And all those who supported and helped spread this libel owe the state of Israel an apology. The best way to counter lies is with the truth. That is why I commend your decision to establish the Israel Action Network and dedicate resources to fight this battle for truth. We must fight these lies and slanders together to ensure that truth prevails.

The threat from Iran and its proxies, and the continued assault on Israel's legitimacy are great perils we must thwart.

Now let me speak about two great opportunities we must seize: peace and prosperity.

The opportunity today to achieve a broader Israeli–Arab peace derives not exclusively but mainly from the perception of a common threat. Today, Arab governments and many throughout the Arab world understand that Iran is a great danger to them as well. This understanding opens up new possibilities for a broader peace that could support our efforts to reach peace with our Palestinian neighbours.

Israelis want to see that the Palestinians are as committed as they are to ending the conflict once and for all. They want to know that just as we are ready to recognise a state for the Palestinian people, the Palestinians are ready to recognise Israel as the state for the Jewish people.

Israel also wants a secure peace. We do not want to vacate more territory only to see Iran walk in and fire thousands of rockets at our cities. That is exactly what happened after we left Lebanon and Gaza. We don't want to see rockets and missiles streaming into a Palestinian state and placed on the hills above Tel Aviv and the hills encircling Jerusalem. If Israel does not maintain a credible security presence in the Jordan Valley for the foreseeable future, this is exactly what will happen. I will not let that happen.

We do not want security on paper. We want security on the ground. Real security. I am willing to make mutual compromises for a genuine peace with the Palestinians, but I will not gamble with the security of the Jewish state. Palestinian leaders who say they want to live peacefully alongside Israel should sit down and negotiate peace with Israel. They should stop placing preconditions and start negotiating peace. The Palestinians may think they can avoid negotiations. They may think that the world will dictate Palestinian demands to Israel. I firmly believe that will not happen because I am confident that friends of Israel, led by the United States, will not let that happen. There is only one path to peace – that is through a negotiated settlement.

We should spend the next year trying to reach an historic agreement for peace and not waste time arguing about marginal issues that will not affect the final peace map in any way. I am confident that if there is goodwill on the Palestinian side, a formula can be found that will enable peace talks to continue. I believe that if we succeed, and I always like to confound the sceptics, and I continue to do that systematically, I believe that peace would unleash tremendous economic opportunities for Israelis, Palestinians, and peoples throughout the region.

But as the last years have shown, Israel has not waited for peace to seize the opportunity to develop a strong economy. As Prime Minister, then as Finance Minister and now again as Prime Minister, I have spent a great deal of time advancing economic reforms and removing obstacles to Israel's economic growth – and I have the political scars to prove it. The reforms that we have been enacting have changed Israel's economy beyond recognition. We are now building fast roads and rail lines that crisscross the country, to connect the Negev and the Galilee to the centre of the country. I intend to complete a rail line that will link the Red Sea with the Mediterranean and the Jordan River to the port of Haifa. This will enable Israel to take advantage of its strategic location as more and more goods are shipped from east to west.

As the world economy becomes more competitive, Israel is well placed to succeed. We are global leaders in high technology. Our scientists win Nobel Prizes. Our innovations in science, medicine, water, energy, communication, agriculture and in many other fields are literally changing the world.

Israel is a wellspring of technological, artistic and cultural creativity. Today, Israel is ranked fifteenth in the world in terms of quality of life by the UN – so you know we are at least fifteenth. And if that does not impress the young people in the audience, here's something else that might. For those of you planning to travel the world, Lonely Planet just ranked Tel Aviv the third most exciting city in the world. I don't agree – that of course is Jerusalem. Still, Israel's best economic days are ahead.

If we hope to thwart dangers and seize opportunities, we must strengthen our unity. The best way to strengthen Jewish unity is to strengthen Jewish identity. By deepening our connection to our shared past, we fortify our bonds to one another and to our state, and thereby strengthen our common future. That is why this year I decided to initiate a national Heritage Plan that will restore and renovate hundreds of Jewish and Israeli sites throughout the country.

I want young people to visit the place where David Ben Gurion declared our independence just as I want them to visit the place where our patriarchs and matriarchs, the mothers and fathers of the Jewish nation, are buried. Talk about distortions, can you imagine that UNESCO tried to deny the Jewish connection to Rachel's Tomb next to Jerusalem and the Tomb of the Patriarchs in Hebron? This absurdity to try to erase our past will fail as we reconnect a new generation of Jews with their history. Our young people will know that we are not foreign interlopers in our own homeland. They will know something that our enemies and politicised international bodies cannot bring themselves to admit: the Jewish people are not strangers in the Land of Israel. Israel is our home. It has always been our home and it will always be our home.

I have also decided to enhance Israel's support for programmes that strengthen Jewish identity in the Diaspora. In my first term as Prime Minister, I decided to invest Israeli government funds in what many then thought was a preposterous idea – that we would pay for young Jews to come on short visits to Israel. Since then, a quarter of a million Jews have come to Israel on Birthright programmes, and we will continue. I am committed to working with Birthright, Masa and Lapid to ensure that every young Jew who wants to can come to Israel.

And I am committed to working with Natan Sharansky and the Jewish Agency to strengthen Jewish identity in the Diaspora.

I know that there are controversial issues that threaten to divide us. We need to resolve these issues in a spirit of compromise and tolerance. As Prime Minister of Israel, I promise you that I will not permit anything to undermine the unity of our people. Israel must always be a place that each and every one of you can call home. Our unity is a critical foundation of our collective strength. The more we speak with one voice, the more that voice will be heard. And in a rapidly changing world, it needs to be heard loud and clear.

At the beginning of the twenty-first century, the fantastic rise of Asia challenges many nations, but it is not a danger. It is a natural shift in global wealth and power that is lifting hundreds of millions of people out of poverty. The great danger we face is not from the battle between East and West but from the aggressive force wedged between them that is spreading its tentacles far and wide. That force is radical Islam, whose fanaticism and savagery knows no bounds. If I can leave you with one message, it is that we must warn others of this peril.

History shows that the most advanced weapons were usually developed by the most advanced societies. Yet today, primitive and barbaric tyrannies that stone women, hang gays, promote terror worldwide, send bombs to synagogues, and advance the most fanatical doctrines can acquire nuclear weapons. If not stopped, this means that the greatest nightmare of all – nuclear terrorism – can become a reality. The civilised world must not let that happen.

As we continue to build a modern and democratic Israel and as we seek peace with all our neighbours, we must also warn the world about this formidable peril. In standing up for modernity against medievalism, the Jewish people and the Jewish state play a vital role in securing our common civilisation. And by helping dispel the shadows of a dark despotism, we can truly fulfil our destiny to be a beacon of light and progress unto all the nations.

BINYAMIN NETANYAHU

'ISRAEL IS WHAT IS RIGHT WITH THE MIDDLE EAST'

—

REMARKS BEFORE A JOINT SESSION OF CONGRESS

WASHINGTON, DC, 24 MAY 2011

Since 2009, Binyamin Netanyahu has been the Prime Minister of Israel. In recent years Israel has faced extensive international criticism for the ongoing construction of settlements in disputed territories occupied since the 1967 war. In addition, President Obama has called for a return to the pre-war borders. There has also been strong diplomatic pressure by the international community for a two-state settlement between Israel and the Palestinian state.

In this speech, Netanyahu addresses these issues before the United States Congress.

—

I am deeply honoured by your warm welcome. And I am deeply honoured that you have given me the opportunity to address Congress a second time.

Mr Vice President, do you remember the time we were the new kids in town?

And I do see a lot of old friends here. And I do see a lot of new friends of Israel here. Democrats and Republicans alike.

Israel has no better friend than America. And America has no better friend than Israel. We stand together to defend democracy. We stand together to advance peace. We stand together to fight terrorism. Congratulations, America, Congratulations, Mr President. You got bin Laden. Good riddance!

In an unstable Middle East, Israel is the one anchor of stability. In a region of shifting alliances, Israel is America's unwavering ally. Israel has always been pro-American. Israel will always be pro-American.

My friends, you don't need to do nation building in Israel. We're already built.

You don't need to export democracy to Israel. We've already got it. You don't need to send American troops to defend Israel. We defend ourselves. You've been very generous in giving us tools to do the job of defending Israel on our own. Thank you all, and thank you President Obama, for your steadfast commitment to Israel's security. I know economic times are tough. I deeply appreciate this.

Support for Israel's security is a wise investment in our common future. For an epic battle is now unfolding in the Middle East, between tyranny and freedom. A great convulsion is shaking the earth from the Khyber Pass to the Straits of Gibraltar. The tremors have shattered states and toppled governments. And we can all see that the ground is still shifting. Now this historic moment holds the promise of a new dawn of freedom and opportunity. Millions of young people are determined to change their future. We all look at them. They muster courage. They risk their lives. They demand dignity. They desire liberty.

These extraordinary scenes in Tunis and Cairo, evoke those of Berlin and Prague in 1989. Yet as we share their hopes, we must also remember that those hopes could be snuffed out as they were in Tehran in 1979. You remember what happened then. The brief democratic spring in Iran was cut short by a ferocious and unforgiving tyranny. This same tyranny smothered Lebanon's democratic Cedar Revolution, and inflicted on that long-suffering country, the medieval rule of Hezbollah.

So today, the Middle East stands at a fateful crossroads. Like all of you, I pray that the peoples of the region choose the path less travelled, the path of liberty. No one knows what this path consists of better than you. This path is not paved by elections alone. It is paved when governments permit protests in town squares, when limits are placed on the powers of rulers, when judges are beholden to laws and not men, and when human rights cannot be crushed by tribal loyalties or mob rule.

Israel has always embraced this path, the Middle East has long rejected it. In a region where women are stoned, gays are hanged, Christians are persecuted, Israel stands out. It is different.

As the great English writer George Eliot predicted over a century ago, that once established, the Jewish state will 'shine like a bright star of freedom amid the despotisms of the East'. Well, she was right. We have a free press, independent courts, an open economy, rambunctious parliamentary debates. You think you guys are tough on one another in Congress? Come spend a day in the Knesset. Be my guest.

Courageous Arab protesters are now struggling to secure these very same rights for their peoples, for their societies. We're proud that over one million Arab citizens of Israel have been enjoying these rights for decades. Of the 300 million Arabs in the Middle East and North Africa, only Israel's Arab citizens enjoy real democratic rights. I want you to stop for a second and think about that. Of those 300 million Arabs, less than one half of 1 per cent are truly free, and they're all citizens of Israel!

This startling fact reveals a basic truth: Israel is not what is wrong about the Middle East. Israel is what is right about the Middle East.

Israel fully supports the desire of Arab peoples in our region to live freely. We long for the day when Israel will be one of many real democracies in the Middle East.

Fifteen years ago, I stood at this very podium, and said that democracy must start to take root in the Arab world. Well, it's begun to take root. This beginning holds the promise of a brilliant future of peace and prosperity. For I believe that a Middle East that is genuinely democratic will be a Middle East truly at peace.

But while we hope and work for the best, we must also recognise that powerful forces oppose this future. They oppose modernity. They oppose democracy. They oppose peace.

Foremost among these forces is Iran. The tyranny in Tehran brutalises its own people. It supports attacks against American troops in Afghanistan and Iraq. It subjugates Lebanon and Gaza. It sponsors terror worldwide.

When I last stood here, I spoke of the dire consequences of Iran developing nuclear weapons. Now time is running out, and the hinge of history may soon turn. For the greatest danger facing humanity could soon be upon us: a militant Islamic regime armed with nuclear weapons. Militant Islam threatens the world. It threatens Islam. I have no doubt that it will ultimately be defeated. It will eventually succumb to the forces of freedom and progress. But like other fanaticisms that were doomed to fail, militant Islam could exact a horrific price from all of us before its inevitable demise.

A nuclear-armed Iran would ignite a nuclear arms race in the Middle East. It would give terrorists a nuclear umbrella. It would make the nightmare of nuclear terrorism a clear and present danger throughout the world. I want you to understand what this means. They could put the bomb anywhere. They could put it on a missile. It could be on a container ship in a port, or in a suitcase on a subway.

Now the threat to my country cannot be overstated. Those who dismiss it are sticking their heads in the sand. Less than seven decades after six million Jews were murdered, Iran's leaders deny the Holocaust of the Jewish people, while calling for the annihilation of the Jewish state.

Leaders who spew such venom should be banned from every respectable forum on the planet. But there is something that makes the outrage even greater: The lack of outrage. In much of the international community, the calls for our destruction are met with utter silence. It is even worse because there are many who rush to condemn Israel for defending itself against Iran's terror proxies.

But not you. Not America. You have acted differently. You've condemned the Iranian regime for its genocidal aims. You've passed tough sanctions against Iran. History will salute you, America.

President Obama has said that the United States is determined to prevent Iran from developing nuclear weapons. He successfully led the Security Council to adopt sanctions against Iran. You in Congress passed even tougher sanctions. These words and deeds are vitally important.

Yet the Ayatollah regime briefly suspended its nuclear programme only once, in 2003, when it feared the possibility of military action. That same year, Muammar Gaddafi gave up his nuclear weapons programme, and for the same reason. The more Iran believes that all options are on the table, the less the chance of confrontation. This is why I ask you to continue to send an unequivocal message: that America will never permit Iran to develop nuclear weapons.

As for Israel, if history has taught the Jewish people anything, it is that we must take calls for our destruction seriously. We are a nation that rose from the ashes of the Holocaust. When we say never again, we mean never again. Israel always reserves the right to defend itself.

My friends, while Israel will be ever vigilant in its defence, we will never give up on our quest for peace. I guess we'll give it up when we achieve it. Israel wants peace. Israel needs peace. We've achieved historic peace agreements with Egypt and Jordan that have held up for decades.

I remember what it was like before we had peace. I was nearly killed in a firefight inside the Suez Canal. I mean that literally. I battled terrorists along both banks of the Jordan River. Too many Israelis have lost loved ones. I know their grief. I lost my brother.

So no one in Israel wants a return to those terrible days. The peace with Egypt and Jordan has long served as an anchor of stability and peace in the heart of the Middle East.

This peace should be bolstered by economic and political support to all those who remain committed to peace.

The peace agreements with Egypt and Jordan are vital. But they're not enough. We must also find a way to forge a lasting peace with the Palestinians. Two years ago, I publicly committed to a solution of two states for two peoples: a Palestinian state alongside the Jewish state.

I am willing to make painful compromises to achieve this historic peace. As the leader of Israel, it is my responsibility to lead my people to peace.

This is not easy for me. I recognise that in a genuine peace, we will be required to give up parts of the Jewish homeland. In Judea and Samaria, the Jewish people are not foreign occupiers. We are not the British in India. We are not the Belgians in the Congo.

This is the land of our forefathers, the Land of Israel, to which Abraham brought the idea of one God, where David set out to confront Goliath, and where Isaiah saw a vision of eternal peace. No distortion of history can deny the 4,000-year-old bond, between the Jewish people and the Jewish land.

But there is another truth: The Palestinians share this small land with us. We seek a peace in which they will be neither Israel's subjects nor its citizens. They should enjoy a national life of dignity as a free, viable and independent people in their own state. They should enjoy a prosperous economy, where their creativity and initiative can flourish.

We've already seen the beginnings of what is possible. In the last two years, the Palestinians have begun to build a better life for themselves. Prime Minister Fayad has led this effort. I wish him a speedy recovery from his recent operation.

We've helped the Palestinian economy by removing hundreds of barriers and roadblocks to the free flow of goods and people. The results have been nothing short of remarkable. The Palestinian economy is booming. It's growing by more than 10 per cent a year.

Palestinian cities look very different today than they did just a few years ago. They have shopping malls, movie theatres, restaurants, banks. They even have e-businesses. This is all happening without peace. Imagine what could happen with peace. Peace would herald a new day for both peoples. It would make the dream of a broader Arab–Israeli peace a realistic possibility.

So now here is the question. You have to ask it. If the benefits of peace with the Palestinians are so clear, why has peace eluded us? Because all six Israeli Prime Ministers since the signing of Oslo accords agreed to establish a Palestinian state. Myself included. So why has peace not been achieved? Because so far, the Palestinians have been unwilling to accept a Palestinian state, if it meant accepting a Jewish state alongside it.

You see, our conflict has never been about the establishment of a Palestinian state. It has always been about the existence of the Jewish state. This is what this conflict is about. In 1947, the United Nations voted to partition the land into a Jewish state and an Arab state. The Jews said yes. The Palestinians said no. In recent years, the Palestinians twice refused generous offers by Israeli Prime Ministers, to establish a Palestinian state on virtually all the territory won by Israel in the Six Day War.

They were simply unwilling to end the conflict. And I regret to say this: they continue to educate their children to hate. They continue to name public squares after terrorists. And worst of all, they continue to perpetuate the fantasy that Israel will one day be flooded by the descendants of Palestinian refugees.

My friends, this must come to an end. President Abbas must do what I have done. I stood before my people, and I told you it wasn't easy for me, and I said: 'I will accept a Palestinian state.' It is time for President Abbas to stand before his people and say: 'I will accept a Jewish state.'

Those six words will change history. They will make clear to the Palestinians that this conflict must come to an end. That they are not building a state to continue the conflict with Israel, but to end it. They will convince the people of Israel that they have a true partner for peace. With such a partner, the people of Israel will be prepared to make a far-reaching compromise. I will be prepared to make a far-reaching compromise.

This compromise must reflect the dramatic demographic changes that have occurred since 1967. The vast majority of the 650,000 Israelis who live beyond the 1967 lines reside in neighbourhoods and suburbs of Jerusalem and Greater Tel Aviv.

These areas are densely populated but geographically quite small. Under any realistic peace agreement, these areas, as well as other places of critical strategic and national importance, will be incorporated into the final borders of Israel.

The status of the settlements will be decided only in negotiations. But we must also be honest. So I am saying today something that should be said publicly by anyone serious about peace. In any peace agreement that ends the conflict, some settlements will end up beyond Israel's borders. The precise delineation of those borders must be negotiated. We will be very generous on the size of a future Palestinian state. But as President Obama said, the border will be different than the one that existed on 4 June 1967. Israel will not return to the indefensible lines of 1967.

We recognise that a Palestinian state must be big enough to be viable, independent and prosperous. President Obama rightly referred to Israel as the homeland of the Jewish people, just as he referred to the future Palestinian state as the homeland of the Palestinian people. Jews from around the world have a right to immigrate to the Jewish state. Palestinians from around the world should have a right to immigrate, if they so choose, to a Palestinian state. This means that the Palestinian refugee problem will be resolved outside the borders of Israel.

As for Jerusalem, only a democratic Israel has protected freedom of worship for all faiths in the city. Jerusalem must never again be divided. Jerusalem must remain the united capital of Israel. I know that this is a difficult issue for Palestinians. But I believe with creativity and goodwill a solution can be found.

This is the peace I plan to forge with a Palestinian partner committed to peace. But you know very well, that in the Middle East, the only peace that will hold is a peace you can defend.

So peace must be anchored in security. In recent years, Israel withdrew from South Lebanon and Gaza. But we didn't get peace. Instead, we got 12,000 rockets fired from those areas on our cities, on our children, by Hezbollah and Hamas. The UN peacekeepers in Lebanon failed to prevent the smuggling of this weaponry. The European observers in Gaza evaporated overnight. So if Israel simply walked out of the territories, the flow of weapons into a future Palestinian state would be unchecked. Missiles fired from it could reach virtually every home in Israel in less than a minute. I want you to think about that too.

Imagine that right now we all had less than sixty seconds to find shelter from an incoming rocket. Would you live that way? Would anyone live that way? Well, we aren't going to live that way either.

The truth is that Israel needs unique security arrangements because of its unique size. Israel is one of the smallest countries in the world. Mr Vice President, I'll grant you this. It's bigger than Delaware. It's even bigger than Rhode Island. But that's about it. Israel on the 1967 lines would be half the width of the Washington Beltway.

Now here's a bit of nostalgia. I first came to Washington thirty years ago as a young diplomat. It took me a while, but I finally figured it out: there is an America beyond the Beltway. But Israel on the 1967 lines would be only nine miles wide. So much for strategic depth.

So it is therefore absolutely vital for Israel's security that a Palestinian state be fully demilitarised. And it is vital that Israel maintain a long-term military presence along the Jordan River. Solid security arrangements on the ground are necessary not only to protect the peace, they are necessary to protect Israel in case the peace unravels. For in our unstable region, no one can guarantee that our peace partners today will be there tomorrow.

And when I say tomorrow, I don't mean some distant time in the future. I mean – tomorrow. Peace can be achieved only around the negotiating table. The Palestinian attempt to impose a settlement through the United Nations will not bring peace. It should be forcefully opposed by all those who want to see this conflict end.

I appreciate the President's clear position on this issue. Peace cannot be imposed. It must be negotiated. But it can only be negotiated with partners committed to peace.

And Hamas is not a partner for peace. Hamas remains committed to Israel's destruction and to terrorism. They have a charter. That charter not only calls for the obliteration of Israel, but says 'kill the Jews wherever you find them'. Hamas's leader condemned the killing of Osama bin Laden and praised him as a holy warrior. Now again I want to make this clear. Israel is prepared to sit down today and negotiate peace with the Palestinian Authority. I believe we can fashion a brilliant future of peace for our children. But Israel will not negotiate with a Palestinian government backed by the Palestinian version of al Qaeda.

So I say to President Abbas: Tear up your pact with Hamas! Sit down and negotiate! Make peace with the Jewish state! And if you do, I promise you this. Israel will not be the last country to welcome a Palestinian state as a new member of the United Nations. It will be the first to do so.

My friends, the momentous trials of the last century, and the unfolding events of this century, attest to the decisive role of the United States in advancing peace and defending freedom. Providence entrusted the United States to be the guardian of liberty. All peoples who cherish freedom owe a profound debt of gratitude to your great nation. Among the most grateful nations is my nation, the people of Israel, who have fought for their liberty and survival against impossible odds, in ancient and modern times alike.

I speak on behalf of the Jewish people and the Jewish state when I say to you, representatives of America, thank you. Thank you for your unwavering support for Israel. Thank you for ensuring that the flame of freedom burns bright throughout the world. May God bless all of you. And may God forever bless the United States of America.

MAHMUD ABBAS

'WE ARE AT THE HEART OF THE ARAB SPRING'

—

REMARKS TO THE PARLIAMENTARY ASSEMBLY

COUNCIL OF EUROPE, STRASBOURG, FRANCE, 6 OCTOBER 2011

M ahmud Abbas has been President of the Palestinian Authority since 2005.
    In these remarks he discusses the conflict with Israel. But he places the Israeli-Palestinian conflict as part of recent events concerning the so-called 'Arab Spring', which began on 18 December 2010 with the self-immolation of Mohamed Bouazizi in Tunisia. Bouazizi was protesting police violence and corruption. Suddenly, protests broke out in several Middle Eastern countries, including Tunisia, Yemen, Saudi Arabia, Egypt, Algeria, Bahrain and elsewhere.

Abbas argues that the revolution under way must include resolution of the Israeli-Palestinian conflict. This is an important argument that is often lost in discussion of the unprecedented events still unfolding in the Middle East. The location for this speech was important, hoping to generate European solidarity and support.

—

In the name of God, the compassionate, the merciful. President Mevlüt Çavusoglu, ladies and gentlemen. It is an honour for me to be with you today, in this historic and venerable House, to speak to you, elected representatives of the countries of Europe, the living conscience of its friendly peoples, embodying the values of freedom, justice and human dignity.

I have come to you from Palestine, the land of peace and the cradle of the three divine messages, and I bring to you a message of peace and love from its people, who have been rooted deeply in this land for thousands of years, devoted to it as their homeland, and continuing, despite the pain and suffering, their epic journey towards the noble goal of freedom and independence.

Two weeks ago, as President of the state of Palestine and Chairman of the Executive Committee of the Palestine Liberation Organization, the sole legitimate representative of the Palestinian people, I asked the Secretary General of the United Nations to accept the accession of the state of Palestine as a full member of the international organisation and I explained in my speech before the General Assembly the reasons for a step such as this.

Two decades have passed since the Madrid Peace Conference, and eighteen years since the signing of the Oslo Agreement in Washington, which was supposed to culminate, by 5 May 1999 at the latest, in a final peace agreement terminating in the establishment of an independent Palestinian state living alongside the state of Israel in peace and security.

Our Palestinian people have been waiting impatiently since that date for implementation of that agreement, but sadly in vain. How much longer must they wait? Despite that, we have seized every opportunity to reach a solution through negotiation, we accepted unreservedly the principle of the Road Map, despite the observations we had about it, but we came up against the prevarication of the Israeli government to negotiate on this basis. Then we accepted the invitation of the former US President George Bush to the Annapolis negotiations, and those negotiations achieved some progress with the acceptance of the former Israeli government, under Prime Minister [Ehud] Olmert, to revert to the 1967 borders based on the principle of equal value and reciprocity in exchange of territory. However, it was not long before the Israeli government changed, resulting in the cessation of negotiations once again.

When US President Barack Obama was elected, we once again began unreserved cooperation with his administration, and we agreed to all the suggestions put forward for a resumption of the negotiations, the latest of which was a round of direct negotiations which Washington initiated in September 2010 on the condition that it resulted in a peace agreement within one year.

We entered into those negotiations with an open heart, and sincere intentions. However, we came up against the prevarication of the government of Mr Netanyahu to negotiate seriously on permanent status issues, insofar as they took advantage of the beginning of the negotiations to embark upon unprecedented intensification of their settlement activity in Jerusalem and other areas in the occupied West Bank.

That government refused to resume negotiations from the point at which they had ended with the former government of Mr Olmert, and insisted on returning to point zero, and refused to apply the terms of reference for the negotiations based on the decisions of international law, and when its representatives sat down at the negotiation table, they refused to discuss the border issue or any permanent status issues.

With regard to security, we had reached an agreement with the former Israeli government and the former American administration, and a number of Arab parties on effective measures to preserve the security of the Palestinians and Israelis via a third party [NATO]. However Mr Netanyahu rejected all this and insisted on an unacceptable concept of security, based on expansion and colonisation, including Jerusalem and the settlement areas and lands situated to the west of the racial separation wall, in addition to the Jordan Valley (i.e. more than 40 per cent of the surface area of the occupied West Bank), and also maintaining military bases inside the West Bank, and we ask ourselves the following: if these requests are agreed to, where will the Palestinian state be?

Peace and settlement activity are incompatible and building settlements in occupied territories and housing settlers there by the occupying forces, this is a flagrant violation of international law and international humanitarian law, and a clear breach of the Geneva agreements, and the agreements between the Palestine Liberation Organisation and the state of Israel.

We are convinced of the need for a halt to the settlement activity as it is one of the necessary conditions for resuming the peace process. This is not a prerequisite but an obligation laid down in the Road Map, and the peace process cannot go ahead if it is built solely on compliance by the Palestinians with their obligations, while Israel flouts all hers.

The settlement expansion has reached a limit representing a serious threat undermining the material foundations of a two-state solution, and since the signing of the Oslo Agreement the number of settlers has increased by 300 per cent, and scarcely any day passes without Israel announcing plans to build thousands of new settlement units.

And what makes things more complicated is the fact that the Netanyahu government is insisting on laying down new and impossible conditions which have no basis in the terms of reference for peace or the resolutions adopted under international law, and the demand that the Palestinians recognise Israel as a 'Jewish' state is an unacceptable precondition, because there is a danger that it will turn the conflict raging in our region into a destructive religious conflict, jeopardising the future of a million and a half Palestinians living in the state of Israel, removing in advance the rights of the Palestinian refugees, forming a cover for expansionist intentions and putting an end to the opportunities for a two-state solution.

We undertook to respect international law and recognised the state of Israel in accordance with a negotiated text recorded in letters exchanged between the two late leaders, Yasser Arafat and Yitzhak Rabin, in 1993, and as far as we were concerned this matter was closed and any attempt to reopen it creates new pretexts for impeding the peace process.

Rather, it is legitimate for us to ask why Israel refuses to recognise our state, the state of Palestine, if it is really serious about accepting a two-state solution.

We have confirmed our acceptance of international law, when our national Palestinian Council was set up in 1988, with the adoption of the Palestinian peace programme which embraces a two-state solution: an independent Palestinian state with its capital in East Jerusalem on Palestinian lands which Israel occupied in June 1967, i.e. on only 22 per cent of the historical territory of Palestine, living side by side in peace and security with the state of Israel.

This difficult and painful step was aimed at achieving a historic compromise which would make it possible to bring about peace between the two peoples.

This programme has become a pillar on which the Arab peace initiative was based, embraced by the Arab League and other member states of the Islamic Cooperation Organisation. This initiative reflects the willingness of all these countries to establish normal relations with Israel as part of a comprehensive and lasting peace to ensure Israel's withdrawal from all the occupied Palestinian and Arab territories to the borders as they stood on 4 June 1967, the establishment of an independent Palestinian state with full sovereignty, with its capital in East Jerusalem, finding a just and agreed solution to the refugee issue, in accordance with UN Resolution 194, and ensuring security and peace for all states and peoples in the region.

We have called and are still calling on the Israelis to seize this opportunity open to them which offers a guarantee for living in peace with the peoples of the region, and which offers them true security for themselves and their children, as it does for us and our children. Peace is what makes security, not military power and not domination and geographical expansion. It is not possible to maintain peace through power, but only through mutual understanding.

In East Jerusalem, the Palestinian inhabitants are subject to a systematic policy of ethnic cleansing, which includes the demolition of houses, the displacement of populations and the withdrawal of identity documents, including from the people's elected representatives, with the aim of forcing them out of their own city; there are restrictions on their freedom to access the holy sites, and continuing excavations which threaten its foundations, quite apart from the resulting stranglehold on the city and its isolation from its Palestinian surroundings by means of the ring of settlements and walls.

The occupying power continues its incursions in areas of the Palestinian National Authority through raids and arrests; free rein has been given to the armed settler militias, who enjoy the special protection of the occupation army, attacking the defenceless Palestinian citizens, targeting their homes, schools, mosques, fields, crops and trees.

It continues to impose its intense blockade on the Gaza Strip, constituting collective sanctions on the rights of the innocent inhabitants; it continues its targeting of the Strip with assassinations, air strikes and artillery shelling, persisting with its war of aggression of three years ago, resulting in mass destruction and huge losses of life and property.

The occupying power is detaining in its prisons more than six thousand Palestinian prisoners, including twenty-one elected representatives from various parliamentary groupings who a few days ago announced a hunger strike in protest at their cruel and humiliating conditions of detention. We wish to see them free to be with their families, just as Gilad Shalit's family wishes to see him free to be once again with them.

Despite the Israeli obstacles, the Palestinian Authority has in recent years worked hard to implement an intensive programme aimed at promoting and strengthening a culture of peace, justice, democracy, to improve the readiness of Palestinian institutions and prepare them for independence, and in accordance with the report by the Ad Hoc Liaison Committee of donor states, and on the basis of the assessments of the World Bank and the International Monetary Fund and the United Nations Mission, this programme has been completely successful in upgrading the performance of the Palestinian institutions to a higher level, which is necessary for administering a successful state.

And the report confirms that Palestine has achieved, in this field, much more than many states which already enjoy full membership of the United Nations.

On the basis of these achievements, and faced with the increasing suffering of our people under the occupation, and in the light of the stalemate in the prospects for the negotiations, our only alternative has been to turn to the international community and call on it to take action to open up new horizons for the peace process, through recognition of the state of Palestine, on the basis of the 4 June 1967 borders, and accept its accession as a full member of the United Nations.

We confirm that by submitting this request, we are not seeking to isolate Israel or delegitimise it; rather we are seeking to obtain legitimacy for our existence as a people with a right to self-determination like any other people.

Our aim is to delegitimise the occupation, settlement activities and apartheid policies. We can also confirm that this step of ours is not a substitute for negotiations, but a positive factor in creating the serious constructive negotiation conditions to bring about fruitful results, and we reconfirm here today our readiness to return to the negotiating table in accordance with a clear reference to international legitimacy and on the basis of a complete cessation of settlement activities.

This explains our positive position on the latest Quartet statement, which redefined the terms of reference for the peace process, especially the two-state principle on the basis of the 1967 borders, and reconfirmed the obligations of both parties under the Road Map. Israel's compliance with these requests will open the way for a resumption of the peace process.

Today 128 member states of the United Nations have recognised the state of Palestine on the basis of the 4 June 1967 borders, and we are proud that seventeen of them are Council of Europe member states. Palestine has diplomatic relations with twenty-four other Council of Europe member states and many of these countries, especially those belonging to the European Union, have confirmed their willingness to recognise the state of Palestine at the appropriate time. We say to you in all sincerity: now is the appropriate time and we appreciate the resolution adopted recently by the European Parliament in this connection and call for it to be implemented.

We also very much appreciate and are proud of the resolution adopted by the Parliamentary Assembly this past Tuesday calling on the six Council of Europe member states which are members of the Security Council to support Palestine's request to become a full member of the United Nations.

Europe has invested a great deal of effort and money in supporting the construction of Palestinian institutions and has given our people considerable aid which it will remember with gratitude and appreciation. Recognition of the state of Palestine and support for its efforts to become a member of the United Nations is a means of protecting its achievements thanks to those efforts and that investment, and it is also a means of strengthening the position of Europe and its leading role in promoting the peace process.

Today we are living in the era of the Arab Spring, and we can see the courage of the Arab peoples, expressing their desire for freedom, democracy and social justice. We Palestinians have always been at the heart of the movement of Arab peoples aspiring to freedom, and we have always been committed to democratic traditions, respecting pluralism and the freedom of opinion and expression, and this has long been a source of pride for us and a source of inspiration for our brothers from other Arab nations. Today we are at the heart of the Arab Spring: we say that the hour of the Palestinian Spring has struck.

And if the essence of the Arab Spring was the people's desire for freedom, then the essence of the Palestinian Spring is to become free of the occupation and achieve freedom and independence, security and stability, and peace in the region.

The promise of our spring was demonstrated by the wonderful sight of hundreds of thousands of people coming out onto the streets of the towns and villages of Palestine and in the Diaspora refugee camps expressing in one voice their wish for Palestine to become state number 194 of the United Nations, and this movement remained peaceful and civilised, despite Israeli attempts at provocation. We today confirm our determination to maintain the peaceful nature of our movement by the people, because we reject violence, and we reject terrorism in all its forms, especially state terrorism, and the terrorism of armed settlers. We shall disappoint their hopes of pushing us towards extremism.

Our people will continue their peaceful resistance against the occupation and settlement activities and against the racial separation wall, providing in this way an inspiring model of the power of defenceless people to confront bullets, tear-gas bombs and bulldozers.

The world which celebrated the Arab Spring today stands before a test of its credibility: will this celebration stop at the borders of Palestine? Or will it manage to overcome double standards and open its arms to embrace the Palestinian Spring? Will it allow Israel to remain a state above the law and above accountability? Will it allow it to continue to reject the resolutions of the Security Council and the General Assembly and the International Court of Justice and violate international law? Our people are waiting for the answer and part of this answer lies with you, elected representatives of the people of Europe. Our people urge you to live up to your responsibilities.

In the midst of this relentless struggle for independence, we shall continue to exert every possible effort to build up our society, consolidate our democratic institutions, and get our house in order. However, we shall strive to protect what has already been achieved in this regard and build on it.

We are particularly proud of the fact that in recent years we have been able to eradicate illiteracy almost totally in Palestine. Our people have helped build up many countries of the world, a people that venerates science, culture and creativity, and we have made valuable progress in extending the education infrastructure at all levels in our country: we now have forty-nine universities and institutes catering for 5 per cent of the total population, and this work will be pursued so as to provide education opportunities for all our children.

Thanks to the appreciated support we have received from the Arab and friendly countries, especially the countries of Europe, we have implemented a number of infrastructure projects, focusing in particular on developing the health services and with special attention to rural and marginalised areas. We have worked and shall continue to work on strengthening judicial authority, the rule of law and maintaining the security and dignity of our citizens.

We have made great strides in the field of women's participation in public life and in decision-making bodies, the executive, the legislative and the judiciary, and in local authority institutions. In this connection, we signed the Convention on the Elimination of All Forms of Discrimination against Women in order to achieve full gender equality.

We have developed a system for monitoring, accountability and administrative and financial reform with the aim of establishing transparency, integrity and good governance, striving to align ourselves with the highest international standards in this field.

In building up our national authority and laying the foundations of our future state, we have chosen the parliamentary democratic system, based on respect for pluralism, equality between citizens, women and men, the rule of law, and protection of freedoms and human rights, and despite the difficulties and external interference and restrictions of the occupation which has placed obstacles and mines on our path to democracy, we have resolved to pursue our commitment to the democratic option, to protecting freedom of organisation and party and trade union work, to strengthening the role of civil society institutions, to protecting freedom of opinion and expression and freedom of publishing and the press and to protecting individual and collective freedoms.

Our success in signing the national reconciliation agreement in Cairo on 4 May constituted a major step towards ending the divisions which had split the unity of our national institutions and had inflicted serious damage on our cause. The essence of this agreement is the formation of a transitional government from among independent national figures which is preparing to run presidential, parliamentary and local elections by May 2012 at the latest.

The reconciliation agreement is a positive achievement for the peace process and not the opposite, and is indispensable for protecting and strengthening Palestinian democracy. What unites Palestinians and Europeans goes beyond links between geographical neighbours on the two shores of the Mediterranean, and goes further than mere trading relations or human interconnections or what has been the result of thousands of years of cultural interaction. Above all, what unites us are the joint values to which our peoples are committed, the values of freedom, brotherhood, equality and justice between all human beings, which the peoples of Europe have championed for centuries, and for which today the Arab peoples, and first and foremost the Palestinians, are struggling.

We look with admiration at what Europe has achieved in the field of establishing the foundations of pluralist democracy, the rule of law and respect for human rights and we look forward to being able to benefit from your experience in this area, so as to develop our own fledgling democracy of which we are very proud. And we look with admiration at this ancient city of Strasbourg which was the site of conflict between the countries of Europe and has become today the centre of the institutions of a united Europe and support for peace.

And in this context, I cannot but express my pride at the partnership agreement which Salim al-Za'nun, Speaker of the Palestinian National Council, signed two days ago, which granted the National Council, the parliament of the Palestinian people in the homeland and the Diaspora, partner for democracy status with the Parliamentary Assembly of the Council of Europe, and we are particularly proud that Palestine, after Morocco, is among the first Arab countries to be granted this status, which will have the most positive effect in strengthening the bonds of friendship and joint cooperation between our peoples and in encouraging the path towards democracy in our Arab region.

I would like to express to you the gratitude of the Palestinian people for the generous support they have received from the countries of Europe to help them build their economy and institutions, and we hope that this role will be strengthened still further through the political role played by Europe in promoting the peace process in our region.

We have always stressed that we want our European friends to be players and not only payers. United Nations Resolution 181 adopted in 1947 announced the setting up of two states. One state, Israel, has come into existence, but the other, Palestine, has not yet seen the light of day. We have come here to ask for this light for our state. This is our legitimate right guaranteed to us by international law. But this does not mean that it is a substitute for negotiations, rather it confirms the necessity of negotiations in order to reach a solution regarding borders, security, refugees, water, settlements, Jerusalem, freeing the prisoners, and also an end to the conflict in accordance with the substance of the Arab peace initiative, to ensure that Israel can live in an ocean of peace that includes all Arabs and Muslims.

We wish to live like other peoples, in freedom and dignity, and we are not seeking to isolate anyone. We wish to protect both the Palestinian and Israeli people from this occupation and colonisation which are destroying the future of both peoples. They have to choose between colonisation and peace. We have chosen peace. You supported the Arab Spring which was seeking democracy and freedom. Now the Palestinian Spring has arrived asking for freedom and an end to the occupation. We deserve your support. We place our trust in you and are confident that you will not abandon us and leave us all on our own. We are depending on you. Thank you.

DOUGLAS ALEXANDER

'THE NEXT DECADE OF THE MIDDLE EAST IS GOING TO BE DEFINED BY OPTIMISM'

—

REMARKS TO THE ROYAL UNITED SERVICES INSTITUTE

LONDON, UNITED KINGDOM, 11 OCTOBER 2011

Douglas Alexander was elected to Parliament in 1997 to represent Paisley and Renfrewshire South for the Labour Party. He held a variety of Cabinet positions from 2006–2010. He has been Shadow Secretary of State for Foreign and Commonwealth Affairs since early 2011.

In this speech he addresses the Arab Spring, discussing its impact on the Middle East and the possible implications for Great Britain. This speech is helpful in sorting out events and offering a perspective on the continuing revolution under way in several countries. Since many of the principals in the Arab Spring have been at the centre of conflict, with little chance to make speeches to the international community, Alexander's remarks also serve as a proxy voice for many without the ability or opportunity to speak, both those seeking power and those merely caught up in the vortex of the violence.

—

It's a pleasure to be speaking to you here at Royal United Services Institute [RUSI] today.

RUSI's up to the minute analysis of the latest developments in the Arab Spring has demonstrated both the great expertise housed here and an ability to apply that expertise to a time of unprecedented change.

The institute's work around the ongoing campaign in Libya, including the recent interim campaign report, shows an appetite for dealing with the very latest issues and tackling the most difficult questions, that is a credit to everyone who works here.

I have been invited to give an autumn perspective on the Arab Spring, to ask, 260 days since the fall of [Zine El] Ben-Ali in Tunisia, how it is unfolding and what Britain is getting right or getting wrong?

I wouldn't be the first to quote Mao's foreign minister, Zhou Enlai, who said, two centuries after the event, that it was 'too early to say' what the consequences of the French Revolution would be.

Today, Harvard professor Joseph Nye talks of a world shaped by the shifting distribution of power from West to East and the growing dispersal of power from state to citizens.

And it is in that latter context that I want to talk today about the Arab Spring.

My argument this afternoon is that the long-term repercussions of the Arab Spring are only beginning to be felt and my concern is that despite getting the short-term decisions generally right, we haven't yet begun to really address the long-term opportunities and threats.

Fareed Zakaria argued in a lecture earlier this year that there were three drivers of the change we have witnessed.

Firstly, a youthful demographic spike – something associated with revolutions for hundreds of years.

Secondly, a growing realisation throughout the Arab world that the West was ambivalent about the old rulers and wouldn't necessarily prop them up in the face of popular discontent, derived from sources as diverse as the Wikileaks cables to President Obama's Cairo speech.

Thirdly, new technology removed the autocrats' monopoly of information.

Satellite television gave people a sense of what was happening in their world that for years the state-controlled broadcasters had failed to show. Online reporting allowed official histories to be challenged. And social networking allowed protesters to see they were not isolated individuals, but powerful majorities.

But if this was a revolution partly driven by technology we must remember what President Obama's Head of the National Institute of Health, Francis Collins, has called 'the first law of technology': that 'a technological advance of a major sort almost always is overestimated in the short run for its consequences – and underestimated in the long run.'

If you look at the whole region of North Africa and the Middle East, I believe that that maxim applies to the political change we have seen since the start of this year.

So while there has been change, the short term can be exaggerated.

In Tunisia, earlier this year, I was impressed by the progress that had been made since the fall of Ben-Ali and I think many hope that small, innovative Arab country has the most straightforward path to a better future.

But elsewhere, the list of issues to worry about is a long one.

In Egypt, [Hosni] Mubarak is gone but his replacements in the Supreme Council of the Armed Forces do not appear to have given up on all the tools, like Emergency Decrees, that he used.

Having just returned from Pakistan, I fear for a situation where a powerful military seeks to protect its economic and political role even after the transition to democracy.

And the killing of twenty-four Coptic Christians in Cairo must be a cause for extreme concern among all the new Egypt's friends, both because of what it says about religious tensions in Egypt and about the interim regime.

And beyond this immediate outbreak of violence, the Egyptian economy shrank by 4.2 per cent in the first quarter of this year compared to a year before. Unemployment runs at around 12 per cent and consumer prices are expected to increase by 13 per cent this year.

In Libya, Labour supported the action to enforce UN Resolutions 1970 and 1973.

There is no doubt that the Libyan campaign took place under the long shadow cast by the decision to authorise military action in Iraq in 2003.

The resulting loss of life and trust from that conflict means that across the country there is real and enduring scepticism about military intervention. But the decision to protect civilians from certain slaughter was, I believe, the right one and Operation Ellamy has been conducted with characteristic professionalism by our forces. They have our abiding admiration and gratitude.

Fighting is ongoing around Sirte as we speak, and we hope that the pro-Gaddafi forces can be forced to surrender with the minimum of bloodshed.

But even after Sirte is taken, stability will be hard won for a post-conflict Libya – the country is awash with weapons and shabab fighters and only 43,000 of 6.5 million Libyans are employed in the oil and gas industry that makes up more than two thirds of the Libyan economy.

In Bahrain last week, in a shocking and reprehensible judgement, a Special Tribunal sentenced a group of medics for treating patients deemed to be part of the protests.

Though there has now been some welcome movement on the sentences of the medics, these actions reinforce the extent to which legitimate grievances are not being met with necessary reform.

In Yemen, the ongoing crisis of leadership risks exacerbating both the humanitarian and security problems that bedevil that country.

In Israel and Palestine, peace, alas, has seemed to move further away in recent months.

Rocket attacks continued over the summer and Prime Minister Netanyahu's poll ratings went up when he rejected President Obama's attempts to restart the peace process.

In Saudi Arabia, a woman being sentenced to ten lashes for driving a car shocked even those who have raised lack of human rights in the kingdom for some time, and for once prompted a response from King Abdullah [bin Abdul-Azizal Saud].

In Iran, many of those who rose up as part of the 2009 protests are still incarcerated, the E3+3 process has made little progress and only a few weeks ago President [Mahmoud] Ahmadinejad was pushing conspiracy theories about 9/11.

And in Syria, President [Bashard al-] Assad's crackdown has included the killing of approximately 2,000 civilians and the detention and torture of thousands more.

Despite diplomatic and economic sanctions from the United States and the European Union, Assad seems no closer to listening to calls to step down from across the international community.

So the protests, the economic chaos, the concerns about al Qaeda taking advantage of instability and the brutal repression of civilians – all of these are still present and may be so for many months yet, even years in some Arab countries.

But my argument is not '*plus ça change* for the Middle East'.

Rather, it is to identify what changes have happened whose long-term consequences we must not underestimate.

The big change, is, I believe, based around the insight that the brittle stability of the last thirty years in the Middle East and North Africa was driven by a politics of pessimism.

Pessimism from each citizen that thought their individual complaints would always be crushed by over-mighty autocrats.

Pessimism from their rulers who trusted oil over the ingenuity of their citizens when it came to building more prosperous economies.

Pessimism from the West that chose the devil we knew for fear of something worse.

And pessimism at the heart of the extremists' offer that said the only possible response was one of self-annihilation and murder.

With the biggest youth bulge in recorded history – 65 per cent of the population under thirty – the next decade of the Middle East is going to be driven by optimism.

Optimism, of course, can have different impacts in different circumstances.

It was optimism that put the West on the right side of history at the time of Tahrir Square and it required optimism to believe that the Libyan operation could be conducted without large-scale civilian casualties or a rallying around Gaddafi.

But it was equally optimism among the pro-Gaddafi forces – that they could push back the rebels or that NATO would lose interest – that is keeping them fighting for so long.

And we do not know what will happen if the optimism surrounding the Palestinian demand for statehood is not turned into meaningful progress towards a two-state solution on the ground.

But we can surely say that a geopolitics of the Middle East driven by optimistic, aspirational populaces rather than pessimistic, sedentary autocrats will have a very different dynamic – yes, with greater potential but also with greater risks.

The second change I would highlight today is a new dynamic in how states relate to each other within the region.

When Turkey is taking quite strong steps in seeking to prevent violence in Syria, when the Arab League is calling for No Fly Zones over an Arab country, when countries like Qatar are taking an ever more activist role ... the era of 'zero problems' diplomacy in the region appears to be over.

Despite not being an Arab country, Turkey clearly now seeks a greater leadership role in this new regional environment.

Egypt has traditionally, as the largest Arab country, sought such a role in the past and is likely to do so again.

But wealthy Gulf states, whose capital investment is sorely needed in a post-Ben-Ali Tunisia, a post-Mubarak Egypt and a post-Gaddafi Libya, may want to continue to play the important regional political role that they have played in relation to Libya and Bahrain.

Not all of these countries always share all of our values.

We disagree regularly over the language used about Israel and about human rights.

But particularly regarding the two non-Arab countries seeking leadership in the Arab world, we should be clear about the difference between disagreement and danger.

Iran has been eclipsed in the last six months by a resurgent Turkey.

And while we should not be uncritical friends of Turkey, we should be clear that there is no equivalence between a democratic NATO ally and a country that supports attacks on our forces and defies the world over its nuclear programme.

In fact, when Indonesia, Pakistan, Bangladesh, Turkey and – we hope – Egypt are all democracies, albeit of different levels of fragility, the Iranian 1979 revolution looks far more like an aberration within the Muslim world than a pioneer.

What then does this autumn perspective mean for Britain's approach?

The bipartisan House of Commons Foreign Affairs Select Committee has characterised the government's foreign policy as being based on 'its declared wish to build strengthened bilateral relationships with emerging powers outside the traditional Euro-Atlantic area, and the increased emphasis it was giving to commercial interests in the UK's foreign relations.'

I was sceptical that such an approach would be sufficient before the Arab Spring – now it looks less and less relevant to the challenges we face.

For my part, I think there are three aspects to the response we need.

Firstly, while other EU members will be understandably focused on the crisis in the Eurozone, it must fall to Britain to be constantly raising the future of North Africa in Brussels.

More radical moves to open European markets to Egypt, Tunisia and a free Libya would benefit European consumers, cement new friendships and help ensure that political optimism isn't met with economic disappointment over the medium term.

Secondly, we need to address the multilateral system to the challenges facing the region. For Europe, it means finding a way to work more effectively with a pre-accession Turkey on diplomatic issues, like Syria, where we have a common cause.

It also means working to strengthen and build formal links with the multi-lateral institutions existing within the region, such as the Gulf Cooperation Council and the Arab League.

And it means using multilateral tools that can promote peace, which is why Labour has said the government should be willing to support the Palestinian call for statehood at the United Nations as part of continuing steps to achieve a comprehensive two-state solution.

Third and finally, we must address our diplomacy not just to states, but to the peoples of the Arab world at their moment of optimism.

BBC Arabic online audiences grew by 300 per cent during the height of the protests in Egypt to 1.6 million.

The World Service Trust is working to support Tunisian TV in the transition to being public service broadcasters, rather than just broadcasting the regime views.

Do these services have an effect? If they didn't, why would BBC Persian televi-sion have been subject to increasing and aggressive jamming from within Iran?

The channel has suffered deliberate attempts to interfere with its signal inter-mittently since its launch in 2009.

The interference intensified on the evening of Saturday 17 September, just as the channel had begun broadcasting a documentary about Iran's Supreme Leader.

The continued attempts of the regime to put pressure on the service show how much they worry about outside broadcasts – and should redouble our support for the work the World Service does.

And – going back to my starting point – that public diplomacy needs to develop for a world of technological change.

In my view, that means Britain's foreign policy needs to be clear that promot-ing unrestricted access to the Internet is in our national interest and promotes our national values.

We need to look at the export licensing of technologies that filter the Internet, support online civil society in countries that continue to restrict Internet access and work with EU partners in providing online journalists the arenas where they can post, free from censorship by their national governments.

In the short run, the West got the major judgements right – choosing to side with protestors in Cairo and Tunis, choosing to protect civilians in Benghazi and choosing to sanction the regime in Damascus.

But short-run change could never be as sweeping as the rhetoric that accompanied the first days of the Arab Spring.

For the long-run challenges, we urgently need to up our game.

But it is those long-run challenges that will define the foreign policy challenges of the next decade: How can we ensure that popular optimism is met with prosperity and not dangerous disappointment? How can we use the moment of exceptional technological change to promote the values we, as a country, believe in? How we can help support the chances of peace between peoples, rather than only brittle truces between states? How we can stop al Qaeda in the Islamic Maghreb from using the instability to its advantage – notwithstanding the body blow to its *raison d'être* that has been dealt by the Arab Spring? This autumn is not too late to start to address these bigger, long-term questions – by next autumn it might be.

Thank you.

HILLARY CLINTON

'THE RIGHT SIDE OF HISTORY'

—

REMARKS AT THE NATIONAL DEMOCRATIC INSTITUTE'S 2011 DEMOCRACY AWARDS

WASHINGTON, DC, 7 NOVEMBER 2011

A native of Illinois and a Republican in her youth, Hillary Rodham met Bill Clinton at Yale Law School in the 1970s, and married him in 1975. A distinguished attorney, she was the first female chair of the Legal Services Corporation and first woman to become a partner at the prestigious Rose Law Firm. As First Lady of Arkansas during her husband's governorship of the state, she led an Education Reform Committee widely credited with raising literacy rates.

Following the 1992 Presidential election and Bill Clinton's accession to the White House, Hillary became First Lady of the United States, and, again, launched a major policy initiative in the form of the Healthcare Reform Commission. The eventual proposal failed to win Congressional approval, and Clinton removed herself from frontline policy-making, reverting to a more traditional, apolitical role as First Lady. In 2000, she was elected to the US Senate seat of the retiring Daniel Patrick Moynihan of New York, winning re-election in 2006. Initially seen as the all-but-inevitable Democratic nominee for President in 2008, she narrowly lost the nomination to Senator Barack Obama. Following his victory in the November general election, President Obama appointed Clinton as United States Secretary of State.

This speech received substantial press coverage for her comments on the Arab Spring. But what didn't receive much notice was the tone of the speech. Speaking before a friendly audience, Clinton showed much personal warmth, mentioning names and recalling past associations. She invoked the memory of former United Nations Ambassador Richard Holbrooke, a much respected and honoured diplomat. The speech shows the power of the personal touch. Clinton reviews United States

policy towards the region, explaining why reform is in the best interest of people in
the Middle East, and that the United States will help those seeking democracy.

———

Thank you. Well, it's a great pleasure for me to be here this evening. And I thank my friend and my predecessor, Madeleine Albright, for not only that kind introduction, but for her extraordinary leadership, and in particular of the National Democratic Institute [NDI]. Thanks also to Shari Bryan and Ken Wollack for inviting me here today. And I want to begin by wishing an Eid Mubarak to Muslims here tonight and around the world.

I think it's important to recognise that back when the streets of Arab cities were quiet, the National Democratic Institute was already on the ground, building relationships, supporting the voices that would turn a long Arab winter into a new Arab Spring. Now, we may not know where and when brave people will claim their rights next, but it's a safe bet that NDI is there now, because freedom knows no better champion. More than a quarter-century old, NDI and its siblings in the National Endowment for Democracy family have become vital elements of America's engagement with the world.

And tonight I want particularly to congratulate the winners of NDI's 2011 Madeleine Albright Award, the women of Appropriate Communication Techniques for Development. Women risked everything to demand their rights for the Egyptian people, and they deserve those rights extended to them. And so we're grateful for their work, and we hope to see the rights that they've fought for and advocated for enshrined in Egypt's new constitution, and we're proud to support efforts like these through our Middle East Partnership Initiative.

Now, tonight it's also a singular, special honour for me to join with you in remembering three friends of NDI, three people I was lucky enough to call my friends as well: Geraldine Ferraro, a trailblazing pioneer, who lived to the fullest her conviction that women belong at the heart of democracy; Chuck Manatt, a passionate chairman of the Democratic National Committee, who understood that some things are too important to belong to any one party, and with his counterpart at the RNC [Republic National Committee], Frank Fahrenkopf, put together a bipartisan coalition to found the National Endowment for Democracy; and of course the indomitable, unforgettable Richard Holbrooke. Now, Richard has many reasons why those of us here tonight applaud and remember him. He died just four days before the desperate act of a Tunisian fruit vendor set the Arab uprisings in motion. And I often wonder what Richard would have made of all that has happened since. I'm sure he would have had a lot to say and even more that he wanted to do to promote the principles that we all cherish. And so these three individuals are very worthy of the awards that you have granted them this evening.

And what a year 2011 has been for freedom in the Middle East and North Africa. We have seen what may well have been the first Arab revolution for democracy, then the second, then the third. And in Yemen, people are demanding a transition to democracy that they deserve to see delivered. And Syrians are refusing to relent until they, too, can decide their own future.

Throughout the Arab world this year, people have given each other courage. Old fears have melted away and men and women have begun making their demands in broad daylight. They have given many of our diplomats courage, too, and I want to single out someone who is here with us tonight. When our Ambassador to Syria was mobbed, assaulted, and threatened, just for meeting with peaceful protestors, he put his personal safety on the line to let the Syrian people know that America stands with them. And he said he was inspired by their bravery. And as he drove into Hama, a city under assault by [Bashar al-] Assad's regime, the people of that city covered his car with flowers. Please join me in giving our own warm welcome to Ambassador Robert Ford and his wife and fellow Foreign Service Officer, Alison Barkley. Thanks to you, Robert, and to you, Alison, for your dedicated service to our country.

Now, in Tunis, Cairo, and a newly free Tripoli, I have met people lifted by a sense that their futures actually do belong to them. In my travels across the region, I have heard joy, purpose, and newfound pride.

But I've also heard questions. I've heard scepticism about American motives and commitments, people wondering if, after decades of working with the governments of the region, America doesn't – in our heart of hearts – actually long for the old days. I've heard from activists who think we aren't pushing hard enough for democratic change, and I've heard from government officials who think we're pushing too hard. I've heard from people asking why our policies vary from country to country, and what would happen if elections bring to power parties we don't agree with or people who just don't like us very much. I've heard people asking America to solve all their problems and others wondering whether we have any role to play at all. And beneath our excitement for the millions who are claiming the rights and freedoms we cherish, many Americans are asking the same questions.

Tonight, I want to ask and answer a few of these tough questions. It's a fitting tribute to people like Gerry Ferraro and Richard Holbrooke and Chuck Manatt. They liked to pose difficult questions and then push us to answer them. And in Richard's case, that meant even following me into a ladies' room in Pakistan one time. As we live this history day by day, we approach these questions with a large dose of humility, because many of the choices ahead are, honestly, not ours to make. Still, it's worth stepping back and doing our best to speak directly to what is on people's minds.

So let me start with one question I hear often: Do we really believe that democratic change in the Middle East and North Africa is in America's interest? That is a totally fair question. After all, transitions are filled with uncertainty. They can be chaotic, unstable, even violent. And, even if they succeed, they are rarely linear, quick, or easy.

As we saw in the Balkans and again in Iraq, rivalries between members of different religions, sects, and tribes can resurface and explode. Toppling tyrants does not guarantee that democracy will follow, or that it will last. Just ask the Iranians who overthrew a dictator thirty-two years ago only to have their revolution hijacked by the extremists who have oppressed them ever since. And even where democracy does takes hold, it is a safe bet that some of those elected will not embrace us or agree with our policies.

And yet, as President Obama said at the State Department in May, 'It will be the policy of the United States to promote reform across the region and to support transitions to democracy.' We believe that real democratic change in the Middle East and North Africa is in the national interest of the United States. And here's why.

We begin by rejecting the false choice between progress and stability. For years, dictators told their people they had to accept the autocrats they knew to avoid the extremists they feared. And too often, we accepted that narrative ourselves. Now, America did push for reform, but often not hard enough or publicly enough. And today, we recognise that the real choice is between reform and unrest.

Last January, I told Arab leaders that the region's foundations were sinking into the sand. Even if we didn't know exactly how or when the breaking point would come, it was clear that the status quo was unsustainable because of changes in demography and technology, high unemployment, endemic corruption and a lack of human rights and fundamental freedoms. After a year of revolutions broadcast on Al Jazeera into homes from Rabat to Riyadh, going back to the way things were in December 2010 isn't just undesirable. It's impossible.

The truth is that the greatest single source of instability in today's Middle East is not the demand for change. It is the refusal to change. That is certainly true in Syria, where a crackdown on small, peaceful protests drove thousands into the streets and thousands more over the borders. It is true in Yemen, where President [Al Abdullah] Saleh has reneged repeatedly on his promises to transition to democracy and suppressed his people's rights and freedoms. And it is true in Egypt. If – over time – the most powerful political force in Egypt remains a roomful of unelected officials, they will have planted the seeds for future unrest, and Egyptians will have missed a historic opportunity.

And so will we, because democracies make for stronger and stabler partners. They trade more, innovate more, and fight less. They help divided societies to air and hopefully resolve their differences. They hold inept leaders accountable at the polls. They channel people's energies away from extremism and toward political and civic engagement. Now, democracies do not always agree with us, and in the Middle East and North Africa they may disagree strongly with some of our policies. But at the end of the day, it is no coincidence that our closest allies – from Britain to South Korea – are democracies.

Now, we do work with many different governments to pursue our interests and to keep Americans safe – and certainly not all of them are democracies. But as the fall of Hosni Mubarak in Egypt made clear, the enduring cooperation we seek will be difficult to sustain without democratic legitimacy and public consent. We cannot have one set of policies to advance security in the here-and-now and another to promote democracy in a long run that never quite arrives.

So for all these reasons, as I said back in March, opening political systems, societies, and economies is not simply a matter of idealism. It is a strategic necessity. But we are not simply acting in our self-interest. Americans believe that the desire for dignity and self-determination is universal – and we do try to act on that belief around the world. Americans have fought and died for these ideals. And when freedom gains ground anywhere, Americans are inspired.

So the risks posed by transitions will not keep us from pursuing positive change. But they do raise the stakes for getting it right. Free, fair, and meaningful elections are essential – but they are not enough if they bring new autocrats to power or disenfranchise minorities. And any democracy that does not include half its population – its women – is a contradiction in terms. Durable democracies depend on strong civil societies, respect for the rule of law, independent institutions, free expression, and a free press. Legitimate political parties cannot have a militia wing and a political wing. Parties have to accept the results of free and fair elections. And this is not just in the Middle East. In Liberia, the leading opposition party is making unsubstantiated charges of fraud and refusing to accept first-round voting in which it came in second. And this is already having harmful consequences on the ground. We urge all parties in Liberia to accept the will of the people in the next round of voting tomorrow. That is what democracy anywhere requires.

And that brings me to my second question. Why does America promote democracy one way in some countries and another way in others? Well, the answer starts with a very practical point: situations vary dramatically from country to country. It would be foolish to take a one-size-fits-all approach and barrel forward regardless of circumstances on the ground. Sometimes, as in Libya, we can bring dozens of countries together to protect civilians and help people liberate their country without a single American life lost. In other cases, to achieve that same goal, we would have to act alone, at a much greater cost, with far greater risks, and perhaps even with troops on the ground.

But that's just part of the answer. Our choices also reflect other interests in the region with a real impact on Americans' lives – including our fight against al Qaeda, defence of our allies, and a secure supply of energy. Over time, a more democratic Middle East and North Africa can provide a more sustainable basis for addressing all three of those challenges. But there will be times when not all of our interests align. We work to align them, but that is just reality.

As a country with many complex interests, we'll always have to walk and chew gum at the same time. That is our challenge in a country like Bahrain, which has been America's close friend and partner for decades. And yet, President Obama and I have been frank, in public and in private, that mass arrests and brute force are at odds with the universal rights of Bahrain's citizens and will not make legitimate calls for reform go away. Meaningful reform and equal treatment for all Bahrainis are in Bahrain's interest, in the region's interest, and in ours – while endless unrest benefits Iran and extremists. The government has recognised the need for dialogue, reconciliation, and concrete reforms. And they have committed to provide access to human rights groups, to allow peaceful protest, and to ensure that those who cross lines in responding to civil unrest are held accountable. King Hamad [bin Isa Al Kalifa] called for an independent commission of inquiry, which will issue its report soon. And we do intend to hold the Bahraini government to these commitments and to encourage the opposition to respond constructively to secure lasting reform.

We also have candid conversations with others in the neighbourhood, like Saudi Arabia – a country that is key to stability and peace – about our view that democratic advancement is not just possible but a necessary part of preparing for the future.

Fundamentally, there is a right side of history. And we want to be on it. And – without exception – we want our partners in the region to reform so that they are on it as well. Now, we don't expect countries to do this overnight, but without reforms, we are convinced their challenges will only grow. So it is in their interest to begin now.

These questions about our interests and consistency merge in a third difficult question: How will America respond if and when democracy brings to power people and parties we disagree with?

We hear these questions most often when it comes to Islamist religious parties. Now, of course, I hasten to add that not all Islamists are alike. Turkey and Iran are both governed by parties with religious roots, but their models and behaviour are radically different. There are plenty of political parties with religious affiliations – Hindu, Christian, Jewish, Muslim – that respect the rules of democratic politics. The suggestion that faithful Muslims cannot thrive in a democracy is insulting, dangerous, and wrong. They do it in this country every day.

Now, reasonable people can disagree on a lot, but there are things that all parties, religious and secular, must get right – not just for us to trust them, but most importantly for the people of the region and of the countries themselves to trust them to protect their hard-won rights.

Parties committed to democracy must reject violence; they must abide by the rule of law and respect the freedoms of speech, religion, association, and assembly; they must respect the rights of women and minorities; they must let go of power if defeated at the polls; and in a region with deep divisions within and between religions, they cannot be the spark that starts a conflagration. In other words, what parties call themselves is less important to us than what they actually do.

We applaud NDI for its work to arrive at a model code of conduct for political parties across the political spectrum and around the globe. We need to reinforce these norms and to hold people accountable for following them.

In Tunisia, an Islamist party has just won a plurality of the votes in an open, competitive election. Its leaders have promised to embrace freedom of religion and full rights for women. To write a constitution and govern, they will have to persuade secular parties to work with them. And as they do, America will work with them, too, because we share the desire to see a Tunisian democracy emerge that delivers for its citizens and because America respects the right of the Tunisian people to choose their own leaders.

And so we move forward with clear convictions. Parties and candidates must respect the rules of democracy, to take part in elections, and hold elective office. And no one has the right to use the trappings of democracy to deny the rights and security of others. People throughout the region worry about this prospect, and so do we. Nobody wants another Iran. Nobody wants to see political parties with military wings and militant foreign policies gain influence. When members of any group seek to oppress their fellow citizens or undermine core democratic principles, we will stand on the side of the people who push back to defend their democracy.

And that brings me to my next question: What is America's role in the Arab Spring? These revolutions are not ours. They are not by us, for us, or against us, but we do have a role. We have the resources, capabilities, and expertise to support those who seek peaceful, meaningful, democratic reform. And with so much that can go wrong, and so much that can go right, support for emerging Arab democracies is an investment we cannot afford not to make.

Now, of course, we have to be smart in how we go about it. For example, as tens of millions of young people enter the job market each year, we recognise that the Arab political awakening must also deliver an economic awakening. And we are working to help societies create jobs to ensure that it does. We are promoting trade, investment, regional integration, entrepreneurship, and economic reforms. We are helping societies fight corruption and replace the old

politics of patronage with a new focus on economic empowerment and opportunity. And we are working with Congress on debt relief for Egypt and loan
guarantees for Tunisia so that these countries can invest in their own futures.

We also have real expertise to offer as a democracy, including the wisdom
that NDI has gleaned from decades of working around the globe to support
democratic transitions. Democracies, after all, aren't born knowing how to run
themselves. In a country like Libya, Gaddafi spent forty-two years hollowing out
every part of his government not connected to oil or to keeping him in power.
Under the Libyan penal code, simply joining an NGO could be punishable
by death. When I travelled last month to Libya, the students I met at Tripoli
University had all sorts of practical, even technical, questions: How do you
form a political party? How do you ensure women's participation in government
institutions? What recommendations do you have for citizens in a democracy?

These are questions NDI and its kindred organisations, many of whom are
represented here tonight, are uniquely qualified to help new democracies answer.
NDI has earned a lot of praise for this work, but also a lot of pushback that
stretches far beyond the Arab world. In part, this resistance comes from miscon-
ceptions about what our support for democracy does and does not include.

The United States does not fund political candidates or political parties. We
do offer training to parties and candidates committed to democracy. We do not
try to shift outcomes or impose an American model. We do support election
commissions, as well as nongovernmental election monitors, to ensure free and
fair balloting. We help watchdog groups learn their trade. We help groups find
the tools to exercise their rights to free expression and assembly, online and off.
And of course we support civil society, the lifeblood of democratic politics.

But in part, the pushback comes from autocrats around the world wondering if the next Tahrir Square will be their capital square, and some are
cracking down when they should be opening up. Groups like NDI are no
strangers to pressure, and neither are the brave local groups you partner with.
And I want you to know that as the pressure on you increases, our support will
not waver.

And I want to offer a special word of thanks for NDI's efforts to empower
women across the Middle East and beyond. Just last week, the World Economic
Forum released a report on the remarkable benefits countries see when they
bridge the social, economic, and political gap separating women from men, and
helping them get there is a priority for the State Department and for me personally. Graduates of NDI training programmes designed to help women run for
office now sit in local councils and parliaments from Morocco to Kuwait.

But we all know a great deal of work lies ahead to help all people, women
and men, find justice and opportunity as full participants in new democratic
societies. Along with our economic and technical help, America will also use

our presence, influence, and global leadership to support change. And later this week, I am issuing new policy guidance to our embassies across the region to structure our efforts.

In Tunisia, Egypt, and Libya, we are working to help citizens safeguard the principles of democracy. That means supporting the forces of reconciliation rather than retribution. It means defending freedom of expression when bloggers are arrested for criticising public officials. It means standing up for tolerance when state-run television fans sectarian tensions. And it means that when unelected authorities say they want to be out of the business of governing, we will look to them to lay out a clear road map and urge them to abide by it.

Where countries are making gradual reforms, we have frank conversations and urge them to move faster. It's good to hold multi-party elections and allow women to take part. It's better when those elections are meaningful and parliaments have real powers to improve people's lives. Change needs to be tangible and real. When autocrats tell us the transition to democracy will take time, we answer, 'Well, then, let's get started.'

And those leaders trying to hold back the future at the point of a gun should know their days are numbered. As Syrians gather to celebrate a sacred holiday, their government continues to shoot people in the streets. In the week since Bashar al-Assad said he accepted the terms of an Arab League peace plan to protect Syrian civilians, he has systematically violated each of its basic requirements. He has not released all detainees. He has not allowed free and unfettered access to journalists or Arab League monitors. He has not withdrawn all armed forces from populated areas. And he has certainly not stopped all acts of violence. In fact, the regime has increased violence against civilians in places like the city of Homs. Now, Assad may be able to delay change. But he cannot deny his people's legitimate demands indefinitely. He must step down; and until he does, America and the international community will continue to increase pressure on him and his brutal regime.

And for all of Iran's bluster, there is no country in the Middle East where the gulf between rulers and ruled is greater. When Iran claims to support democracy abroad, then kills peaceful protestors in the streets of Tehran, its hypocrisy is breathtaking and plain to the people of the region.

And there is one last question that I'm asked, in one form or another, all the time: What about the rights and aspirations of the Palestinians? Israelis and Palestinians are not immune to the profound changes sweeping the region. And make no mistake, President Obama and I believe that the Palestinian people – just like their Arab neighbours, just like Israelis, just like us – deserve dignity, liberty, and the right to decide their own future. They deserve an independent, democratic Palestinian state of their own, alongside a secure Jewish democracy next door. And we know from decades in the diplomatic trenches that the only way to get there is through a negotiated peace – a peace we work every day to achieve, despite all the setbacks.

Of course, we understand that Israel faces risks in a changing region – just as it did before the Arab Spring began. And it will remain an American priority to ensure that all parties honour the peace treaties they have signed and commitments they have made. And we will always help Israel defend itself. We will address threats to regional peace whether they come from dictatorships or democracies. But it would be short-sighted to think either side can simply put peacemaking on hold until the current upheaval is done. The truth is, the stalemate in the Arab–Israeli conflict is one more status quo in the Middle East that cannot be sustained.

This brings me to my last and perhaps most important point of all. For all the hard questions I've asked and tried to answer on behalf of the United States, the most consequential questions of all are those the people and leaders of the region will have to answer for themselves. Because ultimately, it is up to them. It is up to them to resist the calls of demagogues, to build coalitions, to keep faith in the system even when they lose at the polls, and to protect the principles and institutions that ultimately will protect them. Every democracy has to guard against those who would hijack its freedoms for ignoble ends. Our founders and every generation since have fought to prevent that from happening here. The founding fathers and mothers of Arab revolutions must do the same. No one bears a greater responsibility for what happens next.

When Deputy Secretary Bill Burns addressed the National Endowment for Democracy over the summer, he recounted the story of an Egyptian teenager who told her father a few years back that she wanted to spend her life bringing democracy to Egypt. 'Good,' her father said, 'because then you will always have a job.'

Now, we should never fall prey to the belief that human beings anywhere are not ready for freedom. In the 1970s, people said Latin America and East Asia were not ready. Well, the 1980s began proving them wrong. In the 1980s, it was African soil where democracy supposedly couldn't grow. And the 1990s started proving them wrong. And until this year, some people said Arabs don't really want democracy. Well, starting in 2011, that too is being proved wrong. And funnily enough, it proved that Egyptian father right, because we all still have a job to do.

So we have to keep at it. We have to keep asking the tough questions. We have to be honest with ourselves and with each other about the answers we offer. And we cannot waver in our commitment to help the people of the Middle East and North Africa realise their own God-given potentials and the dreams they risked so much to make real.

And on this journey that they have begun, the United States will be their partner. And the many tools at our disposal – the National Endowment and NDI and all of the family of organisations that were created three decades ago to help people make this journey successfully – will be right there.

I heard Madeleine [Albright] say when she introduced me that I defend NDI. Well, I do. And I also defend IRI [International Republican Institute]. I defend those organisations that we have created, that the American taxpayers pay for, who try to do what needs to be done to translate the rhetoric and the calls for democracy into the reality, step by step. And we have to be reminded from time to time that it truly is – or at least can seem to be – a foreign language. Like some of you, I've met with the young people who started these revolutions. And they are still passionate, but perhaps not clear about what it takes to translate that passion into reality within a political system. So there are going to be a lot of bumps along this road. But far better that we travel this path, that we do what we can to make sure that our ideals and values, our belief and experience with democracy, are shared widely and well. It's an exciting time. It's an uncertain time. But it's a good time for the United States of America to be standing for freedom and democracy. And I thank you all for making that journey possible. Thank you very much.

AMR MOUSSA

'VIGOROUS ARAB WORLD IN THE YEARS TO COME'

—

REMARKS AT THE INTERNATIONAL INSTITUTE
FOR STRATEGIC STUDIES

GENEVA, SWITZERLAND, 9 SEPTEMBER 2011

A mr Moussa was Egypt's Minister for Foreign Affairs from 1991–2001. He then became Secretary General of the Arab League, a forum representing twenty-two Arab states. He held that position from 2001–2011. He is now a candidate in the Egyptian Presidential election.

In this speech we turn to an informed insider. His remarks on the Arab Spring are almost always widely reported. Because of Moussa's influential position as a diplomat and politician, with vast knowledge of the region and many of those involved in the revolution, his remarks in Geneva provide insight into the forces behind the conflict and possible outcomes.

These remarks are the version posted on the web. The conclusion indicates that this might be an abbreviated version, an elaborate, fully written, and structured set of talking points.

—

Thank you very much for inviting me to address the International Institute for Strategic Studies annual conference in Geneva which is an opportunity for me to meet this esteemed audience at a very exceptional juncture.

The first point that comes to my mind as a speaker is that we meet today two days before the commemoration of the sad events of 11 September 2001; it will be a decade ago shortly since a heinous act of terrorism was committed, leading to a bloody decade of confrontation and wars, as well as to policies based on doubtful and unsubstantiated theories such as the Clash of Civilisations and the End of History.

This criminal act left all of us, regardless of nationality, geography, religion, colour or creed, in rage, in shame and in disbelief. Disbelief despite the fact that it was live on air from the outset to the end.

A few years earlier, before 9/11, there were celebrations around the world marking the end of the Cold War and the demise of the Soviet Union. We should also recall that in October 1991 the Madrid Conference for peace in the Middle East was held and produced a chain of negotiations and the recognition of the principle of Land for Peace. The world at large and the Middle East in particular was full of hope that a new era of justice and prosperity for all would emerge and a new international order ... a different world order would be established and the world would be heading to a better future.

Unfortunately this did not happen. It continued to be business as usual. Double standards formed the basis for many policies and remained one of the preferred international practices. The clash of civilisations, with special reference to Islam, became a leading world stage line of policy. Major conflicts and issues such as the Arab–Israeli conflict were placed on the backburner of a train going nowhere. The developing nations, with a very few exceptions, remained far behind, especially in Africa. In other words, no change was visible, which led to further frustration and for sentiments of despair to prevail. Questions were raised about the direction of the world, would this indeed be the end of history? In other words, is what we see what we get forever? Could anybody, any people accept this?

This certainly created bitter feelings in many parts of the world especially in the Middle East.

Having said that, I would like to quickly say that the atmosphere of despair and frustration in the Middle East, and in particular in the Arab world, could not and should not be connected to the international causes alone. In fact, the Arab people were enraged, accumulating anger and feelings of rejection because of the policies pursued by the so-called 'elected' leaders, elected time and again through fraud. The misrule, the dictatorial rule, the introduction of ruling family aspirations to perpetuate dynasties, consolidate hegemonies and strengthen their grip on power, in addition to the gathering of enormous wealth, triggered the opposition, then the uprising, then the revolution of the people against those rulers. People went to the streets in an unprecedented move in the Arab world to topple those rulers and put an end to those regimes.

They could not accept any more to be robbed of their present and future by such regimes, insulted and humiliated by those unacceptable policies.

Change was a must and it was time for change. In fact many world powers expected and wanted a change. Some of them went further to force that change within certain parameters.

The greater Middle East was one of those plans for change which meant inter-alia to prepare the ground for the era post the demise of the dictators.

In fact, the big powers enjoyed the full cooperation of many of those leaders and became good friends; however those very leaders were fully rejected by their people.

So the careful handling by some big powers for a change under their auspices coincided with the brave drive by the people in several Arab countries to take matters into their own hands. Revolution occurred and succeeded by the people and for the people, oblivious of any foreign plans or interests.

Hence, what we are witnessing today has no relation to the plans put forward under whatever banner, including in particular the policy of propagating a greater and broader Middle East. Let me tell you that instead of a greater Middle East you will have a vigorous Arab world in the years to come. This will be good for a safer future for the Middle East ... redrawn by its people and the effect of their political landscape.

The changes in Tunisia, Egypt, Yemen, Syria and Libya were genuine, and the change will affect the whole region. Perhaps in different degrees, with different approaches, but all shall fall within the parameters of change in the Arab world. Therefore we shall see a different Middle East in the next few months and years.

In this connection three elements are to be highlighted:

1. Successful popular uprisings in the Arab region want their countries to follow engaging, forthcoming and productive policies that would produce a better region which is peaceful and prosperous.
2. There will be a steady policy towards a new Arab paradigm of more coordination and cooperation, not the contrary.
3. In this connection striving for a fair peace in the Middle East and putting an end to the Arab–Israeli conflict shall continue to enjoy high priority on the Arab agenda. We shall continue to abide by the Arab peace initiative of 2002.

The new revolutionary regimes would be more anxious to reach a fair peace in the Middle East. I see this as a very positive point. In fact the total submission of previous regimes has led nowhere. Those policies were empty and added to the rage of the people. The time has come for a result-oriented peace process.

Time has come for many policy-makers around the world to take the new Arab world more seriously; this new Arab world will be soon in the making, sooner than expected.

I see a new Arab world, vigorous, young, demanding, in a state of production, friendly to the world including the West but not in a state of defeat or submission. The young generation, representing the trigger for the new regimes, need peace and justice and development to prevail. They will have good relations with all those who would help them and those who would present to them genuine help towards achieving their goals.

A win-win situation is what we together should work for. No other formula would succeed.

KING ABDULLAH II OF JORDAN

'THE GATES OF THE FUTURE'

—

OPENING REMARKS FOR THE WORLD ECONOMIC FORUM'S SPECIAL MEETING ON ECONOMIC GROWTH AND JOB CREATION IN THE ARAB WORLD

DEAD SEA, JORDAN, 23 OCTOBER 2011

*A*bdullah II *ascended to the throne of the Hashemite Kingdom of Jordan upon the death of his father, King Hussein. He has actively engaged the forces of the Arab Spring from within, liberalising the economy, holding elections in November 2011, encouraging education of women, and moving toward a British-style Cabinet government. There have been protests and violence in Jordan. Perhaps Abdullah's efforts will preclude a revolution.*

In this speech he offers a path forward and vision for resolution of the region's conflict. The speech was given at a conference to encourage women entrepreneurs, job creation, and small business formation as one solution to the problems in the Middle East.

—

Your Excellencies, ladies and gentlemen:

Before we start this special meeting, I would like to express my sincerest condolences to my brother, the Custodian of the Two Holy Mosques, over the loss of Crown Prince Sultan Bin Abdel Aziz of Saudi Arabia.

Jordan mourns the passing of such an Arab statesman and leader, a champion of the Arab and Muslim cause. May I ask you all to join me for a few seconds of silence. May his soul rest in peace.

Professor [Klaus] Schwab, distinguished guests:

Thank you, and thank you all for being here. It is a vital time for this special meeting on economic growth and job creation in the Arab world. I want to extend a warm welcome to our friends from many continents who join us today.

Professor Schwab, let me thank you personally for your inspired work and loyal friendship to the people of this region. Long before social media, the World Economic Forum was hosting a global conversation. Where good minds meet, smart solutions take root. That is just what I hope will be achieved here, by all of you.

Friends, our region stands today at the gates to the future.

First is the Gate of Dignity ... a passage to the respect our people deserve ... and their right, without exception, to the broad horizons enjoyed by others around the world. Aspiring men and women, young people, pragmatic dreamers, gathered at this gate in the Arab Spring.

Second is the Gate of Opportunity ... an economic opening for millions more of our people – young, old, urban, rural, badia. To widen this gate, entrepreneurs and innovators, educators and policy-makers are desperately needed ... not only to free people from today's economic hardships ... but to clear a path to the 85 million new jobs that the region needs soon.

The third gate is the Gate of Democracy ... not just a political structure but a way of life. An entry to real reform, where people can come together as citizens and stakeholders: assembling in political parties; formulating platforms; building consensus. There is no one path forward from this gate. Solutions must and will be home-grown, in each of our countries.

The fourth gate is the Gate of Peace and Justice ... opening the way out of regional crisis, especially at the heart of the region, the Palestinian–Israeli conflict. Short-sighted leaders may think they can shut this gate. But the future for the Middle East and beyond is with the normalcy of peace ... a two-state solution with a sovereign, viable and independent Palestinian state, on the 1967 borders, with East Jerusalem as its capital, in accordance with UN resolutions, resolving all final status issues ... security and acceptance for Israel ... and a new era of peace and cooperation from the Atlantic to the Indian Ocean.

The four gates of the Arab future are not alternatives. We must pass through them all. Dignity, opportunity, democracy, peace and justice are ultimately inseparable. To cement progress anywhere, we will need progress everywhere.

Your meetings here focus on an area of urgent need: economic growth and jobs. It is hard to find a more central concern for our people – especially our young people, the majority of our population. Today the Middle East has the highest youth unemployment rate of any region in the world. Pockets of poverty make the distress harder ... and families everywhere have felt the impact from global crises in food, energy and even finance. This year's events have opened the way to positive change, but in many places, also created painful economic dislocations. Strategies are urgently needed, and they must take place across the board – in economic life; in politics and policies; in social life and cultural values.

Steve Jobs helped prove that people who 'think different' can change the world. He will be sorely missed. But his inspiration will live on. I believe there are a million men and women, with minds that are no less creative and daring, right here in the Arab world. They are ready for the opportunity to act. And they can, we all can, change our world.

When it comes to getting our people employed, three groups have special roles. One is the private sector, which has a strong interest in getting more people off the unemployment rolls. A secure middle class, optimistic about the future, will anchor our strategic region better than any resource. To get there, we need innovative approaches in all areas. In Jordan, for example, we have seen huge growth in ICT, pioneered by visionaries who saw the possibilities of a new regional market, and supported by national investments in infrastructure and education. There is also great potential in other industries our region needs, such as water and alternative energy – which can in turn open new global markets. Many other possibilities are ripe for initiative and I hope you will discover some here.

The second major player in job growth is government. Let's be clear. Political reform is economic reform. For businesses to invest and expand with confidence, they need a predictable, level playing field ... transparency and accountability ... the rule of law ... and a strong, stable foundation of inclusive political life.

These are key elements of Jordan's reform effort. For us, the Arab Spring has been an opportunity to move our nation's interests forward. We seek a consensual and evolutionary path, engaging citizens at all levels. We have set milestones, and we are keeping to them. New constitutional amendments protect civil rights and freedoms, establish an independent constitutional court, and provide for an independent elections commission. Wide-ranging legislation will implement these and other provisions. We are anticipating new municipal and parliamentary elections in the near future.

The third key group in regional job creation is of course, our people themselves. Building our region's future is a responsibility that belongs to all. This is true in political life, and it is true for our economic future as well. All the jobs that our region needs will not be wished into being. But we can help opportunity grow, by what we do: by strong and growing productivity; new investments and industries; innovation and entrepreneurial spirit. For this, we need everyone.

Employees who do their jobs with dedication and professionalism. Managers who act ethically and competently. CEOs who lead boldly and responsibly. Civil society volunteers and caring young people, who better our communities and help others reach their potential. My friends, we've all seen the soaring archways of classic Islamic architecture. Their design depends on many individual stones ... using the strength of each, working in perfect harmony, to create the whole. It cannot stand, it cannot last, without them all. Today, in our political and economic life, each of us is needed. If we work together, if we lend our full strength to the job, I believe we can make it a future worthy of our great people. My best wishes to you all, for your work today and in the days ahead.

RONALD JAN HEIJN

'THE END OF AN ERA'

—

REMARKS CONCERNING OCCUPY AMSTERDAM

AMSTERDAM, NETHERLANDS, 6 NOVEMBER 2011

*I*n response to the global financial crisis, protests spontaneously erupted worldwide in 2011. In several cities public areas were occupied by those who felt disenfranchised, disaffected or simply left out of the economy. These people became known as the '99 per cent', as opposed to the '1 per cent' alleged to monopolise global wealth and power. Camps of people were set up at St Paul's Church in London, at McPherson Square in Washington, DC, at Wall Street in New York City, and in many major cities around the world. The anger was palpable. The movement demanded radical changes in the world financial system and in their national economies. Political and social change was also part of the Occupy Agenda, which seemed to sweep up many different types of groups with disparate and widespread demands, from anarchists, environmentalists and a variety of informal anti-capitalist groups. Ronald Jan Heijn is a former member of the Dutch international hockey team. He now styles himself as a 'spiritual entrepreneur'.

In these remarks, he explains the reasons for the Occupy Amsterdam Movement. There is some dispute about what he actually said, with conflicting transcripts of his remarks. What follows is a best attempt at capturing his words. Note the claims of international unity and worldwide anger against government, the financial markets, the rich and those with power. Some argue that the Occupy Movement is a large coalition that is unfocused and fuelled by grievances, with little thought for solutions. That may be true. But my own visits to Occupy sites convinced me that Occupy is more than an event. With little to lose, Occupy participants represent a message of anger, desperation and determination. The Occupy Movement may be more than an historical moment. It might be the start of something bigger.

—

We are here all together at a special place in Amsterdam. And also in America, they are in an appropriate place, 'Wall' Street. 'We are standing with our backs against the Wall!'

Therefore ... I think it is a good idea that we all acknowledge that we are now at the end of an era. An era of almost 2000 years. And it is especially the mindset that is now completely inadequate.

Those who are in power want to keep up the existing structures at all costs. But the population has a very strong gut feeling that the time is ripe for a totally different approach. Many governments are still thinking that it is only a matter of a broken engine that needs repair, and that 'we can continue with business as usual' once it is fixed.

But that is impossible! We are at a turning point, and the genie is out of the bottle. It is irreversible, it can never return. So it's not 'just discontent and anger' that people feel. It is a deep fundamental feeling that the situation really has to change now!

In fact, we must be grateful that the bankers have made such a mess, so we could finally wake up from the dream. It appears to be a nightmare. And this huge injustice sinks in: only 2 per cent of the adult world population owns 50 per cent of the property. And 50 per cent of the [poor] adults possess less than 1 per cent! What a shameful unjust distribution!

History has taught us that communism is not the answer, but now we know capitalism is neither. Both systems have fundamental flaws. Therefore, you can also read banners like this all over the world: 'Capitalism in crisis? Capitalism IS the crisis'. Or like this banner on Wall Street: 'The system is not broken, it was built this way!'

Another example of absurd ingrained capitalistic behaviour this past year came out: the unregulated derivative markets have swollen to $600,000 billion. This monster of speculation, this casino, this Fata Morgana is forty times the global trade in goods and services. We lost it completely, ladies and gentlemen!

But it is not only the economy, it concerns a way of thinking that is within the whole society. How we deal with the rainforests, the health care, the famine in Somalia, you name it.

It is the mindset that dictates: Only tangible things count, such as money and matter. It is our physical way of observing, which characterises us. It is all due to the fact that people think: Man is only a physical body, nothing else. However, now we know that man is consciousness. We ARE conscious, and accidentally we have a body – not the other way round. Our ignorance about this comes with enormous consequences.

It is the limited thinking of our ego, our personality. It puts our own interests first and makes us think that status and money are important, and that we will never have enough. It is impossible to satisfy as it cannot stand losses, and is therefore capable of doing anything just to keep up self-preservation.

And above all, it thinks in separation: me and the others. The ego knows rivalry and jealousy, hence it has created a very hostile world – just like the one we all experience around us. Rivalry, separation and commercialisation, that is the real poison in the world and created a society without soul and almost destroyed it.

This is why the world has not actually got an economical, financial, poverty or social problem, but rather a deep spiritual problem: we do not know who we are, where we come from and where we are going. Therefore, above all, it is an existential crisis: we do not know the actual meaning of life!

Although the answer is quite fundamental! Is it to become rich? Or to learn life lessons or to transcend from ignorance to insight, or is it servitude? If the answer is one of the latter, we will probably organise the world in a very different manner, forcing the world economy to be subservient rather than all-important as now.

The reality is certainly much greater then we think. In the new era – which is starting right now – we will discover our consciousness and thus the meaning of life. Everything is energy. We are all connected. We will start sharing when we finally acknowledge that we are all one family!

SLAVOJ ŽIŽEK

'FALSE TERMS, MYSTIFYING OUR PERCEPTION'

—

REMARKS CONCERNING OCCUPY WALL STREET

NEW YORK CITY, NEW YORK, 10 OCTOBER 2011

*S*lavoj Žižek *is a Slovenian philosopher and cultural critic. He has published a number of books examining current events, often from a Marxist perspective. Among his many academic positions, he is Senior Researcher at the Institute of Sociology, University of Ljubljana. He is also the International Director of the Birkbeck Institute for Humanities at the University of London.*

In these remarks, given in New York, he explains the significance and power of the Occupy Movement. The text is from his original speech text and may not correspond to what was actually said. In other words, this is the manuscript of what was made available, not necessarily the remarks as given. However, his work and influence provide some important insights.

—

Don't fall in love with yourselves, with the nice time we are having here. Carnivals come cheap – the true test of their worth is what remains the day after, how our normal daily life will be changed. Fall in love with hard and patient work – we are the beginning, not the end. Our basic message is: the taboo is broken, we do not live in the best possible world, we are allowed and even obliged to think about alternatives. There is a long road ahead, and soon we will have to address the truly difficult questions – questions not about what we do not want, but about what we DO want. What social organisation can replace the existing capitalism? What type of new leaders we need? The twentieth-century alternatives obviously did not work.

So do not blame people and their attitudes: the problem is not corruption or greed, the problem is the system that pushes you to be corrupt. The solution is not 'Main Street, not Wall Street', but to change the system where Main Street cannot function without Wall Street. Beware not only of enemies, but also of false friends who pretend to support us, but are already working hard to dilute our protest. In the same way we get coffee without caffeine, beer without alcohol, ice-cream without fat, they will try to make us into a harmless moral protest. But the reason we are here is that we had enough of the world where to recycle your Coke cans, to give a couple of dollars for charity, or to buy Starbucks cappuccino where 1 per cent goes for the Third World troubles is enough to make us feel good. After outsourcing work and torture, after the marriage agencies started to outsource even our dating, we see that for a long time we were allowing our political engagements also to be outsourced – we want them back.

They will tell us we are un-American. But when conservative fundamentalists tell you that America is a Christian nation, remember what Christianity is: the Holy Spirit, the free egalitarian community of believers united by love. We here are the Holy Spirit, while on Wall Street they are pagans worshipping false idols.

They will tell us we are violent, that our very language is violent: occupation, and so on. Yes we are violent, but only in the sense in which Mahathma Gandhi was violent. We are violent because we want to put a stop on the way things go – but what is this purely symbolic violence compared to the violence needed to sustain the smooth functioning of the global capitalist system?

We were called losers – but are the true losers not there on Wall Street, and were they not bailed out by hundreds of billions of your money? You are called socialists – but in the US, there already is socialism for the rich. They will tell you that you don't respect private property – but the Wall Street speculations that led to the crash of 2008 erased more hard-earned private property than if we were to be destroying it here night and day – just think of thousands of homes foreclosed...

We are not communists, if communism means the system which deservedly collapsed in 1990 – and remember that communists who are still in power run today the most ruthless capitalism [in China]. The success of Chinese communist-run capitalism is an ominous sign that the marriage between capitalism and democracy is approaching a divorce. The only sense in which we are communists is that we care for the commons – the commons of nature, of knowledge – which are threatened by the system.

They will tell you that you are dreaming, but the true dreamers are those who think that things can go on indefinitely the way they are, just with some cosmetic changes. We are not dreamers, we are the awakening from a dream which is turning into a nightmare. We are not destroying anything, we are merely witness to how the system is gradually destroying itself. We all know the classic scene from cartoons: the cat reaches a precipice, but it goes on walking, ignoring the fact that there is no ground under its feet; it starts to fall only when it looks down and notices the abyss. What we are doing is just reminding those in power to look down...

So is the change really possible? Today, the possible and the impossible are distributed in a strange way. In the domains of personal freedoms and scientific technology, the impossible is becoming increasingly possible (or so we are told): 'nothing is impossible', we can enjoy sex in all its perverse versions; entire archives of music, films, and TV series are available for downloading; space travel is available to everyone (with the money...); we can enhance our physical and psychic abilities through interventions into the genome, right up to the techno-gnostic dream of achieving immortality by transforming our identity into a software program. On the other hand, in the domain of social and economic relations, we are bombarded all the time by a: You cannot ... engage in collective political acts (which necessarily end in totalitarian terror), or cling to the old welfare state (it makes you non-competitive and leads to economic crisis), or isolate yourself from the global market, and so on. When austerity measures are imposed, we are repeatedly told that this is simply what has to be done. Maybe, the time has come to turn around these coordinates of what is possible and what is impossible; maybe, we cannot become immortal, but we can have more solidarity and health care?

In mid-April 2011, the media reported that Chinese government has prohibited showing on TV and in theatres films which deal with time travel and alternate history, with the argument that such stories introduce frivolity into serious historical matters – even the fictional escape into alternate reality is considered too dangerous. We in the liberal West do not need such an explicit prohibition: ideology exerts enough material power to prevent alternate history narratives being taken with a minimum of seriousness. It is easy for us to imagine the end of the world – see numerous apocalyptic films – but not the end of capitalism.

In an old joke from the defunct German Democratic Republic, a German worker gets a job in Siberia; aware of how all mail will be read by censors, he tells his friends: 'Let's establish a code: if a letter you will get from me is written in ordinary blue ink, it is true; if it is written in red ink, it is false.' After a month, his friends get the first letter written in blue ink: 'Everything is wonderful here: stores are full, food is abundant, apartments are large and properly heated, movie theatres show films from the West, there are many beautiful girls ready for an affair – the only thing unavailable is red ink.' And is this not our situation till now? We have all the freedoms one wants – the only thing missing is the *red ink*: we *feel free* because we lack the very language to articulate our unfreedom. What this lack of red ink means is that, today, all the main terms we use to designate the present conflict – 'war on terror', 'democracy and freedom', 'human rights', etc. – are FALSE terms, mystifying our perception of the situation instead of allowing us to think it. You, here, you are giving to all of us red ink.

GEORGE W. BUSH

'EMBRYOS ... ARE NOT SPARE PARTS'

—

REMARKS CONCERNING THE VETO OF
THE STEM CELL RESEARCH BILL

WASHINGTON, DC, 19 JULY 2006

D*uring his tenure as President from 2001–2009, George W. Bush faced mounting criticism about his policy to restrict research on embryonic stem cells. This research showed potential to address Parkinson's Disease, Alzheimer's Disease, spinal cord injuries, and many other medical problems. Despite what he perceived as a compromise position allowing research on a limited number of existing stem cell lines, Congress passed the Stem Cell Research Enactment Act of 2005. The original legislation was co-sponsored by Diana DeGette, a Democrat, representing urban Denver, Colorado, and Mike Castle, a Republican, an at-large representative from Delaware. The proposed legislation would have allowed for federal funding of new stem cell lines from discarded embryos originally created as part of human fertility treatments. President Bush vetoed that legislation, the first veto of his administration.*

One core question is this: should biomedical research be politicised? Some charged the President with doing just that. Others felt he should politicise the issue, making it a voting issue for the American public in the 2006 congressional elections. There was also a concern about the international community. Should the United States let other countries, such as the United Kingdom or South Korea, take the lead on stem cell research? Is biomedical research best managed as a national enterprise or an international one? In addition, the moral issues are balanced against practical problems, such as waste avoidance when frozen reproductive materials are thrown away.

In this speech he explains that veto, which Congress failed to override. Later, Bush also vetoed the Stem Cell Research Enactment Act of 2007. The debate surrounding stem cell research was part of a larger debate concerning the politicisation of scientific research.

———

Good afternoon. Congress has just passed and sent to my desk two bills concerning the use of stem cells in biomedical research. These bills illustrate both the promise and perils we face in the age of biotechnology. In this new era, our challenge is to harness the power of science to ease human suffering without sanctioning the practices that violate the dignity of human life.

In 2001, I spoke to the American people and set forth a new policy on stem cell research that struck a balance between the needs of science and the demands of conscience. When I took office, there was no federal funding for human embryonic stem cell research. Under the policy I announced five years ago, my administration became the first to make federal funds available for this research, yet only on embryonic stem cell lines derived from embryos that had already been destroyed.

My administration has made available more than $90 million for research on these lines. This policy has allowed important research to go forward without using taxpayer funds to encourage the further deliberate destruction of human embryos.

One of the bills Congress has passed builds on the progress we have made over the last five years. So I signed it into law. Congress has also passed a second bill that attempts to overturn the balanced policy I set. This bill would support the taking of innocent human life in the hope of finding medical benefits for others. It crosses a moral boundary that our decent society needs to respect, so I vetoed it.

Like all Americans, I believe our nation must vigorously pursue the tremendous possibility that science offers to cure disease and improve the lives of millions. We have opportunities to discover cures and treatments that were unthinkable generations ago. Some scientists believe that one source of these cures might be embryonic stem cell research. Embryonic stem cells have the ability to grow into specialised adult tissues, and this may give them the potential to replace damaged or defective cells or body parts and treat a variety of diseases.

Yet we must also remember that embryonic stem cells come from human embryos that are destroyed for their cells. Each of these human embryos is a unique human life with inherent dignity and matchless value. We see that value in the children who are with us today. Each of these children began his or her life as a frozen embryo that was created for *in vitro* fertilisation, but remained unused after the fertility treatments were complete. Each of these children was adopted while still an embryo, and has been blessed with the chance to grow up in a loving family.

These boys and girls are not spare parts. They remind us of what is lost when embryos are destroyed in the name of research. They remind us that we all begin our lives as a small collection of cells. And they remind us that in our zeal for new treatments and cures, America must never abandon our fundamental morals.

Some people argue that finding new cures for disease requires the destruction of human embryos like the ones that these families adopted. I disagree. I believe that with the right techniques and the right policies, we can achieve scientific progress while living up to our ethical responsibilities. That's what I sought in 2001, when I set forth my administration's policy allowing federal funding for research on embryonic stem cell lines where the life and death decision had already been made.

This balanced approach has worked. Under this policy, twenty-one human embryonic stem cell lines are currently in use in research that is eligible for federal funding. Each of these lines can be replicated many times. And as a result, the National Institutes of Health have helped make more than 700 shipments to researchers since 2001. There is no ban on embryonic stem cell research. To the contrary, even critics of my policy concede that these federally funded lines are being used in research every day by scientists around the world. My policy has allowed us to explore the potential of embryonic stem cells, and it has allowed America to continue to lead the world in this area.

Since I announced my policy in 2001, advances in scientific research have also shown the great potential of stem cells that are derived without harming human embryos. My administration has expanded the funding of research into stem cells that can be drawn from children, adults, and the blood in umbilical cords, with no harm to the donor. And these stem cells are already being used in medical treatments.

With us today are patients who have benefited from treatments with adult and umbilical-cord-blood stem cells. And I want to thank you all for coming.

They are living proof that effective medical science can also be ethical. Researchers are now also investigating new techniques that could allow doctors and scientists to produce stem cells just as versatile as those derived from human embryos. One technique scientists are exploring would involve reprogramming an adult cell. For example, programming a skin cell to function like an embryonic stem cell. Science offers the hope that we may one day enjoy the potential benefits of embryonic stem cells without destroying human life.

We must continue to explore these hopeful alternatives and advance the cause of scientific research while staying true to the ideals of a decent and humane society. The bill I sign today upholds these humane ideals and draws an important ethical line to guide our research. The Fetus Farming Prohibition Act was sponsored by Senators [Rick] Santorum and [Sam] Brownback – both of whom are here. And by Congressman Dave Weldon, along with Nathan Deal. Thank you, Congressmen. This good law prohibits one of the most egregious abuses in biomedical research, the trafficking in human foetuses that are created with the sole intent of aborting them to harvest their parts. Human beings are not a raw material to be exploited, or a commodity to be bought or sold, and this bill will help ensure that we respect the fundamental ethical line.

I'm disappointed that Congress failed to pass another bill that would have promoted good research. This bill was sponsored by Senator Santorum and Senator Arlen Specter and Congressman Roscoe Bartlett. Thanks for coming, Roscoe. It would have authorised additional federal funding for promising new research that could produce cells with the abilities of embryonic cells, but without the destruction of human embryos. This is an important piece of legislation. This bill was unanimously approved by the Senate; it received 273 votes in the House of Representatives, but was blocked by a minority in the House using procedural manoeuvres. I'm disappointed that the House failed to authorise funding for this vital and ethical research.

It makes no sense to say that you're in favour of finding cures for terrible diseases as quickly as possible, and then block a bill that would authorise funding for promising and ethical stem cell research. At a moment when ethical alternatives are becoming available, we cannot lose the opportunity to conduct research that would give hope to those suffering from terrible diseases, and help move our nation beyond the current controversies over embryonic stem cell research.

We must pursue this research. And so I direct the Secretary of Health and Human Services, Secretary Mike Leavitt, and the Director of the National Institutes of Health to use all the tools at their disposal to aid the search for stem cell techniques that advance promising medical science in an ethical and morally responsible way.

Unfortunately, Congress has sent me a bill that fails to meet this ethical test. This legislation would overturn the balanced policy on embryonic stem cell research that my administration has followed for the past five years. This bill would also undermine the principle that Congress, itself, has followed for more than a decade, when it has prohibited federal funding for research that destroys human embryos.

If this bill had become law, American taxpayers would, for the first time in our history, be compelled to fund the deliberate destruction of human embryos. And I'm not going to allow it.

I made it clear to the Congress that I will not allow our nation to cross this moral line. I felt like crossing this line would be a mistake, and once crossed, we would find it almost impossible to turn back. Crossing the line would needlessly encourage a conflict between science and ethics that can only do damage to both, and to our nation as a whole. If we're to find the right ways to advance ethical medical research, we must also be willing, when necessary, to reject the wrong ways. So today, I'm keeping the promise I made to the American people by returning this bill to Congress with my veto.

As science brings us ever closer to unlocking the secrets of human biology, it also offers temptations to manipulate human life and violate human dignity. Our conscience and history as a nation demand that we resist this temptation. America was founded on the principle that we are all created equal, and endowed by our Creator with the right to life. We can advance the cause of science while upholding this founding promise. We can harness the promise of technology without becoming slaves to technology. And we can ensure that science serves the cause of humanity instead of the other way around.

America pursues medical advances in the name of life, and we will achieve the great breakthroughs we all seek with reverence for the gift of life. I believe America's scientists have the ingenuity and skill to meet this challenge. And I look forward to working with Congress and the scientific community to achieve these great and noble goals in the years ahead.

Thank you all for coming and may God bless America.

DIANA DeGETTE

'ETHICAL IMPERATIVE TO HELP CURE DISEASES'

—

RADIO ADDRESS TO THE NATION, IN RESPONSE TO BUSH VETO

WASHINGTON, DC, 23 JULY 2006

E*lected to Congress in 1997 to represent Colorado's First Congressional District, which comprises most of urban Denver, Diana DeGette has been involved in efforts to promote women's rights, equity in health care and choice in decisions on sex and reproduction. She was a co-author of two pieces of legislation to allow Federal funding for embryonic stem cell research. Both bills were vetoed by President Bush.*

After the first veto, DeGette was asked to address the American people via radio to explain the need for this research. She argues the President fails on both moral and practical grounds. There are policy failings too. DeGette believes that the President's veto only hurts the American public. Her stinging criticism of President Bush was carried by virtually every news organisation in the world.

—

Good morning. This is Congresswoman Diana DeGette of Colorado.

Scientists agree: we are on the brink of cures for diseases that affect hundreds of millions around the world. Imagine the heartache we can save the world if we were to eradicate diabetes, Parkinson's or Lou Gehrig's disease. And the most exciting recent breakthroughs – the discovery of embryonic stem cells – may allow us to do just that.

Opponents of stem cell research often point to adult stem cells as a suitable alternative. However, legitimate scientists disagree. Dr Harold Varmus, the former head of our National Institutes of Health, said, 'Compared to adult stem cells, embryonic stem cells have a much greater potential, according to all existing scientific literature.'

Because of this great potential, Congressman Mike Castle and I introduced legislation to expand embryonic stem cell research. This narrowly drawn legislation would allow couples who have undergone *in vitro* fertilisation techniques to donate the excess embryos left over for ethical medical research.

Let me be clear: these are not embryos that would be used for *in vitro* fertilisation or donated to other couples. These are excess embryos that would have been discarded as medical waste. It makes more sense to allow them to be donated to give life and health to people in need.

Fortunately, most members of Congress understood the great potential of this research, and refused to become distracted by the distortions of stem cell research opponents. Both Houses of Congress supported our legislation, with strong bipartisan majorities. The bill received the support of prominent Americans like Nancy Reagan, Michael J. Fox and Senate Majority Leader Bill Frist. Almost three out of every four Americans support this research.

But, on Wednesday, the President exercised the first veto of his presidency on this law. President Bush has signed bills to give subsidies to big oil, to give tax cuts to the wealthiest few, and subsidies to HMOs [Health Maintenance Organisations] but he could not find it in his heart to give hope to America's families, proudly boasting that he was protecting America from crossing a 'moral line'.

I, too, want to talk about morality. A moral society has an ethical imperative to help cure diseases that affect 110 million Americans and their families. We owe that to the child with Type I diabetes, the brother with Parkinson's, the police officer paralysed by a criminal's bullet.

I am tempted to point out the obvious – the President's veto had nothing to do with morals. It had everything to do with cold, calculated, cynical political gain ... the kind of politics that snuffs out the candle of hope, and that condemns the disabled and the sick.

The President's veto is a sad sidebar in a debate that has been about ethical scientific research and hope. The veto has backfired already, putting the spotlight on his stubborn resistance to facts. This last-gasp effort to stop stem cell research will be viewed by historians as a sign more of the weakness of the opponents than a roadblock to progress.

The time for this research is at hand. Public support for ethical stem cell research will only grow. This issue will be a top priority in upcoming elections. Americans remember the words of Dr Martin Luther King, Jr who said, 'We are tied together in the single garment of destiny, caught in an inescapable web of mutuality.'

If someone is ill, then we must heal them. If someone is paralysed, then we must help that person become mobile. If someone is losing his or her memory, we must fight to save it. We cannot stand back and ignore a valuable research tool that might work medical miracles. We won't turn our backs on those in need. We will pass this bill.

This fight is just beginning.

Thank you for listening.

MITT ROMNEY

'FREEDOM AND RELIGION
ENDURE TOGETHER, OR PERISH ALONE'

—

REMARKS AT THE G.H.W. BUSH
PRESIDENTIAL LIBRARY

COLLEGE STATION, TEXAS, 6 DECEMBER 2007

S on of Governor George Romney of Michigan, Mitt Romney was CEO of Bain and Company and headed the Salt Lake Organizing Committee for the 2002 Winter Olympics. A Massachusetts resident, he ran for the United States Senate against the late Senator Teddy Kennedy in 1994, styling himself a liberal Republican, and won 41 per cent of the vote, the best performance by a Republican candidate in any of Kennedy's re-election contests. Following his stewardship of the Winter Olympics, Romney successfully ran for Governor of Massachusetts, again describing himself as a 'moderate' with 'progressive views', including support for abortion rights. In 2008, he ran for the Republican Presidential nomination, winning several primaries and caucuses. Following an impressive performance by Senator John McCain in the Super Tuesday primaries, Romney suspended his campaign, claiming that he did not want to weaken the party's general election chances with a protracted internal battle. This withdrawal, however, was seen by some commentators as a strategic retreat.

Romney is now running for the 2012 Republican Party nomination for President, in what has proved to be an unpredictable race at the time of this writing. Although Romney was at first considered the frontrunner, evangelical Christians who compose a sizeable proportion of the Republican primary electorate have expressed suspicion, both of his 'flip-flopping' and his membership of the Church of Jesus Christ of Latter Day Saints, commonly called 'The Mormons'. It has been argued that his faith should disqualify Romney from the Republic Party nomination.

In this speech he discusses those concerns. He covers some of the same ground as Obama's Philadelphia speech earlier in this volume, and John F. Kennedy's speech to Southern Baptist leaders in Houston in 1960, addressing concerns regarding his Catholicism. His answer is that religion and government are not always inseparable. In fact, they must somehow work together.

The title of the speech is 'Faith in America'. It is a contribution to a valuable, often heated, contemporary dialogue, exploring the lines that can, perhaps must be, drawn between individual religious beliefs and the process of governance within a constitutional framework.

—

Thank you, Mr President [G.H.W. Bush], for your kind introduction.

It is an honour to be here today. This is an inspiring place because of you and the First Lady, and because of the film exhibited across the way in the Presidential Library. For those who have not seen it, it shows the President as a young pilot, shot down during the Second World War, being rescued from his life-raft by the crew of an American submarine. It is a moving reminder that when America has faced challenge and peril, Americans rise to the occasion, willing to risk their very lives to defend freedom and preserve our nation. We are in your debt. Thank you, Mr President.

Mr President, your generation rose to the occasion, first to defeat Fascism and then to vanquish the Soviet Union. You left us, your children, a free and strong America. It is why we call yours the greatest generation. It is now my generation's turn. How we respond to today's challenges will define our generation. And it will determine what kind of America we will leave our children, and theirs.

America faces a new generation of challenges. Radical violent Islam seeks to destroy us. An emerging China endeavours to surpass our economic leadership. And we are troubled at home by government overspending, overuse of foreign oil, and the breakdown of the family.

Over the last year, we have embarked on a national debate on how best to preserve American leadership. Today, I wish to address a topic which I believe is fundamental to America's greatness: our religious liberty. I will also offer perspectives on how my own faith would inform my presidency, if I were elected.

There are some who may feel that religion is not a matter to be seriously considered in the context of the weighty threats that face us. If so, they are at odds with the nation's founders, for they, when our nation faced its greatest peril, sought the blessings of the Creator. And further, they discovered the essential connection between the survival of a free land and the protection of religious freedom. In John Adams's words: 'We have no government armed with power capable of contending with human passions unbridled by morality and religion... Our constitution was made for a moral and religious people.'

Freedom requires religion just as religion requires freedom. Freedom opens the windows of the soul so that man can discover his most profound beliefs and commune with God. Freedom and religion endure together, or perish alone.

Given our grand tradition of religious tolerance and liberty, some wonder whether there are any questions regarding an aspiring candidate's religion that are appropriate. I believe there are. And I will answer them today.

Almost fifty years ago another candidate from Massachusetts explained that he was an American running for President, not a Catholic running for President. Like him, I am an American running for President. I do not define my candidacy by my religion. A person should not be elected because of his faith nor should he be rejected because of his faith.

Let me assure you that no authorities of my church, or of any other church for that matter, will ever exert influence on presidential decisions. Their authority is theirs, within the province of church affairs, and it ends where the affairs of the nation begin.

As Governor, I tried to do the right as best I knew it, serving the law and answering to the Constitution. I did not confuse the particular teachings of my church with the obligations of the office and of the Constitution – and of course, I would not do so as President. I will put no doctrine of any church above the plain duties of the office and the sovereign authority of the law.

As a young man, Lincoln described what he called America's 'political religion' – the commitment to defend the rule of law and the Constitution. When I place my hand on the Bible and take the oath of office, that oath becomes my highest promise to God. If I am fortunate enough to become your President, I will serve no one religion, no one group, no one cause and no one interest. A President must serve only the common cause of the people of the United States.

There are some for whom these commitments are not enough. They would prefer it if I would simply distance myself from my religion, say that it is more a tradition than my personal conviction, or disavow one or another of its precepts. That I will not do. I believe in my Mormon faith and I endeavour to live by it. My faith is the faith of my fathers – I will be true to them and to my beliefs.

Some believe that such a confession of my faith will sink my candidacy. If they are right, so be it. But I think they underestimate the American people. Americans do not respect believers of convenience. Americans tire of those who would jettison their beliefs, even to gain the world.

There is one fundamental question about which I often am asked. What do I believe about Jesus Christ? I believe that Jesus Christ is the Son of God and the Saviour of mankind. My church's beliefs about Christ may not all be the same as those of other faiths. Each religion has its own unique doctrines and history.

These are not bases for criticism but rather a test of our tolerance. Religious tolerance would be a shallow principle indeed if it were reserved only for faiths with which we agree.

There are some who would have a presidential candidate describe and explain his church's distinctive doctrines. To do so would enable the very religious test the founders prohibited in the Constitution. No candidate should become the spokesman for his faith. For if he becomes President he will need the prayers of the people of all faiths.

I believe that every faith I have encountered draws its adherents closer to God. And in every faith I have come to know, there are features I wish were in my own: I love the profound ceremony of the Catholic Mass, the approachability of God in the prayers of the Evangelicals, the tenderness of spirit among the Pentecostals, the confident independence of the Lutherans, the ancient traditions of the Jews, unchanged through the ages, and the commitment to frequent prayer of the Muslims. As I travel across the country and see our towns and cities, I am always moved by the many houses of worship with their steeples, all pointing to heaven, reminding us of the source of life's blessings.

It is important to recognise that while differences in theology exist between the churches in America, we share a common creed of moral convictions. And where the affairs of our nation are concerned, it's usually a sound rule to focus on the latter – on the great moral principles that urge us all on a common course. Whether it was the cause of abolition, or civil rights, or the right to life itself, no movement of conscience can succeed in America that cannot speak to the convictions of religious people.

We separate church and state affairs in this country, and for good reason. No religion should dictate to the state nor should the state interfere with the free practice of religion. But in recent years, the notion of the separation of church and state has been taken by some well beyond its original meaning. They seek to remove from the public domain any acknowledgment of God. Religion is seen as merely a private affair with no place in public life. It is as if they are intent on establishing a new religion in America – the religion of secularism. They are wrong.

The founders proscribed the establishment of a state religion, but they did not countenance the elimination of religion from the public square. We are a nation 'Under God' and in God, we do indeed trust.

We should acknowledge the Creator as did the Founders – in ceremony and word. He should remain on our currency, in our pledge, in the teaching of our history, and during the holiday season, nativity scenes and menorahs should be welcome in our public places. Our greatness would not long endure without judges who respect the foundation of faith upon which our Constitution rests. I will take care to separate the affairs of government from any religion, but I will not separate us from 'the God who gave us liberty'.

Nor would I separate us from our religious heritage. Perhaps the most important question to ask a person of faith who seeks a political office, is this: does he share these American values: the equality of humankind, the obligation to serve one another, and a steadfast commitment to liberty?

They are not unique to any one denomination. They belong to the great moral inheritance we hold in common. They are the firm ground on which Americans of different faiths meet and stand as a nation, united.

We believe that every single human being is a child of God – we are all part of the human family. The conviction of the inherent and inalienable worth of every life is still the most revolutionary political proposition ever advanced. John Adams put it that we are 'thrown into the world all equal and alike'.

The consequence of our common humanity is our responsibility to one another, to our fellow Americans foremost, but also to every child of God. It is an obligation which is fulfilled by Americans every day, here and across the globe, without regard to creed or race or nationality.

Americans acknowledge that liberty is a gift of God, not an indulgence of government. No people in the history of the world have sacrificed as much for liberty. The lives of hundreds of thousands of America's sons and daughters were laid down during the last century to preserve freedom, for us and for freedom-loving people throughout the world. America took nothing from that century's terrible wars – no land from Germany or Japan or Korea; no treasure; no oath of fealty. America's resolve in the defence of liberty has been tested time and again. It has not been found wanting, nor must it ever be. America must never falter in holding high the banner of freedom.

These American values, this great moral heritage, is shared and lived in my religion as it is in yours. I was taught in my home to honour God and love my neighbour. I saw my father march with Martin Luther King. I saw my parents provide compassionate care to others, in personal ways to people nearby, and in just as consequential ways in leading national volunteer movements. I am moved by the Lord's words: 'For I was an hungered, and ye gave me meat: I was thirsty, and ye gave me drink: I was a stranger, and ye took me in: naked, and ye clothed me...'

My faith is grounded on these truths. You can witness them in Ann's and my marriage and in our family. We are a long way from perfect and we have surely stumbled along the way, but our aspirations, our values, are the self-same as those from the other faiths that stand upon this common foundation. And these convictions will indeed inform my presidency.

Today's generations of Americans have always known religious liberty. Perhaps we forget the long and arduous path our nation's forbears took to achieve it. They came here from England to seek freedom of religion. But upon finding it for themselves, they at first denied it to others. Because of their diverse beliefs,

Ann Hutchinson was exiled from Massachusetts Bay, a banished Roger Williams founded Rhode Island, and two centuries later, Brigham Young set out for the West. Americans were unable to accommodate their commitment to their own faith with an appreciation for the convictions of others to different faiths. In this, they were very much like those of the European nations they had left.

It was in Philadelphia that our founding fathers defined a revolutionary vision of liberty, grounded on self-evident truths about the equality of all, and the inalienable rights with which each is endowed by his Creator.

We cherish these sacred rights, and secure them in our constitutional order. Foremost do we protect religious liberty, not as a matter of policy, but as a matter of right. There will be no established church, and we are guaranteed the free exercise of our religion.

I'm not sure that we fully appreciate the profound implications of our tradition of religious liberty. I have visited many of the magnificent cathedrals in Europe. They are so inspired, so grand, so empty. Raised up over generations, long ago, so many of the cathedrals now stand as the postcard backdrop to societies just too busy or too 'enlightened' to venture inside and kneel in prayer. The establishment of state religions in Europe did no favour to Europe's churches. And though you will find many people of strong faith there, the churches themselves seem to be withering away.

Infinitely worse is the other extreme, the creed of conversion by conquest: violent Jihad, murder as martyrdom ... killing Christians, Jews, and Muslims with equal indifference. These radical Islamists do their preaching not by reason or example, but in the coercion of minds and the shedding of blood. We face no greater danger today than theocratic tyranny, and the boundless suffering these states and groups could inflict if given the chance.

The diversity of our cultural expression, and the vibrancy of our religious dialogue, has kept America in the forefront of civilised nations even as others regard religious freedom as something to be destroyed.

In such a world, we can be deeply thankful that we live in a land where reason and religion are friends and allies in the cause of liberty, joined against the evils and dangers of the day. And you can be certain of this: any believer in religious freedom, any person who has knelt in prayer to the Almighty, has a friend and ally in me. And so it is for hundreds of millions of our countrymen: we do not insist on a single strain of religion – rather, we welcome our nation's symphony of faith.

Recall the early days of the First Continental Congress in Philadelphia, during the fall of 1774. With Boston occupied by British troops, there were rumours of imminent hostilities and fears of an impending war. In this time of peril, someone suggested that they pray. But there were objections. They were too divided in religious sentiments, what with Episcopalians and Quakers, Anabaptists and

Congregationalists, Presbyterians and Catholics. Then Sam Adams rose, and said he would hear a prayer from anyone of piety and good character, as long as they were a patriot. And so together they prayed, and together they fought, and together, by the grace of God, they founded this great nation. In that spirit, let us give thanks to the divine author of liberty. And together, let us pray that this land may always be blessed with freedom's holy light. God bless this great land, the United States of America.

SARAH PALIN

'A GROUND UP CALL TO ACTION'

—

REMARKS AT THE INAUGURAL
TEA PARTY CONVENTION

NASHVILLE, TENNESSEE, 6 FEBRUARY 2010

Sarah Louise Palin, born in Idaho in 1964, moved to Alaska with her family as a baby. After studying in Hawaii and Idaho, she returned to Wasilla, Alaska. In 1992, Palin embarked on a political career, winning election to Wasilla City Council as a Republican. Four years later, she was elected Mayor of Wasilla, and in 2002, ran in the Republican primary for Lieutenant Governor, coming second in a field of five candidates. In 2006, she was elected as Alaska's first female Governor. Two years later, Senator John McCain shocked the press and public by selecting her as his Vice-Presidential nominee, making Palin both the first woman to run on a Republican national ticket, and the first Alaskan to be nominated by either major party in a Presidential election. Although her nomination and a well-received convention address provided a brief poll boost for McCain's campaign, Palin appeared ill-informed when subjected to intensive interviews. Criticised for lacking foreign policy experience or knowledge, she invoked Alaska's proximity to Russian-held territory in her defence, and seemed incapable of providing a specific response when asked what newspapers she read. Rumours abounded of conflict between the Palin and McCain camps, and later reports claimed that she seemed bored and depressed during briefing sessions.

In July 2009, Palin resigned from the Governorship, intensifying the debate as to whether she was preparing for a Presidential campaign in 2012. She has not, however, entered the race, and since her resignation, has focused on authorship and media appearances, publishing two bestselling books and presenting the TV series 'Sarah Palin's Alaska'. As the 2012 Republican primary race remains competitive, some pundits have suggested the possibility that a deadlocked Republican convention might turn to Governor Palin as a draft nominee. Such a draft, however, has not occurred since the nomination of Democrat Hubert Humphrey in 1968, following the assassination of Bobby Kennedy.

Palin has also endorsed the populist Tea Party movement, launched in 1999 as a loose coalition of conservatives and libertarians disaffected with the current political system. The name is drawn from the Boston Tea Party of 1773, a rebellion against the taxation policies of King George III. Much like the Occupy Movement, there is a level of anger and disappointment that defines the Tea Party. Also, like the Occupy Movement, the Tea Party movement covers a broad array of issues which do not reflect the views of every member.

Palin's appearance at this event generated much press coverage, especially when she said that the movement was the future of America. Please note the conversational, folksy style, verbalising an outsider's status and an accessibility that separates the Tea Party from the two mainstream, hierarchical political organisations. The appeal here is to the common man, the American who feels left out but wants to get involved. Supposedly, the speech was made without notes. However, reporters concentrated on filming her hands during this speech. She had scribbled notes on them. One Democratic Party activist in Virginia, Sandra Sterne, said that, 'Far from speaking off the cuff, Palin spoke off the palm.'

Sometimes the sentences are incomplete but note the style in this speech: warm, informal, conversational, patriotic, unapologetic. Some of the thoughts are unfinished, incomplete or interrupted in the flow of narrative. Palin and the Tea Party are outsiders, hoping to reclaim the spirit of the American Founding Fathers and to kick out current political leaders, often regardless of party. The language is about empowerment, less taxation, fewer regulations and more accountability to voters.

———

I am so proud to be an American! Thank you so much for being here tonight!

Do you love your freedom?!

If you love your freedom, think of that.

Any of you here serving in uniform, past or present, raise your hand. We're going to thank you for our freedom. God bless you guys! We salute you! We honour you. Thank you.

I am so proud to be American. Thank you. Gosh, thank you.

Happy birthday, Ronald Reagan!

Well, a special hello to the C-SPAN viewers. You may not be welcome in those health care negotiations, but you have an invitation to the Tea Party.

Very good to be here in Tennessee, the volunteer state. It's the home of good country music and good southern barbecue and – great to be at the Tea Party

Convention. I guess down here that's some southern sweet tea. And you know up in Alaska, we have a smaller version of Tea Party up there. We call it 'iced tea'. And I am a big supporter of this movement. I believe in this movement. Got lots of friends and family in the lower 48 who attend these events and across the country just knowing that this is the movement and America is ready for another revolution – and you are a part of this.

I look forward to attending more Tea Party events in the near future. It is just so inspiring to see real people – not politicos, not inside-the-Beltway professionals – come out and stand up and speak out for common-sense conservative principles.

And today, I want to start off with a special shout-out to American's newest Senator, thanks to you, Scott Brown (recently elected a Senator from Massachusetts). Now in many ways Scott Brown represents what this beautiful movement is all about. You know, he was just a guy with a truck and a passion to serve our country. He looked around and he saw that things weren't quite right in Washington. So, he stood up and he decided that he was going to do his part to put our government back on the side of the people. And it took guts. And it took a lot of hard work. But with grassroots support, Scott Brown carried the day.

And it has been so interesting now to watch the aftermath of the Massachusetts Chowder Revolution. The White House blames the candidate – their candidate. And Nancy Pelosi, she blamed the Senate Democrats. And Rahm Emanuel, he criticised a pollster. And yet again, President Obama found some way to make this all about George Bush. You know, considering the recent conservative election sweep, it's time that they stop blaming everyone else. When you're 0-for-3, you'd better stop lecturing and start listening.

The only place that the left hasn't placed the blame is on their agenda. So, some advice for our friends on that side of the aisle: that's where you got to look because that's what got you into this mess – the Obama–Pelosi–Reid agenda. It's going to leave us less secure, more in debt, and more under the thumb of big government. And that is out of touch, and it's out of date. And if Scott Brown is any indication, it's running out of time.

Because from Virginia to New Jersey to Massachusetts, voters are sending a message up and down the East Coast and in good places like Nevada and Connecticut and Colorado, Michigan, North Dakota – they've got the Liberal left – that establishment – running scared. The bottom line is this: it's been a year now. They own this now and voters are going to hold them accountable. Because out here in the cities and in the towns across this great country, we know that we've got some big problems to solve. We've gotten tired now of looking backward. We want to look forward. And from here, my friends, the – the future – it looks really good. It looks really good because if there's hope in Massachusetts, there's hope everywhere.

Brown's victory – it's exciting, and it's a sign of more good things to come. A lot of great common-sense conservative candidates, they're going to put it all on the line in 2010. This year, there are going to be some tough primaries. And I think that's good. Competition in these primaries is good. Competition makes us work harder and be more efficient and produce more. And I hope you'll get out there and work hard for the candidates who reflect your values, your priorities – because despite what the pundits want you to think, contested primaries aren't civil war. They're democracy at work, and that's beautiful.

I was the product of a competitive primary where, running for governor, I faced five guys in the party, and we put our ideas and our experience out there on the table for a debate, and then we allowed, of course, the voters to decide. And that is a healthy process, and it gives Americans the kind of leadership that they want and deserve. And so in 2010, I tip my hat to anyone with the courage to throw theirs in the ring, and may the best ideas and candidates win.

But while I hope that you're going to give these candidates that you choose your best effort, please understand that they're human. There's no perfect candidate, and they're going to disappoint occasionally. And when they do, let them know, but don't get discouraged and sit it out, because the stakes are too high. The stakes are too high right now, and your voice is too important. So work hard for these candidates, but put your faith in ideas.

And in that spirit, I caution against allowing this movement to be defined by any one leader or politician. The Tea Party movement is not a top-down operation. It's a ground-up call to action that is forcing both parties to change the way that they're doing business, and that's beautiful. This is about the people. This is about the people, and it's bigger than any king or queen of a Tea Party. And it's a lot bigger than any charismatic guy with a teleprompter.

The soul of this movement is the people – everyday Americans who grow our food and run our small businesses, teach our kids, and fight our wars. They're folks in small towns and cities across this great nation who saw what was happening – and they saw and were concerned, and they got involved. Like you, they go to town hall meetings, and they write op-eds. They run for local office. You all have the courage to stand up and speak out. You have a vision for the future, one that values conservative principles and common-sense solutions. And if that sounds like you, then you probably too are feeling a bit discouraged by what you see in Washington, DC.

Now in recent weeks, many of us have grown even more uneasy about our administration's approach to national security, the most important role ascribed to our federal government. Let me say, too, it's not politicising our security to discuss our concerns, because Americans deserve to know the truth about the threats that we face and what the administration is or isn't doing about them. So let's talk about them.

New terms used like 'overseas contingency operation' instead of the word 'war'. That reflects a worldview that is out of touch with the enemy that we face. We can't spin our way out of this threat. It's one thing to call a pay raise a job created or saved. It's quite another to call the devastation that a homicide bomber can inflict a 'manmade disaster'. And I just say, come on, Washington. If nowhere else, national security – that's one place where you got to call it like it is.

And in that spirit we should acknowledge that on Christmas Day, the system did not work. Abdul Mutallab passed through airport security with a bomb, and he boarded a flight hell-bent on killing innocent passengers. This terrorist trained in Yemen with al Qaeda, his American visa was not revoked until after he tried to kill hundreds of passengers. On Christmas Day, the only thing that stopped this terrorist was blind luck and brave passengers. Really, it was a Christmas miracle, and that is not the way that the system is supposed to work.

What followed was equally disturbing. After he was captured, he was questioned for only fifty minutes. We had a choice in how to do this. The choice was, only question him for fifty minutes and then read his Miranda Rights. The administration says then, there are no downsides or upsides to treating terrorists like civilian criminal defendants.

But a lot of us would beg to differ. For example, there are questions we would have liked this foreign terrorist to answer before he lawyered up and invoked our US Constitutional right to remain silent. *Our* US Constitutional rights. Our rights that you, sir [to male veteran in audience], fought and were willing to die for to protect in our Constitution. The rights that my son, as an infantry-man in the United States Army, is willing to die for. The protections provided – thanks to you, sir – we're going to bestow them on a terrorist who hates our Constitution and tries to destroy our Constitution and our country? This makes no sense because we have a choice in how we're going to deal with the terrorists. We don't have to go down that road.

There are questions that we would have like answered before he lawyered up like: 'Where exactly were you trained and by whom? You – you're bragging about all these other terrorists just like you. Who are they? When and where will they try to strike next? The events surrounding the Christmas Day plot reflect the kind of thinking that led to September 11th. That ... the ... threat then, as the USS *Cole* was attacked, our embassies were attacked, it was treated like an international crime spree, not like an act of war. We're seeing that mindset again settle into Washington. That scares me for my children and for your children. Treating this like a mere law enforcement matter places our country at grave risk. Because that's not how radical Islamic extremists are looking at this. They know we're at war. And to win that war, we need a Commander-in-Chief, not a professor of law standing at the lectern.

It's that same kind of misguided thinking that is seen throughout the administration's foreign policy decisions. Our President spent a year reaching out to hostile regimes, writing personal letters to dangerous dictators, and apologising for America. And what do we have to show for that? Here's what we have to show. North Korea tested nuclear weapons and longer-range ballistic missiles. Israel, a friend and a critical ally, now question[s] the strength of our support. Plans for a missile defence system in Europe? They've been scrapped. Relations with China and Russia are no better. And relations with Japan – that key Asian ally – they're in the worse shape in years.

And around the world, people who are seeking freedom from oppressive regimes wonder if America is still that beacon of hope for their cause. The administration cut support for democracy programmes, and where the President has not been clear, I ask, where is his clear and where is his strong voice of support for the Iranians who are risking all in their opposition to [Iranian President Mahmoud] Ahmadinejad? Just that shortlist – that shortlist. And you know, it's no wonder that our President only spent about 9 per cent of his State of the Union Address discussing national security and foreign policy, because there aren't a whole lot of victories that he could talk about that night. And that's just a shortlist.

There are so many challenges in front of us, and it can seem overwhelming. But despite these challenges, we have hope that we can move things in the right direction. But it's going to require the administration to change course. We need a foreign policy that distinguishes America's friends from her enemies and recognises the true nature of the threats that we face.

We need a strong national defence. I think you would agree with me – Reagan used to talk about that 'peace through strength'. And in that respect, I applaud the President for following at least a part of the recommendations made by our commanders on the ground to send in some more reinforcements to Afghanistan. Now though, he, we, must spend less time courting our adversaries, spending more time working with our allies. And we must build effective coalitions capable of confronting dangerous regimes like Iran and North Korea. It's time for more than just tough talk. Just like you – probably just so tired of hearing the talk, talk, talk. Tired of hearing the talk.

It's time for some tough actions, like sanctions on Iran. And in places in the world where people are struggling and oppressed and they're fighting for freedom, America must stand with them. We need a clear foreign policy that stands with the people and for democracy – one that reflects both our values and our interests, and it is in our best interests, because democracies – they don't go to war with each other. They can settle their differences peacefully.

The lesson of the last year is this: foreign policy can't be managed through the politics of personality. And our President would do well to take note of an observation John F. Kennedy had made once he was in office: that all the world's problems aren't his predecessor's fault. The problems that we face in the real world require real solutions. And we'd better get to it, because the risks that they pose are great and they're grave. However, as Barry Goldwater said: 'We can be conquered by bombs ... but we can also be conquered by neglect by ignoring our constitution and disregarding the principles of limited government.'

And in the past year, his words rang true. Washington has now replaced private irresponsibility with public irresponsibility. The list of companies and industries that the government is crowding out and bailing out and taking over, it continues to grow. First it was the banks, mortgage companies, financial institutions, then automakers. Soon, if they had their way, health care, student loans.

Today, in the words of Congressman Paul Ryan, the 700 billion dollar 'TARP [Troubled Asset Relief Program] has morphed into crony capitalism at its worse'. And it's becoming a 'slush fund' for the Treasury Department's favourite big players, just as we had been warned about. And while people on Main Street look for jobs, people on Wall Street – they're collecting billions and billions in your bailout bonuses. Among the top seventeen companies that received your bailout money, 92 per cent of the senior officers and directors – they still have their good jobs.

And everyday Americans are wondering: Where are the consequences? They helped to get us into this worst economic situation since the Great Depression. Where are the consequences?

When Washington passed a $787 billion 'stimulus bill', we were nervous because they just spent $700 billion to bail out Wall Street. And on the state level, as a governor, we knew that a lot of that money came with fat strings attached. The federal government was going to have more control over our states. They were going to disrespect the 10th Amendment of our Constitution by essentially bribing us with, 'Take this federal money' (and then we're going to be able to mandate a few more things on you though).

I joined with other conservative governors around the nation in rejecting some of those dollars. Legislators – turned out to be, though, nothing for applause because – nothing to applaud because – legislators then were threatening lawsuits if governors didn't take the money. And I vetoed some of the funds – I knew we couldn't maintain the programmes, that we were going to pay for it with these – these borrowed, printed up, invented dollars out of nowhere. But lawsuits were threatened – even in Alaska, in a Republican-controlled legislature, my veto was overridden and the money poured into those states. And I believe we will see this play out in our states: the federal government will have taken more control over the people who live in our states.

Now I understand wanting to believe that this is all free money. And for some I guess it's tough to tell people 'no' in tough times. Plus, remember our administration promised that it would be good stewards of taxpayer dollars.

Remember? Remember Vice President [Joe] Biden. He was put in charge of a tough, unprecedented oversight effort. That's how it was introduced. You know why? Because nobody messes with Joe.

Now, this was all part of that hope and change and transparency. And now a year later I've got to ask those supporters of all that: How's that hopey-changey stuff working out for you? See, I tried to look into that transparency thing, but Joe's meetings with the transparency and accountability board – it was closed to the public. Yeah, they held the transparency meeting behind closed doors. So, not sure if anybody's messing with Joe, but here is what I do know: a lot of that stimulus cash – it ended up in some pretty odd places, including districts that didn't even exist; and programmes that really don't have a whole lot to do with stimulating the economy.

Nearly $6 million was given to a Democrat pollster who had already made millions during the Democrats' presidential primary. Nearly $10 million was spent to update the stimulus web site. And one state even spent a million bucks to put up signs that advertised that they were spending the federal stimulus projects. Or as someone put it: This was a million-dollar effort using your money to tell you it's spending your money. And it didn't create a single job.

These uses of stimulus funds don't sound targeted and they don't sound timely, as we were promised. They just sound wasteful. And in the case of those signs, kind of ridiculous. All of that – I don't know about you, but seeing those cheques written for some of these pet projects of Congressmen and those in the White House – did you feel very stimulated?

And then it turns out that Washington got the price tag wrong. All of these projects and programmes, they cost tens and tens of billions of dollars more than we were told. It's now closer to $860 billion. Add this to the fact that the White House can't even tell us how many jobs were actually created. Depending on who you ask, it's anywhere from thousands to two million.

But one number we are sure of is the unemployment number. And that's at 9.7, which is well above the 8 per cent mark that we were promised our stimulus package would go to avoid. And underemployment now is 16.5 per cent. You've got all these people who have just kind of given up right now, and they're not even enrolling in some of these programmes. Tough to count them.

Folks, I won't go into all of it tonight, but the list of broken promises is long. Candidate Obama pledged to end closed-door, sweetheart deals and no-bid contracts once and for all. But just last month his administration awarded a $25 million no-bid contract to a Democrat donor. Is that hope? Nope. It's not hope.

That's the same old, same old in Washington, DC. And instead of changing the way Washington does business, we got the 'Cornhusker Kickback' and the 'Louisiana Purchase' and millions of tax breaks for union bosses' desires. The promised ban on lobbyists in this new administration, he handed out waivers left and right, and there are more than forty former lobbyists who now work at the top levels in this administration. And these days most members of Congress, they don't get to read the bill before they have to vote on it, much less the pledge that a bill wouldn't be signed into law until we all had five days to review it online.

So see, it's easy to understand why Americans are shaking their heads when Washington has broken trust with the people that these politicians are (supposed) to be serving. We're drowning in national debt and many of us have had enough.

Now the foundational principles in all of this, it's easy to understand. It really is – even though I think DC would just love for us to believe that this is all way over our heads. Somebody in Tennessee, somebody up there in Alaska, she'll never understand what we're talking about here in DC. No, this is all pretty simple stuff. When our families, when our small businesses, we start running our finances into the red, what do we do? We tighten our belts and we cut back budgets. Isn't that what we teach our children – to live within our means? It's what [husband] Todd and I do when we have to make payroll, buy new equipment for our commercial fishing business. We have to plan for the future, meet a budget.

But in Washington, why is it just the opposite of that? This week, they unveiled a record-busting, mind-boggling $3.8 trillion federal budget. And they keep borrowing, and they keep printing these dollars, and they keep making us more and more beholden to foreign countries, and they keep making us take these steps towards insolvency. Now what they're doing in proposing these big new programmes with giant price tags, they're sticking our kids with the bill. And that's immoral. That's generational theft. We're stealing the opportunities from our children.

And freedom lovers around this country need to be aware that all of this makes us more beholden to other countries. It makes us less secure. It makes us less free. And that should tick us off. So folks, with all these serious challenges ahead, we've got private-sector job creation that has got to take place and got these economic woes and – and health care, the war on terror.

But as the saying goes, if you can't ride two horses at once, you shouldn't be in the circus. So here's some advice for those in DC who want to shine in the greatest show on earth. Too often when big government and big business get together and cronyism sets in, well, it benefits insiders, not everyday Americans. The administration and Congress should do what we did up there in Alaska when the good old boys started making back room deals that were benefiting big oil and not the citizens of the state. And the citizens of the state then, Alaskans, we got together and we put government back on the side of the people. And a lot of the bigwigs, they started getting in trouble and some of the bigwigs ended up going to jail over their back room deals.

Our government needs to adopt a pro-market agenda that doesn't pick winners and losers, but it invites competition and it levels the playing field for everyone. Washington has got to, across the board, lower taxes for small businesses so that our mom and pops can reinvest and hire people so that our businesses can thrive. They should support competition, support innovation, reward hard work.

And they should do all that they can to make sure that the game is fair without that undue corrupt influence. And then they need to get government out of the way. If they would do this, our economy, it would roar back to life and for instance on health care, we need bipartisan solutions to help families, not increase taxes. Remember that red reset button that America through Secretary Clinton, she gave to Putin. Remember that? I think we should ask for that back and hand it instead to Congress. And say, no, start all over on this health care scheme and pass meaningful, market-based reforms that incorporate some simple steps that have broad support – the best ideas, not back room deals but things like insurance purchases across state lines and the tort reform that we've talked about.

Those things that are common-sense steps towards reform that the White House and leaders on the Democrats' side of the aisle in Congress, they don't want to consider. So it makes you wonder, what truly is their motivation? What is their intention if they won't consider even these common-sense, broad-based support ideas that would work? And to create jobs. Washington should jumpstart energy projects. I said it during the campaign and I'll say it now: We need an 'all of the above' approach to energy policy. That means proven conventional resource development and support for nuclear power. And I was thankful that the President at least mentioned nuclear power in the State of the Union.

But, again, we need more than words. We need a plan to turn that goal into a reality and that way we can pave the way for projects that will create jobs. Those are real job creators and deliver carbon-free energy. And while we're at it, let's expedite the regulatory and permitting and legal processes for on- and offshore drilling. Instead of paying billions of dollars, hundreds of billions of dollars that now are being sent to foreign regimes, we should be drilling here and drilling now instead of relying on them to develop their resources for us. So what we've got to do is axe that plan for cap-and-tax, that policy that's going to kill jobs and is going to pass the burden of paying for it onto our working families.

And finally, if we're going to get serious about fiscal restraint, then we've got to make Washington start walking the walk. After putting us on a track to quadruple the deficit, the proposed spending freeze, maybe it's a start, but it's certainly not enough. As Senator John Thune said, it's like putting a Band-Aid on a self-inflicted gunshot wound.

We need to go further. Cut spending. Don't just simply slow down a spending spree. And we've got to axe the plans for a second stimulus when the first hasn't even been measured for any success yet. Kill the plans for the second stimulus and be aware that now that second stimulus is being referred to as a 'jobs bill'. Now these aren't the only ways to rein in spending, and alone, they're not going to be enough, not enough to tackle the insane debt and the deficits that we face. But they are a good way to start and to show that we're serious about getting our financial house in order.

Now like a lot of you, perhaps, I have spent the last year thinking about how – how to best serve. How – How can I help our country? How can I make sure that I, that you, that we're not in a position of nobody being able to succeed? When they try to tell us to sit down and shut up, how can we best serve? In 2008, I had the honour – really of a lifetime – the honour of a lifetime, running alongside John McCain. I ... look at him as an American hero. And nearly sixty million Americans voted for us. They cast their ballot for the things that we are talking about tonight: lower taxes, smaller government, transparency, energy independence and strong national security.

And while no, our votes did not carry the day, it was still a call to serve our country. Those voters wanted us to keep on fighting and take the gloves off. And they wanted common-sense conservative solutions. And they wanted us to keep on debating. And each of us who is here today, we're living proof that you don't need an office or a title to make a difference. And you don't need a proclaimed leader, as if we're all just a bunch of sheep and we're looking for a leader to progress this movement.

That is what we're fighting for. It is what we are fighting about. It is what we believe in and that's what this movement is all about. When people are willing to meet halfway and stand up for common-sense solutions and values, then we want to work with them. And in that spirit, I applaud Independents and Democrats like Bart Stupak who stood up to tough partisan pressure and he wanted to protect the sanctity of life and the rights of the soon to be born. I applaud him for that.

When we can work together, we will. But when the work of Washington violates our – our conscience – and when the work and efforts in Washington, DC, violate our Constitution, then we will stand up and we will be counted – because we are the loyal opposition. And we have a vision for the future of our country, too, and it is a vision anchored in time-tested truths: that the government that governs least, governs best. And that the Constitution – the Constitution provides the best road map towards a more perfect union. And that only a limited government can expand prosperity and opportunity for all. And that freedom is a God-given right and it is worth fighting for. God bless you. And that America's finest, our men and women in uniform, are a force for good throughout the world – and that is nothing to apologise for.

These are enduring truths and these enduring truths have been passed down from Washington to Lincoln to Reagan and now to you. But while this movement, our roots there, in our spirit, too, they are historic. The current form of this movement is fresh and it's young and it's fragile. We are now the keepers of an honourable tradition of conservative values and good works. And we must never forget that it is a sacred trust to carry these ideas forward. It demands civility and it requires decent, constructive, issue-oriented debate.

Opponents of this message, they're seeking to marginalise this movement. They want to paint us as ideologically extreme and the counterpoint to liberal intolerance and outrageous conspiracy theorists aimed at our own government and unethical shameless tactics like considering a candidate's children fair game.

But unlike the elitists who denounce this movement – they just don't want to hear the message – I've travelled across this great country and I've talked to the patriotic men and women who make up the Tea Party movement. And they are good and kind and selfless and they are deeply concerned about our country. And today I ask only this: let's make this movement a tribute to their good example and make it worthy of their hard work and their support.

Do not let us have our heads turned from the important work before us and do not give others an excuse to be able to turn their eyes from this. Let us not get bogged down in the small squabbles. Let us get caught up in the big ideas.

To do so would be a fitting tribute to Ronald Reagan, especially tonight, as he would have turned ninety-nine. No longer with us, his spirit lives on and his American dream endures. He knew the best of our country is not all gathered in Washington, DC. It is here in our communities where families live, and children learn, and children with special needs are welcomed in this world and embraced. And thank you for that.

The best of America can be found in places where patriots are brave enough and free enough to be able to stand up and speak up; and where small businesses grow our economy one job at a time; and folks like Reagan, we know that America is still that 'shining city on a hill'. I do believe that God 'shed his grace on thee'. We know that our best days are yet to come. Tea Party Nation, we know that there is nothing wrong with America that together we can't fix as Americans.

So from the bottom of my heart and speaking on behalf of millions and millions and millions of Americans who want to encourage this movement, this movement is about the people. Who can argue [with] a movement that is about the people and for the people? Remember, all political power is inherent in the people, and government is supposed to be working for the people. That is what this movement is about.

From the bottom of my heart, I thank you for being part of the solution. God bless you, Tea Partiers and God bless the USA. Thank you. God bless you guys.

CHRIS CHRISTIE

'EARNED AMERICAN EXCEPTIONALISM'

—

REMARKS AT THE RONALD REAGAN
PRESIDENTIAL LIBRARY

SIMI VALLEY, CALIFORNIA, 27 SEPTEMBER 2011

H*older of a Bachelor of Arts degree from the University of Delaware and a Juris Doctor from Seton Hall University School of Law, Chris Christie was admitted to the New Jersey State Bar and the Bar of the United States District Court, District of New Jersey, in 1987. In private practice, he specialised in election law, appellate practice, securities and government affairs. His political career began in 1994, with his election to the Morris County Board of Chosen Freeholders. In 1995, he ran in the Republican primary for a seat in the New Jersey General Assembly, but was heavily defeated by the incumbent. Returning to the private sector, he worked as a lobbyist for some years, until his nomination as United States Attorney for New Jersey in 2001. Although objections were raised to his nomination, owing to his lack of prosecutorial experience and active role as a fundraiser for President George W. Bush's 2000 Presidential campaign, he was unanimously confirmed by the US Senate, taking office in January 2002. He soon proved an effective public prosecutor, winning a number of high-profile corruption cases in a state famed for political malfeasance and abuse of public funds. In the 2009 off-year elections, Christie announced his candidacy for the Governorship of New Jersey, defeating incumbent Democrat John Corzine by a slim margin.*

A Republican with a populist rhetorical touch and a quick-witted bruiser in debate, Christie has been mentioned as a possible candidate for higher office. In 2011 he said he would not seek the presidential nomination in 2012, but, like Palin, is considered a possible draft pick should no clear nominee emerge from the primaries. This speech at the Ronald Reagan Library was examined for his analysis of the

Obama administration and his vision for the future of America. It became a hit with
Republicans looking for a Reaganesque leader for future national elections. This is a
speech that will be examined for years to come.

—

Mrs Reagan, distinguished guests. It is an honour for me to be here at the Reagan Library to speak to you today. I want to thank Mrs Reagan for her gracious invitation. I am thrilled to be here.

Ronald Reagan believed in this country. He embodied the strength, perseverance and faith that has propelled immigrants for centuries to embark on dangerous journeys to come here, to give up all that was familiar for all that was possible.

He judged that as good as things were and had been for many Americans, they could and would be better for more Americans in the future.

It is this vision for our country that guided his administration over the course of eight years. His commitment to making America stronger, better and more resilient is what allowed him the freedom to challenge conventional wisdom, reach across party lines and dare to put results ahead of political opportunism.

Everybody in this room and in countless other rooms across this great country has his or her favourite Reagan story. For me, that story happened thirty years ago, in August 1981. The air traffic controllers, in violation of their contracts, went on strike. President Reagan ordered them back to work, making clear that those who refused would be fired. In the end, thousands refused, and thousands were fired.

I cite this incident not as a parable of labour relations but as a parable of principle. Ronald Reagan was a man who said what he meant and meant what he said. Those who thought he was bluffing were sadly mistaken. Reagan's demand was not an empty political play; it was leadership, pure and simple.

Reagan said it best himself, 'I think it convinced people who might have thought otherwise that I meant what I said. Incidentally, I would have been just as forceful if I thought management had been wrong in the dispute.'

I recall this pivotal moment for another reason as well. Most Americans at the time and since no doubt viewed Reagan's firm handling of the PATCO [air traffic controllers' union] strike as a domestic matter, a confrontation between the president and a public sector union. But this misses a critical point.

To quote a phrase from another American moment, the whole world was watching. Thanks to newspapers and television – and increasingly the Internet and social media – what happens here doesn't stay here.

Another way of saying what I have just described is that Americans do not have the luxury of thinking that what we have long viewed as purely domestic matters have no consequences beyond our borders. To the contrary. What we say and what we do here at home affects how others see us and in turn affects what it is they say and do.

America's role and significance in the world is defined, first and foremost, by who we are at home. It is defined by how we conduct ourselves with each other. It is defined by how we deal with our own problems. It is determined in large measure by how we set an example for the world.

We tend to still understand foreign policy as something designed by officials in the State Department and carried out by ambassadors and others overseas. And to some extent it is. But one of the most powerful forms of foreign policy is the example we set.

This is where it is instructive to harken back to Ronald Reagan and the PATCO affair. President Reagan's willingness to articulate a determined stand and then carry it out at home sent the signal that the occupant of the Oval Office was someone who could be predicted to stand by his friends and stand up to his adversaries.

If President Reagan would do that at home, leaders around the world realised that he would do it abroad as well. Principle would not stop at the water's edge. The Reagan who challenged Soviet aggression, or who attacked a Libya that supported terror was the same Reagan who stood up years before to PATCO at home for what he believed was right.

All this should and does have meaning for us today. The image of the United States around the world is not what it was, it is not what it can be and it is not what it needs to be. This country pays a price whenever our economy fails to deliver rising living standards to our citizens – which is exactly what has been the case for years now.

We pay a price when our political system cannot come together and agree on the difficult but necessary steps to rein in entitlement spending or reform our tax system.

We pay a price when special interests win out over the collective national interest. We are seeing just this in the partisan divide that has so far made it impossible to reduce our staggering deficits and to create an environment in which there is more job creation than job destruction.

This is where the contrast between what has happened in New Jersey and what is happening in Washington, DC is the most clear.

In New Jersey over the last twenty months, you have actually seen divided government that is working. To be clear, it does not mean that we have no argument or acrimony. There are serious disagreements, sometimes expressed loudly – Jersey style.

Here is what we did. We identified the problems. We proposed specific means to fix them. We educated the public on the dire consequences of inaction. And we compromised, on a bipartisan basis, to get results. We took action.

How so, you ask? Leadership and compromise.

Leadership and compromise is the only way you can balance two budgets with over $13 billion in deficits without raising taxes while protecting core services.

Leadership and compromise is the only way you reform New Jersey's pension and health benefits system that was collectively $121 billion underfunded.

Leadership and compromise is the only way you cap the highest property taxes in the nation and cap the interest arbitration awards of some of the most powerful public sector unions in the nation at no greater than a 2 per cent increase.

In New Jersey we have done this, and more, because the executive branch has not sat by and waited for others to go first to suggest solutions to our state's most difficult problems.

Being a mayor, being a governor, being a President means leading by taking risk on the most important issues of the day. It has happened in Trenton.

In New Jersey we have done this with a legislative branch, held by the opposite party, because it is led by two people who have more often put the interests of our state above the partisan politics of their caucuses.

Our bipartisan accomplishments in New Jersey have helped to set a tone that has taken hold across many other states. It is a simple but powerful message – lead on the tough issues by telling your citizens the truth about the depth of our challenges. Tell them the truth about the difficulty of the solutions. This is the only effective way to lead in America during these times.

In Washington, on the other hand, we have watched as we drift from conflict to conflict, with little or no resolution.

We watch a President who once talked about the courage of his convictions, but still has yet to find the courage to lead.

We watch a Congress at war with itself because they are unwilling to leave campaign-style politics at the Capitol's door. The result is a debt ceiling limitation debate that made our democracy appear as if we could no longer effectively govern ourselves.

And still we continue to wait and hope that our President will finally stop being a bystander in the Oval Office. We hope that he will shake off the paralysis that has made it impossible for him to take on the really big things that are obvious to all Americans and to a watching and anxious world community.

Yes, we hope. Because each and every time the President lets a moment to act pass him by, his failure is our failure too. The failure to stand up for the bipartisan debt solutions of the Simpson Bowles Commission, a report the President asked for himself ... the failure to act on the country's crushing unemployment ... the failure to act on ever expanding and rapidly eroding entitlement programmes ... the failure to discern pork barrel spending from real infrastructure investment.

The rule for effective governance is simple. It is one Ronald Reagan knew by heart. And one that he successfully employed with Social Security and the Cold

War. When there is a problem, you fix it. That is the job you have been sent to do and you cannot wait for someone else to do it for you.

We pay for this failure of leadership many times over. The domestic price is obvious: growth slows, high levels of unemployment persist, and we make ourselves even more vulnerable to the unpredictable behaviour of skittish markets or the political decisions of lenders.

But, there is also a foreign policy price to pay. To begin with, we diminish our ability to influence the thinking and ultimately the behaviour of others. There is no better way to persuade other societies around the world to become more democratic and more market-oriented than to show that our democracy and markets work better than any other system.

Why should we care?

We should care because we believe, as President Reagan did, that democracy is the best protector of human dignity and freedom. And we know this because history shows that mature democracies are less likely to resort to force against their own people or their neighbours.

We should care because we believe in free and open trade, as exports are the best creators of high-paying jobs here and imports are a means to increase consumer choice and keep prices down.

Around the world – in the Middle East, in Asia, in Africa and Latin America – people are debating their own political and economic futures, right now.

We have a stake in the outcome of their debates. For example, a Middle East that is largely democratic and at peace will be a Middle East that accepts Israel, rejects terrorism, and is a dependable source of energy.

There is no better way to reinforce the likelihood that others in the world will opt for more open societies and economies than to demonstrate that our own system is working.

A lot is being said in this election season about American exceptionalism. Implicit in such statements is that we are different and, yes, better, in the sense that our democracy, our economy and our people have delivered. But for American exceptionalism to truly deliver hope and a sterling example to the rest of the world, it must be demonstrated, not just asserted. If it is demonstrated, it will be seen and appreciated and ultimately emulated by others. They will then be more likely to follow our example and our lead.

At one time in our history, our greatness was a reflection of our country's innovation, our determination, our ingenuity and the strength of our democratic institutions. When there was a crisis in the world, America found a way to come together to help our allies and fight our enemies. When there was a crisis at home, we put aside parochialism and put the greater public interest first. And in our system, we did it through strong presidential leadership. We did it through Reagan-like leadership.

Unfortunately, through our own domestic political conduct of late, we have failed to live up to our own tradition of exceptionalism. Today, our role and ability to affect change has been diminished because of our own problems and our inability to effectively deal with them.

To understand this clearly, one need only look at comments from the recent meeting of the European finance ministers in Poland. Here is what the Finance Minister of Austria had to say:

'I found it peculiar that, even though the Americans have significantly worse fundamental data than the Eurozone, that they tell us what we should do. I had expected that, when [Secretary Timothy Geithner] tells us how he sees the world, that he would listen to what we have to say.'

You see, without strong leadership at home – without our domestic house in order – we are taking ourselves out of the equation. Over and over, we are allowing the rest of the world to set the tone without American influence.

I understand full well that succeeding at home, setting an example, is not enough. The United States must be prepared to act. We must be prepared to lead. This takes resources – resources for defence, for intelligence, for homeland security, for diplomacy. The United States will only be able to sustain a leadership position around the world if the resources are there – but the necessary resources will only be there if the foundations of the American economy are healthy.

So our economic health is a national security issue as well.

Without the authority that comes from that exceptionalism – earned American exceptionalism – we cannot do good for other countries, we cannot continue to be a beacon of hope for the world to aspire to for their future generations.

If Ronald Reagan faced today's challenges we know what he would do. He would face our domestic problems directly, with leadership and without political calculation.

We would take an honest and tough approach to solving our long-term debt and deficit problem through reforming our entitlement programmes and our tax code.

We would confront our unemployment crisis by giving certainty to business about our tax and regulatory future.

We would unleash American entrepreneurship through long-term tax reform, not short-term tax gimmickry.

And we would reform our K-12 education system by applying free market reform principles to education – rewarding outstanding teachers; demanding accountability from everyone in the system; increasing competition through choice and charters; and making the American free public education system once again the envy of the world.

The guiding principle should be simple and powerful – the educational interests of children must always be put ahead of the comfort of the status quo for adults.

The United States must also become more discriminating in what we try to accomplish abroad. We certainly cannot force others to adopt our principles through coercion. Local realities count; we cannot have forced makeovers of other societies in our image. We need to limit ourselves overseas to what is in our national interest so that we can rebuild the foundations of American power here at home – foundations that need to be rebuilt in part so that we can sustain a leadership role in the world for decades to come.

The argument for getting our own house in order is not an argument for turning our back on the world.

We cannot and should not do that. First of all, our economy is dependent on what we export and import. And as we learned the hard way a decade ago, we as a country and a people are vulnerable to terrorists armed with box-cutters, bombs, and viruses, be they computer generated or man-made. We need to remain vigilant, and be prepared to act with our friends and allies, to discourage, deter or defend against traditional aggression; to stop the spread of nuclear materials and weapons and the means to deliver them; and to continue to deprive terrorists of the ways, means and opportunity to succeed.

I realise that what I am calling for requires a lot of our elected officials and a lot of our people. I plead guilty. But I also plead guilty to optimism.

Like Ronald Reagan, I believe in what this country and its citizens can accomplish if they understand what is being asked of them and how we all will benefit if they meet the challenge.

There is no doubt in my mind that we, as a country and as a people, are up for the challenge. Our democracy is strong; our economy is the world's largest. Innovation and risk-taking is in our collective DNA. There is no better place for investment. Above all, we have a demonstrated record as a people and a nation of rising up to meet challenges.

Today, the biggest challenge we must meet is the one we present to ourselves. To not become a nation that places entitlement ahead of accomplishment. To not become a country that places comfortable lies ahead of difficult truths. To not become a people that thinks so little of ourselves that we demand no sacrifice from each other. We are a better people than that; and we must demand a better nation than that.

The America I speak of is the America Ronald Reagan challenged us to be every day. Frankly, it is the America his leadership helped us to be. Through our conduct, our deeds, our demonstrated principles and our sacrifice for each other and for the greater good of the nation, we became a country emulated throughout the world. Not just because of what we said, but because of what we did both at home and abroad.

If we are to reach real American exceptionalism, American exceptionalism that can set an example for freedom around the world, we must lead with purpose and unity.

In 2004, Illinois State Senator Barack Obama gave us a window into his vision for American leadership. He said, 'Now even as we speak, there are those who are preparing to divide us – the spin masters, the negative ad pedlars who embrace the politics of "anything goes". Well, I say to them tonight, there is not a liberal America and a conservative America – there is the United States of America. There is not a Black America and a White America and Latino America and Asian America – there's the United States of America.'

Now, seven years later, President Obama prepares to divide our nation to achieve re-election. This is not a leadership style, this is a re-election strategy. Telling those who are scared and struggling that the only way their lives can get better is to diminish the success of others. Trying to cynically convince those who are suffering that the American economic pie is no longer a growing one that can provide more prosperity for all who work hard. Insisting that we must tax and take and demonise those who have already achieved the American Dream. That may turn out to be a good re-election strategy for President Obama, but is a demoralising message for America. What happened to State Senator Obama? When did he decide to become one of the 'dividers' he spoke of so eloquently in 2004? There is, of course, a different choice.

That choice is the way Ronald Reagan led America in the 1980s. That approach to leadership is best embodied in the words he spoke to the nation during his farewell address in 1989. He made clear he was not there just marking time. That he was there to make a difference. Then he spoke of the city on the hill and how he had made it stronger. He said, 'I've spoken of the shining city all my political life, but I don't know if I ever quite communicated what I saw when I said it. But in my mind it was a tall proud city built on rocks stronger than oceans, wind-swept, God-blessed, and teeming with people of all kinds living in harmony and peace, a city with free ports that hummed with commerce and creativity, and if there had to be city walls, the walls had doors and the doors were open to anyone with the will and the heart to get here. That's how I saw it and see it still.'

That is American exceptionalism. Not a punch line in a political speech, but a vision followed by a set of principled actions that made us the envy of the world. Not a re-election strategy, but an American revitalisation strategy.

We will be that again, but not until we demand that our leaders stand tall by telling the truth, confronting our shortcomings, celebrating our successes and, once again, leading the world because of what we have been able to actually accomplish.

Only when we do that will we finally ensure that our children and grandchildren will live in a second American century. We owe them, as well as ourselves and those who came before us, nothing less.

Thank you again for inviting me – God bless you and God bless the United States of America.

JOHN HOWARD

'UNBEARABLE GRIEF AND PAIN'

—

REMARKS AT THE BALI MEMORIAL SERVICE

AUSTRALIAN CONSULATE, BALI, 18 OCTOBER 2002

John Winston Howard sat in the Australian House of Representatives for over thirty years, holding the Division of Bennelong, New South Wales, for the Liberal Party. It must be noted that the 'Liberal Party' is something of a misnomer in this case, as the Australian 'Liberals' are in fact the mainstream party of the centre-right, and could well be deemed conservatives, alternating, as they do, as party of government and opposition with the left-wing Labour Party.

Howard served as Treasurer of Australia in the administration of Prime Minister Malcolm Fraser from 1977 to 1983. After Fraser's defeat in the 1983 election, Howard became deputy leader of the Opposition after losing the party leadership race to Andrew Peacock. After some years of intra-party tension, Peacock failed to dislodge Howard from the Deputy Leadership, and resigned, thus elevating Howard to the post of Liberal leader. The next thirteen years saw the party remaining on the opposition benches, with Peacock returning as leader, only to lose the post to Howard once again. Finally, in 1996, after a record thirteen years in opposition, the Liberal-National Coalition defeated the Labour government of Paul Keating. Howard remained in office as Prime Minister from 11 March 1996 to 3 December 2007, making him the second-longest serving Prime Minister in Australian history: however, upon his party's defeat in the 2007 election, he also became the second Prime Minister in Australian history to lose his Parliamentary seat while in office.

On 12 October 2002, bombs were detonated in the tourist spot of Katu on the Indonesian island of Bali. Eighty-eight Australians were killed in the attack, along with thirty-eight Indonesians. A further 210 people were injured. This act of terrorism has been called 'Australia's 9/11'.

Howard's comments, made in Bali, attempt to find meaning in these deaths and somehow heal a grieving nation.

—

As the sun sets over this beautiful island we gather here in sorrow, in anguish, in disbelief and in pain.

There are no words that I can summon to salve in any way the hurt and the suffering and the pain being felt by so many of my fellow countrymen and women and by so many of the citizens of other nations.

I can say, though, to my Australian countrymen and women, that there are 19 and a half million Australians who are trying, however inadequately, to feel for you and to support you at this time of unbearable grief and pain.

The wanton, cruel and barbaric character of what occurred last Saturday night has shocked our nation to the core and now the anguish that so many are feeling, the painful process of identification which has prolonged that agony for so many, the sense of bewilderment and disbelief that so many young lives with so much before them should have been taken away in such blind fury, hatred and violence...

I can on behalf of all the people of Australia declare to you that we will do everything in our power to bring to justice those who were responsible for this foul deed.

We will work with our friends in Indonesia to do that and we will work with others to achieve an outcome of justice.

Can I say to our Balinese friends, the lovely people of Bali, who have been befriended over the decades, by the generations of so many Australians who have come here, we grieve for you, we feel for you, we thank you from the bottom of our hearts for the love and support you have extended to our fellow countrymen and women over these past days.

As the chaplain said, there will be scars left on people for the rest of their life, both physical and emotional.

Our nation has been changed by this event.

Perhaps we may not be so carefree as we have been in the past, but we will never lose our openness, our sense of adventure.

The young of Australia will always travel, they will always seek fun in different parts of the world, they will always reach out to the young of other nations, they will always be open, fun-loving and decent men and women.

So as we grapple inadequately and in despair to try and comprehend what has happened, let us gather ourselves together, let us wrap our arms not only around our fellow Australians but our arms around the people of Indonesia, of Bali, let us wrap our arms around the people of other nations and the friends and relatives of the nationals of other countries who died in this horrible event.

It will take a long time for these foul deeds to be seen in any kind of context, they can never be understood, they can never be excused.

Australia has been affected very deeply but the Australian spirit has not been broken, the spirit remains strong and free and open and tolerant.

I know that is what all of those who lost their lives would have wanted and I know that is what those who grieve for them want.

MARGARET THATCHER

'FREEDOM AND OPPORTUNITY
FOR ORDINARY PEOPLE'

—

VIDEO EULOGY FOR RONALD REAGAN

NATIONAL CATHEDRAL, WASHINGTON, DC, 11 JUNE 2004

Margaret Thatcher was elected to Parliament as a Conservative representing Finchley in 1959. She served as Secretary of State for Education and Science under the late Prime Minister Sir Edward Heath. After Heath's loss of the 1974 general election, Thatcher challenged him for the party leadership in 1975, defeating the former Prime Minister on the first ballot, and his preferred successor, Willie Whitelaw, on the second, becoming Leader of the Opposition. Though she had once opined that Britain would not elect a female leader in her lifetime, Thatcher proved herself wrong in 1979, by dislodging the beleaguered Labour government of James Callaghan.

Margaret Thatcher was the longest-serving UK Prime Minister of the twentieth century, holding office from 1979 to 1990. She was appointed to the House of Lords as Baroness Thatcher of Kestaven in 1992. Her lingering influence on the British body politic is so profound that some dubbed reformist Labour leader Tony Blair 'the true inheritor of Thatcher's legacy'. Thatcher was a sworn anti-communist and anti-fascist, making her a natural ally of US President Ronald Reagan. This alliance manifested both in opposition to the pre-Perestroika Soviet Union, and, when both had left office, vocal support for Western intervention in the ethnic slaughter of the Bosnian war. In addition to shared ideals and ideology, Thatcher and Reagan always appeared to be warm natural friends.

Thatcher gave this eulogy to Ronald Reagan at his funeral in Washington, DC, via video. She sat in the audience near Mikhail Gorbachev, the former President of the Soviet Union. Thatcher summarises Reagan's accomplishments and his vision, as *well as his historic impact on world affairs and the advancement of freedom. She also argues that Reagan changed the way we think about government.*

———

We have lost a great President, a great American, and a great man. And I have lost a dear friend.

In his lifetime Ronald Reagan was such a cheerful and invigorating presence that it was easy to forget what daunting historic tasks he set himself. He sought to mend America's wounded spirit, to restore the strength of the free world, and to free the slaves of communism. These were causes hard to accomplish and heavy with risk.

Yet they were pursued with almost a lightness of spirit. For Ronald Reagan also embodied another great cause – what Arnold Bennett once called 'the great cause of cheering us all up'. His politics had a freshness and optimism that won converts from every class and every nation – and ultimately from the very heart of the evil empire.

Yet his humour often had a purpose beyond humour. In the terrible hours after the attempt on his life, his easy jokes gave reassurance to an anxious world. They were evidence that in the aftermath of terror and in the midst of hysteria, one great heart at least remained sane and jocular. They were truly grace under pressure.

And perhaps they signified grace of a deeper kind. Ronnie himself certainly believed that he had been given back his life for a purpose. As he told a priest after his recovery, 'Whatever time I've got left now belongs to the Big Fella Upstairs.'

And surely it is hard to deny that Ronald Reagan's life was providential, when we look at what he achieved in the eight years that followed.

Others prophesied the decline of the West; he inspired America and its allies with renewed faith in their mission of freedom.

Others saw only limits to growth; he transformed a stagnant economy into an engine of opportunity.

Others hoped, at best, for an uneasy cohabitation with the Soviet Union; he won the Cold War – not only without firing a shot, but also by inviting enemies out of their fortress and turning them into friends.

I cannot imagine how any diplomat, or any dramatist, could improve on his words to Mikhail Gorbachev at the Geneva summit: 'Let me tell you why it is we distrust you.' Those words are candid and tough and they cannot have been easy to hear. But they are also a clear invitation to a new beginning and a new relationship that would be rooted in trust.

We live today in the world that Ronald Reagan began to reshape with those words. It is a very different world with different challenges and new dangers. All in all, however, it is one of greater freedom and prosperity, one more hopeful than the world he inherited on becoming President.

As Prime Minister, I worked closely with Ronald Reagan for eight of the most important years of all our lives. We talked regularly both before and after his presidency. And I have had time and cause to reflect on what made him a great President.

Ronald Reagan knew his own mind. He had firm principles – and, I believe, right ones. He expounded them clearly, he acted upon them decisively.

When the world threw problems at the White House, he was not baffled, or disorientated, or overwhelmed. He knew almost instinctively what to do.

When his aides were preparing option papers for his decision, they were able to cut out entire rafts of proposals that they knew 'the Old Man' would never wear.

When his allies came under Soviet or domestic pressure, they could look confidently to Washington for firm leadership.

And when his enemies tested American resolve, they soon discovered that his resolve was firm and unyielding. Yet his ideas, though clear, were never simplistic. He saw the many sides of truth.

Yes, he warned that the Soviet Union had an insatiable drive for military power and territorial expansion; but he also sensed it was being eaten away by systemic failures impossible to reform.

Yes, he did not shrink from denouncing Moscow's 'evil empire'. But he realised that a man of goodwill might nonetheless emerge from within its dark corridors.

So the President resisted Soviet expansion and pressed down on Soviet weakness at every point until the day came when communism began to collapse beneath the combined weight of these pressures and its own failures. And when a man of goodwill did emerge from the ruins, President Reagan stepped forward to shake his hand and to offer sincere cooperation.

Nothing was more typical of Ronald Reagan than that large-hearted magnanimity – and nothing was more American.

Therein lies perhaps the final explanation of his achievements. Ronald Reagan carried the American people with him in his great endeavours because there was perfect sympathy between them. He and they loved America and what it stands for – freedom and opportunity for ordinary people.

As an actor in Hollywood's golden age, he helped to make the American dream live for millions all over the globe. His own life was a fulfilment of that dream. He never succumbed to the embarrassment some people feel about an honest expression of love of country.

He was able to say 'God Bless America' with equal fervour in public and in private. And so he was able to call confidently upon his fellow countrymen to make sacrifices for America – and to make sacrifices for those who looked to America for hope and rescue.

With the lever of American patriotism, he lifted up the world. And so today the world – in Prague, in Budapest, in Warsaw, in Sofia, in Bucharest, in Kiev and in Moscow itself – the world mourns the passing of the Great Liberator and echoes his prayer: 'God Bless America'.

Ronald Reagan's life was rich not only in public achievement, but also in private happiness. Indeed, his public achievements were rooted in his private happiness. The great turning point of his life was his meeting and marriage with Nancy.

On that we have the plain testimony of a loving and grateful husband: 'Nancy came along and saved my soul'. We share her grief today. But we also share her pride – and the grief and pride of Ronnie's children.

For the final years of his life, Ronnie's mind was clouded by illness. That cloud has now lifted. He is himself again – more himself than at any time on this earth. For we may be sure that the Big Fella Upstairs never forgets those who remember Him. And as the last journey of this faithful pilgrim took him beyond the sunset, and as heaven's morning broke, I like to think – in the words of Bunyan – that 'all the trumpets sounded on the other side'.

We here still move in twilight. But we have one beacon to guide us that Ronald Reagan never had. We have his example. Let us give thanks today for a life that achieved so much for all of God's children.

BARACK OBAMA

'[LIVING] UP TO OUR CHILDREN'S EXPECTATIONS'

—

REMARKS AT THE MEMORIAL SERVICE
FOR SHOOTING VICTIMS

TUCSON, ARIZONA, 12 JANUARY 2011

On 8 January 2011, at a constituent event in Tucson, Arizona, United States Representative Gabrielle Giffords and eighteen other people were shot by a lone gunman. Giffords, shot point blank in the head, survived. Six people died, including a United States Judge and a nine-year-old girl. Four days later, President Obama spoke at a nationally televised memorial service. Speaking for the nation, Obama tried to find meaning in these deaths and provide solace for those in shock and grief. Giffords continued to serve in Congress until 25 January 2012, when she resigned to receive further treatment for her injuries.

—

Thank you. Thank you very much. Please, please be seated.

To the families of those we've lost; to all who called them friends; to the students of this university, the public servants who are gathered here, the people of Tucson and the people of Arizona: I have come here tonight as an American who, like all Americans, kneels to pray with you today and will stand by you tomorrow.

There is nothing I can say that will fill the sudden hole torn in your hearts. But know this: The hopes of a nation are here tonight. We mourn with you for the fallen. We join you in your grief. And we add our faith to yours that Representative Gabrielle Giffords and the other living victims of this tragedy will pull through.

Scripture tells us:

There is a river whose streams make glad the city of God,

the holy place where the Most High dwells.

God is within her, she will not fall;

God will help her at break of day.

On Saturday morning, Gabby, her staff and many of her constituents gathered outside a supermarket to exercise their right to peaceful assembly and free speech. They were fulfilling a central tenet of the democracy envisioned by our founders – representatives of the people answering questions to their constituents, so as to carry their concerns back to our nation's capital. Gabby called it 'Congress on Your Corner' – just an updated version of government of and by and for the people.

And that quintessentially American scene, that was the scene that was shattered by a gunman's bullets. And the six people who lost their lives on Saturday – they, too, represented what is best in us, what is best in America.

Judge John Roll served our legal system for nearly forty years. A graduate of this university and a graduate of this law school [University of Arizona], Judge Roll was recommended for the federal bench by John McCain twenty years ago, appointed by President George H.W. Bush and rose to become Arizona's chief federal judge.

His colleagues described him as the hardest-working judge within the Ninth Circuit. He was on his way back from attending Mass, as he did every day, when he decided to stop by and say hi to his representative. John is survived by his loving wife, Maureen, his three sons and his five beautiful grandchildren.

George and Dorothy Morris – 'Dot' to her friends – were high school sweethearts who got married and had two daughters. They did everything together – travelling the open road in their RV, enjoying what their friends called a fifty-year honeymoon. Saturday morning, they went by the Safeway to hear what their Congresswoman had to say. When gunfire rang out, George, a former Marine, instinctively tried to shield his wife. Both were shot. Dot passed away.

A New Jersey native, Phyllis Schneck retired to Tucson to beat the snow. But in the summer, she would return East, where her world revolved around her three children, her seven grandchildren and two-year-old great-granddaughter. A gifted quilter, she'd often work under a favourite tree, or sometimes she'd sew aprons with the logos of the Jets and the Giants – to give out at the church where she volunteered. A Republican, she took a liking to Gabby, and wanted to get to know her better.

Dorwan and Mavy Stoddard grew up in Tucson together – about seventy years ago. They moved apart and started their own respective families. But after both were widowed they found their way back here, to, as one of Mavy's daughters put it, 'be boyfriend and girlfriend again'. When they weren't out on the road in their motor home, you could find them just up the road, helping folks in need at the Mountain Avenue Church of Christ. A retired construction worker, Dorwan spent his spare time fixing up the church along with his dog, Tux. His final act of selflessness was to dive on top of his wife, sacrificing his life for hers.

Everything – everything – Gabe Zimmerman did, he did with passion. But his true passion was helping people. As Gabby's outreach director, he made the cares of thousands of her constituents his own, seeing to it that seniors got the Medicare benefits that they had earned, that veterans got the medals and the care that they deserved, that government was working for ordinary folks. He died doing what he loved – talking with people and seeing how he could help. And Gabe is survived by his parents, Ross and Emily, his brother, Ben, and his fiancée, Kelly, who he planned to marry next year.

And then there is nine-year-old Christina Taylor Green. Christina was an A student; she was a dancer; she was a gymnast; she was a swimmer. She decided that she wanted to be the first woman to play in the Major Leagues, and as the only girl on her Little League team, no one put it past her.

She showed an appreciation for life uncommon for a girl her age. She'd remind her mother, 'We are so blessed. We have the best life.' And she'd pay those blessings back by participating in a charity that helped children who were less fortunate.

Our hearts are broken by their sudden passing. Our hearts are broken – and yet, our hearts also have reason for fullness.

Our hearts are full of hope and thanks for the thirteen Americans who survived the shooting, including the Congresswoman many of them went to see on Saturday.

I have just come from the University Medical Centre, just a mile from here, where our friend Gabby courageously fights to recover even as we speak. And I want to tell you – her husband Mark [Kelly] is here and he allows me to share this with you – right after we went to visit, a few minutes after we left her room and some of her colleagues in Congress were in the room, Gabby opened her eyes for the first time. Gabby opened her eyes for the first time. Gabby opened her eyes. Gabby opened her eyes, so I can tell you she knows we are here. She knows we love her. And she knows that we are rooting for her through what is undoubtedly going to be a difficult journey. We are there for her.

Our hearts are full of thanks for that good news, and our hearts are full of gratitude for those who saved others. We are grateful to Daniel Hernandez – a volunteer in Gabby's office.

And, Daniel, I'm sorry, you may deny it, but we've decided you are a hero because – you ran through the chaos to minister to your boss, and tended to her wounds and helped keep her alive.

We are grateful to the men who tackled the gunman as he stopped to reload. Right over there.

We are grateful for petite Patricia Maisch, who wrestled away the killer's ammunition, and undoubtedly saved some lives.

And we are grateful for the doctors and nurses and first responders who worked wonders to heal those who'd been hurt. We are grateful to them.

These men and women remind us that heroism is found not only on the fields of battle. They remind us that heroism does not require special training or physical strength. Heroism is here, in the hearts of so many of our fellow citizens, all around us, just waiting to be summoned – as it was on Saturday morning. Their actions, their selflessness poses a challenge to each of us. It raises a question of what, beyond prayers and expressions of concern, is required of us going forward. How can we honour the fallen? How can we be true to their memory?

You see, when a tragedy like this strikes, it is part of our nature to demand explanations – to try and pose some order on the chaos and make sense out of that which seems senseless. Already we've seen a national conversation commence, not only about the motivations behind these killings, but about everything from the merits of gun safety laws to the adequacy of our mental health system. And much of this process, of debating what might be done to prevent such tragedies in the future, is an essential ingredient in our exercise of self-government.

But at a time when our discourse has become so sharply polarised – at a time when we are far too eager to lay the blame for all that ails the world at the feet of those who happen to think differently than we do – it's important for us to pause for a moment and make sure that we're talking with each other in a way that heals, not in a way that wounds.

Scripture tells us that there is evil in the world, and that terrible things happen for reasons that defy human understanding. In the words of Job, 'When I looked for light, then came darkness.' Bad things happen, and we have to guard against simple explanations in the aftermath.

For the truth is none of us can know exactly what triggered this vicious attack. None of us can know with any certainty what might have stopped these shots from being fired, or what thoughts lurked in the inner recesses of a violent man's mind. Yes, we have to examine all the facts behind this tragedy. We cannot and will not be passive in the face of such violence. We should be willing to challenge old assumptions in order to lessen the prospects of such violence in the future. But what we cannot do is use this tragedy as one more occasion to turn on each other.

That we cannot do. That we cannot do.

As we discuss these issues, let each of us do so with a good dose of humility. Rather than pointing fingers or assigning blame, let's use this occasion to expand our moral imaginations, to listen to each other more carefully, to sharpen our instincts for empathy and remind ourselves of all the ways that our hopes and dreams are bound together.

After all, that's what most of us do when we lose somebody in our family – especially if the loss is unexpected. We're shaken out of our routines. We're forced to look inward. We reflect on the past: Did we spend enough time with an aging parent? we wonder. Did we express our gratitude for all the sacrifices that they made for us? Did we tell a spouse just how desperately we loved them, not just once in a while but every single day?

So sudden loss causes us to look backward – but it also forces us to look forward; to reflect on the present and the future, on the manner in which we live our lives and nurture our relationships with those who are still with us.

We may ask ourselves if we've shown enough kindness and generosity and compassion to the people in our lives. Perhaps we question whether we're doing right by our children, or our community, whether our priorities are in order.

We recognise our own mortality, and we are reminded that in the fleeting time we have on this Earth, what matters is not wealth, or status, or power, or fame – but rather, how well we have loved – and what small part we have played in making the lives of other people better.

And that process – that process of reflection, of making sure we align our values with our actions – that, I believe, is what a tragedy like this requires.

For those who were harmed, those who were killed – they are part of our family, an American family 300 million strong. We may not have known them personally, but surely we see ourselves in them. In George and Dot, in Dorwan and Mavy, we sense the abiding love we have for our own husbands, our own wives, our own life partners. Phyllis – she's our mom or our grandma; Gabe our brother or son. In Judge Roll, we recognise not only a man who prized his family and doing his job well, but also a man who embodied America's fidelity to the law.

And in Gabby – in Gabby, we see a reflection of our public-spiritedness; that desire to participate in that sometimes frustrating, sometimes contentious, but always necessary and never-ending process to form a more perfect union.

And in Christina – in Christina we see all of our children. So curious, so trusting, so energetic, so full of magic. So deserving of our love. And so deserving of our good example.

If this tragedy prompts reflection and debate – as it should – let's make sure it's worthy of those we have lost. Let's make sure it's not on the usual plane of politics and point-scoring and pettiness that drifts away in the next news cycle.

The loss of these wonderful people should make every one of us strive to be better. To be better in our private lives, to be better friends and neighbours and co-workers and parents. And if, as has been discussed in recent days, their death helps usher in more civility in our public discourse, let us remember it is not because a simple lack of civility caused this tragedy – it did not – but rather because only a more civil and honest public discourse can help us face up to the challenges of our nation in a way that would make them proud.

We should be civil because we want to live up to the example of public servants like John Roll and Gabby Giffords, who knew first and foremost that we are all Americans, and that we can question each other's ideas without questioning each other's love of country and that our task, working together, is to constantly widen the circle of our concern so that we bequeath the American Dream to future generations.

They believed – they believed, and I believe that we can be better. Those who died here, those who saved life here – they help me believe. We may not be able to stop all evil in the world, but I know that how we treat one another, that's entirely up to us.

And I believe that for all our imperfections, we are full of decency and goodness, and that the forces that divide us are not as strong as those that unite us.

That's what I believe, in part because that's what a child like Christina Taylor Green believed.

Imagine – imagine for a moment, here was a young girl who was just becoming aware of our democracy; just beginning to understand the obligations of citizenship; just starting to glimpse the fact that some day she, too, might play a part in shaping her nation's future. She had been elected to her student council. She saw public service as something exciting and hopeful. She was off to meet her Congresswoman, someone she was sure was good and important and might be a role model. She saw all this through the eyes of a child, undimmed by the cynicism or vitriol that we adults all too often just take for granted.

I want to live up to her expectations. I want our democracy to be as good as Christina imagined it. I want America to be as good as she imagined it. All of us – we should do everything we can to make sure this country lives up to our children's expectations.

As has already been mentioned, Christina was given to us on September 11th, 2001, one of fifty babies born that day to be pictured in a book called 'Faces of Hope'. On either side of her photo in that book were simple wishes for a child's life. 'I hope you help those in need,' read one. 'I hope you know all the words to the National Anthem and sing it with your hand over your heart.' 'I hope you jump in rain puddles.'

If there are rain puddles in Heaven, Christina is jumping in them today. And here on this Earth – here on this Earth, we place our hands over our hearts, and we commit ourselves as Americans to forging a country that is forever worthy of her gentle, happy spirit.

May God bless and keep those we've lost in restful and eternal peace. May He love and watch over the survivors. And may He bless the United States of America.

THE WORDS OF OUR TIME

LIST OF SOURCES

MORAL AUTHORITY

1. Aung San Suu Kyi, 'The hard life must be worthwhile' (2010 remarks when freed from house arrest in Burma) http://www.prachatai.com/english/node/2144. Some audience reactions have been removed.

2. Barack Obama, 'We can move beyond some of our old racial wounds' (2008 Philadelphia speech about religion and politics) http://www.npr.org/templates/story/story.php?storyId=88478467

3. Václav Havel, 'A sense of solidarity' (2002 remarks about Cuba at Florida International University) http://cubanexilequarter.blogspot.com/2011/12/vaclav-havels-speech-in-miami-addressed.html

UK GOVERNANCE

4. Tony Blair, 'We are at our best when at our boldest' (2002 Labour Party Conference speech) speech provided by Labour Party. *The Guardian* also provided a full text in two parts: http://www.guardian.co.uk/politics/2002/oct/01/labourconference.labour14 and http://www.guardian.co.uk/politics/2001/oct/02/labourconference.labour7. I have combined lines into paragraphs.

5. Tony Blair, 'Britain is not a follower. It is a leader.' (2007 resignation speech) http://www.telegraph.co.uk/news/1551095/Blairs-resignation-speech-in-full.html. I have combined lines into paragraphs.

6. Dan Hannan, 'A devalued Prime Minister, of a devalued government' (2009 European Parliament speech) http://tazforum.thetazzone.com/viewtopic.php?f=6&p=127579

7. David Cameron, 'This country needs change' (2010 Conservative Party Conference speech) Party Conference transcript and *Telegraph* and *Guardian* copy at http://www.telegraph.co.uk/news/politics/david-cameron/8046342/David-Camerons-Conservative-conference-speech-in-full.html and http://www.guardian.co.uk/politics/2010/oct/06/david-cameron-speech-tory-conference I have combined lines into paragraphs.

8. Nick Clegg, 'We will not lose our soul' (2010 Liberal Democrat Party Conference speech) Party Conference transcript and *Guardian* at http://www.guardian.co.uk/politics/2010/sep/20/nick-clegg-speech-liberal-democrat. I have combined lines into paragraphs.

9. Ed Miliband, 'The new generation of Labour is different' (2010 Labour Party Conference speech) Labour Party Conference transcript and BBC at http://www.bbc.co.uk/news/uk-politics-11426411. I have combined lines into paragraphs.

A CHANGING WORLD

10. Nelson Mandela, 'Massive poverty and obscene inequality are the terrible scourges of our time' (2005 London speech on global poverty) http://news.bbc.co.uk/2/hi/uk_news/politics/4232603.stm

11. Ellen Johnson Sirleaf, 'The resilience of our people' (2006 inaugural speech as Liberia's President) http://allafrica.com/stories/200601170106.html

12. Evo Morales, 'The confrontation of two cultures' (2003 speech at conference in Mexico) http://site.www.umb.edu/faculty/salzman_g/Strate/2006-01-09.htm. This web site has explanation of confusion of dates and two translations of the speech. The date I have is correct.

13. Luiz Inácio Lula da Silva, 'Hunger cannot wait' (2003 speech at G8 Summit) http://www.narconews.com/Issue31/article797.html

14. Hugo Chavez, 'Yesterday, the devil came here' (2006 speech at the United Nations) http://www.archive.org/details/Hugo_Chavez_ http://www.commondreams.org/views06/0920-22.htm and UN_Sept_20_2006_eng_trans

15. Vladimir Putin, 'History has given Russia a unique opportunity' (2009 speech at Davos) http://online.wsj.com/article/SB123317069332125243.html

16. Nicolas Sarkozy, 'A crisis of the denaturing of capitalism' (2010 speech at Davos) https://members.weforum.org/pdf/Sarkozy_en.pdf

17. Benazir Bhutto, 'The moving finger of history' (2003 speech at World Political Forum). I made some slight changes to create paragraphs and see http://www.ppp.org.pk/mbb/speeches/speeche51.html

18. Manmohan Singh, 'We are building a new India' (2010 Indian Independence Day speech) http://www.satp.org/satporgtp/countries/india/document/papers/2010/aug15pm.htm

THE GLOBAL FINANCIAL CRISIS

19. Henry Paulson, 'China's emergence as a global leader' (2008 speech at National Committee for US–China Relations) Treasury Department copy of remarks and http://www.ncuscr.org/files/Paulson%20Remarks_0.pdf

20. Alphonso Jackson, 'Housing is central to the human condition' (2007 speech in Macau) Department of Housing and Urban Development copy of remarks and http://archives.hud.gov/remarks/jackson/speeches/2007-07-10a.cfm. Note: HUD has the name of the group wrong on the web site. The speech was to the Asian Real Estate Society, not the American Real Estate Society.

21. David Cameron, 'Britain remains a great economic power' (2010 foreign policy speech at Lord Mayor's Banquet) http://www.number10.gov.uk/news/speech-to-lord-mayors-banquet. I have combined lines into paragraphs.

22. Michael Bear, 'We now live in a new world' (2011 speech at Lord Mayor's Dinner for the City of London's Bankers and Merchants) http://www.cityoflondon.gov.uk/NR/rdonlyres/09A9A9AE-F409-4FC1-9702-FCECD594C6D4/0/MC_LM_TandIuntrackedv6.pdf

23. George Osborne, 'The British Dilemma' (2011 speech at Lord Mayor's Dinner for the City of London's Bankers and Merchants) http://www.ft.com/intl/cms/s/0/e36b230a-9773-11e0-af13-00144feab49a.html#axzz1nnp6OyEd. I have combined lines into paragraphs.

24. Ben Bernanke, 'This economic healing will take a while' (2011 remarks to the Federal Reserve Bank of Kansas City Economic Summit) http://www.federalreserve.gov/newsevents/speech/bernanke20110826a.htm

25. David Cameron, 'To protect Britain's national interests' (2011 comments to the House of Commons after European Council Meeting) http://politicsdownanddirty.blogspot.com/2011/06/statement-on-european-council-meeting.html and http://conservativehome.blogs.com/parliament/2011/12/david-camerons-statement-on-the-european-council-to-the-house-of-commons-.html. I have combined some lines into paragraphs.

THE WAR ON TERRORISM

26. George W. Bush, 'Either you are with us, or you are with the terrorists' (2001 speech before a Joint Session of Congress) http://www.washingtonpost.com/wp-srv/nation/specials/attacked/transcripts/bushaddress_092001.html

27. Tony Blair, 'The kaleidoscope has been shaken' (2001 Party Conference speech) http://www.guardian.co.uk/politics/2001/oct/02/labourconference.labour6 and http://www.guardian.co.uk/politics/2001/oct/02/labourconference.labour7. I have combined lines into paragraphs.

28. George W. Bush, 'The threat comes from Iraq' (2002 Cincinnati speech) http://www.guardian.co.uk/world/2002/oct/07/usa.iraq

29. Robin Cook, 'The right of this place to vote' (2003 resignation speech) http://news.bbc.co.uk/2/hi/2859431.stm

GLOBALISATION

30. Pope Benedict XVI, 'Faith and reason' (2006 lecture on Christianity and Islam) Vatican transcript of remarks, complete with footnotes at http://www.zenit.org/article-16955?l=english and *Guardian* at http://www.guardian.co.uk/world/2006/sep/15/religion.uk. The Vatican version has the footnotes.

31. Barack Obama, 'A new beginning' (2008 Cairo University remarks on US-Islamic relations) http://www.whitehouse.gov/the-press-office/remarks-president-cairo-university-6-04-09

32. David Cameron, 'We must build stronger societies' (20011 Munich speech on multiculturalism) http://www.number10.gov.uk/news/pms-speech-at-munich-security-conference. I have combined lines into paragraphs.

ISRAEL AND PALESTINE

33. Mahmud Abbas, 'Worthy of a genuine state' (2003 speech before the Palestinian Legislative Council) http://www.bitterlemons.org/docs/abbasspeech.html

34. Binyamin Netanyahu, 'We want to see a parallel commitment' (2010 speech in New Orleans on Israel's security) http://jewishpost.com/news/Israeli-PM-Netanyahu-speaking-before-the-GA-asembly-in-New-Orleans.html. Some audience reactions and some interaction with the audience have been removed.

35. Binyamin Netanyahu, 'Israel is what is right with the Middle East' (2011 Remarks to a Joint Session of Congress) http://www.jpost.com/DiplomacyAndPolitics/Article.aspx?id=222056

36. Mahmud Abbas, 'We are at the heart of the Arab Spring' (2011 remarks to the European Council). This speech keeps appearing and disappearing on the web, http://unispal.un.org/UNISPAL.nsf/47D4E277B48D9D3685256DDC00612265/76DBBD49E69DF4AD852579210 04624C3

ARAB SPRING

37. Douglas Alexander, 'The next decade of the Middle East is going to be defined by optimism' (2011 remarks to the Royal Services Institute on events in the Middle East) http://www.labour.org.uk/autumn-perspective-on-arab-spring

38. Hillary Clinton, 'The right side of history' (2011 remarks to the National Democratic Institute concerning the Arab Spring) http://www.state.gov/secretary/rm/2011/11/176750.htm

39. Amr Moussa, 'Vigorous Arab world in the years to come' (2011 remarks to the International Institute for Strategic Studies) http://www.iiss.org/conferences/global-strategic-review/global-strategic-review-2011/keynote-address/

40. King Abdullah II of Jordan, 'The gates of the future' (2011 remarks to World Economic Forum) http://www.jordanembassyus.org/new/jib/speeches/hmka/hmka10222011.htm

THE OCCUPY MOVEMENT

41. Ronald Jan Heijn, 'The end of an era' (2011 remarks at Occupy Amsterdam on the views and influence of the Occupy Movement) http://www.wereldopdrift.nl/speech-at-occupy-amsterdam/

42. Slavoj Žižek, 'False terms, mystifying our perception' (2011 remarks to Occupy Wall Street on legitimacy of Occupy Protests http://www.versobooks.com/blogs/736. This is the original text, not remarks as delivered. There is video of the speech as given.

SCIENCE AND POLITICS

43. George W. Bush, 'Embryos ... are not spare parts' (2006 remarks on stem cell policy) http://www.presidentialrhetoric.com/speeches/07.19.06.html

44. Diana DeGette, 'Ethical imperative to help cure diseases' (2006 response to Presidential veto of stem cell legislation) http://www.house.gov/list/press/coo1_degette/radioaddress.html

OPPOSITION VOICES IN AMERICA'S 2012 PRESIDENTIAL ELECTION

45. Mitt Romney, 'Freedom and religion endure together, or perish alone' (2007 speech on faith and American politics) http://www.npr.org/templates/story/story.php?storyId=16969460

46. Sarah Palin, 'A ground-up call to action' (2010 remarks to the inaugural Tea Party Convention) http://www.americanrhetoric.com/speeches/sarahpalin2010teapartykeynote.htm

47. Chris Christie, 'Earned American exceptionalism' (2011 remarks at Reagan Library about the up-coming American presidential election) http://dailycaller.com/2011/09/27/chris-christies-reagan-library-speech-full-text/

EULOGY

48. John Howard, 'Unbearable grief and pain' (2002 eulogy for Australian victims of Bali terrorist attack) http://www.smh.com.au/articles/2002/10/18/1034561270521.html
49. Margaret Thatcher, 'Freedom and opportunity for ordinary people' (2004 remarks via video at Reagan funeral) http://news.bbc.co.uk/2/hi/americas/3797947.stm and http://www.margaret-thatcher.org/document/110360. This is a transcript of video remarks.
50. Barack Obama, '[Living] up to our children's expectations' (2011 eulogy for Tucson shooting victims, including Congresswoman Gabby Giffords) http://www.whitehouse.gov/the-press-office/2011/01/12/remarks-president-barack-obama-memorial-service-victims-shooting-tucson

INDEX

Coming soon from Biteback

AMERICA AND THE IMPERIALISM OF IGNORANCE

ANDREW ALEXANDER

American incomprehension of the outside world has been the chief
problem in international affairs since the end of World War II. *In
America and the Imperialism of Ignorance*, veteran political journalist
Andrew Alexander constructs a meticulous case, including evidence
gleaned from the steady opening up of Soviet archives, demonstrating
why this is so. He describes six decades in which war was not the last
resort of diplomacy but an early option and sees little hope of a change
in approach.

368pp paperback, £14.99
Available from all good bookshops or order from
www.bitebackpublishing.com